SENECA
VIII

LCL 62

SENECA

HERCULES FURENS · TROADES
MEDEA · HIPPOLYTUS · OEDIPUS

WITH AN ENGLISH TRANSLATION BY

FRANK JUSTUS MILLER

HARVARD UNIVERSITY PRESS
CAMBRIDGE, MASSACHUSETTS
LONDON, ENGLAND

First published 1917
Reprinted 1927, 1938, 1953, 1960, 1968, 1979, 1998

LOEB CLASSICAL LIBRARY® is a registered trademark
of the President and Fellows of Harvard College

ISBN 0-674-99069-2

Printed in Great Britain by St Edmundsbury Press Ltd,
Bury St Edmunds, Suffolk, on acid-free paper.
Bound by Hunter & Foulis Ltd, Edinburgh, Scotland.

CONTENTS

EDITORIAL NOTE (1979)

Of much important work that has appeared since the Bibliography on pages xiii – xvi was drawn up the following items
call for special mention.

B. Axelson, *Korruptelenkult* (a textual study of Hercules
Oetaeus), Lund 1967

G. Carlsson, *Die Überlieferung der Seneca-Tragödien*, Lund
1926; 'Zu Senecas Tragödien,' *Kung. Hum. Vet. i Lund*
(Ars.), Lund 1929, 39–72

M. Coffey, 'Seneca, *Tragedies*, 1922–1955,' *Lustrum* 2 (1957)
113–186

C. D. N. Costa, edition of *Medea*, Oxford 1973

G. C. Giardina, edition of the tragedies (2 vols), Bologna 1966

P. Grimal, edition of the *Phaedra*, Paris 1965

C. J. Herington, 'Senecan Tragedy,' *Arion* 5 (1966) 422–471

C. W. Mendell, *Our Seneca*, New Haven 1941

R. H. Philp, 'The manuscript tradition of Seneca's tragedies,'
CQ 18 (1968) 150–179

T. H. Sluiter, edition of *Oedipus*, Groningen 1941

R. J. Tarrant, edition of *Agamemnon*, Cambridge 1976

G. Viansino, Paravia edition of the tragedies (3 vols), Turin
1965 (vol.1 1968²)

O. Zwierlein, *Die Rezitationsdramen Senecas*, Diss. Berlin 1966

INTRODUCTION

Lucius Annaeus Seneca, commonly called the Philosopher to distinguish him from his father, Marcus Annaeus Seneca, the Rhetorician, was born close to the beginning of the Christian era, whether shortly before or shortly after is not certain. He, as was his father before him, was born at Cordova in Spain, the birthplace also of his brilliant nephew, Marcus Annaeus Lucanus. Other notable Spaniards in Roman literature were Columella, born in Gades, Martial, in Bilbilis, and Quintilian, in Calagurris.

The younger Seneca was brought to Rome in early infancy and received his training there. He was a Senator under Caligula and Claudius, and in 41 A.D., through the machinations of Messalina, was ordered by the emperor into exile at Corsica. Thence he was recalled in 49 through the influence of Agrippina, now the wife of Claudius, and to him was entrusted the education of Agrippina's son, Domitius, afterwards the emperor Nero. During the early years of Nero's reign, the philosopher had a large influence over his pupil and was virtual ruler for a time. But Nero later became jealous of Seneca's wealth and influence, and, seizing upon the

pretence of Seneca's complicity in the conspiracy of
Piso, he forced his old tutor to commit suicide in the
year 65.

In philosophy Seneca was a Stoic, but was influenced also by the teachings of the Pythagoreans.
His literary fame rests largely upon his philosophical
prose works, concerning which Teuffel remarks :
" He started from the Stoic system, but in him its
barren austerity was toned down, the harshness
softened, its crotchets laid aside ; nor did he disdain
additions from other systems. His paramount purpose is the forcible and eloquent presentation and
advocacy of moral principles conducive to the benefit
of the individual and of society."

A group of nine tragedies has also come down to
us, assigned by tradition to Senecan authorship. A
tenth tragedy, the *Octavia*, has been transmitted with
the other nine, but there is fairly good ground for
doubting its authenticity.[1] As to the nine, there is
no good reason for not considering them the work of
Seneca the Philosopher. They agree in general with
the philosophical principles and spirit of the prose
works, exhibit the same stylistic peculiarities (allowing
for the natural difference between prose essay and
dramatic poetry) and by their clear stylistic agreement
among themselves can readily be accepted as the
work of one hand. It should in fairness be said,
however, that all critics are not in agreement as to
the assignment of all the nine tragedies to Seneca.

[1] See note prefixed to the *Octavia*.

INTRODUCTION

The place of the tragedies of Seneca in literature is unique. They stand, with the exception of a few fragments, as the sole surviving representatives of an extensive Roman product in the tragic drama. They therefore serve as the only connecting link between ancient and modern tragedy. They parallel more or less closely the tragedies of Aeschylus, Sophocles, and Euripides ; and the Greek and Roman product in literature along similar lines cannot be better studied than by a comparison of these Senecan plays with their Greek prototypes—a comparison which is not possible in comedy, since, unfortunately, the Greek originals of Plautus and Terence have not come down to us, except in comparatively scanty fragments.

And yet, while Seneca's tragedies do in most cases parallel the Greek tragedies on corresponding themes, a careful comparative analysis of the Greek and the Latin plays shows quite clearly that Seneca did not take the Greeks for his model in any slavish manner, but, on the contrary, is in many instances surprisingly independent of them both in the introduction of new material and in his use of material common to both. So far as we can judge from the extant fragments, the earlier Roman dramatists, Ennius, Pacuvius and Accius, followed their Greek models, especially Euripides, much more closely, almost to the point of sheer translation.

These plays of Seneca are of great value and interest in themselves, first, as independent dramatic literature of no small merit; and second, as an illustration of the literary characteristics of the age of Nero. It has become quite the fashion among literary critics who include Seneca within their range of observation to pass very harsh judgment upon these tragedies. And they are indeed open to criticism from the standpoint of modern taste, with their florid rhetorical style, their long didactic speeches, their almost ostentatious pride of mythologic lore, their over-sensationalism, which freely admits the horrible and uncanny, their insistent employment of the epigram; and, finally, their introduction of situations which would be impossible from the standpoint of the technique of practical drama.

But in answer to the critic of Seneca's rhetorical faults it should be said that these were the faults of his age, an age when form, when rhetorical devices, when mere locution, had come to be magnified unduly; and as to the shortcomings, or rather the overdoings, of these tragedies from the standpoint of dramatic technique, the obvious answer is that these plays were not written for the stage and there is no evidence that they were acted. This was the age of the declaimer, and it is from the standpoint of declamation that we must both explain the composition of the tragedies and attempt an interpretation of their meaning and an appreciation of their style.

Superficially, Seneca's tragedies present no great difficulties to the translator. But a conscientious attempt to interpret them faithfully encounters the greatest difficulties, which are chargeable partly to confusion in the text due to imperfect transmission, but chiefly to the extreme terseness in Seneca's style, especially in his epigrams; for it is in the epigrammatic part of the plays that the difficulties in interpretation chiefly lie. Difficulties in translation arise also from Seneca's fondness for displaying his mythologic lore, frequently resulting in allusions to points so abstruse as to puzzle the reader who is not thoroughly versed in mythology.

But Seneca, for all his rhetorical liabilities, has some very considerable literary assets. The choruses are, indeed, often prosy, malapropos and disappointing; but here and there we find in these the ring of true poetry, exquisite in its descriptions of natural scenery, genuine in its human touches, and appropriate to the dramatic situation. Such is the chorus in *Hercules Furens* (lines 125 ff.), in *Troades* (1009 ff.), in *Medea* (301 ff.), *Agamemnon* (52 ff.). He has in his *recitativo* passages admirable descriptions of natural scenery and simple life, as in *Hippolytus* (482 ff.); spirited expressions of lofty sentiment, as in *Hercules Furens* (925 ff.); speeches expressing deep and real passion, as throughout the first half of the *Phoenissae*, in *Medea* (199 ff.), *Hercules Furens* (1321 ff.), *Hippolytus* (195 ff., 566 ff., 671 ff.), *Hercules Oetaeus* (1377 ff.), *Troades* (766 ff., 888 ff.); and numerous *sententiae*, terse, epigrammatic statements of general ethical truths, which are well worth remembrance and quotation.

INTRODUCTION

The reader will find many echoes of Vergil, Horace, and Ovid scattered through the plays, which serve to claim the tragedies for Latin literature notwithstanding their Greek models. Looking in the other direction, we find that the influence of Seneca's tragedies upon succeeding literature, especially upon English literature in the case of pre-Elizabethan and Elizabethan drama, is very great. A glance at the bibliography following will show something of the extent and importance of this influence.

The text on which this translation is based is that of Leo (Weidmann, Berlin, 1879) except as otherwise explained in the critical notes. Leo's (*i.e.* the German) punctuation, however, has been freely changed, especially in regard to the continual use of the colon, in order to bring the text into conformity with common English usage.

BIBLIOGRAPHY

I.—THE MANUSCRIPTS

E   *Codex Etruscus* or *Laurentianus*, a manuscript now in the Laurentian Library in Florence. This is the most trustworthy manuscript for the text of the plays. Leo calls it *unicum lectionis universae fundamentum, unicum genuini tragoediarum corporis exemplar.*

To be classed with E, as representing the same recension, are R, T, (both fragments and extracts only), and Σ, a lost copy of E, archetype of M and N.

A   An inferior and corrupt recension, to which the other minor manuscripts belong (A¹, ψ, a).

II.—EDITIONS

Editio Princeps. Andreas Gallicus (printer), at Ferrara. Between 1474 and 1484.

In L. Annaei Senecae Cordubensis Poetae Gravissimi Tragoedias Decem, Amplissima Adversaria quae loco commentarii esse possunt. Ex bibliotheca Martini Antonii Delrii. Antwerpiae: Ex officina Christophori Plantini, Architypographi Regii, 1576.

L. Annaei Senecae Tragoediae, recensuit Johannes Fredericus Gronovius. Lugduni Batavorum, ex officina Elzeviriana, 1661.

L. Annaei Senecae Tragoediae, cum notis integris Gronovii, et selectis Lipsii, Delrii, Gruteri, Commelini, Scaligeri, D. & N. Heinsiorum, Farnabii aliorumque; itemque observationibus nonnullis Hugonis Grotii. Omnia recensuit; notas, animadversationes, atque indicem novum locupletissimumque adiecit; ipsum vero auctoris Syntagma cum MS. codice contulit Johannes Casparus Schroederus. Delphis, apud Adrianum Beman, 1728.

L. Annaei Senecae Tragoediae, recensuerunt Rudolfus Peiper et Gustavus Richter. Teubner, 1867.

L. Annaei Senecae Tragoediae, recensuit et emendavit Fredericus Leo. 2 vols. Berolini: Weidmann, 1878, 1879. Vol. I. De Senecae Tragoediis observationes criticae, 1878. Vol. II. Senecae Tragoedias et Octaviam continens, 1879.

BIBLIOGRAPHY

L. Annaei Senecae Tragoediae, recensuerunt Rudolfus Peiper et Gustavus Richter. Peiperi subsidiis instructus denuo edendas curavit Gustavus Richter. Teubner, 1902.

Three Tragedies: Hercules Furens, Troades, Medea. With Introduction and Notes. By H. M. Kingery. New York: The Macmillan company, 1908.

III.—CRITICAL NOTES (TEXTUAL)

" R. Bentlei notas ad Senecae tragoedias emendandas editioni Gronovianae adscriptas primus edidit A. Stachelscheid in Jahni annalibus (125, p. 481 *sq.*), post eum et copiosius et rectius E. Hedicke in Studiorum Bentleianorum fasciculo altero p. 9 *sq.*" (*Seneca Bentleianus,* Freienwaldiae, 1899.)

Paul Koetschau, "Zu Seneca's Tragoedien," *Philol.* Vol. 61 (1902), p. 133 *seq.*

Mich. Müller, *In Senecae tragoedias quaestiones criticae.* Berolini, 1898.

B. Schmidt, *De Emendandarum Senecae tragoediarum rationibus prosodiacis et metricis.* Berolini, 1860.

—— *Observationes criticae in L. A. Senecae Tragoedias.* Jenae, 1865.

J. Withof, *Praemetium crucium criticarum praecipue ex Seneca tragico.* Lug. Bat. 1749.

IV.—TRANSLATIONS

The Tenne Tragedies of Seneca. Translated into English (1581). Two parts. Printed for the Spenser society, 1887 (Nos. 43, 44).

Les Tragédies de Sénèque. Trad. en vers franç. Par Benoît Baudouyn. Troyes, 1629.

Les Tragédies de Sénèque en latin et en franç. De la traduction de M. de Marolles. Paris, 1659.

Tragedias de Séneca. Traducción en verso de Angel Lasso de la Vega. Madrid, 1783.

Senekas Tragoedien nebst den Fragmenten der übrigen röm. Tragiker. Uebers. von W. A. Swoboda. Three vols. Vienna u. Prague, 1825.

See under Studies and Appreciations—*Die Tragoedien Senecas in Original und Uebersetzung, etc.* By Rudolf Fischer, 1893.

xiv

BIBLIOGRAPHY

The Ten Tragedies of Seneca, with text and notes. Rendered into English Prose as equivalently as the idioms of both languages permit. By Watson Bradshaw. London: Swan, Sonnenschein and Co., 1902.

The Tragedies of Seneca. Rendered into English verse, by Ella Isabel Harris. London: Henry Frowde, 1904.

The Tragedies of Seneca. Translated into English verse, to which have been appended comparative analyses of the corresponding Greek and Roman plays, and a mythological index, by Frank Justus Miller; introduced by an essay on the influence of the tragedies of Seneca upon early English drama, by John Matthews Manly. Chicago: The University of Chicago Press; London: T. Fisher Unwin, 1907.

The Elizabethan Translations of Seneca's Tragedies. By E. M. Spearing, Cambridge, 1912.

V.—STUDIES AND APPRECIATIONS

Post-Augustan Poetry from Seneca to Juvenal. By H. E. Butler. Oxford: Clarendon Press, 1909.

" Senecan Tragedy " in *English Literature and the Classics,* a series of essays collected by G. S. Gordon. Oxford: Clarendon Press, 1912.

Geschichte der Römischen Dichtung. By Otto Ribbeck. (Vol. III. pp. 52–88.) Stuttgart, 1892.

Études sur les Tragiques Grecs. Two vols. By H. Patin. Paris: Hachette et Cie, 1894.

Études de Moeurs et de Critique sur les Poètes Latins de la Décadence. Two vols. By D. Nisard. Paris: Hachette et Cie, 1834, 1878. The tragedies of Seneca are discussed in vol. I. pp. 57–198.

Étude sur la Phèdre de Racine et l'Hippolyte de Sénèque. By August Krug. Progr. des Gymn. Buchsweiler. Colmar, 1883.

Études sur Trois Tragédies de Sénèque, Imitées d'Euripide. By Widal. Aix, 1854.

"The Influence of the Tragedies of Seneca upon Early English Drama." By John M. Manly. In Miller's verse translation, *q.v.*

"Comparative Analyses of Seneca's Tragedies and the Corresponding Greek Dramas." By Frank Justus Miller. In Miller's verse translation, *q.v.*

BIBLIOGRAPHY

"Die Tragoedien Senecas in Original und Uebersetzung."— "Copien Senecas."— "Nachwirkungen Senecas und seiner Copien." In *Zur Kunstentwicklung der englischen Tragoedie von ihren ersten Anfängen bis zu Shakespeare*, by Rudolf Fischer. Strassburg, 1893.

"Seneca's Influence upon 'Gorboduc'." By H. Schmidt. *Modern Language Notes* 2 (1887), pp. 28–35.

Seneca's Influence on Robert Garnier. By Hans Max Schmidt-Wartenburg. Diss. Cornell University, 1888.

A Comparison of the Medea of Euripides and the Medea of Seneca. By Lee Byrne. University of Chicago, Diss., 1899.

Senecas Einfluss auf Jean de La Peruse's Médée und Jean de La Taille's La Famine ou les Gabeonites. By Otto Kulcke. Inaugural Diss. Greifswald, 1884.

"Jean de La Taille's Famine in Verhältnis zu Seneca's Troades." By Otto Kulcke. *Zeitschrift für neufranzösische Sprache und Litteratur.* Supplementheft III, 1885.

"Die Entstehung der Hamlet-Tragoedie. III. Der Urhamlet und Seneca." By G. Sarrazin. *Anglia* 13 (1891).

Sénèque et Hardy. L'influence de Sénèque sur le poète tragique Alexandre Hardy. By Jules Béraneck. Diss. Lpzg. 1880.

Early English Classical Tragedies. Edited with notes and introductions. By John W. Cunliffe. Oxford : Clarendon Press, 1912.

The Influence of Seneca upon Elizabethan Tragedy. John W. Cunliffe. London : Macmillan and Co., 1893. Anastatic reprint published by G. E. Stechert, New York, 1907.

VI.—INDICES

"Index Verborum et Locutionum quae in contextu Tragoed. L.A. Senecae occurrunt." pp. 803 ff. of the text and commentary edition of Johannes Casparus Schroederus, *q.v.*

"Index of Mythological Subjects in the Tragedies of Seneca." By Frank Justus Miller. In Miller's verse translation, pp. 499 ff.

Index Verborum quae in Senecae fabulis necnon in Octavia Praetexta reperiuntur, Oldfather, Pease, Canter. Urbana 1918 (repr. 1964)

HERCULES FURENS

DRAMATIS PERSONAE

HERCULES, *son of Jupiter and Alcmena, but the reputed son of Amphitryon.*

JUNO, *sister and wife of Jupiter, and queen of Heaven.*

AMPHITRYON, *husband of Alcmena.*

THESEUS, *king of Athens and friend of Hercules.*

LYCUS, *the usurping king of Thebes, who has, prior to the opening of the play, slain King Creon in battle.*

MEGARA, *wife of Hercules and daughter of Creon.*

CHORUS *of Thebans.*

THE SCENE is laid before the princely palace of Hercules at Thebes, on the day of the return of the hero from the lower world.

ARGUMENT

THE jealous wrath of Juno, working through Eurystheus, has imposed twelve mighty and destructive tasks on Hercules, her hated stepson. But these, even to the last and worst, the bringing of Cerberus to the upper world, he has triumphantly accomplished. Abandoning her plan of crushing him by toils like these, she will turn his hand against himself, and so accomplish his destruction. Upon the day of his return from hell she brings a madness on him, and so precipitates the tragedy which forms the action of the play.

HERCVLES FVRENS

IVNO

Soror Tonantis (hoc enim solum mihi
nomen relictum est) semper alienum Iovem
ac templa summi vidua deserui aetheris
locumque caelo pulsa paelicibus dedi;
tellus colenda est, paelices caelum tenent.
hinc Arctos alta parte glacialis poli
sublime classes sidus Argolicas agit;
hinc, qua tepenti[1] vere laxatur dies,
Tyriae per undas vector Europae nitet;
illinc timendum ratibus ac ponto gregem   10
passim vagantes exerunt Atlantides.
ferro minax hinc terret Orion deos
suasque Perseus aureus stellas habet;
hinc clara gemini signa Tyndaridae micant
quibusque natis mobilis tellus stetit.
nec ipse tantum Bacchus aut Bacchi parens
adiere superos; ne qua pars probro vacet,
mundus puellae serta Cnosiacae gerit.

[1] *So Richter, with AE*[a]*: Leo* recenti, *E*[1]*Σ.*

4

HERCULES FURENS

JUNO

THE sister of the Thunderer (for this name only is left to me), I have abandoned Jove, always another's lover; widowed, have left the spaces of high heaven and, banished from the sky, have given up my place to harlots; I must dwell on earth, for harlots hold the sky.[1] Yonder the Bear, high up in the icy North, a lofty constellation, guides the Argive ships; yonder, where in the warm springtime the days grow long, he [2] shines who bore the Tyrian Europa across the waves; there the Atlantides,[3] far wandering, put forth their band dreadful to ships and sea alike. Here Orion with threatening sword terrifies the gods, and golden Perseus has his stars; the bright constellation of the twin Tyndaridae shines yonder, and they at whose birth the unsteady land stood firm.[4] And not alone has Bacchus himself or the mother of Bacchus attained the skies; that no place might be free from outrage, the heavens wear the crown of the Cretan maid.[5]

---

[1] In Greek mythology the constellations which the poet names all have their place in the sky as the result of some amorous intrigue of Jupiter.   [2] The Bull.

[3] The reference would be more naturally to the Hyades as bringers of stormy weather; but nevertheless the Pleiades are evidently meant, since three of these had been beloved of Jove. See Index *s.v.* "Pleiades."

[4] See Index *s.v.* "Delos."   [5] Ariadne.

Sed vetera querimur : una me dira ac fera
Thebana tellus sparsa nuribus impiis   20
quotiens novercam fecit !   escendat licet
meumque victrix teneat Alcmene locum,
pariterque natus astra promissa occupet,—
in cuius ortus mundus impendit diem
tardusque Eoo Phoebus effulsit mari
retinere mersum iussus Oceano iubar,—
non sic abibunt odia ; vivaces aget
violentus iras animus et saevus dolor
aeterna bella pace sublata geret.

Quae bella ?   quidquid horridum tellus creat   30
inimica, quidquid pontus aut aer tulit
terribile dirum pestilens atrox ferum,
fractum atque domitum est.   superat et crescit malis
iraque nostra fruitur ; in laudes suas
mea vertit odia ; dum nimis saeva impero,
patrem probavi, gloriae feci locum.
qua Sol reducens quaque deponens diem
binos propinqua tinguit Aethiopas face,
indomita virtus colitur et toto deus
narratur orbe.   monstra iam desunt mihi   40
minorque labor est Herculi iussa exequi,
quam mihi iubere ; laetus imperia excipit.
quae fera tyranni iura violento queant
nocere iuveni ?   nempe pro telis gerit
quae timuit et quae fudit ; armatus venit
leone et hydra.   nec satis terrae patent ;
effregit ecce limen inferni Iovis
6

[19] But I lament ancient wrongs; one land, the
baneful and savage land of Thebes, scattered thick
with shameless mistresses, how oft has it made me
stepdame! Yet, though Alcmena be exalted and in
triumph hold my place; though her son, likewise,
obtain his promised star (for whose begetting [1] the
world lost a day, and Phoebus with tardy light shone
forth from the Eastern sea, bidden to keep his
bright car sunk beneath Ocean's waves), not in such
fashion shall my hatred have its end; my angry
soul shall keep up a long-living wrath, and my raging
smart, banishing peace, shall wage unending wars.

[30] What wars? Whatever fearsome creature the
hostile earth produces, whatever the sea or the air
has borne, terrific, dreadful, noxious, savage, wild,
has been broken and subdued. He rises anew and
thrives on trouble; he enjoys my wrath; to his own
credit he turns my hate; imposing too cruel tasks,
I have but proved his sire, but given room for
glory. Where the Sun, as he brings back, and
where, as he dismisses day, colours both Ethiop races
with neighbouring torch, his unconquered valour is
adored, and in all the world he is storied as a god.
Now I have no monsters left, and 'tis less labour for
Hercules to fulfil my orders than for me to order;
with joy he welcomes my commands. What cruel
biddings of his tyrant [2] could harm this impetuous
youth? Why, he bears as weapons what he once
fought and overcame; he goes armed by lion and by
hydra.[3] Nor is earth vast enough for him; behold,
he has broken down the doors of infernal Jove, and

---

[1] See Index *s.v.* "Hercules."

[2] See Index *s.v.* "Eurystheus."

[3] *i.e.* by the lion's skin, which he used as a shield, and by
the hydra's poisonous gall in which he dipped his arrow-points.

et opima victi regis ad superos refert.   48

vidi ipsa, vidi nocte discussa inferum   50

et Dite domito spolia iactantem patri

fraterna.   cur non vinctum et oppressum trahit

ipsum catenis paria sortitum Iovi

Ereboque capto potitur et retegit Styga ?   54

parum est reverti; foedus umbrarum perit,   49

patefacta ab imis manibus retro via est   55

et sacra dirae mortis in aperto iacent.

at ille, rupto carcere umbrarum ferox,

de me triumphat et superbifica manu

atrum per urbes ducit Argolicas canem.

viso labantem Cerbero vidi diem   60

pavidumque Solem ; me quoque invasit tremor,

et terna monstri colla devicti intuens

timui imperasse.

              Levia sed nimium queror ;

caelo timendum est, regna ne summa occupet

qui vicit ima— sceptra praeripiet patri.

nec in astra lenta veniet ut Bacchus via ;

iter ruina quaeret et vacuo volet

regnare mundo.   robore experto tumet,

et posse caelum viribus vinci suis

didicit ferendo ; subdidit mundo caput   70

nec flexit umeros molis immensae labor

meliusque collo sedit Herculeo polus.

8

brings back to the upper world the spoils [1] of a
conquered king. I myself saw, yes, saw him, the
shadows of nether night dispersed and Dis overthrown, proudly displaying to his father a brother's
spoils. Why does he not drag forth, bound and
loaded down with fetters, Pluto himself, who drew a
lot equal to Jove's? Why does he not lord it over
conquered Erebus and lay bare the Styx? It is not
enough merely to return; the law of the shades has
been annulled, a way back has been opened from the
lowest ghosts, and the mysteries of dread Death lie
bared. But he, exultant at having burst the prison
of the shades, triumphs over me, and with arrogant
hand leads through the cities of Greece that dusky
hound. I saw the daylight shrink at sight of Cerberus,
and the sun pale with fear; upon me, too, terror came,
and as I gazed upon the three necks of the conquered
monster I trembled at my own command.

[63] But I lament too much o'er trivial wrongs. 'Tis
for heaven we must fear, lest he seize the highest
realms who has overcome the lowest—he will snatch
the sceptre from his father. Nor will he come to
the stars by a peaceful journey as Bacchus did; he
will seek a path through ruin, and will desire to rule
in an empty universe. He swells with pride of
tested might, and has learned by bearing them that
the heavens can be conquered by his strength; he
set his head beneath the sky, nor did the burden of
that immeasurable mass bend his shoulders, and the
firmament rested better on the neck of Hercules.[2]

---

[1] In Roman custom *spolia opima* were gained when a king
met an opposing king in battle, conquered, and despoiled him.
In this case the "spoil" was Cerberus; the "king," Pluto,
brother of Jupiter.

[2] *i.e.* than it had on Atlas' shoulders.

immota cervix sidera et caelum tulit
et me prementem.   quaerit ad superos viam.

Perge, ira, perge et magna meditantem opprime,
congredere, manibus ipsa dilacera tuis ;
quid tanta mandas odia ?   discedant ferae,
ipse imperando fessus Eurystheus vacet.
Titanas ausos rumpere imperium Iovis
emitte, Siculi verticis laxa specum,   80
tellus gigante Doris excusso tremens
supposita monstri colla terrifici levet,
sublimis alias Luna concipiat feras.[1]
sed vicit ista.   quaeris Alcidae parem ?
nemo est nisi ipse ; bella iam secum gerat.
adsint ab imo Tartari fundo excitae
Eumenides, ignem flammeae spargant comae,
viperea saevae verbera incutiant manus.

I nunc, superbe, caelitum sedes pete,
humana temne.   iam Styga et manes feros   90
fugisse credis ?   hic tibi ostendam inferos.
revocabo in alta conditam caligine,
ultra nocentum exilia, discordem deam,
quam munit ingens montis oppositi specus ;
educam et imo Ditis e regno extraham
quidquid relictum est ; veniet invisum Scelus
suumque lambens sanguinem Impietas ferox
Errorque et in se semper armatus Furor—
hoc hoc ministro noster utatur dolor !

[1] *Leo deletes this line.*

10

Unshaken, his back upbore the stars and the sky and
me down-pressing. He seeks a way to the gods above.

⁷⁵ Then on, my wrath, on, and crush this plotter
of big things; close with him, thyself rend him in
pieces with thine own hands. Why to another entrust
such hate? Let the wild beasts go their ways, let
Eurystheus rest, himself weary with imposing tasks.
Set free the Titans¹ who dared invade the majesty
of Jove; unbar Sicily's mountain cave, and let the
Dorian land,² which trembles whenever the giant
struggles, set free the buried frame of that dread
monster; let Luna³ in the sky produce still other
monstrous creatures. But he has conquered such as
these. Dost then seek Alcides' match? None is
there save himself; now with himself let him war.
Rouse the Eumenides from the lowest abyss of Tartarus; let them be here, let their flaming locks drop
fire, and let their savage hands brandish snaky whips.

⁸⁹ Go now, proud one, seek the abodes of the immortals and despise man's estate. Dost think that
now thou hast escaped the Styx and the cruel ghosts?
Here will I show thee infernal shapes. One in deep
darkness buried, far down below the place of banishment of guilty souls, will I call up—the goddess
Discord, whom a huge cavern, barred by a mountain,
guards; I will bring her forth, and drag out from
the deepest realm of Dis whatever thou hast left;
hateful Crime shall come and reckless Impiety, stained
with kindred blood, Error, and Madness, armed ever
against itself—this, this be the minister of my smarting
wrath!

---

¹ For this whole passage see Index *s.v.* "Titans" and
"Giants."   ² Sicily.
³ The Nemean lion and other monsters were supposed to
have fallen from the moon.

Incipite, famulae Ditis, ardentem citae   100
concutite pinum et agmen horrendum anguibus
Megaera ducat atque luctifica manu
vastam rogo flagrante corripiat trabem.
hoc agite, poenas petite vitiatae Stygis
concutite pectus, acrior mentem excoquat
quam qui caminis ignis Aetnaeis furit.
ut possit animo captus Alcides agi,
magno furore percitus, nobis [1] prius
insaniendum est—Iuno, cur nondum furis?
me me, sorores, mente deiectam mea   110
versate primam, facere si quicquam apparo
dignum noverca.   vota mutentur mea ;
natos reversus videat incolumes precor
manuque fortis redeat.   inveni diem,
invisa quo nos Herculis virtus iuvet.
me vicit et se vincat et cupiat mori
ab inferis reversus.   hic prosit mihi
Iove esse genitum.   stabo et, ut certo exeant
emissa nervo tela, librabo manu,
regam furentis arma, pugnanti Herculi   120
tandem favebo.   scelere perfecto licet
admittat illas genitor in caelum manus !

    Movenda iam sunt bella ; clarescit dies
ortuque Titan lucidus croceo subit.

CHORVS

Iam rara micant sidera prono
languida mundo ; nox victa vagos
contrahit ignes luce renata,

        [1] *So A : Leo* vobis.

12

[100] Begin, handmaids of Dis, make haste to brandish the burning pine; let Megaera lead on her band bristling with serpents and with baleful hand snatch a huge faggot from the blazing pyre. To work! claim vengeance for outraged Styx. Shatter his heart; let a fiercer flame scorch his spirit than rages in Aetna's furnaces. That Alcides may be driven on, robbed of all sense, by mighty fury smitten, mine must be the frenzy first—Juno, why rav'st thou not? Me, ye sisters, me first, bereft of reason, drive to madness, if I am to plan some deed worthy a stepdame's doing. Let my request be changed; may he come back and find his sons unharmed, that is my prayer, and strong of hand may he return. I have found the day when Hercules' hated valour is to be my joy. Me has he overcome; now may he overcome himself and long to die, though late returned from the world of death. Herein may it profit me that he is the son of Jove. I will stand by him and, that his shafts may fly from string unerring, I'll poise them with my hand, guide the madman's weapons, and so at last be on the side of Hercules in the fray. When he has done this crime, then let his father admit those hands to heaven!

[123] Now must my war be set in motion; the sky is brightening and the shining sun steals up in saffron dawn.

CHORUS

Now stars shine few and faint in the sinking sky; vanquished night draws in her wandering fires as the

13

cogit nitidum Phosphoros agmen;
signum celsi glaciale poli
septem stellis Arcados ursae [1]   130
lucem verso temone vocat.
iam caeruleis evectus equis
Titan summa prospicit Oeta;
iam Cadmeis incluta Bacchis
aspersa die dumeta rubent
Phoebique fugit reditura soror.
labor exoritur durus et omnes
agitat curas aperitque domos.

Pastor gelida cana pruina
grege dimisso pabula carpit;   140
ludit prato liber aperto
nondum rupta fronte iuvencus,
vacuae reparant ubera matres;
errat cursu levis incerto
molli petulans haedus in herba;
pendet summo stridula ramo
pennasque novo tradere soli
gestit querulos inter nidos
Thracia paelex, turbaque circa
confusa sonat murmure mixto   150
testata diem.
carbasa ventis credit dubius
navita vitae, laxos aura
complente sinus. hic exesis
pendens scopulis aut deceptos

     [1] *Leo deletes this line.*

14

new day is born, and Phosphor brings up the rear of
the shining host; the icy sign high in the north, the
Bears of Arcas, with their seven stars, with wheeling
pole [1] summons the dawn. Now, upborne by his azure
steeds, Titan peeps forth from Oeta's crest; now the
rough brakes, made famous by Theban Bacchants,
touched by the dawn, flush red, and Phoebus' sister [2]
flees away, to return again. Hard toil arises, sets all
cares astir, opens all doors.

[139] The shepherd, turning out his flock, plucks
pasturage still white with frosty rime. In the
open mead the young bullock sports at will, his
forehead not yet broken with young horns; the kine
at leisure fill again their udders; the sportive kid
with unsteady, aimless course wanders on the soft
turf; perched on the topmost bough, shrill-voiced,
amid her complaining young, the Thracian paramour [3]
is eager to spread her wings to the morning sun; and
all around a mingled throng sounds forth, proclaim-
ing the dawn of day with varied notes. The sailor,
life ever at risk, commits his canvas to the winds, while
the breeze fills its flapping folds. Here the fisher,
perched on the wave-worn rocks, either rebaits his

---

[1] The poet has mixed two conceptions of these constellations:
(1) the Great Bear and Arctophylax, the "bear-keeper";
(2) the "Wain" and the "Ox-driver" (Boötes).
[2] Phoebe, the moon-goddess.
[3] Philomela, the nightingale, forced to be the mistress of
the Thracian Tereus.

instruit hamos aut suspensus
spectat pressa praemia dextra;
sentit tremulum linea piscem.
   Haec, innocuae quibus est vitae
tranquilla quies et laeta suo   160
parvoque domus; spes immanes   161
urbibus errant trepidique metus.   163
ille superbos aditus regum
durasque fores expers somni
colit, hic nullo fine beatas
componit opes gazis inhians
et congesto pauper in auro;
illum populi favor attonitum
fluctuque magis mobile vulgus   170
aura tumidum tollit inani;
hic clamosi rabiosa fori
iurgia vendens improbus iras
et verba locat.   novit paucos
secura quies, qui velocis
memores aevi tempora numquam
reditura tenent.   Dum fata sinunt
vivite laeti; properat cursu
vita citato volucrique die
rota praecipitis vertitur anni;   180
durae peragunt pensa sorores
nec sua retro fila revolvunt.
at gens hominum flatur rapidis
obvia fatis incerta sui;
Stygias ultro quaerimus undas.

16

cheated hooks or, with firm grip, watches anxiously
for his prize; meantime, his line feels the quivering
fish.

159 Such are the tasks of those whose is the peaceful
calm of harmless lives, whose home rejoices in the tiny
store that is its own; overweening hopes stalk abroad
in cities, and trembling fears. One, sleepless, haunts
the haughty vestibules and unfeeling doors of his
rich patrons; another endlessly heaps up abundant
wealth, gloats over his treasures, and is still poor
amid piled-up gold. Yonder dazed wretch, with
empty wind puffed up, popular applause and the mob
more shifting than the sea uplift; this, trafficking in
the mad wrangles of the noisy court, shamelessly lets
out for hire his passions and his speech. Known to
but few is untroubled calm, and they, mindful of
time's swift flight, hold fast the days that never will
return. While the fates permit, live happily; life
speeds on with hurried step, and with winged days
the wheel of the headlong year is turned. The harsh
sisters [1] ply their tasks, yet do they not spin backward
the threads of life. But men are driven, each one uncertain of his own, to meet the speeding fates; we seek
the Stygian waves of our own accord. With heart too

[1] The Parcae.

nimium, Alcide, pectore forti
properas maestos visere manes;
certo veniunt tempore Parcae.
nulli iusso cessare licet,
nulli scriptum proferre diem;   190
recipit populos urna citatos.

Alium multis gloria terris
tradat et omnes fama per urbes
garrula laudet caeloque parem
tollat et astris; alius curru
sublimis eat; me mea tellus
lare secreto tutoque tegat.
venit ad pigros cana senectus,
humilique loco sed certa sedet
sordida parvae fortuna domus;   200
alte virtus animosa cadit.

Sed maesta venit crine soluto
Megara parvum comitata gregem,
tardusque senio graditur Alcidae parens.

AMPHITRYON

O magne Olympi rector et mundi arbiter,
iam statue tandem gravibus aerumnis modum
finemque cladi.   nulla lux umquam mihi
secura fulsit; nullus e nati datur
labore fructus;[1] finis alterius mali
gradus est futuri.   protinus reduci novus

[1] *Leo supplies* nullus . . . fructus *as necessary to the sense.*

brave, Alcides, thou dost haste to visit the grieving ghosts; at the appointed time the Parcae come. No one may linger when they command, no one may postpone the allotted day; the urn receives the nations hurried to their doom.

192 Let glory laud another to many lands, and let babbling fame sing his praise through every city and lift him to a level with the stars of heaven; let another fare towering in his car; but me let my own land, beside my lonely, sheltered hearth, protect. The inactive reach hoary age, and in a lowly estate but secure stands the mean lot of a humble home; from a lofty height ambitious courage falls.

202 But sad Megara comes hither with streaming hair, her flock of children round her, and, slow with age, the father of Alcides moves.

[*Enter from the palace* MEGARA *with her children, and* AMPHITRYON. *They take their stand at the altar.*]

AMPHITRYON

O mighty ruler of Olympus, judge of all the world, set now at length a limit to our crushing cares, an end to our disasters. No day has ever dawned for me untroubled; no reward from my son's toil is ever given; the end of one ill is but the step to one beyond. Straightway on his return a new foe is

19

paratur hostis; antequam laetam domum   210
contingat, aliud iussus ad bellum meat;
nec ulla requies tempus aut ullum vacat,
nisi dum iubetur.   sequitur a primo statim
infesta Iuno; numquid immunis fuit
infantis aetas?   monstra superavit prius
quam nosse posset.   gemina cristati caput
angues ferebant ora, quos contra obvius
reptabat infans igneos serpentium
oculos remisso lumine ac placido intuens;
artos serenis vultibus nodos tulit,   220
et tumida tenera guttura elidens manu
prolusit hydrae.   Maenali pernix fera,
multo decorum praeferens auro caput,
deprensa cursu est; maximus Nemeae timor
pressus lacertis gemuit Herculeis leo.
quid stabula memorem dira Bistonii gregis
suisque regem pabulum armentis datum,
solitumque densis hispidum Erymanthi iugis
Arcadia quatere nemora Maenalium suem,
taurumque centum non levem populis metum?   230
inter remotos gentis Hesperiae greges
pastor triformis litoris Tartesii
peremptus, acta est praeda ab occasu ultimo;
notum Cithaeron pavit Oceano pecus.
penetrare iussus solis aestivi plagas
et adusta medius regna quae torret dies
utrimque montes solvit ac rupto obice
latam ruenti fecit Oceano viam.

ready for him; before he can reach his happy home, bidden to another struggle he sets forth; there is no chance to rest, no time left free, save while fresh commands are being given. From his very birth relentless Juno has pursued him; was even his infancy exempt? He conquered monsters before he could know that they were monsters. Serpents twain with crested heads advanced their fangs against him; the infant crawled to meet them, gazing at the snakes' fiery eyes with mild and gentle look; with serene face he raised their close-coiled folds and, crushing their swollen throats with his baby hands, he practised for the hydra. The nimble hind of Maenalus, raising her head bounteously adorned with gold, was caught by his long pursuit;[1] the lion, mightiest dread of Nemea, crushed by the arms of Hercules roared his last. Why should I tell of the horrid stalls of the Bistonian herd and the king[2] given as food to his own cattle? of the shaggy boar of Maenalus, whose wont it was on the thick-wooded heights of Erymanthus to harry the groves of Arcady? or of the bull, the crushing terror of a hundred towns?[3] Among his herds in the distant land of Spain the three-shaped shepherd[4] of the Tartesian shore was killed and his cattle driven as spoil from the farthest west; Cithaeron has fed the herd once to Ocean known. When bidden[5] to enter the regions of the summer sun, those scorched realms which midday burns, he clove the mountains on either hand and, rending the barrier, made a wide path[6] for Ocean's rushing stream.

[1] Hercules chased the hind a year before he caught her.
[2] See Index *s.v.* " Diomedes."
[3] The hundred towns of Crete.   [4] Geryon.
[5] This was not one of the twelve labours ordered by Eurystheus. See Index *s.v.* " Hercules."
[6] The Straits of Gibraltar.

21

post haec adortus nemoris opulenti domos
aurifera vigilis spolia serpentis tulit ;　　　　240
quid ?　saeva Lernae monstra, numerosum malum,
non igne demum vicit et docuit mori,
solitasque pennis condere obductis diem
petit ab ipsis nubibus Stymphalidas ?
non vicit illum caelibis semper tori
regina gentis vidua Thermodontiae ;
nec ad omne clarum facinus audaces manus
stabuli fugavit turpis Augei labor.

　Quid ista prosunt ?　orbe defenso caret.
sensere terrae pacis auctorem suae　　　　250
abesse.　rursus prosperum ac felix scelus
virtus vocatur ; sontibus parent boni,
ius est in armis, opprimit leges timor.
ante ora vidi nostra truculenta manu
natos paterni cadere regni vindices
ipsumque, Cadmi nobilis stirpem ultimam,
occidere, vidi regium capiti decus
cum capite raptum.　quis satis Thebas fleat ?
ferax deorum terra, quem dominum tremis ?
e cuius arvis eque fecundo sinu　　　　260
stricto iuventus orta cum ferro stetit
cuiusque muros natus Amphion Iove
struxit canoro saxa modulatu trahens,
in cuius urbem non semel divum parens
caelo relicto venit, haec quae caelites
recepit et quae fecit et (fas sit loqui)
fortasse faciet, sordido premitur iugo.

22

Next he essayed the rich grove's dwellings and bore
off the watchful dragon's golden spoil.[1] Lerna's fell
monster, pest manifold, did he not quell at last by
fire and teach to die? And the Stymphalian birds,
wont to hide the day with veiling wings, did he not
bring down from the very clouds? Thermodon's
unwed queen[2] of ever virgin couch could not prevail
against him, nor did his hands, bold to attempt all
glorious deeds, shirk the foul labour of the Augean
stalls.

[249] But what avails all this? He is banished from
the world which he defended. All the earth has
felt that the giver of its peace is lost to it. Once
again prosperous and successful crime goes by the
name of virtue; good men obey the bad, might is
right and fear oppresses law. Before my eyes I saw
the sons, defenders of their father's[3] kingdom, fall
dead by the murderer's[4] hand, and the king himself
fall, last scion of Cadmus' famous line; I saw the
royal crown that decked his head torn from him,
head and all. Who could lament Thebes enough?
O land, fertile in gods, before what lord dost thou
tremble now? The city from whose fields and fecund
bosom a band of youth[5] stood forth with swords
ready drawn, whose walls Jove's son, Amphion, built,
drawing its stones by his tuneful melodies—to which
not once alone came the father of the gods, quitting
the sky—this city, which has welcomed gods and
has created gods and (may the word be lawful)
perchance will yet create them, is oppressed by a

---

[1] The golden apples of the Hesperides.
[2] Hippolyte, queen of the Amazons.
[3] Creon. [4] Lycus.
[5] *i.e.* they who sprang from Cadmus' sowing of the dragon's
teeth.

Cadmea proles atque Ophionium genus,
quo reccidistis? tremitis ignavum exulem,
suis carentem finibus, nostris gravem. 270
qui scelera terra quique persequitur mari
ac saeva iusta sceptra confringit manu
nunc servit absens fertque quae fieri vetat,
tenetque Thebas exul Herculeas Lycus!
sed non tenebit; aderit et poenas petet
subitusque ad astra emerget; inveniet viam
aut faciet. adsis sospes et remees precor
tandemque venias victor ad victam domum!

MEGARA

Emerge, coniunx, atque dispulsas manu
abrumpe tenebras; nulla si retro via 280
iterque clusum est, orbe diducto redi
et quidquid atra nocte possessum latet
emitte tecum. dirutis qualis iugis
praeceps citato flumini quaerens iter
quondam stetisti, scissa cum vasto impetu
patuere Tempe—pectore impulsus tuo
huc mons et illuc cessit et rupto aggere
nova cucurrit Thessalus torrens via—
talis, parentes liberos patriam petens,
erumpe rerum terminos tecum efferens, 290
et quidquid avida tot per annorum gradus
abscondit aetas redde et oblitos sui
lucisque pavidos ante te populos age.
indigna te sunt spolia, si tantum refers
24

shameful yoke. O seed of Cadmus and Ophion's race, to what depths have you fallen! You tremble before a dastard exile, of his own land deprived, to ours a burden. But he who avenges crime on land and sea, who with righteous hand breaks cruel sceptres, now far away endures a master[1] and brooks what he elsewhere forbids—and Lycus, the exile, rules the Thebes of Hercules! But not for long; he will be present with us and exact punishment, and suddenly to the sight of the stars will he come forth. He will find a way—or make one. Oh, be present and return in safety, I pray, and come at last victorious to thy vanquished home!

MEGARA

Come forth, my husband, burst through the darkness shivered by thy hand; if there is no backward way, and the road is closed, rend earth asunder and return; and whatever lies hid in the hold of murky night, let forth with thee. Even as once, rending the hills asunder, seeking for the rushing stream[2] a headlong path, thou stoodst, what time Tempe, cleft by that mighty shock, opened wide— before the thrust of thy breast, this way and that the mountain yielded and through the broken mass the Thessalian torrent raced in its new bed—even so, seeking thy parents, children, fatherland, burst through, bearing away with thee the bounds of things; and all that greedy time through all the march of years has hidden away, restore; and drive out before thee the self-forgetting dead, peoples that fear the light. Unworthy of thee is the spoil, if thou

---

[1] Eurystheus.

[2] The Peneus river, a passage for which Hercules is said to have forced between Olympus and Ossa.

quantum imperatum est.   magna sed nimium loquor
ignara nostrae sortis.   unde illum mihi
quo te tuamque dexteram amplectar diem
reditusque lentos nec mei memores querar?
tibi, o deorum ductor, indomiti ferent
centena tauri colla ; tibi, frugum potens,   300
secreta reddam sacra ; tibi muta fide
longas Eleusin tacita iactabit faces.
tum restitutas fratribus rebor meis
animas et ipsum regna moderantem sua
florere patrem.   si qua te maior tenet
clausum potestas, sequimur. aut omnes tuo
defende reditu sospes aut omnes trahe—
trahes nec ullus eriget fractos deus.

AMPHITRYON

  O socia nostri sanguinis, casta fide
servans torum natosque magnanimi Herculis,   310
meliora mente concipe atque animum excita.
aderit profecto, qualis ex omni solet
labore, maior.

MEGARA

          Quod nimis miseri volunt
hoc facile credunt.

AMPHITRYON

          Immo quod metuunt nimis
numquam moveri posse nec tolli putant.
prona est timoris semper in peius fides.
26

bringst back only what was commanded. But I speak too frowardly, all ignorant of the fate in store for us. Oh, whence shall come that day for me when I shall clasp thee and thy right hand and lament thy long-delayed returns that have no thought of me? To thee, O leader of the gods, a hundred bulls never broken to the yoke shall yield their necks; to thee, goddess of fruits,[1] will I perform thy secret rites; to thee in speechless faith silent Eleusis shall toss long trains of torches. Then shall I deem their lives restored unto my brothers, my father himself governing his own realm and flourishing. But if some greater power is holding thee in durance, we follow thee. Either defend us all by thy safe return, or drag us all with thee—thou wilt drag us down, nor will any god lift up our broken house.

AMPHITRYON

O ally of my blood, preserving with chaste faith the couch and children of the great-souled Hercules, have better thought and rouse thy courage. Surely he will come home, as is his wont from every task, the greater.

MEGARA

What the wretched overmuch desire, they easily believe.

AMPHITRYON

Nay, what they fear overmuch they think can never be set aside or done away. Fear's trust inclineth ever to the worse.

---

[1] Ceres.

SENECAE TRAGOEDIAE

MEGARA

Demersus ac defossus et toto insuper
oppressus orbe quam viam ad superos habet?

AMPHITRYON

Quam tunc habebat cum per arentem plagam
et fluctuantes more turbati maris   320
adit harenas bisque discedens fretum
et bis recurrens, cumque deserta rate
deprensus haesit Syrtium brevibus vadis
et puppe fixa maria superavit pedes.

MEGARA

Iniqua raro maximis virtutibus
fortuna parcit; nemo se tuto diu
periculis offerre tam crebris potest.
quem saepe transit casus, aliquando invenit.
   Sed ecce saevus ac minas vultu gerens
et qualis animo est talis incessu venit.   330
aliena dextra sceptra concutiens Lycus.

LYCVS

Vrbis regens opulenta Thebanae loca
et omne quidquid uberi cingit solo
obliqua Phocis, quidquid Ismenos rigat,
quidquid Cithaeron vertice excelso videt,
et bina findens Isthmos exilis freta,[1]
non vetera patriae iura possideo domus

[1] *Leo deletes this line.*

MEGARA

Submerged, deep-buried, crushed beneath all the world, what way has he to upper air?

AMPHITRYON

The same he had when across the parched desert and the sands, billowing like the stormy sea, he made his way, and across the strait with twice-receding, twice-returning waves; and when, his barque abandoned, he was stranded, a prisoner on Syrtes' shoals, and, though his vessel was held fast, he crossed o'er seas on foot.[1]

MEGARA

Unrighteous fortune seldom spares the highest worth; no one with safety can long front so frequent perils. Whom calamity oft passes by she finds at last.

[*Enter* LYCUS.]

329 But see, ferocious and with threats upon his brow, the same in gait and spirit, Lycus comes, brandishing another's sceptre in his hand.

LYCUS

Ruling the rich domains of Thebes and all that sloping Phocis encompasses with its rich soil, whatever Ismenus waters, whatever Cithaeron views from his high peak, and slender Isthmus, keeping asunder its twin straits, no ancient rights of an ancestral home

---

[1] Hercules was once wrecked off the African coast and made his way on foot to the shore.

29

ignavus heres; nobiles non sunt mihi
avi nec altis inclitum titulis genus,
sed clara virtus. qui genus iactat suum, 340
aliena laudat. rapta sed trepida manu
sceptra obtinentur; omnis in ferro est salus;
quod civibus tenere te invitis scias
strictus tuetur ensis. alieno in loco
haut stabile regnum est; una sed nostras potest
fundare vires iuncta regali face
thalamisque Megara. ducet e genere inclito
novitas colorem nostra. non equidem reor
fore ut recuset ac meos spernat toros;
quod si impotenti pertinax animo abnuet, 350
stat tollere omnem penitus Herculeam domum.
invidia factum ac sermo populeris premet?
ars prima regni est posse invidiam pati.[1]
temptemus igitur, fors dedit nobis locum;
namque ipsa, tristi vestis obtentu caput
velata, iuxta praesides astat deos
laterique adhaeret verus Alcidae sator.

MEGARA

Quidnam iste, nostri generis exitium ac lues,
novi parat? quid temptat?

LYCVS

O clarum trahens
a stirpe nomen regia, facilis mea 360

---

[1] *So E:* ad invidiam *A :* te invidiam *ψ : to avoid the hiatus,*
Leo suggests posse rumores pati *or* plebis invidiam pati.

do I possess, a slothful heir; not mine are noble
ancestors, nor a race illustrious with lofty titles, but
valour glorious. Who vaunts his race, lauds what
belongs to others. But usurped sceptres are held in
anxious hand; all safety is in arms; what thou
knowest thou holdest against the will of citizens, the
drawn sword must guard. On alien soil kingship
stands not sure; but one there is who can set my
power on firm foundations, if joined to me in royal
wedlock by torch and couch—Megara. From her
noble line my newness shall gain richer hue. Nor
do I think she will refuse and scorn my bed; but
if stubbornly and with headstrong will she shall
decline, it is my resolve to give to utter ruin the
whole house of Hercules. Shall hatred and the
common people's talk restrain my hand? 'Tis the first
art of kings, the power to suffer hate. Let us make
trial, therefore; chance has given us occasion;
for Megara herself, her head close-veiled in mourning vestments, stands by the altar of her protecting
gods, and close by her side keeps the true sire of
Hercules.

MEGARA

What new thing plans that fellow, that destruction and pestilence of our race? What does he
attempt?

LYCUS

O thou whose illustrious name is drawn from
royal stock, graciously listen to my words a little

31

parumper aure verba patienti excipe.
si aeterna semper odia mortales gerant
nec coeptus umquam cedat ex animis furor,
sed arma felix teneat infelix paret,
nihil relinquent bella ; tum vastis ager
squalebit arvis, subdita tectis face
altus sepultas obruet gentes cinis.
pacem reduci velle victori expedit,
victo necesse est—particeps regno veni ;
sociemur animis, pignus hoc fidei cape—   370
continge dextram.   quid truci vultu siles ?

MEGARA

  Egone ut parentis sanguine aspersam manum
fratrumque gemina caede contingam ?   prius
extinguet ortus, referet occasus diem,
pax ante fida nivibus et flammis erit
et Scylla Siculum iunget Ausonio latus,
priusque multo vicibus alternis fugax
Euripus unda stabit Euboica piger.
patrem abstulisti, regna, germanos, larem
patrium—quid ultra est ?   una res superest mihi 380
fratre ac parente carior, regno ac lare—
odium tui, quod esse cum populo mihi
commune doleo.   pars quota ex illo mea est ?
dominare tumidus, spiritus altos gere ;
sequitur superbos ultor a tergo deus.
Thebana novi regna ; quid matres loquar
passas et ausas scelera ?   quid geminum nefas
32

while with patient ear. If mortals should cherish everlasting hate and if mad rage, once felt, should never drop from our hearts, but if the victor should keep and the vanquished prepare arms, nothing will wars leave us ; then on the wasted farms the fields will lie untilled, the torch will be set to homes, and deep ashes will overwhelm the buried nations. 'Tis expedient for the victor to wish for peace restored ; for the vanquished 'tis necessity.—Come, share my throne ; let us be joined in purpose ; accept this pledge of faith—touch hands with me. Why in grim-faced silence dost thou stand ?

MEGARA

I touch a hand stained with my father's blood and with my brothers' double murder? Sooner shall the East extinguish, the West bring back, the day ; sooner shall snow and flame be in lasting harmony and Scylla join the Sicilian and Ausonian shores ; and sooner far shall swift Euripus with his alternating tides rest sluggish upon Euboea's strand ! My father hast thou taken from me, my kingdom, brothers, my ancestral home—what is there else? There is one thing left to me, dearer than brother and father, kingdom and home—my hate of thee, which it is my grief that I must share with all the populace. How small a part of it is mine ! Rule on, swollen with pride, lift thy spirits high ; an avenging god pursues the proud. I know the Theban realm ; why mention the crimes which mothers have endured and dared ? Why speak of the

33

mixtumque nomen coniugis nati patris ?
quid bina fratrum castra ?   quid totidem rogos ?
riget superba Tantalis luctu parens   390
maestusque Phrygio manat in Sipylo lapis.
quin ipse torvum subrigens crista caput
Illyrica Cadmus regna permensus fuga
longas reliquit corporis tracti notas.
haec te manent exempla.   dominare ut libet
dum solita regni fata te nostri vocent.

LYCVS

Agedum efferatas rabida voces amove
et disce regum imperia ab Alcide pati.
ego rapta quamvis sceptra victrici geram
dextra regamque cuncta sine legum metu   400
quas arma vincunt, pauca pro causa loquar
nostra.   cruento cecidit in bello pater ?
cecidere fratres ?   arma non servant modum;
nec temperari facile nec reprimi potest
stricti ensis ira ; bella delectat cruor.
sed ille regno pro suo, nos improba
cupidine acti ?   quaeritur belli exitus,
non causa.   sed nunc pereat omnis memoria ;
cum victor arma posuit, et victum decet
deponere odia.   non ut inflexo genu   410
regnantem adores petimus ; hoc ipsum placet
animo ruinas quod capis magno tuas ;
es rege coniunx digna ; sociemus toros.

34

double infamy and the confused names of husband,
son and sire?[1] Why speak of the brothers'[2] twofold camps? the two funeral-pyres? The daughter
of Tantalus, presumptuous mother,[3] stiffens with
grief and, mournful on Phrygian Sipylus, drips tears
—a stone. Nay, Cadmus himself reared a head fierce
with its crest and, traversing Illyria's realm in flight,
left the long trail of his dragging body.[4] Thee
do such precedents of doom await. Lord it as thou
wilt, if only the accustomed destinies of our realm
summon thee.

LYCUS

Come, mad woman, have done with this wild talk,
and learn from Alcides to endure the commands of
kings. Although I wield a sceptre seized by my
victorious hand, though I rule all things without fear
of laws which arms o'ermaster, still will I say a few
words in mine own cause. 'Twas in a cruel war thy
father fell, sayest thou? thy brothers, too? Arms
observe no bounds; nor can the wrath of the sword,
once drawn, be easily checked or stayed; war de-
lights in blood. But he fought for his realm, sayest
thou; we, impelled by insatiable ambition? Of war
men ask the outcome, not the cause. But now let all
the past be forgotten; when the victor has laid down
his arms, it is meet that the vanquished, too, lay
down his hate. That thou on bended knee shouldst
pray to me as thy sovereign I do not ask; this of
itself is pleasing to me, that thou dost take thy
overthrow with a high spirit. Worthy art thou to
be a king's mate; then let us wed.

---

[1] The reference is to Oedipus. [2] Eteocles and Polynices.
[3] Niobe. [4] Cadmus was changed into a serpent.

MEGARA

Gelidus per artus vadit exangues tremor.
quod facinus aures pepulit? haut equidem horrui,
cum pace rupta bellicus muros fragor
circumsonaret, pertuli intrepide omnia ;
thalamos tremesco ; capta nunc videor mihi.
gravent catenae corpus et longa fame
mors protrahatur lenta ; non vincet fidem   420
vis ulla nostram. moriar, Alcide, tua.

LYCVS

Animosne mersus inferis coniunx facit?

MEGARA

Inferna tetigit, posset ut supera assequi.

LYCVS

Telluris illum pondus immensae premit.

MEGARA

Nullo premetur onere, qui caelum tulit.

LYCVS

Cogere.

MEGARA

Cogi qui potest nescit mori.

HERCULES FURENS

MEGARA

Cold horror creeps through my bloodless limbs.
What outrage has struck my ears? No terror felt I
when peace was broken and war's loud crash rang
around our walls; dauntlessly I bore it all; but
marriage—I shudder at it; now do I indeed seem
captive. Let chains load down my body, and let me
die a lingering death by slow starvation; still shall
no power o'ercome my loyalty. Alcides, I shall die
thine own.

LYCUS

Does a husband buried in the depths produce
such spirit?

MEGARA

He reached the depths that he might gain the
heights.

LYCUS

The weight of the boundless earth crushes him.

MEGARA

By no weight will he be crushed who upbore the
heavens.

LYCUS

Thou shalt be forced.

MEGARA

Who can be forced has not learned how to die.

LYCVS

Effare potius, quod novis thalamis parem
Regale munus.

MEGARA

Aut tuam mortem aut meam.

LYCVS

Moriere demens.

MEGARA

Coniugi occurram meo.

LYCVS

Sceptrone nostro famulus est potior tibi?   130

MEGARA

Quot iste famulus tradidit reges neci.

LYCVS

Cur ergo regi servit et patitur iugum?

MEGARA

Imperia dura tolle—quid virtus erit?

LYCVS

Obici feris monstrisque virtutem putas?

LYCUS

Say rather, what royal gift I shall prepare for my new bride.

MEGARA

Thy death or mine.

LYCUS

Fool, thou shalt die.

MEGARA

So shall I meet my husband.

LYCUS

Is a slave more to thee than I, a king?

MEGARA

How many kings has that slave given to death!

LYCUS

Why, then, does he serve a king and endure the yoke?

MEGARA

Do away with harsh commands—what then will valour be?

LYCUS

To oppose oneself to beasts and monsters think'st thou valour?

SENECAE TRAGOEDIAE

MEGARA

Virtutis est domare quae cuncti pavent.

LYCVS

Tenebrae loquentem magna Tartareae premunt.

MEGARA

Non est ad astra mollis e terris via.

LYCVS

Quo patre genitus caelitum sperat domos?

AMPHITRYON

Miseranda coniunx Herculis magni, sile;
partes meae sunt reddere Alcidae patrem   440
genusque verum.   post tot ingentis viri
memoranda facta postque pacatum manu
quodcumque Titan ortus et labens videt,
post monstra tot perdomita, post Phlegram impio
sparsam cruore postque defensos deos
nondum liquet de patre?   mentimur Iovem?
Iunonis odio crede.

LYCVS

           Quid violas Iovem?
mortale caelo non potest iungi genus.

40

HERCULES FURENS

MEGARA

'Tis valour's part to subdue what all men fear.

LYCUS

The shades of Tartarus bury the braggart deep.

MEGARA

There is no easy way to the stars from earth.

LYCUS

Who is his father that he hopes for a home in heaven?

AMPHITRYON

Unhappy wife of great Hercules, be still; 'tis my place to restore to Alcides his father and true lineage. [*To* LYCUS.] After all the great hero's memorable deeds, after peace has been gained by his hand for all that the sun, rising and setting, sees, after so many monsters tamed, after Phlegra [1] stained with impious blood, after his protection of the gods, is not his fathering yet clear? Claim we Jove falsely? Then believe Juno's hate.

LYCUS

Why blaspheme Jove? The race of mortals cannot mate with heaven.

---

[1] The scene of the battle between the giants and the gods. Hercules fought on the side of the gods.

AMPHITRYON

Communis ista pluribus causa est deis.

LYCVS

Famuline fuerant ante quam fierent dei ?   450

AMPHITRYON

Pastor Pheraeos Delius pavit greges—

LYCVS

Sed non per omnes exul erravit plagas.

AMPHITRYON

Quem profuga terra mater errante edidit?

LYCVS

Num monstra saeva Phoebus aut timuit feras ?

AMPHITRYON

Primus sagittas imbuit Phoebi draco.

LYCVS

Quam gravia parvus tulerit ignoras mala?

AMPHITRYON

E matris utero fulmine eiectus puer
mox fulminanti proximus patri stetit.

HERCULES FURENS

AMPHITRYON

That is the common origin of many gods.

LYCUS

But were they slaves [1] ere they became divine?

AMPHITRYON

The Delian as a shepherd tended flocks at Pherae—[2]

LYCUS

But he did not in exile roam o'er all the world.

AMPHITRYON

What? He whom an exiled mother brought forth on a roaming isle?

LYCUS

Did Phoebus encounter savage monsters or wild beasts?

AMPHITRYON

A dragon was the first to stain Phoebus' shafts.

LYCUS

Knowest thou not what heavy ills he bore in infancy?

AMPHITRYON

Ripped by a thunderbolt from his mother's womb, a boy [3] in after-time stood next his sire, the

[1] As was Hercules to Eurystheus.
[2] The reference is to Apollo's year of servitude to Admetus.
[3] Bacchus.

quid ?   qui gubernat astra, qui nubes quatit,
non latuit infans rupis Idaeae specu ?   460
sollicita tanti pretia natales habent
semperque magno constitit nasci deum.

LYCVS

Quemcumque miserum videris, hominem scias.

AMPHITRYON

Quemcumque fortem videris, miserum neges.

LYCVS

Fortem vocemus cuius ex umeris leo,
donum puellae factus, et clava excidit
fulsitque pictum veste Sidonia latus ?
fortem vocemus cuius horrentes comae
maduere nardo, laude qui notas manus
ad non virilem tympani movit sonum,   470
mitra ferocem barbara frontem premens ?

AMPHITRYON

Non erubescit Bacchus effusos tener
sparsisse crines nec manu molli levem
vibrare thyrsum, cum parum forti gradu
auro decorum syrma barbarico trahit.
post multa virtus opera laxari solet.

LYCVS

Hoc Euryti fatetur eversi domus
pecorumque ritu virginum oppressi greges ;

Thunderer. What? he who rules the stars, who shakes the clouds, did he not lie hid in infancy in a cave of rocky Ida? Such lofty birth must pay its price of care, and ever has it cost dear to be born a god.

LYCUS

Whome'er thou shalt see wretched, know him man.

AMPHITRYON

Whome'er thou shalt see brave, call him not wretched.

LYCUS

Are we to call him brave from whose shoulders fell the lion's skin and club, made present for a girl,[1] and whose side shone resplendent, decked out in Tyrian robes? Call him brave, whose bristling locks dripped with nard, who busied those famous hands with unmanly strummings on the tambourine, whose warlike brow a barbaric turban crowned?

AMPHITRYON

But dainty Bacchus does not blush to sprinkle with perfume his flowing locks, nor in his soft hand to brandish the slender thyrsus, when with mincing gait he trails his robe gay with barbaric gold. After much toil, valour still seeks relief.

LYCUS

That fact the ruined house of Eurytus confesses, and the flocks of maidens harried like so many sheep; no

[1] Omphale.

hoc nulla Iuno, nullus Eurystheus iubet;
ipsius haec sunt opera.

AMPHITRYON

               Non nosti omnia;   480
ipsius opus est caestibus fractus suis
Eryx et Eryci iunctus Antaeus Libys,
et qui hospitali caede manantes foci
bibere iustum sanguinem Busiridis;
ipsius opus est vulneri et ferro invius
mortem coactus integer Cycnus pati,
nec unus una Geryon victus manu.
eris inter istos—qui tamen nullo stupro
laesere thalamos.

LYCVS

             Quod Iovi hoc regi licet.
Iovi dedisti coniugem, regi dabit;   490
et te magistro non novum hoc discet nurus,
etiam viro probante, meliorem sequi.
sin copulari pertinax taedis negat,
vel ex coacta nobilem partum feram.

MEGARA

Vmbrae Creontis et penates Labdaci
et nuptiales impii Oedipodae faces,
nunc solita nostro fata coniugio date.
nunc, nunc, cruentae regis Aegypti nurus,
adeste multo sanguine infectae manus.
dest una numero Danais—explebo nefas.   500

46

Juno, no Eurystheus ordered this; these works are his very own.

AMPHITRYON

Thou knowest not all; his own work it is that Eryx was crushed by his own gauntlets and that Libyan Antaeus shared Eryx' fate; that the altars which dripped with the blood of strangers drank, and justly, too, Busiris' blood; his own work is Cycnus, though proof against wound and sword, forced to suffer death untouched by wounds; and threefold Geryon by one hand overcome. Thou shalt share the fate of these—and yet they never defiled with lust the marriage-bed.

LYCUS

What is Jove's right is a king's right, too. Thou gavest thy wife [1] to Jove, to a king shall he give his [2]; and taught by thy example thy daughter shall learn this old-time lesson—when the husband also gives consent, to take the better man. But should she stubbornly refuse to wed me by the torches' rite, even by force will I get me a noble stock from her.

MEGARA

Ye shades of Creon, ye household gods of Labdacus, ye nuptial torches of incestuous Oedipus, now to our union grant its accustomed doom. Now, now, ye bloody daughters of King Aegyptus, be present here, your hands deep-stained in blood. One Danaïd is lacking from the tale—I will complete the crime.

---

[1] Alcmena.   [2] Megara.

LYCVS

Coniugia quoniam pervicax hostra abnuis
regemque terres, sceptra quid possint scies.
complectere aras—nullus eripiet deus
te mihi, nec orbe si remolito queat
ad supera victor numina Alcides vehi.
congerite silvas ; templa supplicibus suis
iniecta flagrent, coniugem et totum gregem
consumat unus igne subiecto rogus.

AMPHITRYON

Hoc munus a te genitor Alcidae peto,
rogare quod me deceat, ut primus cadam.   510

LYCVS

Qui morte cunctos luere supplicium iubet
nescit tyrannus esse.   diversa inroga :
miserum veta perire, felicem iube.
ego, dum cremandis trabibus accrescit rogus,
sacro regentem maria votivo colam.

AMPHITRYON

Pro numinum vis summa, pro caelestium
rector parensque, cuius excussis tremunt
humana telis, impiam regis feri
compesce dextram—quid deos frustra precor ?
ubicumque es, audi, nate.   cur subito labant   520
agitata motu templa ?   cur mugit solum ?
infernus imo sonuit e fundo fragor.[1]
audimur, est est sonitus Herculei gradus.

[1] *Leo deletes this line.*

HERCULES FURENS

LYCUS

Since my suit thou dost stubbornly refuse and threatenest thy king, now shalt thou know what royal power can do. Embrace the altar—no god shall snatch thee from me, not though earth's mass could be pushed aside and Alcides brought back in triumph to the upper world. [*To attendants.*] 'Heap high the logs; let the temple fall blazing on its suppliants; apply the torch and let one pyre consume the wife and all her brood.

AMPHITRYON

This boon as father of Alcides I ask of thee, which becomes me well to ask, that I be first to fall.

LYCUS

He who inflicts on all the penalty of death knows not how to be a king. Impose contrasting penalties : forbid the wretched, command the happy man to die. Now while the pyre feeds on the burning beams, with promised gifts will I worship him who rules the sea. [*Exit.*

AMPHITRYON

O mightiest of gods, O ruler and sire of the immortals, at whose hurtling bolts mortals tremble, check thou the impious hand of this mad king—why make vain prayers unto the gods? Where'er thou art, hear thou, my son. But why with sudden motion does the rocking temple totter? Why does earth rumble? Infernal crashing has sounded from the lowest pit. Our prayer is heard ; it is, it is the resounding tread of Hercules !

49

O Fortuna viris invida fortibus,
quam non aequa bonis praemia dividis.
" Eurystheus facili regnet in otio ;
Alcmena genitus bella per omnia
monstris exagitet caeliferam manum :
serpentis resecet colla feracia,
deceptis referat mala sororibus,   530
cum somno dederit pervigiles genas
pomis divitibus praepositus draco."

Intravit Scythiae multivagas domos
et gentes patriis sedibus hospitas,
calcavitque freti terga rigentia
et mutis tacitum litoribus mare.
illic dura carent aequora fluctibus,
et qua plena rates carbasa tenderant,
intonsis teritur semita Sarmatis.
stat pontus, vicibus mobilis annuis,   540
navem nunc facilis nunc equitem pati.
illic quae viduis gentibus imperat,
aurato religans ilia balteo,
detraxit spolium nobile corpori
et peltam et nivei vincula pectoris,
victorem posito suspiciens genu.

Qua spe praecipites actus ad inferos,
audax ire vias inremeabiles,
vidisti Siculae regna Proserpinae ?
illic nulla noto nulla favonio   550

HERCULES FURENS

O Fortune, jealous of the brave, in allotting thy
favours how unjust art thou unto the good ! " Let
Eurystheus lord it in untroubled ease ; let Alcmena's
son in endless wars employ on monsters the hand that
bore the heavens ; let him cut off the hydra's teeming necks ; let him bring back the apples from the
cheated sisters when the dragon, set to watch over
the precious fruit, has given his ever-waking eyes to
sleep." [1]

[533] He invaded the wandering homes of Scythia
and nations strangers to their ancestral haunts ; [2] he
trod the sea's frozen ridge, a still ocean with silent
shores.   There the frozen waters are without waves,
and where but now ships had spread full sail, a path
is worn by the long-haired Sarmatae.   There lies
the sea, changing as seasons change, ready to bear
now ship, now horseman.   There she [3] who rules o'er
tribes unwed, with a golden girdle about her loins,
stripped the glorious spoil from her body, her shield
and the bands of her snow-white breast, on bended
knee looking up to her victor.

[547] With what hope, driven headlong to the
depths, bold to tread ways irretraceable, didst thou
see Sicilian Proserpina's realms ?   There beneath
no southern, no western wind do the seas rise

---

[1] A supposed quotation from Fortune's decree.
[2] These were nomadic tribes.
[3] Hippolyte, queen of the Amazons.

consurgunt tumidis fluctibus aequora;
non illic geminum Tyndaridae genus
succurrunt timidis sidera navibus :
stat nigro pelagus gurgite languidum,
et cum Mors avidis pallida dentibus
gentes innumeras manibus intulit,
uno tot populi remige transeunt.

Evincas utinam iura ferae Stygis
Parcarumque colos non revocabiles.
hic qui rex populis pluribus imperat,   560
bello cum peteres Nestoream Pylon,
tecum conseruit pestiferas manus
telum tergemina cuspide praeferens :
effugit tenui vulnere saucius
et mortis dominus pertimuit mori.
fatum rumpe manu, tristibus inferis
prospectus pateat lucis et invius
limes det faciles ad superos vias !

Immites potuit flectere cantibus
umbrarum dominos et prece supplici   570
Orpheus, Eurydicen dum repetit suam.
quae silvas et aves saxaque traxerat
ars, quae praebuerat fluminibus moras,
ad cuius sonitum constiterant ferae,
mulcet non solitis vocibus inferos
et surdis resonat clarius in locis.
deflent Eurydicen Threiciae nurus,[1]

---

[1] *Placed after 580 in A :* Tartareae nurus *Withof:* Elysiae *Bentley.*

with swollen waves; there the stars of the twin Tyndaridae come not to the aid of timorous ships; sluggish stands the mere [1] with black abyss, and, when Death, pale-visaged with greedy teeth, has brought countless tribes to the world of shades, one ferryman transports those many peoples.

[558] Oh, that thou mayest o'ercome the laws of cruel Styx, and the relentless distaffs of the Fates. He [2] who as king lords it o'er countless peoples, what time thou wast making war on Pylos, Nestor's land, brought to combat with thee his plague-dealing hands, brandishing his three-forked spear, yet fled away, with but a slight wound smitten, and, though lord of death, feared he would die. Fate's bars burst thou with thy hands; to the sad nether regions open a view of light, and let the trackless path [3] now give easy passage to the upper world!

[569] Orpheus had power to bend the ruthless lords of the shades by song and suppliant prayer, when he sought back his Eurydice. The art which had drawn the trees and birds and rocks, which had stayed the course of rivers, at whose sound the beasts had stopped to listen, soothes the underworld with unaccustomed strains, and rings out clearer in those unhearing realms. Eurydice the Thracian brides bewail; even the gods,

---

[1] The Styx.
[2] Pluto. The reference is to the combat of Hercules against Pluto in defence of the Pylians.
[3] *i.e.* between life and death.

deflent et lacrimis difficiles dei,
et qui fronte nimis crimina tetrica
quaerunt ac veteres excutiunt reos   580
flentes Eurydicen iuridici sedent.
tandem mortis ait " vincimur" arbiter,
" evade ad superos, lege tamen data—
tu post terga tui perge viri comes,
tu non ante tuam respice coniugem,
quam cum clara deos obtulerit dies
Spartanique aderit ianua Taenari."
odit verus amor nec patitur moras ;
munus dum properat cernere, perdidit.

    Quae vinci potuit regia carmine,   590
haec vinci poterit regia viribus.

HERCVLES

  O lucis almae rector et caeli decus,
qui alterna curru spatia flammifero ambiens
inlustre latis exeris terris caput,
da, Phoebe, veniam, si quid inlicitum tui
videre vultus ; iussus in lucem extuli
arcana mundi.   tuque, caelestum arbiter
parensque, visus fulmine opposito tege ;
et tu, secundo maria qui sceptro regis,
imas pete undas.   quisquis ex alto aspicit   600
terrena, facie pollui metuens nova,
aciem reflectat oraque in caelum erigat
portenta fugiens.   hoc nefas cernant duo,
qui advexit et quae iussit.   in poenas meas

whom no tears can move, bewail her; and they who with awful brows investigate men's crimes and sift out ancient wrongs, as they sit in judgment [1] bewail Eurydice. At length death's lord exclaims: "We own defeat; go forth to the upper world, yet by this appointed doom—fare thou as comrade behind thy husband, and thou, look not back upon thy wife until bright day shall have revealed the gods of heaven, and the opening of Spartan Taenarus shall be at hand." True love hates delay and brooks it not; while he hastes to look upon his prize, 'tis lost.

590 The realm which could be overcome by song, that realm shall strength have power to overcome.

[*Enter* HERCULES, *just returned from the lower world, accompanied by* THESEUS; *apparently, also, he is leading the dog,* CERBERUS, *though this point seems less clear as the play develops.*]

HERCULES

O lord of kindly light, glory of heaven, who in thy flame-bearing car dost circle both spaces [2] of the sky, and dost show thy shining face to the broad lands, pardon, O Phoebus, if any unlawful sight thine eyes have seen; at another's bidding have I brought to light the hidden things of earth. And thou, O judge and sire of heavenly beings, hide thy face behind thy thunderbolt; and thou who, next in power, dost control the seas, flee to thy lowest waters. Whoever from on high looks down on things of earth, and would not be defiled by a strange, new sight, let him turn away his gaze, lift his eyes to heaven, and shun the portent. Let only two look on this monster—him who brought and her

---

[1] It is impossible to reproduce in translation the obvious pun in *Eurydicen iuridici.*

[2] *i.e.* the upper and lower hemispheres.

atque in labores non satis terrae patent
Iunonis odio.   vidi inaccessa omnibus,
ignota Phoebo quaeque deterior polus
obscura diro spatia concessit Iovi;
et, si placerent tertiae sortis loca,
regnare potui.   noctis aeternae chaos   610
et nocte quiddam gravius et tristes deos
et fata vidi, morte contempta redi.
quid restat aliud ?   vidi et ostendi inferos.
da si quid ultra est, iam diu pateris manus
cessare nostras, Iuno ; quae vinci iubes ?
    Sed templa quare miles infestus tenet
limenque sacrum terror armorum obsidet ?

AMPHITRYON

    Vtrumne visus vota decipiunt meos,
an ille domitor orbis et Graium decus
tristi silentem nubilo liquit domum ?   620
estne ille natus ?   membra laetitia stupent.
o nate, certa at sera Thebarum salus,
teneone in auras editum an vana fruor
deceptus umbra ?   tune es ?   agnosco toros
umerosque et alto nobilem trunco manum.

HERCVLES

    Vnde iste, genitor, squalor et lugubribus
amicta coniunx ?   unde tam foedo obsiti
paedore nati ?   quae domum clades gravat ?
56

who ordered it. To appoint me penalties and tasks
earth is not broad enough for Juno's hate. I have
seen places unapproached by any, unknown to
Phoebus, those gloomy spaces which the baser pole
hath yielded to infernal Jove ; and if the regions of
the third estate pleased me, I might have reigned.
The chaos of everlasting night, and something worse
than night, and the grim gods and the fates—all
these I saw and, having flouted death, I have come
back. What else remains ? I have seen and revealed the lower world. If aught is left to do,
give it to me, O Juno ; too long already dost
thou let my hands lie idle. What dost thou bid
me conquer ?

616 But why do hostile soldiers guard the shrine
and dreadful arms beset the sacred portal ?

AMPHITRYON

Can it be that my hopes deceive my sight, or
has that world-subduer, the pride of Greece, come
back from the silent halls of mournful gloom ? Is that
my son ? My limbs are numb with joy. O son, sure,
though late, deliverance of Thebes, do I really clasp
thee risen to upper air, or am I mocked, enjoying
but an empty shade ? Is it thou indeed ? Aye, now
I recognize the bulging thews, the shoulders, the
hand famed for its huge club.

HERCULES

Whence this squalid garb, father ? Why is my
wife clad in mourning weeds ? Why are my sons
covered with loathsome rags ? What disaster overwhelms my house ?

AMPHITRYON

Socer est peremptus, regna possedit Lycus,
natos parentem coniugem leto petit.　　　　630

HERCVLES

Ingrata tellus, nemo ad Herculeae domus
auxilia venit? vidit hoc tantum nefas
defensus orbis?—cur diem questu tero?
mactetur hostia, hanc ferat virtus notam
fiatque summus hostis Alcidae Lycus.
ad hauriendum sanguinem inimicum feror,
Theseu; resiste, ne qua vis subita ingruat.
me bella poscunt, differ amplexus, parens,
coniunxque differ. nuntiet Diti Lycus
me iam redisse.

THESEVS

　　　　　　Flebilem ex oculis fuga,　　　640
regina, vultum, tuque nato sospite
lacrimas cadentes reprime. si novi Herculem,
Lycus Creonti debitas poenas dabit.
lentum est dabit—dat; hoc quoque est lentum—
　　dedit.

AMPHITRYON

Votum secundet qui potest nostrum deus
rebusque lapsis adsit. O magni comes
magnanime nati, pande virtutum ordinem,
quam longa maestos ducat ad manes via,
ut vincla tulerit dura Tartareus canis.

HERCULES FURENS

The father of thy wife is slain; Lycus has seized the throne; thy sons, thy father, thy wife he claims for death.

HERCULES

O ungrateful land, was there none to aid the house of Hercules? Did it see this monstrous wrong, the world I succoured?—but why waste the day in idle plaints? Let the victim [1] be offered up, let my manhood bear this brand of shame, and let the final foe of Hercules be—Lycus. I haste me, Theseus, to drain his detested blood; remain thou here, lest some unexpected force assail. War summons me; delay thy embraces, father; wife, delay them. Let Lycus take the news to Dis that now I have returned.

[*Exit* HERCULES.]

THESEUS

Banish that tearful look from thine eyes, O queen, and do thou,[2] since thy son is safe, check thy falling tears. If I know Hercules, Lycus shall pay the penalty he owes to Creon. "Shall pay" is slow—he pays; that, too, is slow—he has paid.

AMPHITRYON

May the god who can, fulfil our desire and favour our fallen estate. And do thou, great-hearted companion of our great son, unfold his heroic deeds in order; tell how long a way leads to the gloomy shades, and how the Tartarean dog bore his galling bonds.

---

[1] *i.e.* Lycus.   [2] To Amphitryon.

Memorare cogis acta securae quoque   650
horrenda menti. vix adhuc certa est fides
vitalis aurae, torpet acies luminum
hebetesque visus vix diem insuetum ferunt.

AMPHITRYON

Pervince, Theseu, quidquid alto in pectore
remanet pavoris neve te fructu optimo
frauda laborum ; quae fuit durum pati,
meminisse dulce est. fare casus horridos.

THESEVS

Fas omne mundi teque dominantem precor
regno capaci teque quam amotam inrita
quaesivit Enna mater, ut iura abdita   660
et operta terris liceat impune eloqui.
Spartana tellus nobile attollit iugum,
densis ubi aequor Taenarus silvis premit ;
hic ora solvit Ditis invisi domus
hiatque rupes alta et immenso specu
ingens vorago faucibus vastis patet
latumque pandit omnibus populis iter.
non caeca tenebris incipit primo via ;
tenuis relictae lucis a tergo nitor
fulgorque dubius solis adflicti cadit   670
et ludit aciem. nocte sic mixta solet
praebere lumen primus aut serus dies.

HERCULES FURENS

Thou dost force me to recall deeds which strike
terror to my soul even in security. Scarcely yet
do I trust assuredly to breathe the vital air; the
sight of my eyes is dimmed, and my dull vision can
scarce bear the unaccustomed light.

AMPHITRYON

But, Theseus, master whate'er of dread yet dwells
deep in thy heart and rob not thyself of toils'
best fruit; things 'twas hard to bear 'tis pleasant to
recall. Tell thou the awful tale.

THESEUS

All the world's holy powers, and thou[1] who rulest
the all-holding realm, and thou[2] whom, stolen
from Enna, thy mother sought in vain, may it be
right, I pray, boldly to speak of powers hidden away
and buried beneath the earth.

[662] The Spartan land a famous ridge uplifts where
Taenarus with its dense forests invades the sea. Here
the home of hateful Pluto unbars its mouth; a high
cliff cracks asunder, and a huge chasm, a bottomless
abyss, spreads its vast jaws wide and opens for all
peoples a broad path. Not in utter darkness does the
way first begin; a slender gleam of the light left
behind and a doubtful glow as of the sun in eclipse
falls there and cheats the vision. Such light the day
mingled with night is wont to give, at early dawn or
at late twilight. From here ample spaces spread out,

---

[1] Pluto.   [2] Proserpina.

hinc ampla vacuis spatia laxantur locis,
in quae omne versum properat humanum genus.
nec ire labor est ; ipsa deducit via.
ut saepe puppes aestus invitas rapit,
sic pronus aer urguet atque avidum chaos,
gradumque retro flectere haut umquam sinunt
umbrae tenaces.   intus immensi sinus
placido quieta labitur Lethe vado   680
demitque curas, neve remeandi amplius
pateat facultas, flexibus multis gravem
involvit amnem, qualis incertis vagus
Maeander undis ludit et cedit sibi
instatque dubius litus an fontem petat.
palus inertis foeda Cocyti iacet ;
hic vultur, illic luctifer bubo gemit
omenque triste resonat infaustae strigis.
horrent opaca fronde nigrantes comae,
taxum imminentem qua tenet segnis Sopor   690
Famesque maesta tabido rictu iacet
Pudorque serus conscios vultus tegit.
Metus Pavorque furvus et frendens Dolor
aterque Luctus sequitur et Morbus tremens
et cincta ferro Bella ; in extremo abdita
iners Senectus adiuvat baculo gradum.

AMPHITRYON

Estne aliqua tellus Cereris aut Bacchi ferax ?

void regions, whereto the entire human race turns
and hastens. It is no toil to go; the road itself draws
them down. As oft-times the waves sweep on unwilling ships, so does the downward breeze drive, and
the greedy void, and never do the clutching shades
permit a backward step. Within the abyss, Lethe,
measureless in sweep, glides smoothly on with placid
stream, and takes away our cares; and, that there
may be no power to retrace the path, with windings
manifold it takes its sluggish way, even as the
vagrant Maeander with its inconstant waters plays
along, now retreats upon itself, now presses on, in
doubt whether to seek the seashore or its source.
The foul pool of Cocytus' sluggish stream lies here;
here the vulture, there the dole-bringing owl utters
its cry, and the sad omen of the gruesome screech-
owl sounds. The leaves shudder, black with gloomy
foliage where sluggish Sleep clings to the overhanging yew, where sad Hunger lies with wasted jaws, and
Shame, too late, hides her guilt-burdened face. Dread
stalks there, gloomy Fear and gnashing Pain, sable
Grief, tottering Disease and iron-girt War; and last
of all slow Age supports his steps upon a staff.

AMPHITRYON

Is any land there fruitful of corn or wine?

THESEVS

Non prata viridi laeta facie germinant
nec adulta leni fluctuat Zephyro seges;
non ulla ramos silva pomiferos habet: 700
sterilis profundi vastitas squalet soli
et foeda tellus torpet aeterno situ,
rerumque maestus finis et mundi ultima.[1]
immotus aer haeret et pigro sedet
nox atra mundo.   cuncta maerore horrida
ipsaque morte peior est mortis locus.

AMPHITRYON

Quid ille opaca qui regit sceptro loca,
qua sede positus temperat populos leves?

THESEVS

Est in recessu Tartari obscuro locus,
quem gravibus umbris spissa caligo alligat.   710
a fonte discors manat hinc uno latex,
alter quieto similis (hunc iurant dei)
tacente sacram devehens fluvio Styga;
at hic tumultu rapitur ingenti ferox
et saxa fluctu volvit Acheron invius
renavigari.   cingitur duplici vado
adversa Ditis regia, atque ingens domus
umbrante luco tegitur.   hic vasto specu
pendent tyranni limina, hoc umbris iter,
haec porta regni.   campus hanc circa iacet,   720

---

[1] *Leo deletes this line.*

64

HERCULES FURENS

No meadows bud, joyous with verdant view, no
ripened corn waves in the gentle breeze; not any
grove has fruit-producing boughs; the barren desert
of the abysmal fields lies all untilled, and the foul
land lies torpid in endless sloth—sad end of things,
the world's last estate. The air hangs motionless and
black night broods over a sluggish world. All things
are with grief dishevelled, and worse than death
itself is the abode of death.

AMPHITRYON

What of him who holds sway over the dark realm?
Where sits he, governing his flitting tribes?

THESEUS

There is a place in a dark recess of Tartarus, which
with a heavy pall dense mists enshroud. Hence flow
from a single source two streams, unlike: one, a placid
river (by this do the gods swear), with silent current
bears on the sacred Styx; the other with mighty
roar rushes fiercely on, rolling down rocks in its
flood, Acheron, that cannot be recrossed. The royal
hall of Dis stands opposite, girt by a double moat,
and the huge house is hid by an o'ershadowing grove.
Here in a spacious cavern the tyrant's doors over-
hang; this is the road for spirits, this is the kingdom's
gate. A plain lies round about this where sits the

in quo superbo digerit vultu sedens
animas recentes dira maiestas dei.
frons torva, fratrum quae tamen speciem gerat
gentisque tantae, vultus est illi Iovis,
sed fulminantis; magna pars regni trucis
est ipse dominus, cuius aspectus timet
quidquid timetur.

AMPHITRYON

       Verane est fama inferis
tam sera reddi iura et oblitos sui
sceleris nocentes debitas poenas dare?
quis iste veri rector atque aequi arbiter?   730

THESEVS

Non unus alta sede quaesitor sedens
iudicia trepidis sera sortitur reis.
aditur illo Cnosius Minos foro,
Rhadamanthus illo, Thetidis hoc audit socer.
quod quisque fecit, patitur; auctorem scelus
repetit suoque premitur exemplo nocens.
vidi cruentos carcere includi duces
et impotentis terga plebeia manu
scindi tyranni. quisquis est placide potens
dominusque vitae servat innocuas manus   740
et incruentum mitis imperium regit
animoque parcit, longa permensus diu
felicis aevi spatia vel caelum petit
vel laeta felix nemoris Elysii loca,
iudex futurus. sanguine humano abstine
quicumque regnas; scelera taxantur modo
maiore vestra.

66

god, where with haughty mien his awful majesty assorts the new-arriving souls. Lowering is his brow, yet such as wears the aspect of his brothers and his high race; his countenance is that of Jove, but Jove the thunderer; chief part of that realm's grimness is its own lord, whose aspect whate'er is dreaded dreads.

AMPHITRYON

Is the report true that in the underworld justice, though tardy, is meted out, and that guilty souls who have forgot their crimes suffer due punishment? Who is that lord of truth, that arbiter of justice?

THESEUS

Not one inquisitor alone sits on the high judgment-seat and allots his tardy sentences to trembling culprits. In yonder court they pass to Cretan Minos' presence, in that to Rhadamanthus', here the father [1] of Thetis' spouse gives audience. What each has done, he suffers; upon its author the crime comes back, and the guilty soul is crushed by its own form of guilt. I have seen bloody chiefs immured in prison; the insolent tyrant's back torn by plebeian hands. He who reigns mildly and, though lord of life, keeps guiltless hands, who mercifully and without bloodshed rules his realm, checking his own spirit, he shall traverse long stretches of happy life and at last gain the skies, or else in bliss reach Elysium's joyful land and sit in judgment there. Abstain from human blood, all ye who rule: with heavier punishment your sins are judged.

[1] Aeacus, father of Peleus.

AMPHITRYON

   Certus inclusos tenet
locus nocentes? utque fert fama, impios
supplicia vinclis saeva perpetuis domant?

THESEVS

 Rapitur volucri tortus Ixion rota;   750
cervice saxum grande Sisyphia sedet;
in amne medio faucibus siccis senex
sectatur undas, alluit mentum latex,
fidemque cum iam saepe decepto dedit,
perit unda in ore; poma destituunt famem.
praebet volucri Tityos aeternas dapes
urnasque frustra Danaides plenas gerunt;
errant furentes impiae Cadmeides
terretque mensas avida Phineas avis.

AMPHITRYON

 Nunc ede nati nobilem pugnam mei.   760
patrui volentis munus an spolium refert?

THESEVS

 Ferale tardis imminet saxum vadis,
stupent ubi undae, segne torpescit fretum.
hunc servat amnem cultu et aspectu horridus
pavidosque manes squalidus vectat senex.
inpexa pendet barba, deformem sinum
nodus coercet, concavae squalent [1] genae;

[1] *So E: Richter, with A,* lucent: *Leo conjectures* fulgent.

HERCULES FURENS

AMPHITRYON

Does any certain place enclose the guilty? and, as rumour has it, do sinners suffer cruel punishments in bonds unending?

THESEUS

Ixion whirls, racked on a flying wheel; a huge stone rests on the neck of Sisyphus; in mid-stream an old man [1] with parched lips catches at the waves; the water bathes his chin and, when at last it has given him, though oft deceived, a pledge of faith, the wave perishes at his lips; fruits mock his hunger. To the vulture Tityos gives never-ending feasts; the Danaïdes bear their brimming urns in vain; the impious Cadmeïds roam in their madness, and the ravenous bird [2] torments Phineus at his board.

AMPHITRYON

Now tell my son's famous struggle. Is it his willing uncle's gift, or his spoil, he brings?

THESEUS

A rock funereal o'erhangs the slothful shoals, where the waves are sluggish and the dull mere is numbed. This stream an old man tends, clad in foul garb and to the sight abhorrent, and ferries over the quaking shades. His beard hangs down unkempt; a knot ties his robe's misshapen folds; haggard his sunken cheeks; himself his own boatman, with a long

---

[1] Tantalus.
[2] The harpy.

regit ipse longo portitor conto ratem.
hic onere vacuam litori puppem applicans
repetebat umbras; poscit Alcides viam   770
cedente turba; dirus exclamat Charon:
" quo pergis, audax? siste properantem gradum."
non passus ullas natus Alcmena moras
ipso coactum navitam conto domat
scanditque puppem. cumba populorum capax
succubuit uni; sidit et gravior ratis
utrimque Lethen latere titubanti bibit.
tum victa trepidant monstra, Centauri truces
Lapithaeque multo in bella succensi mero;
Stygiae paludis ultimos quaerens sinus   780
fecunda mergit capita Lernaeus labor.

    Post haec avari Ditis apparet domus:
hic saevus umbras territat Stygius canis,
qui terna vasto capita concutiens sono
regnum tuetur. sordidum tabo caput
lambunt colubrae, viperis horrent iubae
longusque torta sibilat cauda draco.
par ira formae. sensit ut motus pedum,
attollit hirtas angue vibrato comas
missumque captat aure subrecta sonum,   790
sentire et umbras solitus. ut propior stetit
Iove natus, antro sedit incertus canis
leviterque timuit—ecce latratu gravi
loca muta terret; sibilat totos minax
serpens per armos. vocis horrendae fragor
per ora missus terna felices quoque

pole he directs his craft. Now, having discharged his load, he is turning his boat towards the bank, seeking the ghosts again; Alcides demands passage, while the crowd draws back. Fierce Charon cries: "Whither in such haste, bold man? Halt there thy hastening steps." Brooking no delay, Alcmena's son o'erpowers the ferryman with his own pole and climbs aboard. The craft, ample for whole nations, sinks low beneath one man; as he takes his seat the o'erweighted boat with rocking sides drinks in Lethe on either hand. Then the monsters he had conquered are in a panic, the fierce Centaurs and the Lapithae whom too much wine had inflamed to war; and, seeking the farthest fens of the Stygian swamp, Lerna's labour [1] plunges deep his fertile heads.

[782] Next after this there appears the palace of greedy Dis. Here the savage Stygian dog frightens the shades; tossing back and forth his triple heads, with huge bayings he guards the realm. Around his head, foul with corruption, serpents lap, his shaggy mane bristles with vipers, and in his twisted tail a long snake hisses. His rage matches his shape. Soon as he feels the stir of feet he raises his head, rough with darting snakes, and with ears erect catches at the onsped sound, wont as he is to hear even the shades. When the son of Jove stood closer, within his cave the dog crouches hesitant and feels a touch of fear. Then suddenly, with deep bayings, he terrifies the silent places; the snakes hiss threateningly along all his shoulders. The clamour of his dreadful voice, issuing from triple throats, fills even the

---

[1] The Hydra.

exterret umbras.   solvit a laeva feros
tunc ipse rictus et Cleonaeum caput
opponit ac se tegmine ingenti tegit,
victrice magnum dextera robur gerens.   800
huc nunc et illuc verbere assiduo rotat,
ingeminat ictus.   domitus infregit minas
et cuncta lassus capita summisit canis
antroque toto cessit.   extimuit sedens
uterque solio dominus et duci iubet;
me quoque petenti munus Alcidae dedit.

Tum gravia monstri colla permulcens manu
adamaṇte texto vincit; oblitus sui
custos opaci pervigil regni canis
componit aures timidus et patiens trahi   810
erumque fassus, ore summisso obsequens,
utrumque cauda pulsat anguifera latus.
postquam est ad oras Taenari ventum et nitor
percussit oculos lucis ignotae novus,
resumit animos victus et vastas furens
quassat catenas; paene victorem abstulit
pronumque retro vexit et movit gradu.
tunc et meas respexit Alcides manus;
geminis uterque viribus tractum canem
ira furentem et bella temptantem inrita   820
intulimus orbi.   vidit ut clarum diem
et pura nitidi spatia conspexit poli,
oborta nox est, lumina in terram dedit;[1]
compressit oculos et diem invisum expulit

[1] *Leo deletes this line.*

72

blessed shades with dread. Then from his left arm
the hero looses the fierce-grinning jaws, thrusts out
before him the Cleonaean [1] head and, beneath that
huge shield crouching, plies his mighty club with
victorious right hand. Now here, now there, with
unremitting blows he whirls it, redoubling the
strokes. At last the dog, vanquished, ceases his
threatenings and, spent with struggle, lowers all his
heads and yields all wardship of the cavern. Both
rulers [2] shiver on their throne, and bid lead the dog
away. Me also they give as boon to Alcides' prayer.

[807] Then, stroking the monster's sullen necks, he
binds him with chains of adamant. Forgetful of
himself, the watchful guardian of the dusky realm
droops· his ears, trembling and willing to be led,
owns his master, and with muzzle lowered follows
after, beating both his sides with snaky tail. But when
he came to the Taenarian borders, and the strange
gleam of unknown light smote on his eyes, though
conquered he regained his courage and in frenzy
shook his ponderous chains. Almost he bore his
conqueror away, back dragging him, forward bent,
and forced him to give ground. Then even to my
aid Alcides looked, and with our twofold strength we
drew the dog along, mad with rage and attempting
fruitless war, and brought him out to earth. But
when he saw the bright light of day and viewed the
clear spaces of the shining sky, black night rose
over him and he turned his gaze to ground, closed
tight his eyes and shut out the hated light; back-

---

[1] *i.e.* of the Nemean lion, so called from Cleonae, near
Nemea, in Argolis.   [2] Pluto and Proserpina.

faciemque retro flexit atque omni petit
cervice terram ; tum sub Herculeas caput
abscondit umbras.   densa sed laeto venit
clamore turba frontibus laurum gerens
magnique meritas Herculis laudes canit.

CHORVS

Natus Eurystheus properante partu   830
iusserat mundi penetrare fundum ;
derat hoc solum numero laborum,
tertiae regem spoliare sortis.
ausus es caecos aditus inire,
ducit ad manes via qua remotos
tristis et nigra metuenda silva,
sed frequens magna comitante turba.

Quantus incedit populus per urbes
ad novi ludos avidus theatri ;
quantus Eleum ruit ad Tonantem,   840
quinta cum sacrum revocavit aestas ;
quanta, cum longae redit hora nocti
crescere et somnos cupiens quietos
libra Phoebeos tenet aequa currus,
turba secretam Cererem frequentat
et citi tectis properant relictis
Attici noctem celebrare mystae,
tanta per campos agitur silentes
turba ; pars tarda graditur senecta,
tristis et longa satiata vita ;   850
pars adhuc currit melioris aevi,

ward he turned his face and with all his necks
sought the earth ; then in the shadow of Hercules
he hid his head.—But see, a dense throng comes
on, glad shouting, with laurel wreaths upon their
brows and chanting the well-won praises of great
Hercules.

Eurystheus, brought to the light by birth untimely, had bidden thee explore the world's foundations ; this only was lacking to thy tale of labours,
to despoil the king of the third estate. Thou wast
bold to enter the blind approach, where a way leads
to the far-off shades, a gloomy way and fearsome with
dark woods, but crowded with vast accompanying
throngs.

838 Great as the host that moves through city streets,
eager to see the spectacle in some new theatre ; great
as that which pours to the Elean [1] Thunderer, when
the fifth summer has brought back the sacred games ;
great as the throng which (when the time comes
again for night to lengthen and the balanced Scales,[2]
yearning for quiet slumber, check Phoebus' car)
surges to Ceres' secret rites, and the initiates of
Attica, quitting their homes, swiftly hasten to celebrate their night—so great is the throng that is led
through the silent plains. Some go slow with age,
sad and sated with long life ; some still can run,

---

[1] i.e. Olympian. The reference is to the Olympic games,
celebrated in honour of Zeus.   [2] See Index.

virgines nondum thalamis iugatae
et comis nondum positis ephebi,
matris et nomen modo doctus infans.
his datum solis, minus ut timerent,
igne praelato relevare noctem;
ceteri vadunt per opaca tristes.
qualis est vobis animus, remota
luce cum maestus sibi quisque sensit
obrutum tota caput esse terra?   860
stat chaos densum tenebraeque turpes
et color noctis malus ac silentis
otium mundi vacuaeque nubes.

    Sera nos illo referat senectus;
nemo ad id sero venit, unde numquam,
cum semel venit, potuit reverti;
quid iuvat durum properare fatum?
omnis haec magnis vaga turba terris
ibit ad manes facietque inerti
vela Cocyto.   tibi crescit omne,   870
et quod occasus videt et quod ortus
—parce venturis—tibi, mors, paramur.
sis licet segnis, properamus ipsi;
prima quae vitam dedit hora, carpit.

    Thebis laeta dies adest.
aras tangite, supplices,
pingues caedite victimas;
permixtae maribus nurus
sollemnes agitent choros;
cessent deposito iugo   880
arvi fertilis incolae.

being of happier age—maidens, not yet in wedlock joined, youths with locks still unshorn, and babes that have but lately learned the name of " mother." To these last alone, that they be not afraid, 'tis given to lessen night's gloom by torches borne ahead ; the rest move sadly through the dark. O ye dead, what thoughts are yours when, light now banished, each has sorrowing felt his head o'erwhelmed 'neath all the earth ? There are thick chaos, loathsome murk, night's baleful hue, the lethargy of a silent world and empty clouds.

864 Late may old age bear us thither! None comes too late unto that land, whence never, when once come, can he return. Why does it please us to hasten cruel fate ? For all this throng which wanders up and down the earth's vast spaces shall go to the world of shades and shall set sail on Cocytus' lifeless stream. For thee, O Death, all things are growing ; all that the setting sun, all that the rising, sees—oh, spare thou those who are sure to come—for thee are we all preparing. Though thou be slow, we hasten of ourselves ; the hour which first gave life is plucking it away.

875 Thebes' joyful day is here. Lay hold on the altars, ye suppliants ; slay the fat victims ; let husbands and wives together start up the festal dance ; let the tillers of the fertile field lay by the yoke and rest.

Pax est Herculea manu
Auroram inter et Hesperum,
et qua sol medium tenens
umbras corporibus negat ;
quodcumque alluitur solum
longo Tethyos ambitu,
Alcidae domuit labor.
transvectus vada Tartari
pacatis redit inferis ;   890
iam nullus superest timor;
nil ultra iacet inferos.
  Stantes, sacrificus, comas
dilecta tege populo.

HERCVLES

Victrice dextra fusus adverso Lycus
terram cecidit ore ; tum quisquis comes
fuerat tyranni iacuit et poenae comes.
nunc sacra patri victor et superis feram
caesisque meritas victimis aras colam.
  Te te laborum socia et adiutrix precor,   900
belligera Pallas, cuius in laeva ciet
aegis feroces ore saxifico minas ;
adsit Lycurgi domitor et rubri maris,
tectam virente cuspidem thyrso gerens,
geminumque numen Phoebus et Phoebi soror,
soror sagittis aptior, Phoebus lyrae,
fraterque quisquis incolit caelum meus
non ex noverca frater.

HERCULES FURENS

882 Peace reigns by the hand of Hercules from the land of the dawn to the evening star, and where the sun, holding mid-heaven, gives to shapes no shadows. Whatever land is washed by Tethys' far-reaching circuit Alcides' toil has conquered. He has crossed the streams of Tartarus, subdued the gods of the underworld, and has returned. And now no fear remains; naught lies beyond the underworld.

893 Now, priest, bedeck thy bristling[1] hair with his well-loved poplar.

[*Enter* HERCULES, *fresh from the slaying of* LYCUS.]

HERCULES

Felled by my conquering hand, Lycus face down has smitten the earth. Next, whoever had been the tyrant's comrade lies low, the comrade also of his punishment. And now as victor will I bring offerings to my father and to the heavenly gods, slay victims, and honour the altars with due sacrifice.

900 Thee, thee, O ally and helper of my toils, I pray, O warlike Pallas, on whose left arm the targe with its petrifying face sends forth fierce threats; may he, too, be near, the tamer[2] of Lycurgus and the ruddy sea,[3] who bears a spear-point hidden beneath his vine-wreathed staff; and ye, twin deities, Phoebus and Phoebus' sister, the sister more ready with her arrows, Phoebus with his lyre; and whatever brother of mine dwells in the sky—but not a brother from my stepdame born.

[1] *i.e.* with the divine afflatus. Compare Virgil's description of the Sibyl, *Aeneid* VI. 48: *non comptae mansere comae.*

[2] Bacchus.

[3] Which Bacchus crossed when he conquered India.

Huc appellite
greges opimos; quidquid Indorum seges [1]
Arabesque odoris quidquid arboribus legunt   910
conferte in aras; pinguis exundet vapor.
populea nostras arbor exornet comas,
te ramus oleae fronde gentili tegat,
Theseu; Tonantem nostra adorabit manus,
tu conditores urbis et silvestria
trucis antra Zethi, nobilis Dircen aquae
laremque regis advenae Tyrium coles.
date tura flammis.

AMPHITRYON

Nate, manantes prius
manus cruenta caede et hostili expia.

HERCVLES

Vtinam cruore capitis invisi deis   920
libare possem; gratior nullus liquor
tinxisset aras; victima haut ulla amplior
potest magisque opima mactari Iovi,
quam rex iniquus.

AMPHITRYON

Finiat genitor tuos
opta labores, detur aliquando otium
quiesque fessis.

[1] *Leo conjectures a lacuna here, and suggests that some such line
as this has fallen out after 909 :*

praestat colonis igne propioris dei.

HERCULES FURENS

[*To his attendants.*]

908 Hither drive fat herds; whatever the fields of the Indians produce, whatever fragrant thing the Arabs gather from their trees, heap on the altars; let the rich smoke roll on high. Let wreaths of poplar bedeck our hair; but thee, O Theseus, an olive-branch, with thy own race's leaves, shall crown. The Thunderer shall my hand adore; do thou [1] invoke the founders of our city, the wooded caves of savage Zethus, Dirce of far-famed water, and the Tyrian house-gods of our pilgrim king. [2] Heap incense on the flames.

AMPHITRYON

O son, first purify thy hands, dripping with thy slaughtered foeman's blood.

HERCULES

Would that I could pour out to the gods the blood of the man I hate; no more pleasing stream had stained the altars; no greater, richer victim can be sacrificed to Jove than an unrighteous king.

AMPHITRYON

Pray that thy father end thy toils, that at last rest and repose be given to the weary.

---

[1] Addressed to Amphitryon. [2] Cadmus.

81

                    Ipse concipiam preces
Iove meque dignas :   stet suo caelum loco
tellusque et aequor ; astra inoffensos agant
aeterna cursus ; alta pax gentes alat ;
ferrum omne teneat ruris innocui labor   930
ensesque lateant ; nulla tempestas fretum
violenta turbet, nullus irato Iove
exiliat ignis, nullus hiberna nive
nutritus agros amnis eversos trahat.
venena cessent, nulla nocituro gravis
suco tumescat herba.   non saevi ac truces
regnent tyranni.   si quod etiamnum est scelus
latura tellus, properet, et si quod parat
monstrum, meum sit.

                          Sed quid hoc ?   medium diem
cinxere tenebrae.   Phoebus obscuro meat   940
sine nube vultu.   quis diem retro fugat
agitque in ortus ?   unde nox atrum caput
ignota profert ?   unde tot stellae polum
implent diurnae ?   primus en noster labor
caeli refulget parte non minima leo
iraque totus fervet et morsus parat.
iam rapiet aliquod sidus ; ingenti minax
stat ore et ignes efflat et rutila iubam
cervice iactans quidquid autumnus gravis
hiemsque gelido frigida spatio refert   950
uno impetu transiliet et verni petet
frangetque tauri colla.

HERCULES FURENS

Myself will I frame prayers worthy of Jupiter and me: May heaven abide in its own place, and earth and sea; may the eternal stars hold on their way unhindered; may deep peace brood upon the nations; may the harmless country's toil employ all iron, and may swords lie hid; may no raging tempest stir up the sea, no fires leap forth from angered Jove, no river, fed by winter's snows, sweep away the up-torn fields. Let poisons cease to be. Let no destructive herb swell with harmful juice. May savage and cruel tyrants rule no more. If earth is still to produce any wickedness, let her make haste, and if she is preparing any monster, let it be mine.[1]

[The madness planned by juno *begins to come upon him.]*

[939] But what is this? Shadows have begirt mid-day. Phoebus fares with darkened face though there be no cloud. Who puts the day to flight and drives it back to dawn? Whence does an unfamiliar night rear its black head? Whence do so many stars fill the sky though it is day? See where the lion, my first toil, glows in no small part of heaven, is all hot with rage, and makes ready his fangs. Forthwith he will seize some star; threatening he stands with gaping jaws, and breathes forth fires, and shakes the mane upon his flaming neck; whatever stars sickly autumn and cold winter with its frozen tracts bring back, with one bound will he o'erleap, and attack and crush the neck of the vernal Bull.

---

[1] *i.e.* to destroy, as he had destroyed so many other earth-born monsters.

SENECAE TRAGOEDIAE

AMPHITRYON

Quod subitum hoc malum est?
quo, nate, vultus huc et huc acres refers
acieque falsum turbida caelum vides?

HERCVLES

Perdomita tellus, tumida cesserunt freta,
inferna nostros regna sensere impetus;
immune caelum est, dignus Alcide labor.
in alta mundi spatia sublimis ferar,
petatur aether; astra promittit pater.
quid, si negaret? non capit terra Herculem   960
tandemque superis reddit. en ultro vocat
omnis deorum coetus et laxat fores,
una vetante. recipis et reseras polum?
an contumacis ianuam mundi traho?
dubitatur etiam? vincla Saturno exuam
contraque patris impii regnum impotens
avum resolvam; bella Titanes parent,
me duce furentes; saxa cum silvis feram
rapiamque dextra plena Centauris iuga.
iam monte gemino limitem ad superos agam;   970
videat sub Ossa Pelion Chiron suum,
in caelum Olympus tertio positus gradu
perveniet aut mittetur.

AMPHITRYON

Infandos procul
averte sensus; pectoris sani parum
magni tamen compesce dementem impetum.

---

¹ *i.e.* Jove has promised to deify his son. This is one of
the chief themes in *Hercules Oetaeus.*

84

HERCULES FURENS

AMPHITRYON

What sudden ill is this? Why, my son, dost turn thy keen eyes now here, now there, and look upon an unreal sky with troubled gaze?

HERCULES

The earth has been subdued, the swollen seas are at rest, the infernal realms have felt my onset; heaven is as yet untried, a task worthy of Alcides. To the lofty regions of the universe on high let me make my way, let me seek the skies; the stars are my father's promise.[1] And what if he should not keep his word? Earth has not room for Hercules, and at length restores him unto heaven. See, the whole company of the gods of their own will summons me, and opens wide the door of heaven, with one alone forbidding. And wilt thou unbar the sky and take me in? Or shall I carry off the doors of stubborn heaven? Dost even doubt my power? I'll free Saturn from his bonds, and against my unfilial[2] father's lawless sway I'll loose my grandsire. Let the Titans prepare war, with me to lead their rage; rocks, woods and all, will I bring, and with my right hand I'll snatch up ridges full of Centaurs. Now with twin mountains I'll construct a pathway to the realms above; Chiron shall see his own Pelion 'neath Ossa, and Olympus, set as third in order, shall reach clean to heaven—or else I'll hurl it there!

AMPHITRYON

Have done with these horrible imaginings! Repress the mad fury of thy proud heart, no longer sane.

[2] Jove with his two brothers had driven their father, Saturn, from the throne.

HERCVLES

Quid hoc? Gigantes arma pestiferi movent.
profugit umbras Tityos ac lacerum gerens
et inane pectus quam prope a caelo stetit.
labat Cithaeron, alta Pellene tremit
marcentque [1] Tempe. rapuit hic Pindi iuga,   980
hic rapuit Oeten, saevit horrendum Mimans.
flammifera Erinys verbere excusso sonat
rogisque adustas propius ac propius sudes
in ora tendit. saeva Tisiphone, caput
serpentibus vallata, post raptum canem
portam vacantem clausit opposita face.—

Sed ecce proles regis inimici latet,
Lyci nefandum semen; inviso patri
haec dextra iam vos reddet. excutiat leves
nervus sagittas—tela sic mitti decet   990
Herculea.

AMPHITRYON

Quo se caecus impegit furor?
vastum coactis flexit arcum cornibus
pharetramque solvit, stridet emissa impetu
harundo—medio spiculum collo fugit
vulnere relicto.

HERCVLES

Ceteram prolem eruam
omnesque latebras. quid moror? maius mihi

[1] *So Richter, with A : Leo, with E*, Macetum.

86

HERCULES FURENS

What's this? The baleful Giants are taking arms. Tityos has escaped the shades and, with breast all torn and empty, has almost reached the sky. Cithaeron is tottering, lofty Pellene .quakes, and Tempe's beauty fades. Here one Giant has seized Pindus' peak, there one has seized Oete, while horribly Mimas rages. Fiery Erinys cracks her brandished scourge, and closer, closer yet, holds out before my face brands burnt on funeral pyres. Cruel Tisiphone, her head with snakes encircled, since the dog was stolen away has blocked the empty gate with her outstretched torch.

[*He catches sight of his children.*]

987 But look! here lurk the children of the king, my enemy, the abominable spawn of Lycus; to your detested father this hand forthwith shall send you. Let my bowstring discharge swift arrows—so it is meet that the shafts of Hercules should fly.

AMPHITRYON

To what deed is his blind fury driven? He has bent his huge bow, the tips drawn close together; he has opened his quiver; shrilly sings the shaft, discharged with force—it has struck the neck full in the middle and sped out past the wound.

HERCULES

The rest of the brood will I rout out and all their hiding-places. Why delay? A greater

87

bellum Mycenis restat, ut Cyclopia
eversa manibus saxa nostris concidant.

Huc eat et illuc valva deiecto obice
rumpatque postes; culmen impulsum labet.   1000
perlucet omnis regia; hic video abditum
natum scelesti patris.

AMPHITRYON

           En blandas manus
ad genua tendens voce miseranda rogat—
scelus nefandum, triste et aspectu horridum!
dextra precantem rapuit et circa furens
bis ter rotatum misit; ast illi caput
sonuit, cerebro tecta disperso madent.
at misera, parvum protegens natum sinu,
Megara furenti similis e latebris fugit.

HERCVLES

Licet tonantis profuga condaris sinu,   1010
petet undecumque temet haec dextra et feret.

AMPHITRYON

Quo, misera, pergis? quam fugam aut latebram
    petis?

struggle awaits me at Mycenae, that there, by
these hands overthrown, the Cyclopean rocks may
fall.

[*He begins to tear at the doors of the shrine in which
his remaining sons have taken refuge.*]

⁹⁹⁹ Let the doors fly, one here, one there, the
barriers cast down and burst the posts asunder; let
the smitten roof reel. The whole palace is alight; I
see hiding there the son of a cursed sire.

[*He seizes the child and drags him from the scene.*]

AMPHITRYON

[*Standing where he can see what is going on
within the palace.*]

See, how he stretches out coaxing hands to his
father's knees, and with piteous voice begs—oh,
impious crime, grim and horrid sight! With his
right hand he has caught the pleading child, and,
madly whirling him again and yet again, has hurled
him; his head crashed loudly against the stones; the
room is drenched with scattered brains. But Megara,
poor woman, sheltering her little son within her
bosom, flees like a mad creature from her hiding-
place.

HERCULES

[*Behind the scene to* MEGARA, *also behind the scene.*]

Though thou run and hide in the Thunderer's
bosom, everywhence shall this hand seek thee and
hale thee forth.

AMPHITRYON [*to* MEGARA]

Whither dost thou flee, poor child? What flight
or what hiding-place dost thou seek? There is no

89

nullus salutis Hercule infesto est locus.
amplectere ipsum potius et blanda prece
lenire tempta.

MEGARA

Parce iam, coniunx, precor,
agnosce Megaram. natus hic vultus tuos
habitusque reddit ; cernis, ut tendat manus ?

HERCVLES

Teneo novercam. sequere, da poenas mihi
iugoque pressum libera turpi Iovem ;
sed ante matrem parvulum hoc monstrum
    occidat.   1020

MEGARA

Quo tendis amens ? sanguinem fundes tuum ?

AMPHITRYON

Pavefactus infans igneo vultu patris
perit ante vulnus, spiritum eripuit timor
in coniugem nunc clava libratur gravis—
perfregit ossa, corpori trunco caput
abest nec usquam est.

Cernere hoc audes, nimis
vivax senectus ? si piget luctus, habes
mortem paratam ; pectus in tela indue,
vel stipitem istuc caede nostrorum inlitum
converte. falsum ac nomini turpem tuo   1030
remove parentem, ne tuae laudi obstrepat.

90

place safe from Hercules enraged. Embrace him, rather, and essay to calm him with soothing prayers.

THE VOICE OF MEGARA

Husband, spare me now, I beg. See, I am Megara. This is thy son, with thine own looks and bearing. See, how he stretches out his hands.

THE VOICE OF HERCULES

I have caught my stepdame. Come, pay me thy debt, and free o'ermastered Jove from a degrading yoke.[1] But before the mother let this little monster perish.

THE VOICE OF MEGARA

What wouldst thou, madman? Thine own blood wilt thou shed?

AMPHITRYON

Stricken with terror of his sire's blazing eyes, the child died ere he felt the blow; fear snatched his life away. Against his wife now he poises his heavy club—her bones are crushed, her head is gone from her mangled body, gone utterly.

1026 [*To himself.*] Darest thou abide this sight, O too stubborn age? If thou art weary of grief, death thou hast ready; expose thy breast to those shafts, or turn against it that club smeared with our children's gore. [*Calling to* HERCULES.] Make away with thy pretended sire, this blot upon thy name, lest he make discord midst thy praise.

[1] He imagines that Megara is Juno, and now he will pay off old scores both in his own and Jove's interests.

CHORVS

Quo te ipse, senior, obvium morti ingeris?
quo pergis amens? profuge et obtectus late
unumque manibus aufer Herculeis scelus.

HERCVLES

Bene habet, pudendi regis excisa est domus.
tibi hunc dicatum, maximi coniunx Iovis,
gregem cecidi; vota persolvi libens
te digna, et Argos victimas alias dabit.

AMPHITRYON

Nondum litasti, nate; consumma sacrum.
stat ecce ad aras hostia, expectat manum   1040
cervice prona. praebeo occurro insequor;
macta—quid hoc est? errat acies luminum
visusque marcor hebetat; an video Herculis
manus trementes? vultus in somnum cadit
et fessa cervix capite summisso labat;
flexo genu iam totus ad terram ruit,
ut caesa silvis ornus aut portum mari
datura moles.
                    Vivis an leto dedit
idem tuos qui misit ad mortem furor?

HERCULES FURENS

CHORUS

Why, old man, dost wantonly challenge death?
Whither wouldst go, senseless? Flee and securely
hide thee, and save the hands of Hercules from the
one crime left.

[*Re-enter* HERCULES.]

HERCULES

'Tis well; the shameless king's house is utterly
destroyed. To thee, wife of almighty Jove, have I
slaughtered this devoted flock; vows worthy of
thee have I paid right joyfully, and Argos[1] shall
give still other victims.

AMPHITRYON

Not yet hast thou made full atonement, son;
complete the sacrifice. See, a victim stands before
the altar; with bent neck he awaits the stroke. I
offer myself to death, I run to meet it, I follow after
it; smite—but what is this? The glance of his
eyes wanders, and faintness dulls his vision. Do
I see the hands of Hercules a-tremble? His eyelids
fall in slumber, and his tired neck sinks beneath
his drooping head; now his knees give way and his
whole body goes crashing to the ground, like an
ash-tree felled in the woods, or a falling mass of
rock that will give a breakwater to the sea.

[*To* HERCULES.]

1048 Livest thou still, or has that same madness given
thee to death which sent thy kindred to their doom?

[*He examines the prostrate body.*]

----

[1] Eurystheus was lord of Argos.

sopor est ; reciprocos spiritus motus agit. 1050
detur quieti tempus, ut somno gravi
vis victa morbi pectus oppressum levet.
removete, famuli, tela, ne repetat furens.

CHORVS

Lugeat aether magnusque parens
aetheris alti tellusque ferax
et vaga ponti mobilis unda,
tuque ante omnes qui per terras
tractusque maris fundis radios
noctemque fugas ore decoro,
fervide Titan ; obitus pariter 1060
tecum Alcides vidit et ortus
novitque tuas utrasque domos.
Solvite tantis animum monstris,
solvite superi, caecam in melius
flectite mentem. tuque, o domitor
Somne malorum, requies animi,
pars humanae melior vitae,
volucre o matris genus Astraeae,
frater durae languide Mortis,
veris miscens falsa, futuri 1070
certus et idem pessimus auctor,
pax errorum, portus vitae,
lucis requies noctisque comes,
qui par regi famuloque venis,
pavidum leti genus humanum
cogis longam discere noctem—
placidus fessum lenisque fove,
preme devinctum torpore gravi ;
sopor indomitos alliget artus
nec torva prius pectora linquat, 1080
quam mens repetat pristina cursum.

He sleeps ; his chest heaves with measured breathing. Let him have time for rest, that deep slumber may break the force of his madness and relieve his troubled heart. Ye slaves, remove his weapons, lest in rage he seek them yet again.

CHORUS

Let heaven mourn, and the great father of high heaven, and fertile earth, and wandering waves of the restless main ; and thou above all, who over the lands and stretches of the sea dost shed thy rays, and dispellest night with comely face, O glowing Sun ; equally with thee hath Alcides seen the lands of thy setting and thy rising, and hath known both thy dwellings.

1063 O free his soul from such monstrous ills, free him, ye gods, and turn to better things his darkened spirit. And do thou, O Sleep, vanquisher of woes, rest of the soul, the better part of human life, thou winged son of thy mother Astraea, sluggish brother of cruel Death, thou who dost mingle false with true, sure yet gloomy guide [1] to what shall be ; O thou, who art peace after wanderings, haven of life, day's respite and night's comrade, who comest alike to king and slave, who dost compel the human race, trembling at death, to prepare for unending night— sweetly and gently soothe his weary spirit; hold him fast bound in heavy stupor ; let slumber chain his untamed limbs, and leave not his savage breast until his former mind regain its course.

[1] Perhaps because dreams are generally of evil.

En fusus humi saeva feroci
corde volutat somnia ; nondum est
tanti pestis superata mali ;
clavaeque gravi lassum solitus
mandare caput quaerit vacua
pondera dextra, motu iactans
bracchia vano.   nec adhuc omnes
expulit aestus, sed ut ingenti
vexata noto servat longos   1090
unda tumultus et iam vento
cessante tumet [1] * * pelle insanos
fluctus animi, redeat pietas
virtusque viro.   vel sit potius
mens vesano concita motu ;
error caecus qua coepit eat ;
solus te iam praestare potest
furor insontem.   proxima puris
sors est manibus nescire nefas.

    Nunc Herculeis percussa sonent   1100
pectora palmis, mundum solitos
ferre lacertos verbera pulsent
victrice manu ; gemitus vastos
audiat aether, audiat atri
regina poli vastisque ferox
qui colla gerit vincta catenis
imo latitans Cerberus antro ;
resonet maesto clamore chaos
latique patens unda profundi
et qui medius tua tela tamen   1110
senserat aer ; [2]
pectora tantis obsessa malis

---

[1] *Leo recognizes a lacuna here with Withof, and suggests the
completion of the sentence thus:* sic pristina adhuc quatit ira
virum.

[2] et qui . . . aer, *deleted by B. Schmidt, followed by Leo.*

¹⁰⁸² See, prone on the ground, he revolves in his fierce heart his savage dreams; not yet has the baleful power of so great woe been overcome; wont to recline his weary head on his heavy club, he feels for its ponderous trunk with empty hand, tossing his arms in fruitless movement. Not yet has he dispelled all his surging madness, but as the waves, stirred up by a mighty wind, still keep their long, tumultuous roll, and still are swollen though the wind has ceased, [so does his former rage still rack the hero.] Banish [1] the mad passions of thy soul; let the hero's piety and manly courage come again. Or rather, let his mind still be stirred by uncontrolled emotion; let his blind error go on the way it has begun; madness alone can now make thee innocent. Next best to guiltless hands is ignorance of guilt.

¹¹⁰⁰ Now let Hercules' breast resound beneath the blows of his palms; let those arms that were wont to upbear the universe be smitten by his victorious hands; let the heavens hear his mighty groans, let the queen of the dark world hear, and fierce Cerberus, crouching in his lowest cave, his necks still bound with chains; let Chaos re-echo the outcries of his grief, and the spreading waves of the broad deep, and mid-air which no less had felt thy shafts; the breast beset by so great ills must by no light blow be

---

[1] The poet wavers in his conception of the person addressed throughout this passage (1092–1121).

non sunt ictu ferienda levi,
uno planctu tria regna sonent.
et tu collo decus ac telum
suspensa diu, fortis harundo,
pharetraeque graves, date saeva fero
verbera tergo ; caedant umeros
robora fortes stipesque potens
duris laceret [1] pectora nodis :   1120
plangant tantos arma dolores.

Ite infaustum genus, o pueri,   1135
noti per iter triste laboris,   1136
non vos patriae laudis comites   1122
ulti saevos vulnere reges,
non Argiva membra palaestra
flectere docti fortes caestu   1125
fortesque manu nondumque ferae   1130
terga iubatae [2] * * iam tamen ausi   1126
telum Scythicis leve corytis
missum certa librare manu
tutosque fuga figere cervos—   1129
ite ad Stygios, umbrae, portus   1131
ite, innocuae, quas in primo
limine vitae scelus oppressit
patriusque furor ;   1134
ite, iratos visite reges.   1137

HERCVLES

Quis hic locus, quae regio, quae mundi plaga ?
ubi sum ?   sub ortu solis, an sub cardine
glacialis ursae ?   numquid Hesperii maris   1140
extrema tellus hunc dat Oceano modum ?

---

[1] laceret *Leo :* oneret *MSS.*
[2] *Leo assumes a lacuna here which he supplies with the line*
vulnere gaesi frangere torti.

smitten; with one lamentation three kingdoms must
resound.   And thou, brave reed, which hung so long
as ornament and weapon from his neck, and thou,
heavy quiver, lay savage blows on his untamed back;
let the stout oak club mangle his strong shoulders and
with its hard knots bruise his breast; let his weapons
make lament for his mighty woes.

[1135] Go ye, ill-fated brood, ye boys, along the gloomy
way of your father's famous task, not destined to be
partakers of his praise by taking bloody vengeance
on savage kings; never taught in Argive wrestling
school to ply the limbs, brave with boxing-glove
and brave with hand, never yet taught to wound
the maned lion with well-hurled javelin, but yet
already bold to poise and throw with steady hand the
slender Scythian dart, and shoot the deer that seek
safety in flight—go to the haven of the Styx, go,
harmless shades whom on the very threshold of life
your sire's mad crime o'ercame; go, go to the presence
of the angered kings.[1]

HERCULES

[*Waking up in his right mind.*]

What place is this?   What region, what quarter
of the world?   Where am I?   Beneath the sun's
rising or beneath the wheeling course of the frozen
Bear?   Is this the boundary set to Ocean's stream
by that farthest land on the western sea?   What air

---

[1] *i.e.* the lords of death, angry because Hercules had defied
them.

quas trahimus auras ?   quod solum fesso subest ?
certe redimus—
                Unde prostrata ad domum
video cruenta corpora ?   an nondum exuit
simulacra mens inferna ?   post reditus quoque
oberrat oculis turba feralis meis ?
pudet fateri—paveo ; nescio quod mihi,
nescio quod animus grande praesagit malum.
ubi es, parens ?   ubi illa natorum grege
animosa coniunx ?   cur latus laevum vacat   1150
spolio leonis ?   quonam abit tegimen meum
idemque somno mollis Herculeo torus ?
ubi tela ?   ubi arcus ?   arma quis vivo mihi
detrahere potuit ?   spolia quis tanta abstulit
ipsumque quis non Herculis somnum horruit ?
libet meum videre victorem, libet.
exurge, virtus, quem novum caelo pater
genuit relicto, cuius in fetu stetit
nox longior quam nostra—
                Quod cerno nefas ?
nati cruenta caede confecti iacent,   1160
perempta coniunx.   quis Lycus regnum obtinet ?
quis tanta Thebis scelera moliri ausus est [1]
Hercule reverso ?   quisquis Ismeni loca,
Actaea quisquis arva, qui gemino mari
pulsata Pelopis regna Dardanii colis,
succurre, saevae cladis auctorem indica.
ruat ira in omnes ; hostis est quisquis mihi
non monstrat hostem.   victor Alcidae, lates ?

---

[1] *Leo deletes this line.*

is this I breathe ? What soil lies beneath my weary frame ? Surely I have returned to earth—

[*His eyes fall on his murdered children.*]

1143 How is it that I see bloody corpses lying before my house ? Is my mind not yet free from infernal phantoms ? Even after my return do troops of ghastly things still throng before my eyes? With shame I confess it—I am afraid ; something, some great calamity my heart forebodes. Where art thou, father ? Where is my wife, so proud of her brood of sons ? Why is my left shoulder bare of the lion's spoil ? Whither has it gone, that shield of mine, at once a soft couch, too, for the sleep of Hercules? Where are my shafts ? my bow ? Who has been able to steal away my arms while I still live ? Who has gained so great spoils of me, and has not shuddered at even a sleeping Hercules ? Glad would I be to see my conqueror, glad. Come forth, thou brave hero, whom my sire, leaving heaven, has begotten, a later son, at whose begetting night stood still, longer than at mine—

[*He recognizes his dead wife and children.*]

1159 What horror do I see ? My sons, with bloody murder destroyed, lie here, my wife lies slain. What Lycus holds sway now ? Who has dared perpetrate such outrages in Thebes, though Hercules has returned ? Whoever dwellest by Ismenus' stream, on Attic plains, in the kingdom of Dardanian Pelops, lapped by two seas, come to my aid, tell me the doer of this cruel murder. On all let mine anger sweep; my foeman is he who points not out the foe. Vanquisher of Alcides, hidest thou ? Come

procede, seu tu vindicas currus truces
Thracis cruenti sive Geryonae pecus   1170
Libyaeve dominos, nulla pugnandi mora est.
en nudus asto, vel meis armis licet
petas inermem.   Cur meos Theseus fugit
paterque vultus ?   ora cur condunt sua ?
differte fletus ; quis meos dederit neci
omnes simul, profare—quid, genitor, siles ?
at tu ede, Theseu, sed tua, Theseu, fide.
uterque tacitus ora pudibunda obtegit
furtimque lacrimas fundit.   in tantis malis
quid est pudendum ?   numquid Argivae impotens
dominator urbis, numquid infestum Lyci   1181
pereuntis agmen clade nos tanta obruit ?
per te meorum facinorum laudem precor,
genitor, tuique nominis semper mihi
numen secundum, fare.   quis fudit domum ?
cui praeda iacui ?

AMPHITRYON

Tacita sic abeant mala.

HERCVLES

Vt inultus ego sim ?

AMPHITRYON

Saepe vindicta obfuit.

out; whether thou dost seek vengeance for the savage horses of the b'oody Thracian,[1] or for Geryon's flock, or the Libyan heroes,[2] I am ready for the fray. Here I stand defenceless, e'en though with my own arms thou shouldst assail me armourless.

[1173] Why does Theseus avoid my eyes, why does my father? Why do they hide their faces? Postpone your tears. Who has given my loved ones to death, all of them at once, tell me—why, father, art thou silent? But do thou tell, Theseus! Nay, Theseus, tell me by thy loyalty!—They both in silence turn away and hide their faces as if in shame, while tears steal down their cheeks. In woes so great what room is there for shame? Has the ruthless lord[3] of Argos, has the hostile band of dying Lycus, in ruin so vast overwhelmed me? O father, by the glory of my deeds, I pray thee, and by thy sacred name[4] always next[5] hallowed in my sight, speak out! who has overthrown my house? To whom have I fallen prey?

AMPHITRYON

In silence, as they may, let troubles pass.

HERCULES

And I be unavenged?

AMPHITRYON

Oft vengeance has brought bane.

---

[1] Diomedes.   [2] *e.g.* Antaeus, Busiris.
[3] Eurystheus.   [4] *i.e.* of father.
[5] *i.e.* next to that of Jove, real father of Hercules. The play on the words *nomen* and *numen* cannot be reproduced in English.

HERCVLES

Quisquamne segnis tanta toleravit mala?

AMPHITRYON

Maiora quisquis timuit.

HERCVLES

His etiam, pater,
quicquam timeri maius aut gravius potest?   1190

AMPHITRYON

Cladis tuae pars ista quam nosti quota est '

HERCVLES

Miserere, genitor, supplices tendo manus.
quid hoc?   manus refugit—hic errat scelus.
unde hic cruor?   quid illa puerili madens
harundo leto?   tincta Lernaea est nece—
iam tela video nostra.   non quaero manum.
quis potuit arcum flectere aut quae dextera
sinuare nervum vix recedentem mihi?
ad vos revertor; genitor, hoc nostrum est scelus?
tacuere—nostrum est.

AMPHITRYON

Luctus est istic tuus,   1200
crimen novercae.   casus hic culpa caret.

HERCVLES

Nunc parte ab omni, genitor, iratus tona
oblite nostri vindica sera manu

HERCULES FURENS

Has any e'er borne such woes supinely?

Yes, he who greater woes has feared.

But than these, father, can aught still greater or heavier be feared?

How small the part of thy calamity is that thou knowest!

Have pity, father; see, I stretch out suppliant hands. What? from my hands he started back —here lurks the sin. Whence this blood? What of that shaft, still dripping with the blood of boys? It has been dipped in Hydra's gore—ah, now my own weapons do I recognize. No need to ask the hand that used them! Who could have bent the bow or what hand drawn the string which scarce yields to me? I turn to you again; father, is this my deed? Silent still—'tis mine.

Truly the woe is thine; the crime thy step-dame's. This mischance is free from sin.

Now from every quarter of the sky, O father, thunder in thy wrath; though thou hast forgotten

saltem nepotes.   stelliger mundus sonet
flammasque et hic et ille iaculetur polus ;
rupes ligatum Caspiae corpus trahant
atque ales avida—cur Promethei vacant
scopuli ?   vacat cur vertice immenso feras
volucresque pascens Caucasi abruptum latus
nudumque silvis ?   illa quae pontum Scythen   1210
Symplegas artat hinc et hinc vinctas manus
distendat alto, cumque revocata vice
in se coibunt saxaque in caelum expriment
actis utrimque rupibus medium mare,
ego inquieta montium iaceam mora.
quin structum acervans nemore congesto aggerem
cruore corpus impio sparsum cremo ?
sic, sic agendum est—inferis reddam Herculem.

AMPHITRYON

   Nondum tumultu pectus attonito carens
mutavit iras quodque habet proprium furor,   1220
in se ipse saevit.

HERCVLES

                  Dira Furiarum loca
et inferorum carcer et sonti plaga
decreta turbae, si quod exilium latet
ulterius Erebo, Cerbero ignotum et mihi,
hoc me abde, tellus ; Tartari ad finem ultimum
mansurus ibo.   pectus o nimium ferum !
quis vos per omnem, liberi, sparsos domum
deflere digne poterit ?   hic durus malis
106

me, with tardy hand at least avenge thy grandsons.
Let the starry heavens resound, and the skies dart
lightnings from pole to pole ; let the Caspian crags [1]
claim my fettered body, and let the ravenous bird—
Why are Prometheus' crags unoccupied ?   Why, the
bare, steep side of Caucasus which, on its lofty summit, feeds beasts and birds of prey ? Let those clashing rocks [2] which confine the Scythian sea stretch
my fettered hands apart this way and that o'er the
deep, and, when with recurrent change they come
together and when, as the crags rush from either
side, the rocks force up to heaven the interposing
flood, may I lie there the mountains' tortured curb.
Nay, I will build me a huge pile of logs and burn my
body spattered with impious gore.   Thus, thus must
I do—to the nether gods will I give back Hercules.

AMPHITRYON

His heart, not yet eased of frenzy's tumult, has
shifted its wrath's aim and now, sure sign of madness,
he rages against himself.

HERCULES

Ye dire abodes of fiends, prison-house of the
dead, ye regions set apart for the guilty throng, if
any place of banishment lies hidden away beneath
hell itself, unknown to Cerberus and me, hide me
there, O earth ; to the remotest bounds of Tartarus
will I go and there abide. O heart too fierce ! Who
can weep worthily for you, my children, scattered
through all my house? This face, hardened with

[1] To which Prometheus had been bound, and from which
Hercules released him.
[2] The Symplegades.   See Index.

lacrimare vultus nescit.   huc arcum date,
date huc sagittas, stipitem huc vastum date.   1230
   Tibi tela frangam nostra, tibi nostros, puer,
rumpemus arcus; at tuis stipes gravis
ardebit umbris; ipsa Lernaeis frequens
pharetra telis in tuos ibit rogos.
dent arma poenas.   vos quoque infaustas meis
cremabo telis, o novercales manus.

AMPHITRYON

Quis nomen usquam sceleris errori addidit?

HERCVLES

Saepe error ingens sceleris obtinuit locum.

AMPHITRYON

Nunc Hercule opus est; perfer hanc molem mali.

HERCVLES

Non sic furore cessit extinctus pudor,   1240
populos ut omnes impio aspectu fugem.
arma, arma, Theseu, flagito propere mihi
subtracta reddi.   sana si mens est mihi,
referte manibus tela; si remanet furor,
pater, recede; mortis inveniam viam.

AMPHITRYON

Per sancta generis sacra, per ius nominis
utrumque nostri, sive me altorem vocas
108

woe, has forgotten how to weep. Give my bow
here, give me my arrows, here give me my huge
club.

[*He bends over the corpses and addresses each in turn.*]

¹²³¹ For thee will I break my shafts, for thee,
poor boy, will I rend my bow; but to thy shades my
heavy club shall burn; my quiver itself, full of
Lerna's darts, shall go with thee to thy pyre. So
let my arms pay the penalty. You, too, with my
weapons will I burn, O cursed, O stepdame's hands.

AMPHITRYON

What man anywhere hath laid on error the name
of guilt?

HERCULES

Oft hath great error held the place of guilt.

AMPHITRYON

Now must thou be Hercules; bear thou this
weight of trouble.

HERCULES

Shame, quenched by madness, has not so far
gone from me that with unhallowed presence I
should scare all peoples. Arms, Theseus, my arms!
I pray you quickly give back what you have stolen.
If my mind is sane, give back to my hands their
weapons; if madness still remains, fly, O my father;
I shall find a path to death.

AMPHITRYON

By the holy ties of birth, by the right of both
my names, whether thou dost call me foster-father

seu tu parentem, perque venerandos piis
canos, senectae parce desertae, precor,
annisque fessis; unicum lapsae domus   1250
firmamen, unum lumen afflicto malis
temet reserva.   nullus ex te contigit
fructus laborum; semper aut dubium mare
aut monstra timui; quisquis in toto furit
rex saevus orbe, manibus aut aris nocens,
a me timetur; semper absentis pater
fructum tui tactumque et aspectum peto.

HERCVLES

Cur animam in ista luce detineam amplius
morerque nil est; cuncta iam amisi bona:
mentem arma famam coniugem natos manus,   1260
etiam furorem!   nemo polluto queat
animo mederi; morte sanandum est scelus.

AMPHITRYON

Perimes parentem.

HERCVLES

Facere ne possim, occidam.

AMPHITRYON

Genitore coram?

HERCVLES

Cernere hunc docui nefas.

AMPHITRYON

Memoranda potius omnibus facta intuens
unius a te criminis veniam pete.

110

or true sire, by these grey hairs, which pious sons
revere, spare thyself, I pray, to my lonely age and to
my weary years. Sole prop of my fallen house, sole
light of my woe-darkened life, save thyself for me.
No enjoyment of thee, no fruit of thy toils has fallen
to my lot; but always have I had to fear either the
stormy seas or monsters; every cruel king that rages
in all the world with guilt on his hands or altars is
cause of dread to me; always do I, thy father, yearn
for the joy of touch and sight of thee, my ever-absent
son.

HERCULES

Why I should longer stay my soul in the light
of day, and linger here, there is no cause; all that
was dear to me I've lost: reason, arms, honour,
wife, children, strength—and madness too! No
power could purge a tainted spirit; by death must
sin be healed.

AMPHITRYON

Thou'lt slay thy father.

HERCULES

Lest I do so, I'll die.

AMPHITRYON

Before thy father's eyes?

HERCULES

I have taught him to look on impious deeds.

AMPHITRYON

Nay, rather think upon thy deeds glorious to all,
and seek from thyself pardon for one sin.

HERCVLES

Veniam dabit sibi ipse, qui nulli dedit?
laudanda feci iussus; hoc unum meum est
succurre, genitor; sive te pietas movet
seu triste fatum sive violatum decus   1270
virtutis.   effer arma; vincatur mea
fortuna dextra.

THESEVS

       Sunt quidem patriae preces
satis efficaces, sed tamen nostro quoque
movere fletu.   surge et adversa impetu
perfringe solito.   nunc tuum nulli imparem
animum malo resume, nunc magna tibi
virtute agendum est: Herculem irasci veta

HERCVLES

Si vivo, feci scelera; si morior, tuli.
purgare terras propero.   iamdudum mihi
monstrum impium saevumque et immite ac ferum
oberrat; agedum dextra, conare aggredi   1281
ingens opus, labore bis seno amplius.
ignava cessas, fortis in pueros modo
pavidasque matres?   arma nisi dantur mihi,
aut omne Pindi Thracis excidam nemus
Bacchique lucos et Cithaeronis iuga
mecum cremabo, aut tota cum domibus suis
dominisque tecta, cum deis templa omnibus
Thebana supra corpus excipiam meum
atque urbe versa condar, et, si fortibus   1290
leve pondus umeris moenia immissa incident

HERCULES FURENS

HERCULES

Shall he give remission to himself who to none
other gave it? As for my glorious deeds, at others'
hest I did them; this alone is mine. Help me,
father; whether love move thee, or my sad fate, or
the tarnished glory of my manhood. Bring me my
weapons; by my right hand let fate be vanquished

THESEUS

Enough thy father's prayers have power to move,
but let my weeping move thee, too. Up! and with
thy wonted force break through adversity. Now
get back thy courage which was ne'er unequal to
any hardship; now must thou greatly play the man- ·
forbid Hercules to rage [1]

HERCULES

If I keep to life, I have wrought wrong; if I die,
have borne it. I am in haste to purge the earth.
Long since a monstrous form, impious, savage, in-
exorable, wild, has stalked before my eyes; come,
hand, grapple with this task greater than the last of
all thy labours. Coward, dost thou shrink, brave
against boys alone and trembling mothers? My
arms, I say! Unless they are given me, either I will
cut down all the woods of Thracian Pindus and
Bacchus' groves and Cithaeron's ridges, and along
with my own body I will burn them up; or else all
the dwellings of Thebes with their households and
their masters, the temples with all their gods, I
will pull down upon myself and lie buried 'neath a
city's wreck; and if, hurled on my shoulders, the
walls shall fall with too light a weight, and if, buried

113

septemque opertus non satis portis premar,
onus omne media parte quod mundi sedet
dirimitque superos, in meum vertam caput.

AMPHITRYON

Reddo arma.

HERCVLES

          Vox est digna genitore Herculis
hoc en peremptus spiculo cecidit puer.

AMPHITRYON

Hoc Iuno telum manibus immisit tuis

HERCVLES

Hoc nunc ego utar.

AMPHITRYON

          Ecce quam miserum metu
cor palpitat pectusque sollicitum ferit.

HERCVLES

Aptata harundo est.

AMPHITRYON

          Ecce iam facies scelus   1300
volens sciensque.

HERCVLES

          Pande, quid fieri iubes?

beneath the seven gates, I be not crushed enough,
then all the mass which lies at the centre of the
universe and separates gods from men will I overthrow upon my head.

AMPHITRYON

I return thine arms.

HERCULES

Thy words are worthy the sire of Hercules. See,
slain by this shaft fell my boy.

AMPHITRYON

'Twas Juno shot the arrow by thy hand.

HERCULES

'Tis I who shall use it now.

AMPHITRYON

Oh, how my woeful heart trembles with fear
and smites on my anxious breast!

HERCULES

The shaft is notched.

AMPHITRYON

Ah, now wilt thou sin of thine own will and
knowledge.

HERCULES

Speak out; what wouldst have me do?

115

SENECAE TRAGOEDIAE

AMPHITRYON

Nihil rogamus; noster in tuto est dolor—
natum potes servare tu solus mihi,
eripere nec tu.   maximum evasi metum;
miserum haut potes me facere, felicem potes.
sic statue, quidquid statuis, et causam tuam
famamque in arto stare et ancipiti scias;
aut vivis aut occidis.   hanc animam levem
fessamque senio nec minus fessam malis
in ore primo teneo.   tam tarde patri   1310
vitam dat aliquis?   non feram ulterius moram,
letale ferro pectus impresso [1] induam;
hic, hic iacebit Herculis sani scelus.

HERCVLES

Iam parce, genitor, parce, iam revoca manum.
succumbe, virtus, perfer imperium patris.
eat ad labores hic quoque Herculeos labor:
vivamus.   artus alleva afflictos solo,
Theseu, parentis.   dextra contactus pios
scelerata refugit.

AMPHITRYON

       Hanc manum amplector libens,
hac nisus ibo, pectori hanc aegro admovens   1320
pellam dolores.

HERCVLES

       Quem locum profugus petam?
ubi me recondam quave tellure obruar?
quis Tanais aut quis Nilus aut quis Persica
violentus unda Tigris aut Rhenus ferox

[1] impressum *A*: *Richter* laetare! ferro pectus impresso
induam.

116

HERCULES FURENS

AMPHITRYON

I make no prayer; for me woe is assured—thou alone canst preserve my son to me, but not even thou canst snatch him from me. I have passed my greatest fear; wretched thou canst not make me, but blest, thou canst. Decide, then, as thou wilt decide, but know that in so doing thy cause and fame stand at hazard and doubtful issue; either thou livest or slayest me. This flitting soul, weary with age and no less with woe weary, I hold upon my very lips. So grudgingly does any man grant his father life? [*He seizes a sword and sets its point to his breast.*] I will brook no more delay; with the fatal steel thrust home will I pierce my breast; here, here shall lie the crime of a sane Hercules!

HERCULES

Now hold, father, hold, recall thy hand! Strong soul of mine, yield, do a father's will; add this task also to Hercules' toils—and live! Theseus, lift thou from the ground my father's fainting limbs. My hands defiled shrink from that pious touch.

AMPHITRYON

But this hand I clasp joyfully; by its help I'll walk and, holding it close to my aching heart, banish my griefs.

HERCULES

Whither shall I flee? Where shall I hide me, or in what land bury me? What Tanaïs, what Nile, what Tigris, raging with Persian torrents, what warlike Rhine, or Tagus, turbid with the golden sands

117

Tagusve Hibera turbidus gaza fluens
abluere dextram poterit ?   arctoum licet
Maeotis in me gelida transfundat mare
et tota Tethys per meas currat manus,
haerebit altum facinus.   in quas impius
terras recedes ?   ortum an occasum petes?　　1330
ubique notus perdidi exilio locum.
me refugit orbis, astra transversos agunt
obliqua cursus, ipse Titan Cerberum
meliore vultu vidit.   o fidum caput,
Theseu, latebram quaere longinquam abditam ;
quoniamque semper sceleris alieni arbiter
amas nocentes, gratiam meritis refer
vicemque nostris.   redde me infernis precor
umbris reductum, meque subiectum tuis
substitue vinclis ; ille me abscondet locus—　　1340
sed et ille novit.

THESEVS

　　　　　Nostra te tellus manet.
illic solutam caede Gradivus manum
restituit armis : illa te, Alcide, vocat,
facere innocentes terra quae superos solet.

of Spain, can cleanse this hand? Though cold
Maeotis should pour its northern sea upon me,
though the whole ocean should stream along my
hands, still will the deep stains cling. To what
countries, man of sin, wilt thou betake thee? The
rising or the setting sun wilt seek? Known in every
land, I have lost place for exile. The world shrinks
from my presence, the stars, moving askance, turn
away their courses; Titan himself looked upon Cerberus with kindlier face. O faithful friend, Theseus,
seek a hiding-place for me, remote, obscure; since,
though witness of others' sins, thou dost ever love
the sinners, grant me now grace and recompense
for favours past. Take me back, I pray thee, and
restore me to the nether shades; put me in thy
stead, loaded with thy chains; that place will hide
me—but it, too, knows me!

THESEUS

My land awaits thee. There Gradivus once
cleansed his hands from blood [1] and gave them back
to war; thee, Alcides, does that land call, land which
can free the immortals from their stains.[2]

[1] See Index *s.v.* " Mars."
[2] If Athens could cleanse Mars from blood-guiltiness, she
could do the same for Hercules.

119

TROADES

DRAMATIS PERSONAE

AGAMEMNON. *king of the Greek forces in the war against Troy.*

PYRRHUS, *son of Achilles, one of the active leaders in the final events of the war.*

ULYSSES, *king of Ithaca, one of the most powerful and crafty of the Greek chiefs before Troy.*

CALCHAS, *a priest and prophet among the Greeks.*

TALTHYBIUS, *a Greek messenger.*

AN OLD MAN, *faithful to Andromache.*

ASTYANAX, *little son of Hector and Andromache.*

HECUBA, *widow of Priam, one of the Trojan captives.*

ANDROMACHE, *widow of Hector, a Trojan captive.*

HELENA, *wife of Menelaüs, king of Sparta, and afterwards of Paris, a prince of Troy ; the exciting cause of the Trojan war.*

POLYXENA, *daughter of Hecuba and Priam (persona muta).*

CHORUS *of captive Trojan women.*

THE SCENE is laid on the seashore, with the smouldering ruins of Troy in the background.

THE TIME is the day before the embarkation of the Greeks on their homeward journey.

ARGUMENT

THE *long and toilsome siege of Troy is done. Her stately palaces and massive walls have been overthrown and lie darkening the sky with their still smouldering ruins. Her heroic defenders are either slain or scattered, seeking other homes in distant lands. The victorious Greeks have gathered the rich spoils of Troy upon the shore, among these the Trojan women, who have suffered the usual fate of women when a city is sacked. They await the lot which shall assign them to their Grecian lords and scatter them among the cities of their foes. All things are ready for the start.*

But now the ghost of Achilles has risen from the tomb, and demanded that Polyxena be sacrificed to him before the Greeks shall be allowed to sail away. And Calchas, also, bids that Astyanax be slain, for only thus can Greece be safe from any future Trojan war. And thus the Trojan captives, who have so long endured the pains of war, must suffer still this double tragedy.

TROADES

HECVBA

Qvicvmqve regno fidit et magna potens
dominatur aula nec leves metuit deos
animumque rebus credulum laetis dedit,
me videat et te, Troia.   non umquam tulit
documenta fors maiora, quam fragili loco
starent superbi.   columen eversum occidit
pollentis Asiae, caelitum egregius labor;
ad cuius arma venit et qui [1] frigidum
septena Tanain ora pandentem bibit
et qui renatum primus excipiens diem   10
tepidum rubenti Tigrin immiscet freto,
et quae vagos vicina prospiciens Scythas
ripam catervis Ponticam viduis ferit,[2]
excisa ferro est, Pergamum incubuit sibi.
en alta muri decora congesti [3] iacent
tectis adustis;[4] regiam flammae ambiunt
omnisque late fumat Assaraci domus.
non prohibet avidas flamma victoris manus.
diripitur ardens Troia.   nec caelum patet
undante fumo; nube ceu densa obsitus   20
ater favilla squalet Iliaca dies.

[1] *A: Leo* quae.   [2] *Leo deletes* et quae . . . ferit.
[3] *A: Leo* congestis.   [4] *A : Leo* adusti.

124

TROADES

HECUBA

WHOEVER trusts in sovereignty and strongly lords it
in his princely hall, who fears not the fickle gods and
has given up his trustful soul to joy, on me let him
look and on thee, O Troy.   Never did fortune give
larger proof on how frail ground stand the proud.
O'erthrown and fallen is mighty Asia's prop,[1] famous
work of gods / she to whose assistance came he [2] who
drinks chill Tanaïs, spreading its sevenfold mouths,
he [3] who first greets the new-born day, where mingle
the warm waters of Tigris with the ruddy sea,
and she [4] who sees o'er her borders the wandering
Scythians and with her virgin hordes scourges the
Pontic shore—e'en she by the sword is razed, Pergamum upon herself has fallen.   See! the towering
glories of her high-piled wall lie low, her dwellings
consumed by fire ; the flames lick round her palace,
and all the house of Assaracus smokes on every side.
The flames check not the victor's greedy hands;
Troy is plundered even while she burns.   The very
sky is hidden by billowing smoke; the face of
day, obscured as by an impenetrable cloud, is black
and foul with the ashes of Ilium.   With wrath still

---

[1] Troy, whose walls were built by Neptune and Apollo.
[2] Rhesus.   [3] Memnon.
[4] Penthesilea, queen of the Amazons.

stat avidus irae victor et lentum Ilium
metitur oculis ac decem tandem ferus
ignoscit annis ; horret afflictam quoque,
victamque quamvis videat, haut credit sibi
potuisse vinci.   spolia populator rapit
Dardania ; praedam mille non capiunt rates.

    Testor deorum numen adversum mihi,
patriaeque cineres teque rectorem Phrygum
quem Troia toto conditum regno tegit,   30
tuosque manes quo stetit stante Ilium,
et vos, meorum liberum magni greges,
umbrae minores : quidquid adversi accidit,
quaecumque Phoebas ore lymphato furens
credi deo vetante praedixit mala,
prior Hecuba vidi gravida nec tacui metus
et vana vates ante Cassandram fui.
non cautus ignes Ithacus aut Ithaci comes
nocturnus in vos sparsit aut fallax Sinon.
meus ignis iste est, facibus ardetis meis.   40

    Sed quid ruinas urbis eversae gemis,
vivax senectus ? respice infelix ad hos
luctus recentes ; Troia iam vetus est malum.
vidi execrandum regiae caedis nefas
ipsasque ad aras (maius admissum fide)
Aeacidis arma,[1] cum ferox, scaeva manu
coma reflectens regium torta caput,
alto nefandum vulneri ferrum abdidit ;

---

[1] *So Leo conjectures by way of emending the impossible text :*
maius admissumst scelus Aeacis armis.

126

unglutted the victor stands, eyeing long-lingering
Ilium, and at last, spite of his savage hate, forgives
the ten long years; he quakes even at her ruins and,
though he sees her overthrown, yet trusts not his
own witness that she could have been overthrown.
The plunderer hurries away the Dardan spoils, booty
which a thousand ships cannot contain.

²⁹ I call to witness the divinity of the gods, hostile
to me, the ashes of my country, thee,[1] ruler of Phrygia,
whom, buried beneath thy whole realm, Troy covers,
and the shades of thee [2] with whose standing Ilium
stood, and you, great troops of children mine, ye lesser
shades: whatever disaster has befallen us, whatever
evils Phoebus' bride,[3] raving with frenzied lips,
foretold, though the god forbade that she should
be believed, I, Hecuba, big with child,[4] saw first,
nor did I keep my fears unuttered, and I before
Cassandra was a prophetess unheeded. 'Tis not the
crafty Ithacan,[5] nor the night-prowling comrade [6] of
the Ithacan, who has scattered firebrands 'mongst
you, nor the lying Sinon—mine is that fire, by my
brands are you burning.

⁴¹ But why lamentest thou the downfall of a city
overthrown, old age that clingest too long to life?
Think thou, ill-fated, on these recent griefs; Troy's
fall is now an ancient woe. I saw the accursed
murder of the king and at the very altar (crime past
belief) the arms of Aeacides,[7] when he, with left
hand clutching the old man's hair, bent back the
royal head and into the deep wound savagely thrust
the impious steel; and when with right good will

---

[1] Priam.   [2] Hector's.   [3] Cassandra.
[4] Paris. See Index *s.v.* "Paris" and "Hecuba."
[5] Ulysses.   [6] Diomedes.
[7] Pyrrhus, son of Achilles, and remote descendant of Aeacus.

quod penitus actum cum recepisset libens,
ensis senili siccus e iugulo redit.   50
placare quem non potuit a caede effera
mortalis aevi cardinem extremum premens
superique testes sceleris et quondam [1] sacrum
regni iacentis ? ille tot regum parens
caret sepulcro Priamus et flamma indiget
ardente Troia.   non tamen superis sat est ;
dominum ecce Priami nuribus et natis legens
sortitur urna praedaque en vilis sequar.
hic Hectoris coniugia despondet sibi,
hic optat Heleni coniugem, hic Antenoris ;   60
nec dest tuos, Cassandra, qui thalamos petat.
mea sors timetur, sola sum Danais metus.

 Lamenta cessant ? turba captivae mea,
ferite palmis pectora et planctus date
et iusta Troiae facite.   iamdudum sonet
fatalis Ide, iudicis diri domus.

CHORVS

 Non rude vulgus lacrimisque novum
lugere iubes : hoc continuis
egimus annis, ex quo tetigit
Phrygius Graias hospes Amyclas   70
secuitque fretum pinus matri
sacra Cybebae.
deciens nivibus canuit Ide,
deciens nostris nudata rogis,
et Sigeis trepidus campis
decumas secuit messor aristas,
ut nulla dies maerore caret.

  [1] *So* ψ : *Leo* quoddam.

---

[1] Paris.   [2] *Ibid.*

he had plucked away the deep-driven sword, it came unwetted from the old man's throat. Ah, whose rage might not have been stayed from savage slaughter by one close drawing to the last period of mortal life, by the gods who beheld the crime, and by what was once the sanctuary of a fallen realm? Priam, that father of so many princes, lies unentombed and lacks a funeral torch, though Troy is burning. And yet the gods are not satisfied; behold, the urn by lot is choosing lords for the matrons and maids of Priam's house, and I, a spoil unprized, shall follow some new lord. One promises himself the wife of Hector, one prays that Helenus' wife be his, and one, Antenor's; nor is one wanting who seeks thy couch, Cassandra; my lot is dreaded, I only am a terror to the Greeks.

[63] Do your wailings falter? O throng of mine, captives as ye are, smite breasts with palms, make loud laments, due rites for Troy perform. Long since 'twere time for fatal Ida to resound, home of the ill-omened judge.[1]

CHORUS

No untrained company, stranger to tears, dost thou bid mourn; this have we done for years unceasing, from when the Phrygian guest[2] touched at Grecian Amyclae, and the waves were cleft by the pine sacred to mother Cybele.[3] Ten times has Ida whitened with her snows, ten times been stripped for our funeral pyres, and in the Sigean fields ten harvests has the trembling reaper cut, since when no day has been without its grief. But now we have

---

[3] *i.e.* the pines were cut on Mount Ida, which was sacred to Cybele.

sed nova fletus causa ministrat.
ite ad planctus, miseramque leva,
regina, manum.   vulgus dominam   80
vile sequemur ; non indociles
lugere sumus.

HECVBA

Fidae casus nostri comites,
solvite crinem, per colla fluant
maesta capilli tepido Troiae
pulvere turpes.   complete manus,   102^b
hoc ex Troia sumpsisse licet.[1]   103
paret exertos turba lacertos ;   87
veste remissa substringe sinus
uteroque tenus pateant artus.
cui coniugio pectora velas,   90
captive pudor ?
cingat tunicas palla solutas,
vacet ad crebri verbera planctus
furibunda manus—placet hic habitus,
placet ; agnosco Troada turbam.
iterum luctus redeant veteres,
solitum flendi vincite morem ;
Hectora flemus.

CHORVS

Solvimus omnes lacerum multo
funere crinem ; coma demissa est   100
libera nodo sparsitque cinis
fervidus ora.
cadit ex umeris vestis apertis   104
imumque tegit suffulta latus ;

---

[1] *Leo follows F. Haase in transferring ll. 102^b and 103 to this place.*

new cause for weeping. On with your lamentation,
and do thou, O queen, lift high thy wretched hand.
We, the common throng, will follow our mistress;
well trained in mourning are we.

HECUBA

Trusty comrades of my fate, unbind your locks;
over your sorrowing shoulders let them flow, defiled
with Troy's warm dust. Fill your hands—so much
may we take from Troy. Let the band their bared
arms make ready; let down your robes and bind their
folds; down to the waist let your forms be bared.
For what husband dost veil thy breast, O captive
modesty? Let your mantles gird up the loose-flowing
tunics,[1] let mad hands be free for raining the blows
of woe—'tis well, this attire is well; now do I recognize my Trojan band. Repeat once more your old
lamentations; exceed your wonted manner of weeping; 'tis for Hector we weep.

CHORUS

We have all loosed our locks at many a funeral
torn; our hair has fall'n free from its knot, and
hot ashes have sprinkled our faces. From our
bared shoulders our garments fall and cover only
our loins with their folds. Now naked breasts invite

---

[1] *i.e.* the outer robe (palla) is to be used as a girdle with
which to hold up the loose tunic, and so leave the hands
free.

iam nuda vocant pectora dextras;
nunc, nunc vires exprome, dolor.
Rhoetea sonent litora planctu,
habitansque cavis montibus Echo
non, ut solita est, extrema brevis   110
verba remittat, totos reddat
Troiae gemitus.   audiat omnis
pontus et aether.   saevite, manus,
pulsu pectus tundite vasto,
non sum solito contenta sono;
Hectora flemus.

HECVBA

Tibi nostra ferit dextra lacertos
umerosque ferit tibi sanguineos,
tibi nostra caput dextera pulsat,
tibi maternis ubera palmis   120
laniata iacent.   fluat et multo
sanguine manet quamcumque tuo
funere feci rupta cicatrix.
columen patriae, mora fatorum,
tu praesidium Phrygibus fessis,
tu murus eras umerisque tuis
stetit illa decem fulta per annos;
tecum cecidit summusque dies
Hectoris idem patriaeque fuit.
Vertite planctus; Priamo vestros   130
fundite fletus, satis Hector habet.

CHORVS

Accipe, rector Phrygiae, planctus,
accipe fletus, bis capte senex.
nil Troia semel te rege tulit,
bis pulsari Dardana Graio

our hands; now, now, O Grief, put forth thy strength. Let the Rhoetean shores resound with our mourning, and let Echo, who dwells in the caves of the mountains, not, after her wont, curtly repeat our final words alone, but give back our full mourning for Troy. Let every sea hear us, and sky. Smite, hands, bruise breasts with mighty beating; I am not content with the accustomed sound—'tis for Hector we weep.

HECUBA

For thee [1] my right hand smites my arms, and bleeding shoulders it smites for thee; for thee my hand beats on my head, for thee my breasts with a mother's palms are mangled. Let flow and stream with blood, bleeding afresh, whatever wound I made at thy funeral. O prop of thy country, hindrance of fate, thou bulwark for weary Phrygians, thou wast our country's wall; propped on thy shoulders, ten years she stood; with thee she fell, and Hector's last day was his country's, too.

[130] Turn now your mourning; for Priam shed your tears; Hector has enough.

CHORUS

Receive our mourning, O ruler of Phrygia; receive our tears, twice-captured old man. Naught has Troy suffered but once in thy reign; nay, twice she endured the battering of her Dardanian walls by

[1] Hector.

moenia ferro bisque pharetras
passa Herculeas.   post elatos
Hecubae partus regumque gregem
postrema pater funera cludis
magnoque Iovi victima caesus   140
Sigea premis litora truncus.

HECVBA

Alio lacrimas flectite vestras;
non est Priami miseranda mei
mors, Iliades.   felix Priamus
dicite cunctae.   liber manes
vadit ad imos, nec feret umquam
victa Graium cervice iugum;
non ille duos videt Atridas
nec fallacem cernit Vlixen;
non Argolici praeda triumphi   150
subiecta feret colla tropaeis;
non adsuetas ad sceptra manus
post terga dabit currusque sequens
Agamemnonios aurea dextra
vincula gestans latis fiet
pompa Mycenis.

CHORVS

Felix Priamus dicimus omnes.
secum excedens sua regna tulit;
nunc Elysii nemoris tutis
errat in umbris interque pias   160
felix animas Hectora quaerit.
felix Priamus, felix quisquis
bello moriens omnia secum
consumpta tulit.

---

[1] First, when Hercules captured Troy with the aid of
Telamon during the reign of Laomedon, at which time little

Grecian steel and twice [1] felt the arrows of Hercules.
After Hecuba's sons were borne out to burial, after
that troop of princes, thou, father, dost close the long
funeral train and, slaughtered as a victim to mighty
Jove,[2] on Sigeum's strand headless thou liest.

HECUBA

Otherwhere turn ye your tears; not to be pitied
is my Priam's death, ye Trojans. Cry ye all, " Happy
Priam ! " Free fares he to the deep land of spirits,
nor ever will bear on his conquered neck the yoke of
the Grecians; he does not look upon the two sons
of Atreus, nor behold crafty Ulysses; he will not,
as booty of Argolic triumph, bend neck 'neath their
trophies; he will not yield hands to be bound which
have wielded the sceptre, nor, following the car of
Agamemnon, wearing gold fetters, will he make
show for wide-spreading Mycenae.

CHORUS

" Happy Priam," say we all. With him, in de-
parting, he has taken his kingdom; now in the
peaceful shades of Elysium's grove he wanders, and
happy midst pious souls he seeks for his Hector.
Happy Priam, happy whoe'er, dying in battle, has
with his death made an end of all.

Priam was set on the throne; and second, when in the hands
of Philoctetes they were again used against Troy.
  [2] Priam was slain near the altar of Jupiter in the central
courtyard of his own palace,

SENECAE TRAGOEDIAE

O longa Danais semper in portu mora,
seu petere bellum, petere seu patriam volunt!

Quae causa ratibus faciat et Danais moram,
effare, reduces quis deus claudat vias.

Pavet animus, artus horridus quassat tremor.
maiora veris monstra vix capiunt fidem—
vidi ipse, vidi.   summa iam Titan iuga   170
stringebat ortu, vicerat noctem dies,
cum subito caeco terra mugitu fremens
concussa totos traxit ex imo sinus ;
movere silvae capita et excelsum nemus
fragore vasto tonuit et lucus sacer ;
Idaea ruptis saxa ceciderunt iugis.
nec terra solum tremuit ; et pontus suum
adesse Achillen sensit ac stravit vada.
tum scissa vallis aperit immensos specus
et hiatus Erebi pervium ad superos iter
tellure fracta praebet ac tumulum levat.   180
emicuit ingens umbra Thessalici ducis,
Threicia qualis arma proludens tuis
iam, Troia, fatis stravit aut Neptunium
136

TROADES

[*Enter* TALTHYBIUS.]

TALTHYBIUS

O delay, ever long for Greeks in harbour, whether they would seek war or seek fatherland!

CHORUS

Tell thou what cause delays the Grecian fleet, what god blocks the homeward paths.

TALTHYBIUS

My spirit is afraid; shivering horror makes my limbs to quake. Portents transcending truth scarce gain belief—but I saw it, with my own eyes I saw. The sun was just grazing the hill-tops with his morning rays and day had vanquished night, when suddenly the earth with hidden rumblings rocked convulsive and brought to light her innermost recesses; the woods tossed their tops and the lofty forest and sacred grove resounded with huge crashing; and rocks came falling from the shivered heights of Ida. Nor did the earth only tremble; the sea, too, felt its own Achilles near and stilled its waters. Then was the valley rent asunder, revealing caverns measureless, and yawning Erebus gave passage-way through the cleft earth to the world above and opened up the tomb.[1] Forth leaped the mighty shade of the Thessalian chief, such shape as when, practising for thy fate, O Troy, he laid low the Thracian[2] arms, or smote the son[3] of Neptune with

---

[1] *i.e.* the great tomb of Achilles.
[2] Achilles on his way to Troy defeated Cisseus, father of Hecuba, who was leading Thracian auxiliaries to Troy.
[3] See Index *s.v.* "Cycnus" (ii).

cana nitentem perculit iuvenem coma,
aut cum inter acies Marte violento furens
corporibus amnes clusit et quaerens iter
tardus cruento Xanthus erravit vado,
aut cum superbo victor in curru stetit
egitque habenas Hectorem et Troiam trahens.
implevit omne litus irati sonus: 190
"ite, ite inertes, manibus meis debitos
auferte honores, solvite ingratas rates
per nostra ituri maria.   non parvo luit
iras Achillis Graecia et magno luet.
desponsa nostris cineribus Polyxene
Pyrrhi manu mactetur et tumulum riget."
haec fatus alta voce dimisit [1] diem
repetensque Ditem mersus ingentem specum
coeunte terra iunxit. immoti iacent
tranquilla pelagi, ventus abiecit minas   200
placidumque fluctu murmurat leni mare,
Tritonum ab alto cecinit hymenaeum chorus.

PYRRHVS

  Cum laeta pelago vela rediturus dares,
excidit Achilles cuius unius manu
impulsa Troia, quidquid accessit [2] morae
illo remoto, dubia quo caderet stetit.
velis licet quod petitur ac properes dare,
sero es daturus; iam suum cuncti duces
tulere pretium. quae minor merces potest
tantae dari virtútis? an meruit parum   210
qui, fugere bellum iussus et longa sedens

---

[1] So *Gronovius, with ψ: Leo* alta nocte divisit: *Richter* alta nocte demersit.

[2] So *Richter: Leo* adiecit, *with ω.*

138

white plumes gleaming; or when, amidst the ranks
raging in furious battle, he choked rivers with corpses,
and Xanthus, seeking his way, wandered slowly
along with bloody stream ; or when he stood in his
proud car victorious, plying the reins and dragging
Hector—and Troy. The shout of the enraged hero
filled all the shore : "Go, go, ye cowards, bear off
the honours due to my spirit ; loose your ungrateful
ships to sail away over my [1] seas. At no small price
did Greece avert the wrath of Achilles, and at great
cost shall she avert it. Let Polyxena, once pledged
to me, be sacrificed to my dust by the hand of Pyrrhus
and bedew my tomb." So speaking with deep voice,
he bade farewell to day and, plunging down to Dis
once more, closed the huge chasm as the earth was
again united. The tranquil waters lie motionless,
the wind has given up its threats, the calm sea
murmurs with gentle waves, from the deep the band
of Tritons has sounded the wedding hymn.

[*Enter* PYRRHUS *and* AGAMEMNON.]

PYRRHUS

When thou wast spreading joyful sails for thy
return over the sea, Achilles was quite forgot, who
by his sole hand made Troy to totter, so that—
whate'er delay was added after his death—she but
stood wavering which way to fall. Though thou
shouldst wish and haste to give him what he seeks,
thou wouldst give too late; already have all the
chiefs made choice of their spoils. What meaner
prize can be given to his great worth ? Or was his
desert but slight who, bidden to shun the war and
idly spend a long old age, surpassing the years of the

[1] Because he was the son of the sea-goddess Thetis.

aevum senecta ducere ac Pylii senis
transcendere annos, exuit matris dolos
falsasque vestes, fassus est armis virum?
inhospitali Telephus regno impotens,
dum Mysiae ferocis introitus negat,
rudem cruore regio dextram imbuit
fortemque eandem sensit et mitem manum.
cecidere Thebae, vidit Eetion capi
sua regna victus; clade subversa est pari   220
apposita celso parva Lyrnesos iugo,
captaque tellus nobilis Briseide
et causa litis regibus Chryse iacet
et nota fama Tenedos et quae pascuo
fecunda pingui Thracios nutrit greges
Scyros fretumque Lesbos Aegaeum secans
et cara Phoebo Cilla; quid quas alluit
vernis Caycus gurgitem attollens aquis?

   Haec tanta clades gentium ac tantus pavor,
sparsae tot urbes turbinis vasti modo   230
alterius esset gloria ac summum decus;
iter est Achillis; sic meus venit pater
et tanta gessit bella, dum bellum parat.
ut alia sileam merita, non unus satis
Hector fuisset? Ilium vicit pater,
vos diruistis. inclitas laudes iuvat
et facta magni clara genitoris sequi.
iacuit peremptus Hector ante oculos patris
patruique Memnon, cuius ob luctum parens
pallente maestum protulit vultu diem;   240
suique victor operis exemplum horruit
didicitque Achilles et dea natos mori.
tum saeva Amazon ultimus cecidit metus.

TROADES

ancient Pylian,[1] put off his mother's wiles and those
disguising garments, confessing himself a man by his
choice of arms?[2] When Telephus, unbridled ruler
of inhospitable realm, refused him passage through
warlike Mysia, he with his royal blood first dyed that
inexperienced hand, and found that same hand brave
and merciful.[3] Thebes fell and conquered Eëtion
saw his kingdom taken; by a like disaster little
Lyrnesos, perched on a high hill, was overthrown,
and the land famous for Briseïs' capture; Chryse,
too, lies low, cause of strife for kings, and Tenedos,
well known in fame, and fertile Scyros, which on its
rich pasturage feeds the Thracian flocks, and Lesbos,
cleaving in twain the Aegean sea, and Cilla, sacred to
Phoebus; and what of the lands which the Caÿcus
washes, his waters swollen by the floods of spring?

229 This great overthrow of nations, this widespread
terror, all these cities wrecked as by a tornado's blast,
to another could have been glory and the height of
fame; to Achilles they were but deeds upon the
way. 'Twas thus my father came, and so great wars
he waged while but preparing war. Though I speak
not of other merits, would not Hector alone have
been enough? My father conquered Ilium; you
have plundered it. Proud am I to rehearse my great
sire's illustrious praises and glorious deeds: Hector
lies low, slain before his father's eyes, and Memnon
before his uncle's, in sorrow for whose death his
mother [4] with wan face ushered in a mournful day,
while the victor shuddered at the lesson of his own
work, and Achilles learned that even sons of goddesses
can die. Then fell the fierce Amazon,[5] our latest

[1] Nestor.   [2] See Index s.v. "Achilles."
[3] See "Telephus."   [4] Aurora, goddess of the dawn.
[5] Penthesilea, queen of the Amazons.

141

debes Achilli, merita si digne aestimas,
et si ex Mycenis virginem atque Argis petat.
dubitatur et iam placita nunc subito improbas
Priamique natam Pelei nato ferum
mactare credis ?   at tuam natam parens
Helenae immolasti.   solita iam et facta expeto.

AGAMEMNON

Iuvenile vitium est regere non posse impetum ;   250
aetatis alios fervor hic primus rapit,
Pyrrhum paternus.   spiritus quondam truces
minasque tumidi lentus Aeacidae tuli.
quo plura possis, plura patienter feras.
Quid caede dira nobiles clari ducis
aspergis umbras ? noscere hoc primum decet,
quid facere victor debeat, victus pati.
violenta nemo imperia continuit diu,
moderata durant ; quoque Fortuna altius
evexit ac levavit humanas opes,   260
hoc se magis supprimere felicem decet
variosque casus tremere metuentem deos
nimium faventes.   magna momento obrui
vincendo didici.   Troia nos tumidos facit
nimium ac feroces ? stamus hoc Danai loco,
unde illa cecidit.   fateor, aliquando impotens
regno ac superbus altius memet tuli ;
sed fregit illos spiritus haec quae dare
potuisset aliis causa, Fortunae favor.
tu me superbum, Priame, tu timidum facis   270

dread. Thou art Achilles' debtor, if rightly thou
estimate his worth, even if he should ask a maiden
from Mycenae and from Argos.[1] Dost hesitate and
now of a sudden deem wrong what has already been
approved,[2] and count it cruel to sacrifice Priam's
daughter to Peleus' son ? And yet thine own daughter
for Helen's sake thou, her sire, didst immolate. I
claim but what is already use and precedent.

AGAMEMNON

Ungoverned violence is a fault of youth ; in the
case of others 'tis the first fervour of their years that
sweeps them on, but with Pyrrhus 'tis his father's
heat. The blustering airs and threats of arrogant
Aeacides I once bore unmoved. The greater the
might, the more should be the patience to endure.
[255] Why with cruel bloodshed dost thou besmirch
the noble shade of an illustrious chief? This 'twere
fitting first to learn, what the victor ought to do,
the vanquished, suffer. Ungoverned power no one
can long retain ; controlled, it lasts ; and the higher
Fortune has raised and exalted the might of man, the
more does it become him to be modest in prosperity, to
tremble at shifting circumstance, and to fear the gods
when they are overkind. That greatness can be in
a moment overthrown I have learned by conquering.
Does Troy make us too arrogant and bold? We
Greeks are standing in the place whence she has
fallen. In the past, I grant, I have been headstrong in
government and borne myself too haughtily; but such
pride has been broken by that cause which could
have produced it in another, e'en Fortune's favour.
Thou, Priam, mak'st me proud—and fearful, too.

---

[1] *i.e.* if he should ask for a Grecian maid, even a daughter
of Agamemnon.

[2] Probably a covert allusion to the sacrifice of Iphigenia.

Ego esse quicquam sceptra nisi vano putem
fulgore tectum nomen et falso comam
vinclo decentem?   casus haec rapiet brevis,
nec mille forsan ratibus aut annis decem:
non omnibus fortuna tam lenta imminet.[1]
equidem fatebor (pace dixisse hoc tua,
Argiva tellus, liceat) affligi Phrygas
vincique volui; ruere et aequari solo—
utinam arcuissem.   sed regi frenis nequit
et ira et ardens hostis et victoria   280
commissa nocti.   quidquid indignum aut ferum
cuiquam videri potuit, hoc fecit dolor
tenebraeque, per quas ipse se irritat furor,
gladiusque felix, cuius infecti semel
vecors libido est.   quidquid eversae potest
superesse Troiae, maneat; exactum satis
poenarum et ultra est.   regia ut virgo occidat
tumuloque donum detur et cineres riget
et facinus atrox caedis ut thalamos vocent,
non patiar.   in me culpa cunctorum redit;   290
qui non vetat peccare, cum possit, iubet.

PYRRHVS

Nullumne Achillis praemium manes ferent?

AGAMEMNON

Ferent, et illum laudibus cuncti canent
magnumque terrae nomen ignotae audient.
quod si levatur sanguine infuso cinis,
opima Phrygii colla caedantur greges
fluatque nulli flebilis matri cruor.
quis iste mos est?   quando in inferias homo est

---

[1] *Leo deletes this line.*

271 Should I count sovereignty anything but a name bedecked with empty glamour, a brow adorned with a lying coronet? Brief chance will plunder these, mayhap without the aid of a thousand ships or ten long years: Fate hangs not over all so long. For my part, I will confess—thy pardon for saying it, O Argive land!—I wished to see the Phrygians beaten down and conquered; but overthrown and razed to the ground—would that I could have spared them that. But wrath, the fiery foeman, victory given to night's charge, these cannot be kept in hand. All that any might have deemed unworthy in me or brutal, this resentment wrought and darkness, whereby fury is spurred to greater fury, and the victorious sword, whose blood-lust, when once stained with blood, is madness. All that can survive of ruined Troy let it survive; enough and more of punishment has been exacted. That a royal maid should fall, be offered to a tomb, should water the ashes of the dead, and that men should call foul murder marriage, I will not permit. The blame of all comes back on me; he who, when he may, forbids not sin, commands it.

PYRRHUS

And shall Achilles' ghost gain no reward?

AGAMEMNON

It shall; all shall sing his praises and unknown lands shall hear his mighty name. But if his dust can be appeased only by on-poured blood, let Phrygian cattle, rich spoil, be slain, and let blood flow which will cause no mother's tears. What custom this? When was a human victim offered up

145

impensus hominis? detrahe invidiam tuo
odiumque patri, quem coli poena iubes. 300

O tumide, rerum dum secundarum status
extollit animos, timide cum increpuit metus,
regum tyranne! iamne flammatum geris
amore subito [1] pectus ac veneris novae?
solusne totiens spolia de nobis feres?
hac dextra Achilli victimam reddam suam.
quam si negas retinesque, maiorem dabo
dignamque quam det Pyrrhus; et nimium diu
a caede nostra regia cessat manus
paremque poscit Priamus.

        Haud equidem nego 310
hoc esse Pyrrhi maximum in bello decus,
saevo peremptus ense quod Priamus iacet,
supplex paternus.

        Supplices nostri patris
hostesque eosdem novimus. Priamus tamen
praesens rogavit; tu gravi pavidus metu,
nec ad rogandum fortis, Aiaci preces
Ithacoque mandas clausus atque hostem tremens.

At non timebat tunc tuus, fateor, parens,
interque caedes Graeciae atque ustas rates

---

[1] *So Leo, with* ω: solito ψ: *Leo conjectures* amoris igne:
Richter amoris aestu: *Peiper* amore nuptae.

in honour of human dead ? Save thy father from
scorn and hate, whom thou art bidding us honour by
a maiden's death.

PYRRHUS

O thou swollen with pride so long as prosperity
exalts thy soul, but faint of heart when the alarms
of war resound, tyrant of kings ! Is now thy heart
inflamed with sudden love and of a new mistress ?
Art thou alone so often to bear off our spoils ? With
this right hand will I give to Achilles the victim due.
If thou dost refuse and keep her from me, a greater
will I give, worthy the gift of Pyrrhus ; too long
has my hand refrained from killing kings, and Priam
claims his peer.

AGAMEMNON

Nay, I deny not that 'tis Pyrrhus' most glorious
deed of war that Priam lies slain by thy brutal sword,
and he thy father's suppliant.[1]

PYRRHUS

Yea, I know my father's suppliants—and enemies,
too. And yet in my father's presence Priam prayed ;
thou, quaking with o'ermastering fear, not brave
enough to make thy own plea, didst delegate thy
prayers to Ajax and the Ithacan, staying hid in thy
tent and trembling at thy foe.[2]

AGAMEMNON

But no fear then, I grant it, had thy father, and
mid Grecian carnage and their blazing ships idly he

---

[1] Priam sought out Achilles to ransom Hector's body.
[2] This scene is described in Homer, *Iliad*, bk. IX.

segnis iacebat belli et armorum immemor,   320
levi canoram verberans plectro chelyn.

PYRRHVS

Tunc magnus Hector, arma contemnens tua,
cantus Achillis timuit et tanto in metu
navalibus pax alta Thessalicis fuit.

AGAMEMNON

Nempe isdem in istis Thessalis navalibus
pax alta rursus Hectoris patri fuit.

PYRRHVS

Est regis alti spiritum regi dare.

AGAMEMNON

Cur dextra regi spiritum eripuit tua?

PYRRHVS

Mortem misericors saepe pro vita dabit.

AGAMEMNON

Et nunc misericors virginem busto petis?   330

PYRRHVS

Iamne immolari virgines credis nefas?

AGAMEMNON

Praeferre patriam liberis regem decet.

lay, thoughtless of war and arms, strumming with dainty quill on tuneful lyre.

PYRRHUS

Then mighty Hector, though he scorned thy arms, still feared Achilles' songs, and midst so great general dread deep peace lay on the ship-camp of Thessaly.[1]

AGAMEMNON

Yes, and in that same ship-camp of Thessaly deep peace, again, did Hector's father find.

PYRRHUS

'Tis a high, a kingly act to give life to a king.

AGAMEMNON

Why then from a king did thy right hand take life?

PYRRHUS

The merciful will oft give death instead of life.

AGAMEMNON

And is it now in mercy thou seekest a maiden for the tomb?

PYRRHUS

So *now* thou deemst the sacrifice of maids a crime?

AGAMEMNON

To put country before children befits a king.

[1] *i.e.* in the camp of Achilles' Thessalians, who dwelt in huts by their ships drawn up on the shore.

SENECAE TRAGOEDIAE

Lex nulla capto parcit aut poenam impedit.

AGAMEMNON

Quod non vetat lex, hoc vetat fieri pudor.

PYRRHVS

Quodcumque libuit facere victori licet.

AGAMEMNON

Minimum decet libere cui multum licet.

PYRRHVS

His ista iactas, quos decem annorum gravi
regno subactos Pyrrhus exsolvit iugo?

AGAMEMNON

Hos Scyrus animos—?

PYRRHVS

Scelere quae fratrum caret.

AGAMEMNON

Inclusa fluctu—

PYRRHVS

Nempe cognati maris.   340
Atrei et Thyestae nobilem novi domum.
150

TROADES

PYRRHUS

No law spares the captive or stays the penalty.

AGAMEMNON

What law forbids not, shame forbids be done.

PYRRHUS

Whate'er he will, 'tis the victor's right to do.

AGAMEMNON

Least should he will who has much right.

PYRRHUS

Darest fling such words to those whom, overwhelmed beneath thy heavy sway for ten long years, Pyrrhus freed from the yoke?

AGAMEMNON

Does Scyrus give such airs?

PYRRHUS

'Tis free from the crime of brothers.[1]

AGAMEMNON

Hemmed by the waves—

PYRRHUS

Yes, of a kindred sea.[2] Atreus and Thyestes—well do I know their noble house.

---

[1] A reference to Atreus and Thyestes, father and uncle of Agamemnon, who committed all crimes against each other.

[2] Explained in l. 346 ; and see l. 193 and note.

SENECAE TRAGOEDIAE

AGAMEMNON

Ex virginis concepte furtivo stupro
et ex Achille nate, sed nondum viro—

PYRRHVS

Illo ex Achille, genere qui mundum suo
sparsus per omne caelitum regnum tenet:
Thetide aequor, umbras Aeaco, caelum Iove.

AGAMEMNON

Illo ex Achille, qui manu Paridis iacet.

PYRRHVS

Quem nec deorum comminus quisquam petit.

AGAMEMNON

Compescere equidem verba et audacem malo
poteram domare; sed meus captis quoque   *350*
scit parcere ensis.   potius interpres deum
Calchas vocetur.   fata si poscent, dabo.
    Tu qui Pelasgae vincla solvisti rati
morasque bellis, arte qui reseras polum,
cui viscerum secreta, cui mundi fragor
et stella longa semitam flamma trahens
dant signa fati, cuius ingenti mihi
mercede constant ora: quid iubeat deus
effare, Calchas, nosque consilio rege.

152

TROADES

AGAMEMNON

Thou son of a maiden's secret shame [1] and of
Achilles, but scarce yet a man—

PYRRHUS

Of that Achilles who by right of lineage extends
throughout the realm of the immortals and claims
the universe : the sea through Thetis, through
Aeacus the shades, the heavens through Jove.

AGAMEMNON

Of that Achilles who lies slain by Paris' hand.

PYRRHUS

Whom e'en a god would not contend with face to
face.

AGAMEMNON

I could check thy words and curb thy recklessness by punishment ; but my sword knows how to
spare e'en captives.   Rather, let Calchas, the inter-
preter of the gods, be called.   If the fates demand,
I will give her up.

[*Enter* CALCHAS.]

353 Thou who didst free the Pelasgian fleet from
bonds, and didst end the wars' delays, who by thy
art dost unlock the sky, to whom the entrails' secrets,
to whom the crashing heavens and the star with its
long, flaming trail disclose the fates, thou whose
utterances ever cost me dear : what is God's will,
declare, O Calchas, and by thy wisdom guide us.

---

[1] See Index *s.v.* " Pyrrhus."

SENECAE TRAGOEDIAE

CALCHAS

Dant fata Danais quo solent pretio viam. 360
mactanda virgo est Thessali busto ducis;
sed quo iugari Thessalae cultu solent
Ionidesve vel Mycenaeae nurus,
Pyrrhus parenti coniugem tradat suo.
sic rite dabitur.   non tamen nostras tenet
haec una puppes causa; nobilior tuo,
Polyxene, cruore debetur cruor.
quem fata quaerunt, turre de summa cadat
Priami nepos Hectoreus et letum oppetat.
tum mille velis impleat classis freta. 370

CHORVS

Verum est an timidos fabula decipit
umbras corporibus vivere conditis,
cum coniunx oculis imposuit manum
supremusque dies solibus obstitit
et tristis cineres urna cohercuit?
non prodest animam tradere funeri,
sed restat miseris vivere longius?
an toti morimur nullaque pars manet
nostri, cum profugo spiritus halitu
immixtus nebulis cessit in aera 380
et nudum tetigit subdita fax latus?
    Quidquid sol oriens, quidquid et occidens
novit, caeruleis Oceanus fretis
quidquid bis veniens et fugiens lavat,
aetas Pegaseo corripiet gradu.
quo bis sena volant sidera turbine,
quo cursu properat volvere saecula
astrorum dominus, quo properat modo
obliquis Hecate currere flexibus;

154

TROADES

'Tis at the accustomed price fate grants the Danaï
their voyage.   A maiden must be sacrificed on
the Thessalian chieftain's tomb; but in the garb· in
which Thessalian brides are wed, or Ionian or My-
cenaean, let Pyrrhus lead his father's bride to him.
'Tis so she shall be given duly.   But it is not this
cause alone which delays our ships; blood nobler
than thy blood, Polyxena, is due.   Whom the fates
seek, from the high watch-tower let him fall, Priam's
grandson, Hector's son, and let him perish there.
Then with its thousand sails may the fleet fill the
seas.

CHORUS

Is it true, or does the tale cheat timid souls,
that spirits live on when bodies have been buried,
when the wife has closed her husband's eyes, when
the last day has blotted out the sun, when the
mournful urn holds fast our dust ?   Profits it not to
give up the soul to death, but remains it for wretched
mortals to live still longer ?   Or do we wholly die
and does no part of us remain, when with the fleeting
breath the spirit, mingling with vapours, has passed
into the air, and the lighted fire has touched the
naked body ?
382 All that the rising sun and all that the setting
knows, all that the ocean laves with its blue waters,
twice ebbing and twice flowing, time with the pace
of Pegasus shall gather in.   With such whirlwind
speed as the twelve signs fly along, with such swift
course as the lord [1] of stars hurries on the centuries,
and in such wise as Hecate hastens along her slanting

[1] The sun.

hoc omnes petimus fata nec amplius, 390
iuratos superis qui tetigit lacus,
usquam est. ut calidis fumus ab ignibus
vanescit, spatium per breve sordidus,
ut nubes, gravidas quas modo vidimus,
arctoi Boreae dissicit impetus;
sic hic, quo regimur, spiritus effluet.
post mortem nihil est ipsaque mors nihil,
velocis spatii meta novissima.
spem ponant avidi, solliciti metum;
tempus nos avidum devorat et chaos. 400
mors individua est, noxia corpori
nec parcens animae. Taenara et aspero
regnum sub domino limen et obsidens
custos non facili Cerberus ostio
rumores vacui verbaque inania
et par sollicito fabula somnio.
quaeris quo iaceas post obitum loco?
quo non nata iacent.

ANDROMACHA

Quid, maesta Phrygiae turba, laceratis comas
miserumque tunsae pectus effuso genas 410
fletu rigatis? levia perpessae sumus,
si flenda patimur. Ilium vobis modo,
mihi cecidit olim, cum ferus curru incito
mea membra raperet et gravi gemeret sono
Peliacus axis pondere Hectoreo tremens.

---

[1] The Styx.
[2] *individua* is used here in evident reminiscence of Cicero,

ways, so do we all seek fate, and nevermore does
he exist at all who has reached the pool [1] whereby
the high gods swear. As smoke from burning fires
vanishes, staining the air for one brief moment; as
clouds, which but now we saw lowering, are scattered
by the cold blasts of Boreas, so shall this spirit which
rules our bodies flow away. There is nothing after
death, and death itself is nothing, the final goal of a
course full swiftly run. Let the eager give up their
hopes; their fears, the anxious; greedy time and
chaos engulf us altogether. Death is a something
that admits no cleavage,[2] destructive to the body
and unsparing of the soul. Taenarus and the cruel
tyrant's [3] kingdom and Cerberus, guarding the portal
of no easy passage—all are but idle rumours, empty
words, a tale light as a troubled dream. Dost ask
where thou shalt lie when death has claimed thee?
Where they lie who were never born.

[*Enter* ANDROMACHE, *leading her little son,* ASTYANAX,
and accompanied by an aged man-servant.]

ANDROMACHE

Ye Phrygian women, mournful band, why do
you tear your hair, beat on your wretched breasts,
and water your cheeks with weeping unrestrained?
Trivial woes have we endured if our sufferings can
be told by tears. Ilium has fallen but now for you;
for me she fell long since, when the cruel foeman
behind his swift car dragged limbs—my own, and
his axle-tree, on Pelion hewed, groaned loud, straining beneath Hector's weight. On that day over-

---

de Finibus, I. VI. 17: *atomos . . . id est corpora individua
propter soliditatem.*

[3] Pluto, lord of death.

tunc obruta atque eversa quodcumque accidit
torpens malis rigensque sine sensu fero.
iam erepta Danais coniugem sequerer meum,
nisi hic teneret.   hic meos animos domat
morique prohibet ; cogit hic aliquid deos   420
adhuc rogare, tempus aerumnae addidit.
hic mihi malorum maximum fructum abstulit,
nihil timere.   prosperis rebus locus
ereptus omnis, dira qua veniant habent.
miserrimum est timere, cum speres nihil,

SENEX

Quis te repens commovit afflictam metus ?

ANDROMACHA

Exoritur aliquod maius ex magno malum.
nondum ruentis Ilii fatum stetit.

SENEX

Et quas reperiet, ut velit, clades deus ?

ANDROMACHA

Stygis profundae claustra et obscuri specus   430
laxantur et, ne desit eversis metus,
hostes ab imo conditi Dite exeunt.
solisne retro pervium est Danais iter ?
certe aequa mors est ; turbat atque agitat Phrygas
communis iste terror ; hic proprie meum
exterret animum noctis horrendae sopor.
158

whelmed and ruined, whatever has happened since I bear, benumbed with woe, stony, insensible. And now, escaping the Greeks, I should follow my husband, if this child held me not. He tames my spirit and prevents my death; he forces me still to ask something of the gods, has prolonged my suffering. He has robbed me of the richest fruit of sorrows, the scorn of fear. All chance of happiness has been snatched away from me; calamity has still a door of entrance. Most wretched 'tis to fear when you can hope for naught.

OLD MAN

What sudden terror has stirred thy stricken soul?

ANDROMACHE

Some greater woe from woe already great arises. The fate of falling Ilium is not yet stayed.

OLD MAN

What new disasters, though he wish, will the god discover?

ANDROMACHE

The bars of deep Styx and its darksome caves are opened and, lest terror be wanting to our overthrow, our buried foemen come forth from lowest Dis. To the Greeks only is a backward passage given? Death surely is impartial. That terror [1] disturbs and alarms all Phrygians alike; but this vision [2] of dread night doth terrify my soul alone.

---

[1] Achilles' ghost.　　　　[2] *i.e.* Hector's ghost.

SENECAE TRAGOEDIAE

SENEX

Quae visa portas ? effer in medium metus.

ANDROMACHA

Partes fere nox alma transierat duas
clarumque septem verterant stellae iugum;
ignota tandem venit afflictae quies   440
brevisque fessis somnus obrepsit genis,
si somnus ille est mentis attonitae stupor;
cum subito nostros Hector ante oculos stetit,
non qualis ultro bella in Argivos ferens
Graias petebat facibus Idaeis rates,
nec caede multa qualis in Danaos furens
vera ex Achille spolia simulato tulit,
non ille vultus flammeum intendens iubar,
sed fessus ac deiectus et fletu gravis
similisque nostro, squalida obtectus coma.   450
iuvat tamen vidisse.   tum quassans caput:
"dispelle somnos" inquit " et natum eripe,
o fida coniunx ; lateat, haec una est salus.
omitte fletus! Troia quod cecidit gemis?
utinam iaceret tota, festina, amove
quocumque nostrae parvulam stirpem domus."
mihi gelidus horror ac tremor somnum expulit,
oculosque nunc huc pavida, nunc illuc ferens
oblita nati misera quaesivi Hectorem;
fallax per ipsos umbra complexus abit.   460

O nate, magni certa progenies patris,
spes una Phrygibus, unica afflictae domus,
160

TROADES

What vision hast thou to tell? Speak out thy fears before us all.

Two portions of her course had kindly night well-nigh passed, and the seven stars had turned their shining car; at last long unfamiliar calm came to my troubled heart, and a brief slumber stole o'er my weary cheeks—if, indeed, the stupor of a mind all dazed be slumber—when suddenly Hector stood before my eyes, not in such guise as when, forcing the fight against the Argives, he attacked the Grecian ships with torches from Ida's pines, not as when he raged in copious slaughter against the Danaï and bore off true spoils from a feigned Achilles[1]; not such his face, blazing with battle light, but weary, downcast, heavy with weeping, like my own, covered with matted locks. Even so, 'twas joy to have looked upon him. Then, shaking his head, he said : " Rouse thee from slumber and save our son, O faithful wife ! hide him; 'tis the only hope of safety. Away with tears ! Dost grieve because Troy has fallen ? Would she were fallen utterly ![2] Make haste, remove to any place soever the little scion of our house." Cold horror and trembling banished sleep; quaking with terror, I turned my eyes now here, now there, taking no thought of my son, and piteously seeking Hector; but from my very arms his cheating ghost was gone.

[461] O son, true offspring of a mighty sire, sole hope of Phrygians, sole comfort of our stricken house,

---

[1] Patroclus, who was fighting in the borrowed armour of his friend, Achilles.

[2] He intimates that there is a deeper depth of woe yet to come.

veterisque suboles sanguinis nimium incliti
nimiumque patri similis; hos vultus meus
nabebat Hector, talis incessu fuit
habituque talis, sic tulit fortes manus,
sic celsus umeris, fronte sic torva minax
cervice fusam dissipans iacta comam.
o nate sero Phrygibus, o matri cito,
eritne tempus illud ac felix dies   470
quo Troici defensor et vindex soli
rediviva ponas Pergama et sparsos fuga
cives reducas, nomen et patriae suum
Phrygibusque reddas?   sed mei fati memor
tam magna timeo vota—quod captis sat est,
vivamus.

        Heu me, quis locus fidus meo
erit timori quave te sede occulam?
arx illa pollens opibus et muris deum,
gentes per omnes clara et invidiae gravis,
nunc pulvis altus, strata sunt flamma omnia   480
superestque vasta ex urbe ne tantum quidem,
quo lateat infans.   quem locum fraudi legam?
est tumulus ingens coniugis cari sacer,
verendus hosti, mole quem immensa parens
opibusque magnis struxit, in luctus suos
rex non avarus.   optime credam patri.
sudor per artus frigidus totos cadit;
omen tremesco misera feralis loci.   488

SENEX

Miser occupet praesidia, securus legat.[1]   497

ANDROMACHA

Quid quod latere sine metu magno nequit,   496
ne prodat aliquis?

[1] *The order of ll. 488–498 is Leo's: Richter follows this,
except that he reads l. 491 after 495.*

child of an ancient, too illustrious line, too like thy
father, thou ; such features my Hector had, such was
he in gait, such in bearing; so carried he his brave
hands, so bore he his shoulders high, such august,
commanding look had he as with head thrown
proudly back he tossed his flowing locks. O son,
born too late for the Phrygians, too soon for thy
mother, will that time ever come and that happy day
when, as defender and avenger of the Trojan land,
thou shalt establish Pergama restored, bring back its
scattered citizens from flight, and give again their
name to fatherland and Phrygians ? But, remembering my own lot, I shrink from such proud prayers;
this is enough for captives—may we but live !

[476] Ah me, what place will be faithful to my fears ?
where shall I hide thee ? That citadel, once rich in
treasure and its god-built walls, amongst all nations
famed and envied, is now deep dust, wasted utterly
by fire ; and of that huge city not even enough is
left wherein a child may hide. What place shall
I choose to cheat them ? There is my dear lord's
great tomb, hallowed, awe-inspiring to the foe, which
of huge bulk and at mighty cost his father reared,
a prince not niggardly in his grief. To his sire shall
I best entrust the child. Cold sweat streams down
all my limbs. Ah me ! I shudder at the omen of
the place of death.

OLD MAN

In wretchedness, seize any refuge; in safety,
choose.

ANDROMACHE

What that he cannot hide without great danger
of betrayal ?

SENEX

 Amove testes doli.   492

ANDROMACHA

Si quaeret hostis?

SENEX

   Vrbe in eversa perit;   493
haec causa multos una ab interitu arcuit,   489
credi perisse.

ANDROMACHA

   Vix spei quicquam est super;   490
grave pondus illum magna nobilitas premit.   491
quid proderit latuisse redituro in manus?   494

SENEX

Victor feroces impetus primos habet.   495

ANDROMACHA

Quis te locus, quae regio seducta, invia,   498
tuto reponet? quis feret trepidis opem?
quis proteget? qui semper, etiam nunc tuos, 500
Hector, tuere; coniugis furtum piae
serva et fideli cinere victurum excipe.
succede tumulo, nate—quid retro fugis
tutasque latebras spernis? agnosco indolem;
pudet timere. spiritus magnos fuga
animosque veteres, sume quos casus dedit.
en intuere, turba quae simus super—

164

OLD MAN

Have none to see thy guile.

ANDROMACHE

If the foe inquire?

OLD MAN

He perished in the city's downfall; this cause alone has saved many from destruction—the belief that they have perished.

ANDROMACHE

Scant hope is left; the crushing weight of his noble birth lies heavy on him. What will it profit him to have hidden, when he must fall into their hands?

OLD MAN

The victor's first onslaughts are the deadliest.

ANDROMACHE [*to* ASTYANAX]

What place, what spot, remote and inaccessible, will keep thee safe? Who will bring help in our sore need? Who will protect? O Hector, who didst always shield thine own, shield them even now; guard thou a wife's pious theft and to thy faithful ashes take him to live again. Enter the tomb, my son—why dost thou shrink back and reject this safe hiding-place? I recognize thy breeding; thou art ashamed of fear. But put away thy high spirit and old-time courage; put on such spirit as misfortune grants. See how small

tumulus, puer, captiva ; cedendum est malis.
sanctas parentis conditi sedes age
aude subire.   fata si miseros iuvant,   510
habes salutem ; fata si vitam negant,
habes sepulchrum.

SENEX

           Claustra commissum tegunt ;
quem ne tuus producat in medium timor,
procul hinc recede teque diversam amove.

ANDROMACHA

Levius solet timere, qui propius timet ;
sed, si placet, referamus hinc alio pedem.

SENEX

Cohibe parumper ora questusque opprime ;
gressus nefandos dux Cephallanum admovet.

ANDROMACHA

Dehisce tellus tuque, coniunx, ultimo
specu revulsam scinde tellurem et Stygis   520
sinu profundo conde depositum meum.
adest Vlixes, et quidem dubio gradu
vultuque ; nectit pectore astus callidos.
166

a company of us remains—a tomb, a child, a captive
woman ; we must yield to ills. Come, boldly enter
the sacred home of thy buried father. If the fates
befriend the wretched, thou hast a safe retreat; if
the fates deny thee life, thou hast a tomb.

[ASTYANAX *enters the tomb and the gates are closed
and barred behind him.*]

OLD MAN

The bars protect their charge ; and, that thy fear
may not hale him forth, retire thou far from here
and withdraw thyself apart.

ANDROMACHE

Who fears from near at hand, fears often less ;
but if thou thinkest well, we will betake us elsewhere.

[ULYSSES *is seen approaching.*]

OLD MAN

Be still a little while, utter no word or cry ;
the leader of the Cephallanians hither bends his
accursed steps.

ANDROMACHE

[*With a final appealing look towards the tomb.*]

Yawn deep, O earth, and thou, my husband, rive
the rent earth to its lowest caves and hide the
charge I give thee in the deep bosom of the Styx.
Ulysses is here, with step and look of one in hesitation ; in his heart he weaves some crafty stratagem.

[*Enter* ULYSSES.]

167

SENECAE TRAGOEDIAE

Durae minister sortis hoc primum peto,
ut, ore quamvis verba dicantur meo,
non esse credas nostra; Graiorum omnium
procerumque vox est, petere quos seras domos
Hectorea suboles prohibet; hanc fata expetunt.
sollicita Danaos pacis incertae fides
semper tenebit, semper a tergo timor   530
respicere coget, arma nec poni sinet,
dum Phrygibus animos natus eversis dabit,
Andromacha, vester.   augur haec Calchas canit;
et, si taceret augur haec Calchas, tamen
dicebat Hector, cuius et stirpem horreo;
generosa in ortus semina exurgunt suos.
sic ille magni parvus armenti comes
primisque nondum cornibus findens cutem
cervice subito celsus et fronte arduus
gregem paternum ducit ac pecori imperat;   540
quae tenera caeso virga de trunco stetit,
par ipsa matri tempore exiguo subit
umbrasque terris reddit et caelo nemus;
sic male relictus igne de magno cinis
vires resumit.   est quidem iniustus dolor
rerum aestimator; si tamen tecum exigas,
veniam dabis, quod bella post hiemes decem
totidemque messes iam senex miles timet
aliasque clades rursus ac numquam bene
Troiam iacentem.   magna res Danaos movet,   550
futurus Hector.   libera Graios metu.
168

TROADES

ULYSSES

As the minister of harsh fate I beg this first,
that, although the words are uttered by my lips,
thou count them not my words; it is the voice of all
the Grecian chiefs, whom Hector's son is keeping
from their late home-coming; 'tis the fates demand
him. A fretting mistrust of uncertain peace will
ever possess the Danaï, and fear ever will force them
to look behind and not let them lay down their
arms, so long as thy son, Andromache, and Hector's
shall give heart to the conquered Phrygians. Calchas,
the augur, gives this response; and if Calchas, the
augur, were silent upon this, yet Hector used to say
it, and I dread even a son of his; the generous scion
grows to its parent's likeness. So that little companion of the mighty herd, his first horns not yet
sprouting through the skin, suddenly, with high-
borne neck and proudly lifted brow, leads his father's
herd and rules the drove; the slender shoot which
has sprung up from a lopped-off trunk in a little
while rises to match the parent tree, gives back shade
to the earth and a sacred grove to heaven; so do the
embers of a great fire, carelessly left behind, regain
their strength. I know that grief is no impartial
judge; still, if thou weigh the matter with thyself,
thou wilt forgive a soldier if, after ten winters and
as many harvest seasons, now veteran he fears war,
fears still other bloody battles and Troy never wholly
o'erthrown. A great matter moves the forebodings
of the Danaï—another Hector. Free the Greeks

haec una naves causa deductas tenet,
hac classis haeret.   neve crudelem putes,
quod sorte iussus Hectoris natum petam;
petissem Oresten.   patere quod victor tulit.

ANDROMACHA

Vtinam quidem esses, nate, materna in manu,
nossemque quis te casus ereptum mihi
teneret, aut quae regio—non hostilibus
confossa telis pectus ac vinclis manus
secantibus praestricta, non acri latus   560
utrumque flamma cincta maternam fidem
umquam exuissem.   nate, quis te nunc locus,
fortuna quae possedit? errore avio
vagus arva lustras? vastus an patriae vapor
corripuit artus? saevus an victor tuo
lusit cruore?   numquid immanis ferae
morsu peremptus pascis Idaeas aves?

VLIXES

Simulata remove verba; non facile est tibi
decipere Vlixen; vicimus matrum dolos,
etiam dearum.   cassa consilia amove;   570
ubi natus est?

ANDROMACHA

              Vbi Hector? ubi cuncti Phryges?
ubi Priamus? unum quaeris; ego quaero omnia.

170

from fear. This one cause holds our ships, already launched; this cause stays the fleet. And think me not cruel because, at the bidding of the lot, I seek Hector's son; I would have sought Orestes.[1] Bear thou what thy conqueror has borne.[2]

ANDROMACHE

Oh, that thou wert within thy mother's reach, my son, and that I knew what hap holds thee now snatched from my arms, or what place—not though my breast were pierced with hostile spears, and my hands bound with cutting chains, not though scorching flames hemmed me on either side, would I ever put off a mother's loyalty. O son, what place, what fate, hath gotten thee now? On some pathless way dost thou roam the fields? Has the vast burning of thy fatherland consumed thy frame? or has some rude conqueror revelled in thy blood? Slain by some wild beast's fangs, dost feed the birds of Ida?

ULYSSES

Have done with lies; 'tis not easy for thee to deceive Ulysses; we have out-matched the wiles of mothers and even of goddesses.[3] Away with vain designs; where is thy son?

ANDROMACHE

Where is Hector? Where all the Phrygians? Where is Priam? Thou seekest one; I seek for all.

---

[1] *i.e.* even the son of Agamemnon.
[2] An evident allusion to the sacrifice of Iphigenia by Agamemnon for the public good.
[3] It was Ulysses who had tricked Clytemnestra into letting Iphigenia go to Aulis, and had discovered the disguise under which Thetis had hidden her son, Achilles.

SENECAE TRAGOEDIAE

VLIXES

Coacta dices sponte quod fari abnuis.

ANDROMACHA

Tuta est, perire quae potest debet cupit.

VLIXES

Magnifica verba mors prope admota excutit.

ANDROMACHA

Si vis, Vlixe, cogere Andromacham metu,
vitam minare ; nam mori votum est mihi.

VLIXES

Verberibus igni omnique [1] cruciatu eloqui
quodcumque celas adiget invitam dolor
et pectore imo condita arcana eruet ;   580
necessitas plus posse quam pietas solet.

ANDROMACHA

Propone flammas, vulnera et diras mali
doloris artes et famem et saevam sitim
variasque pestes undique, et ferrum inditum
visceribus istis, carceris caeci luem,
et quidquid audet victor iratus timens.

VLIXES

Stulta est fides celare quod prodas statim. [2]

ANDROMACHA

Animosa nullos mater admittit metus.

[1] omnique *Leo :* morte *MSS.*   [2] *Leo deletes this line.*

172

TROADES

ULYSSES

Thou shalt be forced to tell what of thyself thou wilt not.

ANDROMACHE

She is safe who is able, who ought, who longs to die.

ULYSSES

When death draws near it drives out boastful words.

ANDROMACHE

If thou desirest, Ulysses, to force Andromache through fear, threaten her with life; for 'tis my prayer to die.

ULYSSES

Stripes, fire, and every form of torture shall force thee against thy will, through pain, to speak out what thou concealest, and from thy heart shall tear its inmost secrets; necessity is oft a greater force than love.

ANDROMACHE

Bring on thy flames, wounds, devilish arts of cruel pain, and starvation and raging thirst, plagues of all sorts from every source, and the sword thrust deep within these vitals, the dungeon's pestilential gloom, yea, all a victor dares in rage—and fear.

ULYSSES

'Tis foolish confidence to hide what thou must at once betray.

ANDROMACHE

My dauntless mother-love admits no fears.

173

VLIXES

Hic ipse, quo nunc contumax perstas, amor
consulere parvis liberis Danaos monet.   590
post arma tam longinqua, post annos decem
minus timerem quos facit Calchas metus,
si mihi timerem.   bella Telemacho paras.

ANDROMACHA

Invita, Vlixe, gaudium Danais dabo ;
dandum est ; fatere quos premis luctus, dolor.
gaudete, Atridae, tuque laetifica, ut soles,
refer Pelasgis—Hectoris proles obit.

VLIXES

Et esse verum hoc qua probas Danais fide?

ANDROMACHA

Ita quod minari maximum victor potest
contingat et me fata maturo exitu   600
facilique solvant ac meo condant solo
et patria tellus Hectorem leviter premat,
ut luce cassus inter extinctos iacet
datusque tumulo debita exanimis tulit.

VLIXES

Expleta fata stirpe sublata Hectoris
solidamque pacem laetus ad Danaos feram—

174

TROADES

ULYSSES

This very love, in which thou now dost stubbornly
withstand us, warns the Danaï to take thought for
their little sons. After a war so distant, after ten
years of strife, I should feel less the fears which
Calchas rouses, if 'twas for myself I feared. Thou
art preparing war against Telemachus.

ANDROMACHE

Unwillingly, Ulysses, will I give to the Danaï
cause for joy, but I must give it; confess, O grief,
the woes which thou wouldst conceal. Rejoice, ye
sons of Atreus, and do thou bear joyful tidings to
the Pelasgians as is thy wont—Hector's son is dead.[1]

ULYSSES

What surety givest thou the Danaï that this is
true?

ANDROMACHE

So may the conqueror's worst threat befall, may
fate set me free by an early and easy passing, may I
be buried in my own soil, may his native earth rest
light on Hector, according as my son, deprived of
light, lies amongst the dead and, given to the tomb,
has received the due of those who live no more.[1]

ULYSSES

That the fates have been fulfilled by the removal
of Hector's stock, and that peace is secure, this news
will I joyfully bear to the Danaï— [*Aside.*] What

[1] Andromache first tells Ulysses to report that her son is
dead ; but she is not yet under oath ; in the second statement,
being under oath, she speaks words which give the literal
truth, but seem to say the opposite.

175

quid agis, Vlixe ? Danaidae credent tibi,
tu cui ? parenti—fingit an quisquam hoc parens,
nec abominandae mortis auspicium pavet ?
auspicia metuunt qui nihil maius timent.   610
fidem alligavit iure iurando suam ;
si peierat, timere quid gravius potest?
nunc advoca astus, anime, nunc fraudes, dolos,
nunc totum Vlixen ; veritas numquam perit.
scrutare matrem.   maeret, inlacrimat, gemit ;
sed et huc et illuc anxios gressus refert
missasque voces aure sollicita excipit ;
magis haec timet, quam maeret.   ingenio est opus.

   Alios parentes alloqui in luctu decet :
tibi gratulandum est, misera, quod nato cares,   620
quem mors manebat saeva praecipitem datum
e turre, lapsis sola quae muris manet.

ANDROMACHA

   Reliquit animus membra, quatiuntur, labant
torpetque vinctus frigido sanguis gelu.

VLIXES

   Intremuit ; hac, hac parte quaerenda est mihi ;
matrem timor detexit ; iterabo metum.

   Ite, ite celeres, fraude materna abditum
hostem, Pelasgi nominis pestem ultimam,

176

doest thou, Ulysses? The Danaï will believe thy
word, but whose word, thou? A mother's—or
would any mother feign her offspring's death, and
not shrink from the omen of the abhorrent word?
Yet omens they fear who have naught worse to fear.
She has confirmed her truth by oath; if the oath is
false, what is the worse thing she can be fearing?
Now, my heart, summon up thy craft, thy tricks,
thy wiles, now all Ulysses; truth is never lost.[1]
Watch the mother. She grieves, she weeps, she
groans; now here, now there she wanders restlessly,
straining her ears to catch each uttered word; this
woman's fear is greater than her grief. Now have I
need of skill.

[*To* ANDROMACHE.]

619 Other parents 'twere fitting to console in sorrow;
but thou art to be congratulated, poor soul, that thou
hast lost thy son, for a cruel death awaited him, cast
headlong from the tower which still stands solitary
midst the fallen walls.

ANDROMACHE [*aside*]

Life deserts my limbs, they quake, they fail;
my blood stands still, congealed with icy cold.

ULYSSES [*aside*]

She trembles; by this, yes, by this means must
I test her. Her fear has betrayed the mother; this
fear will I redouble.

[*To his attendants.*]

627 Go, go quickly! This enemy, hidden away by
his mother's guile, this last plague of the Pelasgian

---

[1] *i.e.* it is always to be discovered.

ubicumque latitat, erutam in medium date.
Bene est ! tenetur ! perge, festina, attrahe.   630
quid respicis trepidasque ?   iam certe perit.

ANDROMACHA

Vtinam timerem !   solitus ex longo est metus.
dediscit animus sero [1] quod didicit diu.

VLIXES

Lustrale quoniam debitum muris puer
sacrum antecessit nec potest vatem sequi
meliore fato raptus, hoc Calchas ait
modo piari posse redituras rates,
si placet undas Hectoris sparsi cinis
ac tumulus imo totus aequetur solo.
nunc ille quoniam debitam effugit necem,   640
erit admovenda sedibus sacris manus.

ANDROMACHA

Quid agimus ? animum distrahit geminus timor :
hinc natus, illinc coniugis sacri cinis.
pars utra vincet ?   testor immites deos,
deosque veros coniugis manes mei,
non aliud, Hector, in meo nato mihi
placere quam te.   vivat, ut possit tuos
referre vultus.—prorutus tumulo cinis

---

[1] *So Gronovius, with* A : sicre (*i.e.* scire) E, *and so Richter*
Leo saepe.

name, wherever he is hiding, hunt him out and bring him hither. [*Pretending that the boy is discovered, and then speaking as if to the man who has found him.*] Good! He is caught! Come, make haste and bring him in! [*To* ANDROMACHE.] Why dost thou look around and tremble? Surely he is already dead.

ANDROMACHE

Oh, that I were afraid. 'Tis but my wonted fear, sprung from long use. The mind unlearns but slowly what it has learned for long.

ULYSSES

Since the boy has forestalled the lustral rites we owed the walls and cannot fulfil the priest's command, snatched from us by a better fate, the word of Calchas is that only thus can a peaceful home-coming be granted to our ships, if the waves be appeased by the scattering of Hector's ashes and his tomb be utterly levelled with the ground. Now, since the boy has escaped the death he owed, needs must hands be laid upon his hallowed resting-place.[1]

ANDROMACHE [*aside*]

What shall I do? My mind is distracted by a double fear: here, for my son; there, for my husband's sacred dust. Which shall prevail? I call the unpitying deities to witness, and that true deity, my husband's shade, that in my son naught else endears him to me, Hector, than thyself. May he live, that so he may recall thy face.—But shall thy ashes, torn

---

[1] It need not be supposed that Ulysses suspects that Astyanax is really hidden in the tomb.

mergetur ? ossa fluctibus spargi sinam
disiecta vastis ? potius hic mortem oppetat.—   650
poteris nefandae deditum mater neci
videre ? poteris celsa per fastigia
missum rotari ?   potero, perpetiar, feram,
dum non meus post fata victoris manu
iactetur Hector.—hic suam poenam potest
sentire, at illum fata iam in tuto locant.—
quid fluctuaris ? statue, quem poenae extrahas.
ingrata, dubitas ?   Hector est illinc tuus—
erras—utrimque est Hector ; hic sensus potens,
forsan futurus ultor extincti patris—   660
utrique parci non potest.   quid iam facis ?
serva e duobus, anime, quem Danai timent.

VLIXES

Responsa peragam ; funditus busta eruam

ANDROMACHA

Quae vendidistis ?

VLIXES

Pergam et e summo aggere
traham sepulchra.

ANDROMACHA

Caelitum appello fidem
fidemque Achillis ; Pyrrhe, genitoris tui
munus tuere.

---

¹ *i.e.* it is not really a choice between Hector and the boy,
for Hector in a real sense is in the boy, who is to be another
Hector. *cf.* 470 ff., 550.

from the tomb, be sunk beneath the sea? Shall I
permit thy scattered bones to be flung upon the
vasty deep? Sooner let the boy meet death.—But
canst thou, his mother, see him given up to murder
infamous? Canst see him sent whirling over the
lofty battlements? I can, I will endure it, will suffer
it, so but my Hector after death be not scattered
by the victor's hand.—But he can still feel suffering,
while death has placed the other beyond its reach.
Why dost thou waver? decide whom thou wilt snatch
from vengeance. Ungrateful woman, dost thou hesitate? On that side is thy Hector—nay, herein thou
errest—Hector is in both;[1] but the boy can still
feel pain, and is destined perchance to avenge his
father's death—both cannot be saved. What then?
Save of the two, my soul, him whom the Danaï
dread.

ULYSSES

I will fulfil the oracle; the tomb will I raze to
its foundation.

ANDROMACHE

The tomb ye sold?[2]

ULYSSES

I'll keep right on, and from the mound's top I'll
drag the sepulchre.

ANDROMACHE

To heaven's faith I appeal, and Achilles' faith;
Pyrrhus, protect thy father's gift.

[2] Hector's body had been sold to Priam; here the idea of
ransom is extended to the tomb as well.

VLIXES

> Tumulus hic campo statim
> toto iacebit.

ANDROMACHA

> Fuerat hoc prorsus nefas
> Danais inausum.   templa violastis, deos
> etiam faventes ; busta transierat furor.   670
> resistam, inermes offeram armatis manus,
> dabit ira vires.   qualis Argolicas ferox
> turmas Amazon stravit, aut qualis deo
> percussa Maenas entheo silvas gradu
> armata thyrso terret atque expers sui
> vulnus dedit nec sensit, in medios ruam
> tumuloque cineris socia defenso cadam.

VLIXES

> Cessatis et vos flebilis clamor movet
> furorque cassus feminae ?   iussa ocius
> peragite.

ANDROMACHA

> Me, me sternite hic ferro prius.   680
> repellor, heu me.   rumpe fatorum moras,
> molire terras, Hector, ut Vlixen domes.
> vel umbra satis es—arma concussit manu,
> iaculatur ignes—cernitis, Danai, Hectorem ?
> an sola video ?

VLIXES

> Funditus cuncta eruam.

TROADES

ULYSSES

This mound shall at once lie level with the plain.

ANDROMACHE

Such sacrilege, truly, the Greeks had left undared.
Temples you have profaned, even of your favouring
gods; but our tombs your mad rage had spared. I
will resist, will oppose my unarmed hands against
you, armed; passion will give strength. Like the
fierce Amazon who scattered the Argive squadrons,
or like some god-smit Maenad who, armed with the
thyrsus only, with frenzied march frightens the forest
glades and, beside herself, has given wounds, nor
felt them, so will I rush against you and fall in the
tomb's defence, an ally of its dust.

ULYSSES [to his men]

Do you hold back, and does a woman's tearful
outcry and futile rage move you? My orders—be
quick and do them.

ANDROMACHE [struggling with the men]

Me, me destroy here with the sword sooner. Ah
me, I am thrust back. O Hector, burst the bars
of death, heave up the earth, that thou mayst quell
Ulysses. Even as a shade thou art enough—he [1] has
brandished his arms in his hand, he is hurling firebrands—ye Danaï, do you see Hector? or do I alone
see him?

ULYSSES

I'll pull it down to its foundations, all of it.

[1] In her frenzy she seems to see Hector's ghost.

183

ANDROMACHA

Quid agis ? ruina pariter et natum et virum
prosternis una ?   forsitan Danaos prece
placare poteris.—conditum illidet statim
immane busti pondus—intereat miser
ubicumque potius, ne pater natum obruat   690
prematque patrem natus.

                 Ad genua accido
supplex, Vlixe, quamque nullius pedes
novere dextram pedibus admoveo tuis.
miserere matris et preces placidus pias
patiensque recipe, quoque te celsum altius
superi levarunt, mitius lapsos preme ;
misero datur quodcumque, fortunae datur.
sic te revisat coniugis sanctae torus,
annosque, dum te recipit, extendat suos
Laerta ; sic te iuvenis excipiat[1] tuus,   700
et vota vincens vestra felici indole
aetate avum transcendat, ingenio patrem :
miserere matris.   unicum adflictae mihi
solamen hic est.

VLIXES

Exhibe natum et roga.

ANDROMACHA

Huc e latebris procede tuis,
flebile matris furtum miserae.

      [1] *So A : Leo* aspiciat : *E* accipiat.

TROADES

[Aside, while the men begin to demolish the tomb.]

What art thou doing? dost thou lay low together
in common ruin both son and husband? Perhaps
thou wilt be able to appease the Danaï by prayer.
—But even now the huge weight of the tomb will
crush the hidden boy—poor lad! let him perish no
matter where, so but sire o'erwhelm not son, and son
harm not sire.

[She casts herself at the knees of ULYSSES.*]*

691 At thy knees I fall, a suppliant, Ulysses, and this
hand, which no man's feet have known, I lay upon
thy feet. Pity a mother, calmly and patiently listen
to her pious prayers, and the higher the gods have
exalted thee, the more gently bear down upon the
fallen. What is given to misery is a gift to Fortune.[1]
So may thy chaste wife's couch see thee again; so
may Laertes prolong his years till he welcome thee
home once more; so may thy son succeed thee,
and, by his nature's happy gifts, surpassing all your
prayers, transcend his grandsire's years, his father's
gifts: pity a mother. This one only comfort is left
in my affliction.

ULYSSES

Produce thy son—and pray.

ANDROMACHE

[Going to the tomb, calls ASTYANAX.*]*

Hither from thy hiding-place come out, sad object
of a wretched mother's theft.

*[*ASTYANAX *appears from the tomb.]*

---

[1] *i.e.* Fortune accepts it as an offering to herself, and will
repay it in the hour of your own need.

hic est, hic est terror, Vlixe,
mille carinis. submitte manus
dominique pedes supplice dextra
stratus adora nec turpe puta   710
quidquid miseros fortuna iubet.
pone ex animo reges atavos
magnique senis iura per omnes
incluta terras, excidat Hector,
gere captivum positoque genu,
si tua nondum funera sentis,
matris fletus imitare tuae.

   Vidit pueri regis lacrimas
et Troia prior, parvusque minas
trucis Alcidae flexit Priamus.   720
ille, ille ferox, cuius vastis
viribus omnes cessere ferae,
qui perfracto limine Ditis
caecum retro patefecit iter,
hostis parvi victus lacrimis,
" suscipe " dixit " rector habenas
patrioque sede celsus solio ;
sed sceptra fide meliore tene."
hoc fuit illo victore capi ;
discite mites Herculis iras.   730
an sola placent Herculis arma ?
iacet ante pedes non minor illo
supplice supplex vitamque petit—
regnum Troiae quocumque volet
     Fortuna ferat.

VLIXES

Matris quidem me maeror attonitae movet,
magis Pelasgae me tamen matres movent,
quarum iste magnos crescit in luctus puer

⁷⁰⁷ Here he is, Ulysses, here is the terror of a thousand ships! [*To* ASTYANAX.] Lower thy hands and, prone at thy master's feet, pray thou with appealing touch; and deem naught base which fortune imposes on the wretched. Forget thy royal ancestry, the illustrious sway of thy noble grandsire o'er all lands, forget Hector, too ; play the captive and on bended knee, if thou feelst not yet thine own doom, copy thy mother's tears.

[*She turns to* ULYSSES.]

⁷¹⁸ Troy aforetime also ¹ saw the tears of a boy-king, and little Priam averted the threats of fierce Alcides. He, yes he, fierce warrior, to whose vast strength all savage creatures yielded, who burst through the doors of Dis and made the dark way retraceable, conquered by his small enemy's tears, exclaimed : "Take the reins and rule thy state, sitting high on thy father's throne ; but wield the sceptre with better faith." This it was to be taken by such a conqueror ; learn ye the merciful wrath of Hercules. Or is it the arms alone of Hercules that please thee ? ² See, there lies at thy feet a suppliant, no less than that other suppliant, and pleads for life—as for Troy's throne, let Fortune bear that whithersoe'er she will.

ULYSSES

The grief of a stricken mother moves me, true, and yet the Pelasgian mothers move me more, to whose great sorrow that boy of thine is growing.

¹ Hercules, having taken Troy and slain Laomedon for his breach of faith, spared little Priam, and placed him on the throne of his father.

² *i.e.* if Ulysses would imitate Hercules, let it be in his mercy as well as in his power.

ANDROMACHA

Has, has ruinas urbis in cinerem datae
hic excitabit? hae manus Troiam erigent? 740
nullas habet spes Troia, si tales habet.
non sic iacemus Troes, ut cuiquam metus
possimus esse. spiritus genitor facit?
sed nempe tractus. ipse post Troiam pater
posuisset animos, magna quos frangunt mala.
si poena petitur, quae peti gravior potest?
famulare collo nobili subeat iugum,
servire liceat. aliquis hoc regi negat?

VLIXES

Non hoc Vlixes, sed negat Calchas tibi.

ANDROMACHA

O machinator fraudis et scelerum artifex, 750
virtute cuius bellica nemo occidit,
dolis et astu maleficae mentis iacent
etiam Pelasgi, vatem et insontes deos
praetendis? hoc est pectoris facinus tui.
nocturne miles, fortis in pueri necem,
iam solus audes aliquid et claro die.

VLIXES

Virtus Vlixis Danaidis nota est satis
nimisque Phrygibus. non vacat vanis diem
conterere verbis; ancoras classis legit.

188

TROADES

ANDROMACHE

These ruins, these ruins of a city brought to dust,
shall he wake to life? Shall these hands raise Troy
again? Troy has no hopes if she has but such as these.
Not such our overthrow [1] that we Trojans can be a
fear to any. Does thought of his father rouse pride in
him? 'Twas a father dragged in the dust. That father
himself after Troy's fall would have given up courage,
which great misfortunes break. If revenge be sought,
what greater revenge couldst thou seek? Let the
yoke of bondage be placed upon his high-born neck,
let a slave's lot be granted him. Does any refuse
this to a prince?

ULYSSES

'Tis not Ulysses, but Calchas refuses this to thee.

ANDROMACHE

O thou contriver of fraud, cunning master in
crime, by whose warlike prowess none has ever
fallen, by whose tricks and by the cunning of whose
vicious mind even Pelasgians [2] are undone, dost seek
to hide behind seer and blameless gods? This is
the deed of thine own heart. Thou nocturnal soldier,
brave to do a mere boy to death, at last thou darest
some deed alone and in the open day.

ULYSSES

Ulysses' courage the Danaï know full well, and
all too well the Phrygians. But leisure we lack to
waste the day in empty words; the fleet is weighing
anchor.

[1] *i.e.* we are destroyed not merely in part, but utterly.
[2] Iphigenia, Palamedes, Ajax, may be cited as illustrations.

SENECAE TRAGOEDIAE

ANDROMACHA

Brevem moram largire, dum officium parens   760
nato supremum reddo et amplexu ultimo
avidos dolores satio.

VLIXES

Misereri tui
utinam liceret. quod tamen solum licet,
tempus moramque dabimus. arbitrio tuo
implere lacrimis ; fletus aerumnas levat.

ANDROMACHA

O dulce pignus, o decus lapsae domus
summumque Troiae funus, o Danaum timor,
genetricis o spes vana, cui demens ego
laudes parentis bellicas, annos avi
toties [1] precabar, vota destituit deus.   770
Iliaca non tu sceptra regali potens
gestabis aula, iura nec populis dabis
victasque gentes sub tuum mittes iugum,
non Graia caedes terga, non Pyrrhum trahes ;
non arma tenera parva tractabis manu
sparsasque passim saltibus latis feras
audax sequeris nec stato lustri die,
solemne referens Troici lusus sacrum,
puer citatas nobilis turmas ages ;
non inter aras mobili velox pede,   780
reboante flexo concitos cornu modos,
barbarica prisco templa saltatu coles.
o Marte diro tristius leti genus !
flebilius aliquid Hectoris magni nece
muri videbunt.

---

[1] *Leo's conjecture for* medios *of the MSS. :* *Richter* demens.

190

TROADES

ANDROMACHE

Generously grant a brief delay while I, his mother, do the last service to my son, and with a farewell embrace satisfy my yearning grief.

ULYSSES

Would that I might have compassion on thee; but what alone I may, I will give thee time and respite. Weep thy fill; weeping lightens woe.

ANDROMACHE [to ASTYANAX]

O sweet pledge of love, O glory of our fallen house, last loss of Troy, thou terror of the Danaï, thy mother's vain hope, for whom in my madness I used so oft to pray thy sire's war-earned praises, thy grandsire's years; God has denied my prayers. Thou shalt not with kingly might wield Ilium's sceptre in thy royal hall, shalt not give laws unto the nations, nor send conquered tribes beneath thy yoke; thou shalt not smite fleeing Greeks nor drag Pyrrhus at thy chariot-wheels. Thy slender hand shall wield no boyish weapons, nor shalt thou boldly chase the wild beasts scattered through broad forest-glades, nor on the appointed lustral day, celebrating the sacred festival of the Trojan Game,[1] shalt thou, a princely boy, lead on thy charging squadrons; nor among the altars, with swift and nimble feet, while the curved horn blares out stirring measures, shalt thou at Phrygian shrines celebrate the ancient dance. O mode of death sadder than cruel war! A sight more tearful than great Hector's death shall the walls behold.

[1] *Troiae Ludus* or *Troia* was an equestrian sham-battle said to have been popular among the boys of Troy, described by Virgil, *Aeneid* v. 545 ff., who traces the game as played at Rome back to this ancient source.

VLIXES

Rumpe iam fletus, parens;
magnus sibi ipse non facit finem dolor.

ANDROMACHA

Lacrimis, Vlixe, parva quam petimus mora est;
concede paucas, ut mea condam manu
viventis oculos.   occidis parvus quidem,
sed iam timendus.   Troia te expectat tua;   790
i, vade liber, liberos Troas vide.

ASTYANAX

Miserere, mater.

ANDROMACHA

Quid meos retines sinus
manusque matris cassa praesidia occupas?
fremitu leonis qualis audito tener
timidum iuvencus applicat matri latus,
at ille saevus matre summota leo
praedam minorem morsibus vastis tenens
frangit vehitque, talis e nostro sinu
te rapiet hostis.   oscula et fletus, puer,
lacerosque crines excipe et plenus mei   800
occurre patri; pauca maternae tamen
perfer querelae verba: "si manes habent
curas priores nec perit flammis amor,
servire Graio pateris Andromachen uiro,
crudelis Hector?   lentus et segnis iaces?
redit Achilles."   sume nunc iterum comas

192

TROADES

Break off now thy tears, thou mother; great grief
sets no limit to itself.

ANDROMACHE

For my tears, Ulysses, the respite I ask is small;
grant me a few tears yet, that with my own hand I
may close his eyes while he still lives. [*To* ASTYA-
NAX.] Thou diest, little indeed, but already to be
feared. Thy Troy awaits thee; go, depart in freedom; go, look on Trojans who are free.[1]

ASTYANAX

Pity me, mother.

ANDROMACHE

Why clingest thou to my breast, and graspest the
vain protection of thy mother's hands? As, when
the lion's roar is heard, the young bull draws close
to its mother's trembling flank, but see! the savage
lion thrusts the dam away and, with huge jaws
grasping the lesser booty, crushes and bears it off,
so shall thy enemy snatch thee from my breast.
Now, son, take my kisses and tears, take my torn
locks and, full of me, hasten to thy sire. Yet bear,
too, some few words of a mother's plaint: " If spirits
still feel their former cares, and if love perishes not
in the funeral flames, dost thou permit Andromache
to serve a Greek lord, O cruel Hector? Indifferent
and sluggish dost thou lie? Achilles has come back."
Take now once again these locks, and take these

[1] *i.e.* the boy is to join his kinsmen who have died free
rather than to live enslaved.

et sume lacrimas, quidquid e misero viri
funere relictum est, sume quae reddas tuo
oscula parenti.   matris hanc solacio
relinque vestem ; tumulus hanc tetigit meus   810
manesque cari.   si quod hic cineris latet,
scrutabor ore.

VLIXES

Nullus est flendi modus—
abripite propere classis Argolicae moram.

CHORVS

Quae vocat sedes habitanda captas?
Thessali montes et opaca Tempe,
an viros tellus dare militares
aptior Phthie meliorque fetu
fortis armenti lapidosa Trachin,
an maris vasti domitrix Iolcos?
urbibus centum spatiosa Crete,   820
parva Gortynis sterilisque Tricce,
an frequens rivis levibus Mothone
quae sub Oetaeis latebrosa silvis
misit infestos Troiae ruinis
        non semel arcus?
Olenos tectis habitata raris,
virgini Pleuron inimica divae,
an maris lati sinuosa Troezen?
Pelion regnum Prothoi superbum,
tertius caelo gradus?   (hic recumbens   830
montis exesi spatiosus antro
iam trucis Chiron pueri magister,

tears, all that is left from my poor husband's funeral,
take kisses to deliver to thy sire. This cloak leave
as comfort for thy mother; my tomb has touched it,
and my beloved shades. If any of his dust is hidden
here, I'll hunt it with my lips.

ULYSSES [*to his attendants*]

There is no limit to her weeping—away with this
hindrance to the Argive fleet.

[*Exeunt* ULYSSES *and his attendants, the former leading
the little* ASTYANAX.]

CHORUS

What place of dwelling calls to our captive band?
Thessalian mountains and Tempe's shady vale, or
Phthia, a land more fitted to produce warriors, and
rocky Trachin, famous for its breed of brave herds,
or Iolchos, the vast sea's mistress?[1] Crete, spacious
with her hundred towns, little Gortynis and barren
Tricce, or Mothone, abounding in tiny rills, the land
of caves beneath Oeta's wooded heights which sent
not once only to Troy's fall the deadly bow?[2] Olenos,
land of scattered homes, Pleuron, which the virgin
goddess[3] hates, or Troezen, on the broad sea's curving
shore? Pelion, proud kingdom of Prothoüs, third
step to heaven?[4] (Here, reclining at full length
within his hollowed mountain cave, Chiron, tutor
of a youth already pitiless,[5] with his quill striking

[1] It was from Iolchos that the Argo sailed on its conquest
of the sea. See *Medea*, 596.

[2] *i.e.* of Hercules, who took Troy by the aid of his bow
and arrows, and later, dying on Mount Oeta, gave them to
Philoctetes, who with them assisted in the second fall of Troy.

[3] Diana, who hated this and all Aetolian towns for the sake
of Oeneus, king of Calydon, who had slighted her divinity.

[4] See Index *s.v.* "Pelion."   [5] Achilles.

tinnulas plectro feriente chordas,
tunc quoque ingentes acuebat iras
    bella canendo.)
An ferax varii lapidis Carystos,
an premens litus maris inquieti
semper Euripo properante Chalcis?
quolibet vento faciles Calydnae,
an carens numquam Gonoessa vento   840
quaeque formidat Borean Enispe?
Attica pendens Peparethos ora,
an sacris gaudens tacitis Eleusin?
numquid Aiacis Salamina [1] veram [2]
aut fera notam Calydona saeva,
quasque perfundit subiturus aequor
seguibus terras Titaressos undis?
Bessan et Scarphen, Pylon an senilem?
Pharin an Pisas Iovis et coronis
    Elida claram?   850

    Quolibet tristis miseras procella
mittat et donet cuicumque terrae,
dum luem tantam Troiae atque Achivis
quae tulit, Sparte, procul absit, absit
Argos et saevi Pelopis Mycenae,
Neritos parva brevior Zacyntho
et nocens saxis Ithace dolosis.

    Quod manet fatum dominusque quis te,
aut quibus terris, Hecuba, videndam
ducet? in cuius moriere regno?   860

    [1] *The abrupt change of construction in the names of the places
here following suggests the loss of some words in this passage.
Scaliger conjectures :* quove *iactatae pelago feremur | exules?
ad quae loc , quas ad urbes ?*
    [2] *So Scaliger : Leo* veri, *with MSS. It is* vera *as opposed to
the new Salamis founded by Teucer in Cyprus.*

out tinkling chords, even then whetted the boy's mighty passions by songs of war.)   Or Carystos, rich in many-hued marble, or Chalcis, hard by the shore of the restless sea, where Euripus' racing tides evei flow ?   Calydnae, easy of approach in any wind, or Gonoëssa, never free from winds, and Enispe, which shivers before the northern blast ?   Peparethos, lying close to the Attic shore, or Eleusin, rejoicing in her sacred mysteries ?   Shall we to the true Salamis, home of Ajax, or to Calydon, famed for the wild boar, or to those lands [1] which the Titaressos bathes, destined to flow with its sluggish waters beneath the sea ? [2] or to Bessa, and Scarphe, or Pylos, the old man's [3] home ? to Pharis or Pisae, sacred to Jupiter, and Elis, famed for victors' crowns ?

[851] Let the mournful blasts bear our misery where'er they list and give us to any land if only Sparta, which brought such woe on Troy and the Greeks alike, be far away, and far away be Argos, and Mycenae, home of savage Pelops, and Neritos,[4] smaller than small Zacynthos,[4] and baleful Ithaca with her crafty crags.

[858] What fate, what lord waits for thee, Hecuba, or to what land will he lead thee to be a public show ? In whose kingdom shalt thou die ?

[Enter HELEN.]

[1] Thessaly.
[2] This river, a sluggish affluent of the Peneus, was said to have its rise in the Styx, and plunged beneath the sea on its way thither again.   [3] Nestor
[4] Two small islands near Ithaca, ruled by Ulysses.

197

HELENA

Quicumque hymen funestus, inlaetabilis
lamenta caedes sanguinem gemitus habet
est auspice Helena dignus.   eversis quoque
nocere cogor Phrygibus.   ego Pyrrhi toros
narrare falsos iubeor, ego cultus dare
habitusque Graios.   arte capietur mea
meaque fraude concidet Paridis soror.
fallatur ; ipsi levius hoc equidem reor ;
optanda mors est sine metu mortis mori.
quid iussa cessas agere ?   ad auctorem redit   870
sceleris coacti culpa.

                      Dardaniae domus
generosa virgo, melior afflictos deus
respicere coepit teque felici parat
dotare thalamo ; tale coniugium tibi
non ipsa sospes Troia, non Priamus daret.
nam te Pelasgae maximum gentis decus,
cui regna campi lata Thessalici patent,[1]   878
ad sancta lecti iura legitimi petit.   877
te magna Tethys teque tot pelagi deae
placidumque numen aequoris tumidi Thetis   880
suam vocabunt, te datam Pyrrho socer
Peleus nurum vocabit et Nereus nurum.
depone cultus squalidos, festos cape,
dedisce captam ; deprime horrentes comas
crinemque docta patere distingui manu.
hic forsitan te casus excelso magis
solio reponet.   profuit multis capi.

      [1] *Lines 877 and 878 were transposed by Swoboda.*

TROADES

HELEN [*aside*]

Whatever wedlock, calamitous, joyless, has mourning, murder, blood, and lamentations, is worthy of Helen's auspices. Even in their ruin am I driven to be the Phrygians' bane. It is my task to tell a false tale of marriage [1] with Pyrrhus; mine, to dress the bride in Grecian fashion; by my craft she will be snared and by my treachery will the sister of Paris fall. Let her be deceived; for her I deem this the easier lot; 'tis a death desirable, to die without the fear of death. Why dost hesitate to execute thy orders? To its author returns the blame of a crime compelled.

[*To* POLYXENA.]

871 Thou noble maid of the house of Dardanus, in more kindly wise doth heaven begin to regard the afflicted, and makes ready to dower thee with a happy bridal; such a match neither Troy herself while still secure, nor Priam, could make for thee. For the greatest ornament of the Pelasgian race, whose realm stretches wide over the plains of Thessaly, seeks thee in holy bonds of lawful wedlock. Thee will great Tethys call her own, thee all the goddesses of the deep, and Thetis, calm deity of the swelling sea; wedded to Pyrrhus, Peleus as thy father-in-law shall call thee daughter, and Nereus shall call thee daughter. Put off thy mournful garb, don festal array, forget thou art a captive; smooth thy unkempt locks, and suffer my skilled hand to part thy hair.[2] This fall, perchance, will restore thee to a more exalted throne. Many have profited by captivity.

[1] *i.e.* of Polyxena.
[2] It was in accordance with *Roman* custom to part the bride's hair into six locks.

ANDROMACHA

Hoc derat unum Phrygibus eversis malum—
gaudere.   flagrant strata passim Pergama—
o coniugale tempus! an quisquam audeat   890
negare ? quisquam dubius ad thalamos eat,
quos Helena suadet ? pestis exitium lues
utriusque populi, cernis hos tumulos ducum
et nuda totis ossa quae passim iacent
inhumata campis ? haec hymen sparsit tuus.
tibi fluxit Asiae, fluxit Europae cruor,
cum dimicantes laeta prospiceres viros,
incerta voti.   perge, thalamos appara.
taedis quid opus est quidve solemni face ?
quid igne ? thalamis Troia praelucet novis.   900
celebrate Pyrrhi, Troades, conubia,
celebrate digne : planctus et gemitus sonet.

HELENA

Ratione quamvis careat et flecti neget
magnus dolor sociosque nonnumquam sui
maeroris ipsos oderit, causam tamen
possum tueri iudice infesto meam,
graviora passa.   luget Andromacha Hectorem
et Hecuba Priamum ; solus occulte Paris
lugendus Helenae est.   durum et invisum et grave
    est
servitia ferre ? patior hoc olim iugum,   910
annis decem captiva.   prostratum Ilium est,
versi penates ? perdere est patriam grave,
gravius timere. vos levat tanti mali
comitatus ; in me victor et victus furit.
quam quisque famulam traheret incerto diu
casu pependit; me meus traxit statim

TROADES

ANDROMACHE

This one woe was lacking to the ruined Phrygians—to rejoice. Pergama's ruins lie blazing all around—fit time for marriage! Would any dare refuse? Would any hesitate to go to a bridal when Helen invites? Thou plague, destruction, pest of both peoples, seest thou these tombs of chieftains, the bare bones which everywhere lie unentombed o'er all the plain? These has thy marriage scattered. For thee has flowed Asia's, has flowed Europe's blood, whilst thou gleefully didst look out upon thy warring husbands with wavering prayer. Go on, make ready thy marriages! What need of pine-brands, what of the solemn nuptial torch, what need of fire? For this strange marriage Troy furnishes the torch. Ye Trojan dames, celebrate Pyrrhus' nuptials, celebrate them worthily: let blows and groans resound.

HELEN

Although great grief lacks reason and will not be turned aside, and sometimes hates the very comrades of its suffering, still could I maintain my cause even before a hostile judge, having borne worse things than you. Andromache mourns for her Hector, and Hecuba for her Priam; for Paris alone must Helen mourn in secret. Is it a hard, a hateful, and a galling thing to endure servitude? This yoke have I long endured, for ten years captive. Is Ilium laid low, are your household gods overthrown? It is hard to lose one's native country, harder to fear it. You are comforted by companionship in so great misfortune; against me victor and vanquished rage alike. Which one of you each lord should drag away as his slave, has long hung on uncertain chance; me has

201

sine sorte dominus.   causa bellorum fui
tantaeque Teucris cladis? hoc verum puta,
Spartana puppis vestra si secuit freta ;
sin rapta Phrygiis praeda remigibus fui   920
deditque donum iudici victrix dea,
ignosce praedae.   iudicem iratum mea
habitura causa est ; ista Menelaum manent
arbitria.   nunc hanc luctibus paulum tuis,
Andromacha, omissis flecte—vix lacrimas queo
retinere.

ANDROMACHA

        Quantum est Helena quod lacrimat malum.
cur lacrimat autem ? fare quos Ithacus dolos,
quae scelera nectat ; utrum ab Idaeis iugis
iactanda virgo est, arcis an celsae edito
mittenda saxo ? num per has vastum in mare   930
volvenda rupes, latere quas scisso levat
altum vadoso Sigeon spectans sinu ?
dic, fare, quidquid subdolo vultu tegis.
leviora mala sunt cuncta, quam Priami gener
Hecubaeque Pyrrhus.   fare, quam poenam pares
exprome et unum hoc deme nostris cladibus :
falli.   paratas perpeti mortem vides.

HELENA

Vtinam iuberet me quoque interpres deum
abrumpere ense lucis invisae moras
vel Achillis ante busta furibunda manu   940
occidere Pyrrhi, fata comitantem tua,
Polyxene miseranda, quam tradi sibi
cineremque Achilles ante mactari suum,
campo maritus ut sit Elysio, iubet.

my master dragged away at once, without waiting
for the lot. Have I been the cause of wars and all
this ruin to the Teucrians? Count that the truth
if 'twas a Spartan ship that clove your seas; but if,
swept along by Phrygian oarsmen, I was a helpless
prey, if a triumphant goddess gave me as a reward
to her judge, pity the helpless prey. 'Tis an angry
judge my cause will have; the decision of that case
waits on Menelaüs. But now forget your own woes
a little while, Andromache, and prevail on her [1]—I
can scarce keep from weeping.

ANDROMACHE

How great must be the woe for which Helen
weeps! But why weep? Tell us what tricks, what
crimes the Ithacan is devising. Must the maiden be
cast down from Ida's crags or thrown from the lofty
citadel's high rock? Must she be hurled into the
vasty deep over these cliffs which lofty Sigeum with
sheer sides raises, looking out on his shallow bay?
Speak, speak, whatever it is thou hidest beneath thy
lying looks. All woes are easier to bear than that
Pyrrhus be son-in-law to Hecuba and Priam. Tell
us, explain what suffering thou hast in hand, and
subtract this one from our calamities—ignorance of
our fate. Thou seest us ready to suffer death.

HELEN

Would that the prophet of the gods bade me, too,
end with the sword this lingering, hateful life, or fall
before Achilles' tomb by the mad hand of Pyrrhus,
a companion of thy fate, poor Polyxena, whom
Achilles bids be given to him, and be sacrificed in
presence of his ashes, that in the Elysian fields he
may wed with thee.

[1] Polyxena.

SENECAE TRAGOEDIAE

ANDROMACHA

Vide ut animus ingens laetus audierit necem.
cultus decoros regiae vestis petit
et admoveri crinibus patitur manum.
mortem putabat illud, hoc thalamos putat.
at misera luctu mater audito stupet;
labefacta mens succubuit. assurge, alleva   950
animum et cadentem, misera, firma spiritum.

  Quam tenuis anima vinculo pendet levi!
minimum est quod Hecubam facere felicem potest.
spirat, revixit.   prima mors miseros fugit.

HECVBA

Adhuc Achilles vivit in poenas Phrygum?
adhuc rebellat?   o manum Paridis levem.
cinis ipse nostrum sanguinem ac tumulus sitit.
modo turba felix latera cingebat mea,
lassabar in tot oscula et tantum gregem
dividere matrem; sola nunc haec est super   960
votum, comes, levamen afflictae, quies;
haec totus Hecubae fetus, hac sola vocor
iam voce mater.   dura et infelix age
elabere anima, denique hoc unum mihi
remitte funus.   inrigat fletus genas
imberque victo subitus e vultu cadit.

204

TROADES

ANDROMACHE

See with what joy her mighty soul has heard her doom! The becoming attire of royal robes she seeks, and allows Helen's hand to approach her locks. Death she deemed that other, this, her bridal. But, hearing the woeful news, her wretched mother [1] is in a daze; her tottering reason has given way. Arise, lift up thy courage, poor queen, strengthen thy fainting spirit.

[HECUBA *falls in a faint.*]

952 On how slender a thread her frail life hangs! But very little lacks to bring—happiness to Hecuba. She breathes, she lives again. 'Tis the wretched that death first flees.

HECUBA

Does Achilles still live for vengeance on the Phrygians? Does he still war against them? O hand of Paris, too light! [2] His very ashes and his tomb thirst for our blood. But late a happy throng of children girt me round, and I grew weary of sharing a mother's love among so many kisses and so large a flock; but now this daughter alone is left, object of my prayer, my companion, comfort in affliction, my resting-place; she is Hecuba's entire offspring, hers is the only voice that now calls me mother. O obstinate, unhappy soul, come, slip away, and spare me the sight of this one death at least. Tears overflow my cheeks and from my vanquished eyes a sudden shower falls.

---

[1] Hecuba has been present during this scene, up to this time as a *persona muta*.

[2] Paris should have slain Achilles past all resurrection.

SENECAE TRAGOEDIAE

ANDROMACHA

Nos Hecuba, nos, nos, Hecuba, lugendae sumus, 969
quas mota classis huc et huc sparsas feret; 970
hanc cara tellus sedibus patriis teget.

HELENA

Magis invidebis, si tuam sortem scies.

ANDROMACHA

An aliqua poenae pars meae ignota est mihi?

HELENA

Versata dominos urna captivis dedit.

ANDROMACHA

Cui famula trador? ede; quem dominum voco?

HELENA

Te sorte prima Scyrius iuvenis tulit.

ANDROMACHA

Cassandra felix, quam furor sorti eximit
Phoebusque.

HELENA

Regum hanc maximus rector tenet. 978

HECVBA

Laetare, gaude, nata. quam vellet tuos 967
Cassandra thalamos, vellet Andromache tuos.[1] 968
estne aliquis, Hecubam qui suam dici velit? 979

---

[1] *Leo follows Richter in placing ll. 967, 968 after 978.*

206

TROADES

ANDROMACHE

'Tis we, Hecuba, we, we, Hecuba, who should be mourned, whom the fleet, once started on its way, will scatter to every land; but her the dear soil of her native land will cover.

HELEN

Still more wilt thou envy her when thine own lot thou knowest.

ANDROMACHE

Is any part of my suffering still unknown to me?

HELEN

The urn has whirled and to the captives given lords.

ANDROMACHE

To whom am I given as slave? Speak! Whom do I call master?

HELEN

Thee, by the first lot, the youth [1] of Scyros gained.

ANDROMACHE

Fortunate Cassandra, whom madness and Phoebus from the lot exempt.

HELEN

Her the most mighty king of kings receives.

HECUBA [*to* POLYXENA]

Rejoice and be glad, my daughter! How would Cassandra, how would Andromache long for thy marriage! [*To* HELEN.] Is there anyone who would have Hecuba called his?

[1] Pyrrhus.

HELENA

Ithaco obtigisti praeda nolenti brevis.   980

HECVBA

Quis tam impotens ac durus et iniquae ferus
sortitor urnae regibus reges dedit?
quis tam sinister dividit captas deus?
quis arbiter crudelis et miseris gravis
eligere dominos nescit et matrem Hectoris [1]   985
armis Achillis miscet? ad Vlixen vocor;   987
nunc victa, nunc captiva, nunc cunctis mihi
obsessa videor cladibus—domini pudet,   989
non servitutis.[1]   sterilis et saevis fretis   991
inclusa tellus non capit tumulos meos—
duc, duc, Vlixe, nil moror, dominum sequor;
me mea sequentur fata: non pelago quies
tranquilla veniet, saeviet ventis mare,[2]
et bella et ignes et mea et Priami mala.
dumque ista veniant, interim hoc poenae loco est—
sortem occupavi, praemium eripui tibi.
    Sed en citato Pyrrhus accurrit gradu
vultuque torvo.   Pyrrhe, quid cessas? age   1000
reclude ferro pectus et Achillis tui
coniunge soceros.   perge, mactator senum,
et hic decet te sanguis.   abreptam trahe.

---

[1] *Richter incorporates (bracketed) in his text at this point
a line which Leo deletes:*

    Eligere dominos nescit et [saeva manu   985
    dat iniqua miseris fata? quis] matrem Hectoris   986

and again at l. 990:

    non servitutis. [Hectoris spolium feret   990
    qui tulit Achillis?] sterilis et saevis fretis   991

[2] *Leo thinks that some such additional line as the following is
required by the sense:* sociosque merget, obruent reducem
quoque.

HELEN

To the Ithacan, against his will, hast thou fallen,
a short-lived prize.

HECUBA

Who so reckless and unfeeling, who so cruelly
drawing lots from an unjust urn hath given royalty
to royalty? What god so perverse apportions the
captives? What arbiter, heartless and hard to the
unfortunate, so blindly chooses our lords, and unites
Hector's mother to Achilles' arms?[1] To Ulysses am
I summoned; now indeed do I seem vanquished, now
captive, now beset by all disasters—'tis the master
shames me, not the servitude. That barren land,
hemmed in by stormy seas, does not contain my tomb[2]
—lead, lead on, Ulysses, I hold not back, I follow my
master; but me my fates shall follow: upon the deep
no calm peace shall come; the sea shall rage with
the winds and engulf thy comrades; and thee, e'en
when safe home again, shall wars and fires, my
own and Priam's evil fortunes, o'erwhelm.[3] And
till those shall come, meanwhile this serves in place
of vengeance on thee—I have usurped thy lot, I have
stolen from thee thy prize.[4]

999 But see, Pyrrhus approaches with hurried step
and grim countenance. Pyrrhus, why dost thou
hesitate? Come, plunge thy sword into my breast,
and so unite the parents of thy Achilles' bride. Pro-
ceed, thou murderer of old men, this blood of mine
also becomes thee. [*Pointing to* POLYXENA.] Seize!

[1] After Achilles' death his arms had been awarded to Ulysses.
[2] *i.e.* the place of her burial does not lie in Ithaca, since she
will die before reaching it.
[3] Translating Leo's conjecture.
[4] *i.e.* Ulysses can have but one choice, and this, instead of
being a beautiful young woman, has turned out an ugly old hag.

maculate superos caede funesta deos,
maculate manes—quid precer vobis? precor
his digna sacris aequora; hoc classi accidat
toti Pelasgae, ratibus hoc mille accidat
meae precabor, cum vehar, quidquid rati.

CHORVS

 Dulce maerenti populus dolentum,
dulce lamentis resonare gentes;   1010
lenius luctus lacrimaeque mordent,
turba quas fletu similis frequentat.
semper a semper dolor est malignus;
gaudet in multos sua fata mitti
seque non solum placuisse poenae.
ferre quam sortem patiuntur omnes,
  nemo recusat.
 Tolle felices: miserum, licet sit,
nemo se credet. removete multo
divites auro, removete centum   1020
rura qui scindunt opulenta bubus:
pauperi surgent animi iacentes.
est miser nemo nisi comparatus.
dulce in immensis posito ruinis,
neminem laetos habuisse vultus;
ille deplorat queriturque fatum,
qui secans fluctum rate singulari
nudus in portus cecidit petitos.
aequior casum tulit et procellas,
mille qui ponto pariter carinas   1030
obrui vidit tabulaque vectus
naufraga, terris mare dum coactis
fluctibus Corus prohibet, revertit.
questus est Hellen cecidisse Phrixus,
cum gregis ductor radiante villo
aureo fratrem simul ac sororem

drag her hence! Defile, ye Greeks, the gods above
with deadly slaughter, defile the shades below—nay,
why pray to you? I pray for seas that befit such [1]
rites as these; may such doom befall the whole fleet
of the Pelasgians, may such befall their thousand
ships, as I shall call down on my own when I set sail.

CHORUS

Sweet to the mourner is a host of mourners, sweet
to hear multitudes in lamentation; lighter is the
sting of wailing and of tears which a like throng
accompanies. Ever, ah, ever is grief malicious; glad
is it that its own fate comes on many, and that it
alone is not appointed unto suffering. To bear the
lot which all endure none can refuse.

[1018] Remove the fortunate: unfortunate though
he be, none will so think himself. Remove those blest
with heaps of gold, remove those who plough rich fields
with a hundred oxen: the downcast spirits of the
poor will rise again. No one is unfortunate save as
compared with others. 'Tis sweet to one set in
widespread desolation to see no one with joyful
countenance; but he deplores and complains of his
hard fortune who, while he cleaves the waves in
solitary vessel, has been flung naked into the harbour
he had sought. More calmly has he endured the
tempest and disaster who has seen a thousand vessels
engulfed by the selfsame billows and who comes
back, borne on a piece of wreckage, to safety,
while Corus,[2] controlling the waves, forbids their
onslaught on the land. Phrixus mourned because
Helle fell, when the flock's leader, resplendent with
golden fleece, bore brother and sister on his back

---

[1] *i.e.* savage. [2] The north-west wind.

sustulit tergo medioque iactum
fecit in ponto ; tenuit querelas
et vir et Pyrrha, mare cum viderent,
et nihil praeter mare cum viderent   1040
unici terris homines relicti.
    Solvet hunc questum lacrimasque nostras
sparget huc illuc agitata classis,
cum [1] tuba iussi dare vela nautae
et [1] simul ventis properante remo
prenderint altum fugietque litus.
quis status mentis miseris, ubi omnis
terra decrescet pelagusque crescet,
celsa cum longe latitabit Ide ?
tum puer matri genetrixque nato,   1050
Troia qua iaceat regione monstrans,
dicet et longe digito notabit :
" Ilium est illic, ubi fumus alte
serpit in caelum nebulaeque turpes."
Troes hoc signo patriam videbunt.

NVNTIVS

O dura fata, saeva miseranda horrida !
quod tam ferum, tam triste bis quinis scelus
Mars vidit annis ? quid prius referens gemam,
tuosne potius, an tuos luctus, anus ?

HECVBA

Quoscumque luctus fleveris, flebis meos ;   1060
sua quemque tantum, me omnium clades premit ;
mihi cuncta pereunt : quisquis est Hecubae est miser.

---

[1] *So Richter ; Leo reads with* ω: et tuba . . . cum simul,
*and suggests that some such expression as the following is necessary
here :* caede cum pontus fuerit piatus.

together, and in mid-sea lost half his burden; but
both Pyrrha and her husband [1] checked their mourning, though they saw the sea, and saw nothing else
than sea, left as they were sole remnants of the
human race on earth.

[1042] But the fleet driven this way and that will
separate these our laments and scatter our tears,
when once the sailors, by the trumpet bidden to
spread sail, shall gain the deep, by winds and speeding oarage, and the shore shall flee away. What
will be the wretched captives' feelings when all
the land shall dwindle and the sea loom large, and
lofty Ida shall vanish in the distance? Then son to
mother, mother to her son, pointing to the place
where Troy lies prostrate, will mark it afar with
pointing finger, saying: "Yonder is Ilium where the
smoke curls high to heaven, where the foul vapours
hang." The Trojans by that sign only will see their
fatherland.

[*Enter* MESSENGER.]

MESSENGER

O cruel fate, harsh, pitiable, horrible! What
crime so savage, so grievous, has Mars seen in ten
long years? Which first shall I tell amidst my lamentations, thy woes, Andromache, or thine, thou aged
woman?

HECUBA

Whosoever woes thou weepest, thou wilt weep
mine. Each feels the weight of his own disaster
only, but I the disasters of them all; for me do all
things perish. Whoever is unfortunate is Hecuba's.

---

[1] Deucalion.

NVNTIVS

Mactata virgo est, missus e muris puer
sed uterque letum mente generosa tulit

ANDROMACHA

Expone seriem caedis, et duplex nefas
persequere ; gaudet magnus aerumnas dolor
tractare totas.   ede et enarra omnia.

NVNTIVS

Est una magna turris e Troia super,
adsueta Priamo, cuius e fastigio
summisque pinnis arbiter belli sedens   1070
regebat acies.   turre in hac blando sinu
fovens nepotem, cum metu versos gravi
Danaos fugaret Hector et ferro et face,
paterna puero bella monstrabat senex.
haec nota quondam turris et muri decus,
nunc sola cautes, undique adfusa ducum
plebisque turba cingitur ; totum coit
ratibus relictis vulgus.   his collis procul
aciem patenti liberam praebet loco,
his alta rupes, cuius in cacumine   1080
erecta summos turba libravit pedes.
hunc pinus, illum laurus, hunc fagus gerit
et tota populo silva suspenso tremit.
extrema montis ille praerupti petit,
semusta ille tecta vel saxum imminens
muri cadentis pressit, atque aliquis (nefas)
tumulo ferus spectator Hectoreo sedet.
     Per spatia late plena sublimi gradu
incedit Ithacus parvulum dextra trahens
Priami nepotem, nec gradu segni puer   1090

214

TROADES

The maiden is slain; thrown from the walls the boy. But each met doom with noble spirit.

ANDROMACHE

Expound their deaths in order and relate the twofold crime; great grief hath joy to dwell on all its woes. Out with it, tell us all the tale.

MESSENGER

There is one high tower left of Troy, much used by Priam; upon its battlements and lofty pinnacles he would sit watching the war and directing the embattled lines. On this tower, nestling his grandson in his fond arms, when Hector with sword and torch pursued the Danaï fleeing in abject fear, the old man would point out to the lad his father's battles. Around this tower, once famous, the glory of the walls, but now a solitary ruin, on all sides pours a throng of chiefs and commons, encircling it. The whole host, leaving the ships, assembles here. For some, a far-off hill gives a clear view of the open space; for others, a high cliff, on whose top the eager crowd stands on tiptoe balanced. A pine-tree holds one, a laurel-tree, another, a beech-tree, one; and the whole forest sways with clinging people. One climbs to the highest peak of a steep mountain, another seeks a smouldering roof or stands on an overhanging stone of a crumbling wall, and one (oh, shame!) sits heartlessly to view the show from Hector's tomb

[1088] Now along the plain, on every hand thronged with people, with stately step the Ithacan makes his way, leading by the hand the little grandson of Priam; and with no lagging step does the boy

215

ad alta pergit moenia. ut summa stetit
pro turre, vultus huc et huc acres tulit
intrepidus animo. qualis ingentis ferae
parvus tenerque fetus et nondum potens
saevire dente iam tamen tollit minas
morsusque inanes temptat atque animis tumet ;
sic ille dextra prensus hostili puer
ferox superbit.[1] moverat vulgum ac duces
ipsumque Vlixen. non flet e turba omnium
qui fletur ; ac, dum verba fatidici et preces   1100
concipit Vlixes vatis et saevos ciet
ad sacra superos, sponte desiluit sua
in media Priami regna—

ANDROMACHA

  Quis Colchus hoc, quis sedis incertae Scytha
commisit, aut quae Caspium tangens mare
gens iuris expers ausa ? non Busiridis
puerilis aras sanguis aspersit feri,
nec parva gregibus membra Diomedes suis
epulanda posuit. quis tuos artus leget
tumuloque tradet ?

NVNTIVS

                        Quos enim praeceps locus   1110
reliquit artus ? ossa disiecta et gravi
elisa casu ; signa clari corporis,
et ora et illas nobiles patris notas,
confudit imam pondus ad terram datum ;
soluta cervix silicis impulsu, caput
ruptum cerebro penitus expresso—iacet
deforme corpus.

                    [1] *Leo :* superbe *MSS.*

216

approach the lofty walls. When he stood on the tower's summit, he turned his keen gaze now here, now there, undaunted in spirit. As the cub of some great beast, tiny and young, not yet strong enough to do injury with its fangs, still bristles, bites harmlessly, and swells with rage; so the boy, though in his enemy's grasp, was proudly bold. He had moved the crowd to tears, and the chieftains, and even Ulysses. Of all the throng he alone, for whom they wept, wept not; and while Ulysses rehearsed the words and prayers appointed by the fate-revealing priest,[1] and summoned the cruel gods to the sacrifice, of his own will leaped the boy down into the midst of Priam's kingdom—

ANDROMACHE

What Colchian, what Scythian of shifting home e'er committed crime like this, or what tribe to law unknown by the Caspian sea has dared it? No blood of children stained the altars of Busiris, cruel though he was, nor did Diomedes[2] set limbs of babes for his herds to feast on. Who will take up thy limbs and consign them to the tomb?

MESSENGER

What limbs has that steep place left? His bones were crushed and scattered by the heavy fall; the familiar marks of his noble form, his face, the illustrious likeness of his sire, have been disfigured by his body's weight plunging to earth below; his neck was broken by the crash upon the rock, his skull was crushed, his brains dashed out—he lies a shapeless corpse.

---

[1] Calchas.   [2] See Index *s.v.* " Diomedes."

SENECAE TRAGOEDIAE

ANDROMACHA
Sic quoque est similis patri.

NVNTIVS

Praeceps ut altis cecidit e muris puer
flevitque Achivum turba quod fecit nefas,
idem ille populus aliud ad facinus redit   1120
tumulumque Achillis. cuius extremum latus
Rhoetea leni verberant fluctu vada;
adversa cingit campus et clivo levi
erecta medium vallis includens locum.
crescit theatri more concursus frequens,
implevit omne litus. hi classis moram
hac morte solvi rentur, hi stirpem hostium
gaudent recidi. magna pars vulgi levis
odit scelus, spectatque. nec Troes minus
suum frequentant funus et pavidi metu   1130
partem ruentis ultimam Troiae vident;
cum subito thalami more praecedunt faces
et pronuba illi Tyndaris, maestum caput
demissa. "tali nubat Hermione modo"
Phryges precantur, "sic viro turpis suo
reddatur Helena." terror attonitos tenet
utrosque populos. ipsa deiectos gerit
vultus pudore, sed tamen fulgent genae
magisque solito splendet extremus decor,
ut esse Phoebi dulcius lumen solet   1140
iamiam cadentis, astra cum repetunt vices
premiturque dubius nocte vicina dies.
stupet omne vulgus, et fere cuncti magis
peritura laudant. hos movet formae decus,
218

TROADES

So also is he like his sire.

After the boy fell headlong from the lofty tower,
and the throng of Greeks wept for the crime it
wrought, that same host turned to a second crime
and to Achilles' tomb. Its further side is gently
lapped by Rhoeteum's waters; its front is surrounded by a plain, while a valley, sloping gently
up, hems in the middle space. The surging mass
increases as if thronging to a theatre and has filled
all the shore. Some think that by this death the
fleet's delay is ended; some joy that the foeman's
stock is cut away; the greater part of the heedless
mob detest the crime—and gaze. Nor any less do
the Trojans throng their own funeral and, quaking
with fear, look on at the last act of the fall of Troy;
when suddenly, as at a wedding, the torches come,
leading the way, and the daughter [1] of Tyndareus as
the bride's attendant, with sad and drooping head.
"So may Hermione [2] be wed," the Phrygians pray;
"in such wise may base Helen to her husband be
given back." Terror holds both peoples awe-struck.
The maid herself comes on with eyes in modesty
cast down, but yet her face is radiant and the dying
splendour of her beauty shines beyond its wont;
as Phoebus' light is wont to appear more glorious at
the moment of his setting, when the stars come
back to their stations and the uncertain daylight is
dimmed by the approach of night. Astonished gazes
the whole multitude, for all ever admire the more
what must soon pass from them. Some, her beauty

[1] Helen.   [2] Daughter of Helen and Menelaüs.

hos mollis aetas, hos vagae rerum vices ;
movet animus omnes fortis et leto obvius.
Pyrrhum antecedit ; omnium mentes tremunt,
mirantur ac miserantur.   ut primum ardui
sublime montis tetigit atque alte edito
iuvenis paterni vertice in busti stetit,   1150
audax virago non tulit retro gradum ;
conversa ad ictum stat truci vultu ferox.
tam fortis animus omnium mentes ferit
novumque monstrum est Pyrrhus ad caedem piger.
ut dextra ferrum penitus exacta abdidit,
subitus recepta morte prorupit cruor
per vulnus ingens.   nec tamen moriens adhuc
deponit animos ; cecidit, ut Achilli gravem
factura terram, prona et irato impetu.
uterque flevit coetus ; at timidum Phryges   1160
misere gemitum, clarius victor gemit.
hic ordo sacri.   non stetit fusus cruor
humove summa fluxit ; obduxit statim
saevusque totum sanguinem tumulus bibit.

HECVBA

Ite, ite, Danai, petite iam tuti domos ;
optata velis maria diffusis secet
secura classis.   concidit virgo ac puer ;
bellum peractum est.   quo meas lacrimas feram ?
ubi hanc anilis expuam leti moram ?
natam an nepotem, coniugem an patriam fleam ?
an omnia an me sola ?   mors votum meum,   1170
infantibus, violenta, virginibus venis,

moves; some, her tender youth; some, the shift-ing changes of her fortune; but one and all, her courage, dauntless and death-confronting. On she comes and Pyrrhus follows; the hearts of all are filled with terror, wonder, pity. Soon as the young man reached the summit of the steep mound, and stood upon the high-raised top of his father's tomb, the dauntless maid did not shrink back, but, facing the stroke, stood there with stern look and courageous. A spirit so bold strikes the hearts of all and—strange prodigy—Pyrrhus is slow to kill. When his hand, thrust forth, had buried deep the sword, with the death-stroke her blood leaped out in a sudden stream through the gaping wound. Yet, though in the very act of death, she put not by her spirit; she fell, as if thus to make the earth heavy on Achilles, prone and with angry thud. The throng of both peoples wept; but the Phrygians mourned her with timid lamentation, while the victors wailed aloud. Thus was the rite performed. The shed blood stayed not nor flowed off on the surface of the ground; instantly the savage mound sucked it down and drank the whole draught of gore.

HECUBA

Go, go, ye Danaï, seek now your homes in safety; let your fleet now spread its sails and at ease plough the longed-for sea. A maiden and a boy have fallen; the war is done. But I, whither shall I betake my tears? Where in my old age shall I spew out this lingering life? Daughter or grandson, hus-band or country—which shall I lament? Shall I mourn all or, in my loneliness, myself alone? O death, object of my prayer, to boys and girls every-where thou com'st with speed and savage violence;

ubique properas, saeva; me solam times
vitasque, gladios inter ac tela et faces
quaesita tota nocte, cupientem fugis.
non hostis aut ruina, non ignis meos
absumpsit artus; quam prope a Priamo steti.

NVNTIVS

Repetite celeri maria, captivae, gradu;
iam vela puppis laxat et classis movet.

me alone dost thou fear and shun ; sought midst swords and spears and firebrands the livelong night, thou dost evade my eager search.   No foe, no falling wall, no fire has consumed my limbs ; and yet how near to Priam did I stand !

MESSENGER

Haste to the sea, ye captives ; already the vessels are spreading sail and the fleet is off.

MEDEA

DRAMATIS PERSONAE

MEDEA, *daughter of Aeëtes, king of Colchis, and wife of Jason.*

JASON, *son of Aeson, and nephew of Pelias, the usurping king of Thessaly; organizer and leader of the Argonautic expedition to Colchis in quest of the Golden Fleece.*

CREON, *king of Corinth, who had received into his hospitable kingdom Medea and Jason, fugitives from Thessaly, after Medea had plotted the death of Pelias.*

NURSE *of Medea.*

MESSENGER.

TWO SONS *of Medea and Jason (personae mutae).*

CHORUS OF CORINTHIANS, *friendly to Jason and hostile to Medea.*

THE TIME of the play is confined to the single day of the culmination of the tragedy, the day proposed by Creon for the banishment of Medea and the marriage of Jason to Creusa, daughter of Creon.

THE SCENE is in Corinth, in the court of the house of Jason.

ARGUMENT

ALTHOUGH *the play is confined in time to the final day of catastrophe at Corinth, the background is the whole romantic story of the Argonauts: how Jason and his hero-comrades, at the instigation of Pelias, the usurping king of Thessalian Iolchos, undertook the first voyage in quest of the Golden Fleece; how, after many adventures, these first sailors reached the kingdom of Aeëtes, who jealously guarded the fleece, since upon its possession depended his own kingship; how the three deadly labours were imposed upon Jason before the fleece could be won —the yoking of the fiery bulls, the contest with the giants that sprang from the sown serpent's teeth, and the overcoming of the sleepless dragon that ever guarded the fleece; how, smitten by love of him, the beautiful barbaric Medea, daughter of the king, by the help of her magic aided Jason in all these labours and accompanied him in his flight; how to retard her father's pursuit she slew her brother and scattered his mangled remains in the path as they fled; how again, for love of Jason, she restored his father to youth and tricked Pelias' own daughters into slaying their aged sire; how, for this act, Medea with her husband were exiled from Thessalia and dwelt in Corinth; how, for ten happy years, she lived with her husband and two sons in this alien land, her wild past almost forgotten, her magic untouched.*

But now Jason has been won away from his wife, and is about to wed Creusa, the daughter of Creon, king of Corinth. The wedding festivities have already begun when the play opens and reveals Medea invoking all the powers of heaven and hell in punishment of her false lord.

MEDEA

Di coniugales tuque genialis tori,
Lucina, custos, quaeque domituram freta
Tiphyn novam frenare docuisti ratem,
et tu, profundi saeve dominator maris,
clarumque Titan dividens orbi diem,
tacitisque praebens conscium sacris iubar
Hecate triformis, quosque iuravit mihi
deos Iason, quosque Medeae magis
fas est precari—noctis aeternae chaos,
aversa superis regna manesque impios   10
dominumque regni tristis et dominam fide
meliore raptam, voce non fausta precor.
nunc, nunc adeste, sceleris ultrices deae,
crinem solutis squalidae serpentibus,
atram cruentis manibus amplexae facem,
adeste, thalamis horridae quondam meis
quales stetistis; coniugi letum novae
letumque socero et regiae stirpi date.

Mihi peius aliquid, quod precer sponso, manet—
vivat.   per urbes erret ignotas egens   20
228

MEDEA

Ye gods of wedlock, and thou, Lucina, guardian of the nuptial couch, and thou [1] who didst teach Tiphys to guide his new barque to the conquest of the seas, and thou, grim ruler of the deeps of Ocean, and Titan, who dost portion out bright day unto the world, and thou who dost show thy bright face as witness of the silent mysteries, O three-formed Hecate, and ye gods by whose divinity Jason swore to me, to whom Medea may more lawfully appeal— thou chaos of endless night, ye realms remote from heaven, ye unhallowed ghosts, thou lord [2] of the realm of gloom, and thou, his queen,[3] won by violence but with better [4] faith, with ill-omened speech I make my prayer to you. Be present, be present, ye goddesses [5] who avenge crime, your hair foul with writhing snakes, grasping the smoking torch with your bloody hands, be present now, such as once ye stood in dread array beside my marriage couch ; upon this new wife destruction bring, destruction on this father-in-law and the whole royal stock.

[19] I have yet curse more dire to call down on my husband—may he live. Through unknown cities

---

[1] Minerva.   [2] Pluto.   [3] Proserpina.
[4] *i.e.* than that which Medea had experienced.
[5] The Furies.

exul pavens invisus incerti laris,
iam notus hospes limen alienum expetat,
me coniugem optet quoque non aliud queam
peius precari, liberos similes patri
similesque matri.—parta iam, parta ultio est:
peperi.   querelas verbaque in cassum sero?
non ibo in hostes?   manibus excutiam faces
caeloque lucem.   spectat hoc nostri sator
Sol generis, et spectatur, et curru insidens
per solita puri spatia decurrit poli?   30
non redit in ortus et remetitur diem?
da, da per auras curribus patriis vehi,
committe habenas, genitor, et flagrantibus
ignifera loris tribue moderari iuga;
gemino Corinthos litore opponens moras
cremata flammis maria committat duo.

Hoc restat unum, pronubam thalamo feram
ut ipsa pinum postque sacrificas preces
caedam dicatis victimas altaribus.
per viscera ipsa quaere supplicio viam,   40
si vivis, anime, si quid antiqui tibi
remanet vigoris; pelle femineos metus
et inhospitalem Caucasum mente indue.
quodcumque vidit Pontus aut Phasis nefas,
videbit Isthmos.   effera ignota horrida,
tremenda caelo pariter ac terris mala
mens intus agitat—vulnera et caedem et vagum
230

may he wander, in want, in exile, in fear of life, hated and homeless; may he seek hospitality at strange doors, by now a familiar applicant; may he desire me for wife, and, than which I can pray nothing worse, may his children be like their sire and like their mother.—Already borne, borne is my vengeance! I have borne children! But why frame complaints and idle words? Shall I not go against my enemies? I'll snatch the bridal-torches from their hands and the light from heaven. Does he behold this, the Sun, father of my race, and do men still behold him [1] as, sitting in his chariot, he courses over bright heaven's accustomed spaces? Why does he not return to his rising and measure back the day? Grant, oh, grant that I ride through the air in my father's car; give me the reins, O sire, give me the right to guide thy fire-bearing steeds with the flaming reins; then let Corinth, with her twin shores cause of delay [2] to ships, be consumed by flames and bring the two seas together.

[37] This course alone remains, that I myself bear the wedding torch unto the chamber and, after sacrificial prayers, slay victims on the consecrated altars. Amid the very entrails seek thou a way for punishment, if thou livest, O soul, if there remains to thee aught of thy old-time strength. Away with womanish fears, clothe thy heart with unfeeling Caucasus. Whatever horror Pontus has beheld, or Phasis, Isthmus shall behold. Wild deeds, unheard-of, horrible, calamities at which heaven and earth alike shall tremble, my heart deep within is planning—wounds, slaughter, death, creeping from limb to limb. Ah, too trivial

---

[1] He should be darkened at sight of such wickedness.
[2] *i.e.* by requiring ships to sail around the Peloponnesus.

funus per artus. levia memoravi nimis ;
haec virgo feci. gravior exurgat dolor ;
maiora iam me scelera post partus decent. 50
accingere ira teque in exitium para
furore toto. paria narrentur tua
repudia thalamis. quo virum linques modo ?
hoc quo secuta es. rumpe iam segnes moras ;
quae scelere parta est, scelere linquenda est domus

CHORVS

Ad regum thalamos numine prospero
qui caelum superi quique regunt fretum
adsint cum populis rite faventibus.
primum sceptriferis colla Tonantibus
taurus celsa ferat tergore candido ; 60
Lucinam nivei femina corporis
intemptata iugo placet, et asperi
Martis sanguineas quae cohibet manus,
quae dat belligeris foedera gentibus
et cornu retinet divite copiam,
donetur tenera mitior hostia.
et tu, qui facibus legitimis ades,
noctem discutiens auspice dextera
huc incede gradu marcidus ebrio,
praecingens roseo tempora vinculo. 70
et tu quae, gemini praevia temporis,
tarde, stella, redis semper amantibus,
te matres, avide te cupiunt nurus
quamprimum radios spargere lucidos.

the deeds I have rehearsed; these things I did in
girlhood. Let my grief rise to more deadly strength;
greater crimes become me, now that I am a mother.
Gird thyself with wrath, and prepare thee for deadly
deeds with the full force of madness. Let the story
of thy rejection match [1] the story of thy marriage.
How wilt thou leave thy husband? Even as thou
didst follow him. Break off now dull delay; the
home which by crime was gained, by crime must be
abandoned.

CHORUS

[Chanting the epithalamium for JASON *and* CREUSA.]

May the high gods who rule over heaven, and
they who rule the sea, with gracious divinity attend
on our princes' marriage, amid the people's solemn
applause. First to the sceptre-bearing Thunderers [2]
let the bull with white-shining hide offer his high-
raised neck. Lucina let a heifer appease, snow-white,
untouched by the yoke; and let her [3] who restrains
the bloody hands of rough Mars, who brings peace to
warring nations and holds plenty in her rich horn,
mild goddess, be given a tender victim. And do
thou,[4] who the torches of lawful marriage attendest,
dissipating the night with propitious hand, hither
come, reeling with drunken footstep, binding thy
temples with garlands of roses. And thou star,[5]
forerunner of twilight, who returnest ever slowly
for lovers—thee, mothers, thee, brides eagerly await,
to see thee full soon thy bright beams scattering.

---

[1] In the crimes accompanying each.
[2] The epithet here includes Juno as well as Jupiter.
[3] Pax, goddess of concord.
[4] Hymen.
[5] Hesperus, the evening star.

Vincit virgineus decor
longe Cecropias nurus,
et quas Taygeti iugis
exercet iuvenum modo
muris quod caret oppidum
et quas Aonius latex   80
Alpheosque sacer lavat.
    Si forma velit aspici,
cedent Aesonio duci
proles fulminis improbi
aptat qui iuga tigribus,
nec non, qui tripodas movet,
frater virginis asperae,
cedet Castore cum suo
Pollux caestibus aptior.
    Sic, sic, caelicolae, precor,   90
vincat femina coniuges,
vir longe superet viros.

  Haec cum femineo constitit in choro,
unius facies praenitet omnibus.
sic cum sole perit sidereus decor,
et densi latitant Pleiadum greges
cum Phoebe solidum lumine non suo
orbem circuitis cornibus alligat.
    Talem dum iuvenis conspicit, en rubor
perfudit subito purpureus genas.[1]
ostro sic niveus puniceo color
perfusus rubuit, sic nitidum iubar   100
pastor luce nova roscidus aspicit.

---

[1] *Leo finds a lacuna here and suggests the insertion of* Talem
. . . genas.

234

⁷⁵ Our maiden in beauty far excels the Cecropian [1] brides, and those who on Taÿgetus' ridges are trained after the manner of men by the unwalled city,[2] and those who bathe in Aonia's [3] waters and Alpheus' [4] sacred stream.

⁸² Should he wish to be judged in beauty, all will yield to the son of Aeson, our leader—the ruthless lightning's son [5] who yokes the wild tigers, and he [6] who makes tremble the tripod, the stern virgin's [7] brother; with his twin, Castor, Pollux will yield, more skilful in boxing.

⁹⁰ So, so, ye heaven-dwellers, I pray you, let this bride surpass brides, this husband far excel husbands.

⁹³ When she has taken her stand midst her train of maidens, her one beauty shines more brightly than all. So does starlight splendour wane with the coming of the sun, and the huddled flock of the Pleiades vanish away when Phoebe, shining with borrowed light, with encircling horns encloses her full-orbed disk.[8]

⁹⁸ᵃ While on such beauty the young lover gazes, see, her cheeks are suddenly covered with rosy blushes.[9] So snowy wool, dipped in purple dye, doth redden; so shines the sun when the shepherd at dawn, wet with the dew, beholds it.

---

[1] Athenian.   [2] Sparta.   [3] Boeotian.   [4] Of Elis.
[5] See Index *s.v.* " Bacchus " and " Semele."
[6] Apollo.   [7] Diana.
[8] *cf.* Sappho, 3 :

> ἄστερες μὲν ἀμφὶ κάλαν σελάνναν
> ἂψ ἀπυκρύπτοισι φάεννον εἶδος
> ὅπποτα πλήθοισα μάλιστα λάμπῃ
> γᾶν ἐπὶ παῖσαν.

[9] Translating Leo's suggested supplementary lines.

Ereptus thalamis Phasidis horridi,
effrenae solitus pectora coniugis
invita trepidus prendere dextera,
felix Aeoliam corripe virginem
nunc primum soceris, sponse, volentibus.

Concesso, iuvenes, ludite iurgio,
hinc illinc, iuvenes, mittite carmina ;
rara est in dominos iusta licentia.

Candida thyrsigeri proles generosa Lyaei,   110
multifidam iam tempus erat succendere pinum ;
excute sollemnem digitis marcentibus ignem.
festa dicax fundat convicia fescenninus,
solvat turba iocos—tacitis eat illa tenebris,
si qua peregrino nubit fugitiva marito.

MEDEA

Occidimus, aures pepulit hymenaeus meas.
vix ipsa tantum, vix adhuc credo malum.
hoc facere Iason potuit, erepto patre
patria atque regno sedibus solam exteris
deserere durus?   merita contempsit mea   120
qui scelere flammas viderat vinci et mare ?
adeone credit omne consumptum nefas ?
incerta vaecors mente vaesana feror
partes in omnes ; unde me ulcisci queam ?
utinam esset illi frater !   est coniunx ; in hanc
ferrum exigatur.   hoc meis satis est malis ?
si quod Pelasgae, si quod urbes barbarae
novere facinus quod tuae ignorent manus,

236

[102] Do thou, O bridegroom, rescued from the marriage bonds of barbarous Phasis, wont with fear and reluctant hand to caress an unruly wife, joyfully take to thy arms the Aeolian maid [1]—now at last 'tis with the parents' will.

[107] Sport, youths, with free banter and jesting; let your songs ring out, O youths, in responsive cadence; rarely against our lords is unrebuked licence given.

[110] Comely, noble scion [2] of Lyaeus, the thyrsus-bearer, now is the time to light thy torch of frayed pinewood; toss on high the ritual fire with languishing fingers. Let saucy, sharp wit pour forth festive banterings and let the throng be free with jesting.— Let *her* pass in silent gloom who steals away to wed with a foreign husband.

MEDEA

We are undone! Upon my ears has sounded the marriage-hymn. So great a calamity scarce I myself, scarce even yet can comprehend? Had Jason the heart to do this; having robbed me of my father, native land, and kingdom, could he leave me alone in a foreign land, cruel? Has he scorned my deservings, who saw flames and sea conquered by my crime? Does he think that all my powers of evil are so exhausted? Perplexed, witless, with mind scarce sane, I am tossed to every side. Whence can I get vengeance? I would that he had a brother! [3] A wife he has; into her heart let the sword be driven. Is this enough to offset my woes? All monstrous deeds which Pelasgian, which barbaric cities know, all that thy own hands do not know,

---

[1] Creusa, a descendant of Aeolus.
[2] Hymen, son of Bacchus and Venus.
[3] That he might be slain as her own had been.

nunc est parandum.   scelera te hortentur tua
et cuncta redeant—inclitum regni decus   130
raptum et nefandae virginis parvus comes
divisus ense, funus ingestum patri
sparsumque ponto corpus, et Peliae senis
decocta aeno membra.   funestum impie
quam saepe fudi sanguinem!—et nullum scelus
irata feci; movit infelix amor.

    Quid tamen Iason potuit, alieni arbitri
iurisque factus?   debuit ferro obvium
offerre pectus—melius, a melius, dolor
furiose, loquere.   si potest, vivat meus,   140
ut fuit, Iason; si minus, vivat tamen
memorque nostri muneri parcat meo.
culpa est Creontis tota, qui sceptro impotens
coniugia solvit quique genetricem abstrahit
natis et arto pignore astrictam fidem
dirimit; petatur, solus hic poenas luat
quas debet.   alto cinere cumulabo domum;
videbit atrum verticem flammis agi
Malea longas navibus flectens moras.

NVTRIX

    Sile, obsecro, questusque secreto abditos   150
manda dolori.   gravia quisquis vulnera
patiente et aequo mutus animo pertulit,
referre potuit; ira quae tegitur nocet;
professa perdunt odia vindictae locum.

must be made ready now. Let thine own crimes
urge thee on, and let them all return in memory—
the bright ornament of the kingdom stolen away,
and the wicked girl's little comrade [1] hewn in pieces
with the sword, his murder forced upon his father's
sight, his body scattered over the deep, and the
limbs of aged Pelias seethed in a brazen pot.
Murder and impious bloodshed how often have I
wrought!—and yet no crime have I done in wrath;
'twas ill-omened love that stirred me.

[137] But what else could Jason have done, once made
subject to another's will and power? He should
have bared his breast unto the sword—nay, ah, nay,
mad grief, say not so! If possible, may he live, my
Jason, as once he was; if not, still may he live and,
mindful of me, keep unharmed the gift [2] I gave.
The fault is Creon's, all, who with unbridled sway
dissolves marriages, tears mothers from their children, and breaks pledges bound by straitest oath;
on him be my attack, let him alone pay the penalties
which he owes. I will pile his home high with ashes;
its dark pinnacles wrapt in flames Malea shall see.
where, jutting out, it holds ships in tedious delay.

NURSE

Be silent, I pray thee, and confide to secret
grief thy hidden plaints. Whoe'er has dumbly borne
hard blows with patient and calm soul, has been
able to repay them; it is hidden wrath that harms;
hatred proclaimed loses its chance for vengeance.

---

[1] Absyrtus: see Index.   [2] *i.e.* his life.

MEDEA

Levis est dolor qui capere consilium potest
et clepere sese; magna non latitant mala.
libet ire contra.

NVTRIX

Siste furialem impetum,
alumna; vix te tacita defendit quies.

MEDEA

Fortuna fortes metuit, ignavos premit.

NVTRIX

Tunc est probanda, si locum virtus habet.   160

MEDEA

Numquam potest non esse virtuti locus.

NVTRIX

Spes nulla rebus monstrat adflictis viam.

MEDEA

Qui nil potest sperare, desperet nihil.

NVTRIX

Abiere Colchi, coniugis nulla est fides
nihilque superest opibus e tantis tibi.

MEDEA

Medea superest—hic mare et terras vides
ferrumque et ignes et deos et fulmina.

240

MEDEA

MEDEA

Light is the grief which can take counsel and hide itself; great ills lie not in hiding. 'Tis pleasing to face the foe.

NURSE

Stay this frenzied outburst, my child; even silent calm can scarce defend thee.

MEDEA

Fortune fears the brave, the cowardly overwhelms.

NURSE

If there is place for courage, then should it be approved.

MEDEA

It can never be that for courage there is no place.

NURSE

No hope points out a way for our broken fortunes.

MEDEA

Whoso has naught to hope, let him despair of naught.

NURSE

The Colchians are no longer on thy side, thy husband's vows have failed, and there is nothing left of all thy wealth.

MEDEA

Medea is left—in her thou beholdest sea and land, and sword and fire and gods and thunderbolts.

NVT. Rex est timendus.

MED.   Rex meus fuerat pater.

NVT. Non metuis arma?

MED.   Sint licet terra edita.

NVT. Moriere.

MED.   Cupio.

NVT.   Profuge.

MED.   Paenituit fugae.   170

NVT. Medea,

MED.   Fiam.

NVT.   Mater es.

MED.   Cui sim vides.

NVT. Profugere dubitas?

MED.   Fugiam, at ulciscar prius.

NVT. Vindex sequetur.

MED.   Forsan inveniam moras.

NVTRIX

Compesce verba, parce iam, demens, minis
animosque minue; tempori aptari decet.

MEDEA

Fortuna opes auferre, non animum potest.—
sed cuius ictu regius cardo strepit?
ipse est Pelasgo tumidus imperio Creo.

CREO

Medea, Colchi noxium Aeetae genus,
nondum meis exportat e regnis pedem?   180

NUR. The king is to be feared.

MED.   My father was a king.

NUR. Fearst thou not arms?

MED.   Not though they were sprung from earth.[1]

NUR. Thou'lt die.

MED.   I wish it.

NUR.   Flee!

MED.   Of flight I have repented.

NUR. Medea,

MED.   Will I be.

NUR.   Thou art a mother.

MED.   By whom, thou seest.

NUR. Dost delay flight?

MED.   Flee I shall, but I'll take vengeance first.

NUR. The avenger will pursue.

MED.   Perchance I shall find means to stay him.

NURSE

Check thy words, spare now thy threats, foolish one, and thy proud spirit humble; 'tis well to fit thee to the times.

MEDEA

Fortune can take away my wealth, but not my spirit.—But under whose blows does the king's door upon its hinges creak? It is Creon himself, puffed with Pelasgian power.

[MEDEA *has retired to the back of the stage.* *Exit* NURSE. *Enter* CREON.]

CREON

Medea, Colchian Aeëtes' baleful child, has she not yet taken herself from my realm? She is

---

[1] As when armed warriors sprang from the dragon's teeth sowed in the earth by Jason.

molitur aliquid; nota fraus, nota est manus.
cui parcet illa quemve securum sinet?
abolere propere pessimam ferro luem
equidem parabam; precibus evicit gener.
concessa vita est, liberet fines metu
abeatque tuta.
    Fert gradum contra ferox
minaxque nostros propius affatus petit.
arcete, famuli, tactu et accessu procul,
iubete sileat. regium imperium pati
aliquando discat. vade veloci fuga   190
monstrumque saevum horribile iamdudum avehe.

MEDEA

Quod crimen aut quae culpa multatur fuga?

CREO

Quae causa pellat, innocens mulier rogat.

MEDEA

Si iudicas, cognosce; si regnas, iube.

CREO

Aequum atque iniquum regis imperium feras.[1]

MEDEA

Iniqua numquam regna perpetuo manent.

CREO

I, querere Colchis.

----

[1] *Leo alone of editors gives* si regnas, iube *to Creon, and deletes
l. 195. This omission, especially, is unfortunate, as it leaves
no background for* iniqua *in l. 196.*

244

plotting mischief; I know her guile, I know her power. Whom will she spare? Whom will she let live in peace? I was making ready to rid me of this outrageous pest by the sword's means and with all speed; but the prayers of my daughter's husband have prevailed. I have granted her life; let her free my boundaries from fear, and depart in safety.

[*He sees* MEDEA *approaching.*]

[186] Boldly she moves to meet me, and with threatening mien seeks closer speech. Keep her off, ye slaves, from touch and approach far off; bid her keep silence; let her learn at last to obey a king's commands. [*To* MEDEA.] Hence in swift flight! remove at once thine abominable presence, dire, horrible!

MEDEA

What crime, what fault is punished by my exile?

CREON

What cause expels her—that may an innocent woman ask.

MEDEA

If thou'rt my judge, then hear me; if my king, command.

CREON

A king's commands, just and unjust, thou must obey.

MEDEA

Unjust rule never abides continually.

CREON

Go, complain to the Colchians.

SENECAE TRAGOEDIAE

MEDEA
Redeo; qui avexit, ferat.

CREO
Vox constituto sera decreto venit.

MEDEA
Qui statuit aliquid parte inaudita altera,
aequum licet statuerit, haud aequus fuit.   200

CREO
Auditus a te Pelia supplicium tulit ?
sed fare, causae detur egregiae locus.

MEDEA
Difficile quam sit animum ab ira flectere
iam concitatum, quamque regale hoc putet,
sceptris superbas quisquis admovit manus,
qua coepit, ire, regia didici mea.
quamvis enim sim clade miseranda obruta,
expulsa supplex sola deserta, undique
afflicta, quondam nobili fulsi patre
avoque clarum Sole deduxi genus.   210
quodcumque placidis flexibus Phasis rigat
Pontusque quidquid Scythicus a tergo videt,
palustribus qua maria dulcescunt aquis,
armata peltis quidquid exterret cohors
inclusa ripis vidua Thermodontiis,—

MEDEA

MEDEA

I go; but let him take me who brought me
thence.

CREON

Thy prayer comes too late; my resolve is fixed.

MEDEA

He who has judged aught, with the other side
unheard, may have judged righteously, but was
himself unrighteous.

CREON

Didst thou hear Pelias ere he suffered punishment? But say on; be a hearing granted to thine
excellent case.

MEDEA

How hard it is to turn away from wrath the spirit
when once aroused, and how royal it seems to him
who has grasped the sceptre in his proud hands to
go on as he has begun, I have learned in my own
royal home. For, although I am overwhelmed by
piteous disaster, an exile, suppliant, lonely, forsaken,
on all sides buffeted, once I had glory from my
noble father, and from my grandsire, the Sun, traced
illustrious descent. All the land that Phasis waters
with its calm, winding stream, all that Scythian
Pontus sees behind it, where the sea grows sweet
with marshy waters,[1] all that the unwedded hordes,[2]
crescent-shielded, hemmed by Thermodon's banks,

---

[1] Numerous rivers flow into the eastern part of the Pontus,
depositing much mud. Hence the marshy nature of the
shore. These waters also sweeten the naturally saline water
of the Pontus.

[2] The Amazons.

hoc omne noster genitor imperio regit.
generosa, felix, decore regali potens
fulsi; petebant tunc meos thalamos proci,
qui nunc petuntur. rapida fortuna ac levis
praecepsque regno eripuit, exilio dedit.   220

    Confide regnis, cum levis magnas opes
huc ferat et illuc casus! hoc reges habent
magnificum et ingens, nulla quod rapiat dies:
prodesse miseris, supplices fido lare
protegere. solum hoc Colchico regno extuli,
decus illud ingens Graeciae et florem inclitum,
praesidia Achivae gentis et prolem deum
servasse memet. munus est Orpheus meum,
qui saxa cantu mulcet et silvas trahit,
geminique munus Castor et Pollux meum est   230
satique Borea quique trans Pontum quoque
summota Lynceus lumine immisso videt,
omnesque Minyae; nam ducem taceo ducum,
pro quo nihil debetur; hunc nulli imputo;
vobis revexi ceteros, unum mihi.

    Incesse nunc et cuncta flagitia ingere.
fatebor: obici crimen hoc solum potest,
Argo reversa. virgini placeat pudor
paterque placeat; tota cum ducibus ruet
Pelasga tellus, hic tuus primum gener   240
tauri ferocis ore flammanti occidet.
fortuna causam quae volet nostram premat,
248

fill with alarm—over all this my father rules. High-born, blest of heaven, in royal power and splendour then I shone ; then princes sued for marriage with me, whom now I must sue. Swift and fickle is fortune and, swooping down, has torn me from royalty and given me o'er to exile.

²²¹ Put thy trust in royalty, although light chance hither and thither tosses e'en mighty wealth ! This is the glorious, great privilege of kings, which time can never snatch away—to succour the afflicted, on a safe hearth to shelter suppliants. This only have I brought from my Colchian realm, that by my own self I saved that great glory and illustrious flower of Greece, bulwark of the Achaeans, offspring of gods.[1] Orpheus is my gift, who softens the rocks by his singing and draws trees after him ; mine, too, are the twins, Castor and Pollux, and the sons of Boreas,[2] and Lynceus, who with far-flung gaze sees things removed even beyond Pontus,—and all the Minyans. For of the leader [3] of the leaders I say no word ; for him naught is owing ; 1 count none debtor for his sake. For you I brought back the rest ; him only for myself.

²³⁶ Come on now, and heap all kinds of shameful deeds upon me. I will confess them ; but as for crimes, this only can be charged, the rescue of the Argo. Suppose modesty should please the maiden, suppose her filial duty should please her ; then will the whole Pelasgian land perish with its leaders, and this thy son-in-law will first fall before the fiery breath of the fierce bull.[4] Let what fortune will, oppress me ;

---

[1] The Argonauts.   [2] Zetes and Calaïs.   [3] Jason.
[4] In vivid memory she puts herself back at the parting of the ways, where she was debating in her heart as to her course, and from this standpoint she speaks.

non paenitet servasse tot regum decus.
quodcumque culpa praemium ex omni tuli,
hoc est penes te.   si placet, damna ream ;
sed redde crimen.   sum nocens, fateor, Creo ;
talem sciebas esse, cum genua attigi
fidemque supplex praesidis dextrae peti ;
iterum miseriis angulum ac sedem rogo
latebrasque viles.   urbe si pelli placet,   250
detur remotus aliquis in regnis locus.

CREO

Non esse me qui sceptra violentus geram
nec qui superbo miserias calcem pede,
testatus equidem videor haud clare parum
generum exulem legendo et afflictum et gravi
terrore pavidum, quippe quem poenae expetit
letoque Acastus regna Thessalica optinens.
senio trementem debili atque aevo gravem
patrem peremptum queritur et caesi senis
discissa membra, cum dolo captae tuo   260
piae sorores impium auderent nefas.
potest Iason, si tuam causam amoves,
suam tueri ; nullus innocuum cruor
contaminavit, afuit ferro manus
proculque vestro purus a coetu stetit.
tu, tu malorum machinatrix facinorum,
feminea cui nequitia ad audenda omnia,
robur virile est, nulla famae memoria,
egredere, purga regna, letales simul
tecum aufer herbas, libera cives metu,   270
alia sedens tellure sollicita deos.

250

MEDEA

I repent not the glorious salvation of so many kings. Whatever reward I have won by all my crimes, it is in thy hands. Arraign and condemn me, if 'tis thy pleasure; but give me back my sin.[1] I am guilty, I confess it, Creon; such didst thou know me when I clasped thy knees and as suppliant sought the loyalty of thy protecting hand. Once more, some corner, some abiding-place for my woes I beg, some paltry hiding-place; if from thy city thou art pleased to drive me, let some remote nook in thy realm be given me.

CREON

That I am not one to wield the sceptre with violence nor to trample upon misery with haughty foot, methinks I have not unclearly shown by choosing for son-in-law an exile, crushed and stricken with heavy fear—aye, one whom Acastus, lord of Thessaly, demands for punishment and death. He complains that his father,[2] palsied and weak with age, burdened with years, was taken off, and the murdered old man's limbs torn asunder, when, deceived by thy guile, his[3] pious sisters dared an impious crime. Jason can defend his own cause if it is separate from thine; no blood has stained his innocence, his hand wielded no sword, and he has kept far off and free from company of such as thou. Thou, thou contriver of wickedness, who combinest woman's wanton recklessness and man's strength, with no thought of reputation, away! Purge my kingdom and take thy deadly herbs with thee; free the citizens from fear; abiding in some other land, harry[4] the gods.

---

[1] *i.e.* Jason, for whom she sinned.
[2] Pelias.   [3] *i.e.* Acastus'.
[4] *i.e.* by the power of her witchcraft.

SENECAE TRAGOEDIAE

Profugere cogis? redde fugienti ratem
vel redde comitem. fugere cur solam iubes?
non sola veni. bella si metuis pati,
utrumque regno pelle. cur sontes duos
distinguis? illi Pelia, non nobis iacet;
fugam, rapinas adice, desertum patrem
lacerumque fratrem, quidquid etiam nunc novas
docet maritus coniuges, non est meum.
totiens nocens sum facta, sed numquam mihi.   280

CREO

Iam exisse decuit. quid seris fando moras?

MEDEA

Supplex recedens illud extremum precor:
ne culpa natos matris insontes trahat.

CREO

Vade; hos paterno ut genitor excipiam sinu.

MEDEA

Per ego auspicatos regii thalami toros,
per spes futuras perque regnorum status,
Fortuna varia dubia quos agitat vice,
precor, brevem largire fugienti moram,
dum extrema natis mater infigo oscula
fortasse moriens.

MEDEA

MEDEA

Dost force me to flee? Give back then to the fugitive her ship, yea, give back her comrade.[1] Why dost thou bid me flee alone? I did not come alone. If 'tis war[2] thou fearest, drive us both from thy kingdom. Why make distinction 'twixt two culprits? 'Tis for him Pelias lies dead, and not for me. Add flight, theft, a deserted father, a mangled brother, any crime which e'en now the bridegroom is teaching his new wives[3]—'tis no crime of mine. Full oft have I been made guilty, but never for myself.

CREON

Thy going is already overdue. Why dost contrive delay with words?

MEDEA

Suppliant I make this last prayer to thee as I depart: let not the mother's guilt drag down her guiltless sons.

CREON

Go then; these will I take as father to my fatherly embrace.

MEDEA

By the blest bed of this royal marriage, by thy hopes for the future, and by the estate of thrones, which fickle Fortune disturbs with changeful lot, I pray thee be bountiful of a brief stay of my flight, while I, their mother, imprint on my sons the latest kiss, perchance my dying act.

---

[1] Jason. [2] *i.e.* with Acastus.
[3] She uses the plural with a sneer.

CREO

Fraudibus tempus petis. 290

MEDEA

Quae fraus timeri tempore exiguo potest?

CREO

Nullum ad nocendum tempus angustum est malis.

MEDEA

Parumne miserae temporis lacrimis negas?

CREO

Etsi repugnat precibus infixus timor,
unus parando dabitur exilio dies.

MEDEA

Nimis est, recidas aliquid ex isto licet.
et ipsa propero.

CREO

Capite supplicium lues,
clarum priusquam Phoebus attollat diem
nisi cedis Isthmo.
Sacra me thalami vocant,
vocat precari festus Hymenaeo dies. 300

CHORVS

Audax nimium qui freta primus
rate tam fragili perfida rupit
terrasque suas post terga videns
animam levibus credidit auris,
dubioque secans aequora cursu

MEDEA

CREON

For treachery thou art seeking time.

MEDEA

What treachery can be feared in time so scant?

CREON

No time is too brief for harm to those on evil bent.

MEDEA

Dost refuse a poor mother just a little time for tears?

CREON

Though my ingrained fear bids me refuse thy plea, one day shall be given to prepare for banishment.

MEDEA

'Tis more than enough, though thou retrench it somewhat. I also am in haste.

CREON

With thy life shalt thou pay penalty if before Phoebus brings the bright day thou art not gone from Isthmus.

²⁹⁹ But the marriage rites summon me, summons the festal day to pray to Hymen. [*Exeunt.*

CHORUS

Too venturesome the man who in frail barque first cleft the treacherous seas and, with one last look behind him at the well-known shore, trusted his life to the fickle winds; who, ploughing the waters on an

255

potuit tenui fidere ligno[1]
inter vitae mortisque vias
nimium gracili limite ducto.   308
   Candida nostri saecula patres[2]   329
videre, procul fraude remota.   330
sua quisque piger litora tangens
patrioque senex factus in arvo,
parvo dives, nisi quas tulerat
natale solum, non norat opes.   334
nondum quisquam sidera norat,   309
stellisque quibus pingitur aether   310
non erat usus, nondum pluvias
Hyadas poterat vitare ratis,
non Oleniae lumina caprae,
nec quae sequitur flectitque senex
Attica tardus plaustra Bootes,
nondum Boreas, nondum Zephyrus
nomen habebant.
   Ausus Tiphys pandere vasto
carbasa ponto legesque novas
scribere ventis : nunc lina sinu   320
tendere toto, nunc prolato
pede transversos captare notos,
nunc antemnas medio tutas
ponere malo, nunc in summo
religare loco, cum iam totos
avidus nimium navita flatus
optat et alto rubicunda tremunt
sipara velo.   328
bene dissaepti foedera mundi   335
traxit in unum Thessala pinus

---

[1] *Leo deletes these two lines.*
[2] *Leo and Richter agree in the rearrangement of the following lines ; M. Müller, of the modern editors, defends the traditional order.*

unknown course, could trust to a slender plank, stretching too slight a boundary between the ways of life and death.

329 Unsullied the ages our fathers saw, with crime banished afar. Then every man inactive kept to his own shores and lived to old age on ancestral fields, rich with but little, knowing no wealth save what his home soil had yielded. Not yet could any read the sky and use the stars with which the heavens are spangled; not yet could ships avoid the rainy Hyades; not yet did the fires of the Olenian Goat nor the Attic Wain which slow old Boötes follows and controls, not yet did Boreas, not yet Zephyrus have names.

318 Tiphys made bold to spread his canvas on the vasty deep and to write new laws for the winds: now to spread full-bellied sail, now to haul the forward sheet[1] and catch cross-breezes, now to set the yards in safety midway of the mast, now to bind them at the top, when the too eager sailor prays for winds and aloft the ruddy topsails flutter. The lands, well separated before by nature's laws, the Thessalian ship[2] made one, bade the deep suffer

---

[1] *i.e.* to set the sail sideways.   [2] The Argo.

iussitque pati verbera pontum,
partemque metus fieri nostri
mare sepositum.
    Dedit illa graves improba poenas   340
per tam longos ducta timores,
cum duo montes, claustra profundi,
hinc atque illinc subito impulsu
velut aetherio gemerent sonitu,
spargeret arces nubesque ipsas
mare deprensum.
palluit audax Tiphys et omnes
labente manu misit habenas,
Orpheus tacuit torpente lyra
ipsaque vocem perdidit Argo.
quid cum Siculi virgo Pelori,   350
rabidos utero succincta canes,
omnes pariter solvit hiatus?
quis non totos horruit artus
totiens uno latrante malo?
quid cum Ausonium dirae pestes
voce canora mare mulcerent,
cum Pieria resonans cithara
Thracius Orpheus solitam cantu
retinere ràtes paene coegit
Sirena sequi?   quod fuit huius   360
pretium cursus?   aurea pellis
maiusque mari Medea malum,
merces prima digna carina.
    Nunc iam cessit pontus et omnes
patitur leges ; non Palladia
compacta manu regumque ferens
inclita remos quaeritur Argo ;
quaelibet altum cumba pererrat.
terminus omnis motus et urbes
muros terra posuere nova,   370

blows,[1] and the sequestered sea become a part of
our human fear.

340 Heavy the penalties which that bold barque
paid, brought through long terrors, when two mountains, barriers of the deep, from either side quick
rushing, roared as with sound of thunder, and the
sea, caught between, sprinkled their peaks and the
clouds themselves. Bold Tiphys paled with fear
and let the helm slip wholly from his faltering hand;
Orpheus was still, his lyre mute with amaze, and
the Argo herself lost voice.[2] What, when the maid[3]
of Sicilian Pelorus, her waist begirt with ravenous
dogs, opened all her gaping throats together? Who
did not shudder in every limb when that one monster
howled with so many tongues? What, when the
deadly pests[4] soothed the Ausonian sea with their
tuneful songs, when, sounding back on his Pierian
lyre, Thracian Orpheus well-nigh forced the Siren
to follow, though wont to hold ships spell-bound by
her song? Of this voyage what was the prize?
The golden fleece and Medea, worse evil than the
sea, worthy to be the first ship's merchandise.

364 Now, in our time, the deep has ceased resistance
and submits utterly to law; no famous Argo, framed
by a Pallas' hand, with princes to man its oars, is
sought for; any little craft now wanders at will upon
the deep. All bounds have been removed, cities
have set their walls in new lands, and the world, now

---

[1] *i.e.* of oars.
[2] The Argo's figurehead was made of wood from the talking
oaks of Dodona and had itself power to speak and give timely
warnings.   [3] Scylla.   [4] The Sirens.

nil qua fuerat sede reliquit
pervius orbis:
Indus gelidum potat Araxen,
Albin Persae Rhenumque bibunt.
venient annis saecula seris,
quibus Oceanus vincula rerum
laxet et ingens pateat tellus
Tethysque novos detegat orbes
nec sit terris ultima Thule.

NVTRIX

Alumna, celerem quo rapis tectis pedem?   380
resiste et iras comprime ac retine impetum.
  Incerta qualis entheos gressus tulit
cum iam recepto maenas insanit deo
Pindi nivalis vertice aut Nysae iugis,
talis recursat huc et huc motu effero,
furoris ore signa lymphati gerens.
flammata facies spiritum ex alto citat,
proclamat, oculos uberi fletu rigat,
renidet; omnis specimen affectus capit.   389
quo pondus animi vergat, ubi ponat minas,   390
haeret; minatur aestuat queritur gemit.   391
ubi se iste fluctus franget? exundat furor.   392
non facile secum versat aut medium scelus;
se vincet. irae novimus veteris notas.
magnum aliquid instat, efferum immane impium.
vultum furoris cerno. di fallant metum!

passable throughout, has left nothing where it once
had place: the Indian drinks of the cold Araxes, the
Persians quaff the Elbe and the Rhine. There will
come an age in the far-off years when Ocean shall
unloose the bonds of things, when the whole broad
earth shall be revealed, when Tethys shall disclose
new worlds and Thule not be the limit of the lands.

NURSE

[*Sees* MEDEA *hurrying out of the house.*]

Dear child, whither hurriest thou abroad? Stay,
curb thy passion, check thy impetuous haste.

[MEDEA *goes on without heeding.*]

382 As a maenad uncertainly directs her frenzied
steps when now she raves at the oncoming of the god,
on snowy Pindus' top or on Nysa's ridges, so she runs
now here, now there, with frantic rush, marks of
distracted passion in her face. Her cheeks aflame,
she pants with deep sobs for breath, shouts aloud,
weeps floods of tears, beams with joy; she assumes
the proof of every passion. Whither the weight of
her wrath inclines, where it aims its threats, hangs
still in doubt; she threatens, seethes with rage,
complains, groans aloud. Where will this wave
break itself? Madness o'erflows its bounds. No
simple or half-way crime doth she ponder in her
heart; she will outdo herself. I recognize the marks
of her old-time rage. Something great is impending,
wild, monstrous, impious.

[MEDEA *now approaches.*]

I see madness in her face. May Heaven avert my
fears!

MEDEA

Si quaeris odio, misera, quem statuas modum,
imitare amorem.   regias egone ut faces
inulta patiar?   segnis hic ibit dies,
tanto petitus ambitu, tanto datus?   400
dum terra caelum media libratum feret
nitidusque certas mundus evolvet vices
numerusque harenis derit et solem dies,
noctem sequentur astra, dum siccas polus
versabit Arctos, flumina in pontum cadent,
numquam meus cessabit in poenas furor
crescetque semper.   quae ferarum immanitas,
quae Scylla, quae Charybdis Ausonium mare
Siculumque sorbens quaeve anhelantem premens
Titana tantis Aetna fervebit minis?   410
non rapidus amnis, non procellosum mare
Pontusve Coro saevus aut vis ignium
adiuta flatu possit imitari impetum
irasque nostras; sternam et evertam omnia.

   Timuit Creontem ac bella Thessalici ducis?
amor timere neminem verus potest.
sed cesserit coactus et dederit manus;
adire certe et coniugem extremo alloqui
sermone potuit.   hoc quoque extimuit ferox.
laxare certe tempus immitis fugae   420
genero licebat—liberis unus dies
datus est duobus.   non queror tempus breve;
multum patebit.   faciet hic faciet dies
quod nullus umquam taceat.   invadam deos
et cuncta quatiam.

MEDEA

MEDEA [*aside*]

If thou seekst, poor soul, what limit thou
shouldst set to hate, copy thy love. Can it be that
unavenged I should endure this royal wedding?
Shall this day go idly by so anxiously besought, so
anxiously bestowed? While the central earth shall
bear up the balanced heavens, while the bright
universe shall pursue its unchanging rounds, while
sands lack number, while day attends the sun and
stars the night, while the dry [1] Bears revolve about
the pole, and rivers fall to the sea, my madness shall
never cease its quest of vengeance and shall grow
on for ever. What ferocity of beasts, what Scylla,
what Charybdis, sucking up the Ausonian and Sicilian
waters, or what Aetna, resting heavily on panting
Titan, shall burn with such threats as I? No whirling
river, no storm-tossed sea, no Pontus, raging beneath
the north-west wind, no violence of fire, fanned by
the gale, could imitate the onrush of my wrath. I
shall lay prostrate and destroy all things.

[415] Did he [2] fear Creon and the threats of Thessaly's
king? [3] True love can fear no man. But grant that
under compulsion he yielded and made surrender;
he could at least have come to me, could have spoken
some last words to his wife. This also, though bold
of heart, he feared to do. Surely 'twas in the power
of the king's son-in-law to put off the time of my
cruel banishment—one day was given for my children
twain. But I complain not that the time is short;
it shall stretch far. This day shall do, shall do that
whereof no day shall e'er be dumb. I will storm
the gods, and shake the universe.

---

[1] Because these constellations never set beneath the ocean.
[2] Jason.   [3] Acastus.

SENECAE TRAGOEDIAE

NVTRIX

Recipe turbatum malis.
era, pectus, animum mitiga.

MEDEA

Sola est quies,
mecum ruina cuncta si video obruta;
mecum omnia abeant.   trahere, cum pereas, libet.

NVTRIX

Quam multa sint timenda, si perstas, vide;
nemo potentes aggredi tutus potest.   430

IASON

O dura fata semper et sortem asperam,
cum saevit et cum parcit ex aequo malam!
remedia quotiens invenit nobis deus
periculis peiora; si vellem fidem
praestare meritis coniugis, leto fuit
caput offerendum; si mori nollem, fide
misero carendum.   non timor vicit fidem,
sed trepida pietas; quippe sequeretur necem
proles parentum.   sancta si caelum incolis
Iustitia, numen invoco ac testor tuum: 440
nati patrem vicere.   quin ipsam quoque,
etsi ferox est corde nec patiens iugi,
consulere natis malle quam thalamis reor.
constituit animus precibus iratam aggredi.
atque ecce, viso memet exiluit, furit,
fert odia prae se; totus in vultu est dolor.

264

MEDEA

NURSE

Win back thy woe-troubled heart, my mistress;
calm thy soul.

MEDEA

The only calm for me—if with me I see the
universe o'erwhelmed in ruins; with me let all things
pass away. 'Tis sweet to drag others down when
thou art perishing. [*Exit.*

NURSE [*calling after* MEDEA]

Beware how many perils are to be feared if thou
persist; no one may safely assail the strong.

[*Enter* JASON.]

JASON

O fate, ever hard, and fortune, cruel—when she
rages and when she spares, equally malign! How
often does God find cures for us worse than our
perils; should I resolve to be faithful to my wife
according to her deserts, my life would be forfeited
to death; should I refuse to die, alas! I must be
faithless. It is not fear, but fearful father-love that
has conquered faith; surely my children would share
their parents' death. O holy Justice, if in heaven
thou dwellest, I call thy divinity to witness: the
sons have prevailed upon the sire. Nay, even she
herself, though she is fierce of heart and ill brooks
the yoke, would rather, methinks, take thought for
her sons than for her marriage rights. My mind is
fixed to assail her wrath with prayers. [*Enter* MEDEA.]
And see, at sight of me she starts up, bursts into a
passion, displays her hate; all her anguish is in
her face.

MEDEA

Fugimus, Iason, fugimus.   hoc non est novum,
mutare sedes ; causa fugiendi nova est—
pro te solebam fugere.   discedo exeo,
penatibus profugere quam cogis tuis ;   450
at quo remittis ?   Phasin et Colchos petam
patriumque regnum quaeque fraternus cruor
perfudit arva ?   quas peti terras iubes ?
quae maria monstras ?   Pontici fauces freti
per quas revexi nobilem regum manum
adulterum secuta per Symplegadas ?
parvamne Iolcon, Thessala an Tempe petam ?
quascumque aperui tibi vias, clausi mihi.
quo me remittis ?   exuli exilium imperas
nec das.   eatur.   regius iussit gener ;   460
nihil recuso.   dira supplicia ingere ;
merui.   cruentis paelicem poenis premat
regalis ira, vinculis oneret manus
clausamque saxo noctis aeternae obruat ;
minora meritis patiar.

                        Ingratum caput,
revolvat animus igneos tauri halitus
interque saevos gentis indomitae metus
armifero in arvo flammeum Aeetae pecus,[1]
hostisque subiti tela, cum iussu meo
terrigena miles mutua caede occidit.   470
adice expetita spolia Phrixei arietis
somnoque iussum lumina ignoto dare
insomne monstrum, traditum fratrem neci

[1] *Leo deletes ll. 467, 468.*

MEDEA

We are fleeing, Jason, fleeing. 'Tis no new thing to change our abode; but the cause of flight is new—'twas *for* thee I was wont to flee. I withdraw, I go away, whom thou art forcing to flee forth from thy home; but whither dost thou send me back? Shall I seek Phasis and the Colchians, my father's kingdom, the fields drenched with my brother's blood? What lands dost thou bid me seek? What waters dost thou show to me? The jaws of the Pontic sea through which I brought back the noble band of princes, following thee, thou wanton, through the Clashing Rocks? Is it little Iolcos or Thessalian Tempe I shall seek? All the ways which I have opened for thee I have closed upon myself. Whither dost send me back? Thou imposest exile on an exile, but givest no place. But let me go. A king's son-in-law has commanded it; I'll not refuse. Heap dire penalties upon me; them have I deserved. Let the angry king crush thy mistress with cruel punishments, load her hands with chains, shut her up and bury her in dungeons of eternal darkness; I shall suffer less than I deserve.

465 O ungrateful man, let thy heart recall the bull's fiery breath, and, midst the savage terrors of an unconquered race, the fire-breathing herd on Aeëtes' arm-bearing[1] plain, the weapons of the suddenly appearing foe, when, at my order, the earth-born soldiery fell in mutual slaughter. Think, too, on the long-sought spoil of the ram of Phrixus, the sleepless dragon, bidden to close his eyes in unknown slumber, my brother given up to death,

---

[1] Where the dragon's teeth sowed by Jason sprang up into full-armed warriors.

et scelere in uno non semel factum scelus,
ausasque natas fraude deceptas mea
secare membra non revicturi senis. 476
per spes tuorum liberum et certum larem, 478
per victa monstra, per manus, pro te quibus
numquam peperci, perque praeteritos metus, 480
per caelum et undas, coniugi testes mei,
miserere, redde supplici felix vicem. 482
aliena quaerens regna deserui mea; 477
ex opibus illis, quas procul raptas Scythae 483
usque a perustis Indiae populis agunt,
quas quia referta vix domus gaza capit,
ornamus auro nemora, nil exul tuli
nisi fratris artus.   hos quoque impendi tibi,
tibi patria cessit, tibi pater, frater, pudor—
hac dote nupsi.   redde fugienti sua.

IASON

Perimere cum te vellet infestus Creo, 490
lacrimis meis evictus exilium dedit.

MEDEA

Poenam putabam ; munus ut video est fuga.

IASON

Dum licet abire, profuge teque hinc eripe ;
gravis ira regum est semper.

---

[1] Medea not only slew her brother, but cut him in pieces and
cast them into the sea.   She thinks of each piece as a separate
crime.   Similarly, when her brother's ghost appears to her
(l. 963) it is still in pieces, *dispersis membris.*

crime not done once alone in one act of crime;[1] think on the daughters[2] who, lured by my guile, dared dismember the old man who was never to return to life. By the hopes of thy children, thine established house, by the monsters conquered, by these hands which I have never spared in thy service, by the perils we have undergone, by heaven and sea, witnesses of my marriage, have mercy on me; happy thyself, give thy suppliant her turn at happiness. Seeking a kingdom for another, I have given up my own; of all that wealth which, plundered even from the distant swart tribes of India, the Scythians heap up, that golden treasure which, since the packed palace can scarce contain it, we hang upon the trees,[3] I brought away nothing in my exile save only my brother's limbs. Those also I squandered upon thee; for thee my country has given place, for thee father, brother, maidenhood—with this dower did I wed thee. Give back to the fugitive her own.

JASON

When angry Creon was bent on thy destruction, 'twas by my tears he was prevailed upon to grant thee banishment.

MEDEA

A punishment I deemed it; now, as I see, exile is a boon.

JASON

Depart while still thou mayst; take thyself hence; grievous ever is the wrath of kings.

[2] Of Pelias.
[3] Referring to the golden fleece.

MEDEA

                    Hoc suades mihi,
praestas Creusae; paelicem invisam amoves.

IASON

Medea amores obicit?

MEDEA

                    Et caedem et dolos.

IASON

Obicere tandem quod potes crimen mihi?

MEDEA

Quodcumque feci.

IASON

                    Restat hoc unum insuper,
tuis ut etiam sceleribus fiam nocens.

MEDEA

Tua illa, tua sunt illa; cui prodest scelus   500
is fecit.   omnes coniugem infamem arguant;
solus tuere, solus insontem voca;
tibi innocens sit quisquis est pro te nocens.

IASON

Ingrata vita est cuius acceptae pudet.

MEDEA

Retinenda non est cuius acceptae pudet.

MEDEA

MEDEA

In urging this upon me, thou art Creusa's advocate; thou wouldst remove the rival whom she hates.

JASON

What! Medea charge me with love?

MEDEA

Yes, murder, too, and treachery.

JASON

What crime, pray, canst thou charge to me?

MEDEA

Whatever I have done.

JASON

This one thing remains still for me, to become guilty of thy sins as well.

MEDEA

They are, they are thine own; who profits by a sin has done the sin. Though all should hold thy wife infamous, do thou alone protect her, do thou alone call her innocent; let her be guiltless in thy sight, who for thy sake is guilty.

JASON

Unwelcome is life which one is ashamed to have accepted.

MEDEA

Then one should not keep a life which he is ashamed to have accepted.

IASON

Quin potius ira concitum pectus doma,
placare natis.

MEDEA

Abdico eiuro abnuo.
meis Creusa liberis fratres dabit?

IASON

Regina natis exulum, afflictis potens.

MEDEA

Non veniat umquam tam malus miseris dies 510
qui prole foeda misceat prolem inclitam,
Phoebi nepotes Sisyphi nepotibus.

IASON

Quid, misera, meque teque in exitium trahis?
abscede quaeso.

MEDEA

Supplicem audivit Creo.

IASON

Quid facere possim, loquere.

MEDEA

Pro me?   vel scelus

IASON

Hinc rex et illinc——

MEDEA

JASON

Nay, calm thy wrath-stirred heart; for thy sons
sake be reconciled.

MEDEA

I reject, forswear, disown them! Shall Creusa
bear brothers to my children?

JASON

Yes, a queen, to the sons of exiles; a royal lady to
the fallen.

MEDEA

Never may such ill day come to the wretched,
as shall mingle a base breed with illustrious stock
Phoebus' sons with the sons of Sisyphus.

JASON

Why, wretched woman, dost thou drag both me
and thee to ruin? Begone, I pray thee.

MEDEA

Creon has heard my prayer.

JASON

What can I do? Tell me.

MEDEA

For me? Crime.

JASON

A king on this side and on that——

MEDEA

Est (et hic maior metus [1])
Medea.   nos confligere. [2]   certemus sine,
sit pretium Iason.

IASON

Cedo defessus malis.
et ipsa casus saepe iam expertos time.

MEDEA

Fortuna semper omnis infra me stetit.   520

IASON

Acastus instat.

MEDEA

Propior est hostis Creo;
utrumque profuge.   non ut in socerum manus
armes nec ut te caede cognata inquines
Medea cogit; innocens mecum fuge.

IASON

Et quis resistet, gemina si bella ingruant,
Creo atque Acastus arma si iungant sua?

MEDEA

His adice Colchos, adice et Aeeten ducem,
Scythas Pelasgis iunge; demersos dabo.

IASON

Alta extimesco sceptra.

---

[1] *Reading with Richter.   Leo*, Est et his maior metus: |
Medea.
[2] *The text is obviously corrupt here.   Nothing satisfactory has
been made of* nos confligere; *Leo considers ll. 516–520 an
interpolation; Page suggests* conflige, *used in active sense.*

274

MEDEA

MEDEA

There is (and this more fearsome still) Medea. Let us[1] strive together, and let the prize be Jason.

JASON

I yield, worn with trouble. And do thou thyself beware lest thou tempt fate too often.

MEDEA

Always has every fortune stood beneath my feet.

JASON

Acastus is hard after us.

MEDEA

Nearer foe is Creon; flee them both. That thou arm thy hand against thy father-in-law, and stain thyself with kindred[2] blood, Medea does not compel thee; remain guiltless and escape with me.

JASON

And who will resist if double war assail us, if Creon and Acastus unite their arms?

MEDEA

Add the Colchians to these, add Aeetes, too, to lead them, join Scythians with Pelasgians; to destruction will I give them all.

JASON

I tremble at lofty sceptres.

[1] *i.e.* Creon and me.   [2] Acastus was Jason's cousin.

MEDEA

Ne cupias vide.

IASON

Suspecta ne sint, longa colloquia amputa.   530

MEDEA

Nunc summe toto Iuppiter caelo tona,
intende dextram, vindices flammas para
omnemque ruptis nubibus mundum quate.
nec deligenti tela librentur manu
vel me vel istum; quisquis e nobis cadet
nocens peribit, non potest in nos tuum
errare fulmen.

IASON

Sana meditari incipe
et placida fare.   si quod ex soceri domo
potest fugam levare solamen, pete.

MEDEA

Contemnere animus regias, ut scis, opes   540
potest soletque; liberos tantum fugae
habere comites liceat in quorum sinu
lacrimas profundam.   te novi nati manent.

IASON

Parere precibus cupere me fateor tuis;
pietas vetat; namque istud ut possim pati,
non ipse memet cogat et rex et socer.
haec causa vitae est, hoc perusti pectoris
curis levamen.   spiritu citius queam
carere, membris, luce.

276

MEDEA

See that thou lust not after them.

JASON

Cut short this long discourse, lest it arouse suspicion.

MEDEA

Now, O most high Jupiter, thunder throughout thy heavens, stretch forth thy hand, thine avenging flames prepare, rend the clouds and make the whole world quake. Let thy bolts be poised with hand that chooseth neither me nor him; whichever of us falls will perish guilty; against us thy bolt can make no error.

JASON

Begin to think with reason, and speak with calm. If any solace from my father-in-law's house can soothe thy flight, request it.

MEDEA

To scorn the wealth of kings, my soul, as well thou knowest, hath strength and wont. I ask but this: that I may have my children as comrades of my flight, that in their bosoms I may pour forth my tears. Thee new sons await.

JASON

I confess that right gladly would I yield unto thy prayer, but a father's love forbids; for that I should permit this thing, not Creon himself, my king and father-in-law, could force me. This is my reason for living, this, my heart's comfort, consumed as it is with cares. Sooner could I part with breath, with limbs, with light.

SENECAE TRAGOEDIAE

MEDEA

                Sic natos amat?
bene est, tenetur, vulneri patuit locus.—   550
suprema certe liceat abeuntem loqui
mandata, liceat ultimum amplexum dare ;
gratum est et illud.   voce iam extrema peto,
ne, si qua noster dubius effudit dolor,
maneant in animo verba ; melioris tibi
memoria nostri sedeat ; haec irae data
oblitterentur

IASON

         Omnia ex animo expuli
precorque et ipse, fervidam ut mentem regas
placideque tractes ; miserias lenit quies.

MEDEA

   Discessit. itane est ?   vadis oblitus mei   560
et tot meorum facinorum?   excidimus tibi ?
numquam excidemus.   hoc age, omnes advoca
vires et artes.   fructus est scelerum tibi
nullum scelus putare.   vix fraudi est locus ;
timemur.   hac aggredere, qua nemo potest
quicquam timere.   perge nunc, aude, incipe
quidquid potest Medea, quidquid non potest.
   Tu, fida nutrix, socia maeroris mei
variique casus, misera consilia adiuva.
est palla nobis, munus aetherium, domus   570
decusque regni, pignus Aeetae datum
a Sole generis, est et auro textili
monile fulgens quodque gemmarum nitor
278

MEDEA

MEDEA [*aside*]

Thus does he love his sons? 'Tis well! I have
him! The place to wound him is laid bare. [*To*
JASON.] As I depart, my final message, at least, grant
me to speak; grant me to give the last embrace;
e'en that will be a boon. With my latest utterance
I beg thee now; let not any words my distracted
grief has poured forth remain within thy mind; let
the memory of my better self stay with thee, and
let these words spoken in wrath be quite forgot.

JASON

All have I driven from my mind, and I also make
prayer to thee that thou curb thy hot passion and
be calm; peace soothes the soul's distresses. [*Exit.*

MEDEA

He has gone! Can it be so? Goest thou, forgetful of me and of all the deeds I wrought? Have
we fallen from thy memory? Nay, we shall never
fall therefrom. [*To herself.*] To thy task; summon
up all thy powers and arts. The fruit of thy crimes
is to count nothing crime. There is scant room for
fraud; we are held in fear. There make attack
where no one can fear aught. Haste thee now,
dare, begin whatever Medea can—and cannot—do.

[*To the* NURSE.]

568 Do thou, faithful nurse, comrade of my grief and
of my shifting fortunes, help my unhappy plannings.
I have a robe, a gift from heaven, the glory of our
house and kingdom, given by the Sun to Aeetes as a
pledge of fatherhood; there is also a gleaming necklace of woven gold and a golden band which the

279

distinguit aurum, quo solent cingi comae.
haec nostra nati dona nubenti ferant,
sed ante diris inlita ac tincta artibus.
vocetur Hecate.　sacra letifica appara;
statuantur arae, flamma iam tectis sonet.

CHORVS

Nulla vis flammae tumidive venti
tanta, nec teli metuenda torti,　　　　　　　　580
quanta cum coniunx viduata taedis
　　　ardet et odit;

non ubi hibernos nebulosus imbres
Auster advexit properatque torrens
Hister et iunctos vetat esse pontes
　　　ac vagus errat;

non ubi impellit Rhodanus profundum,
aut ubi in rivos nivibus solutis
sole iam forti medioque vere
　　　tabuit Haemus.　　　　　　　　　590

caecus est ignis stimulatus ira
nec regi curat patiturve frenos
aut timet mortem; cupit ire in ipsos
　　　obvius enses.

Parcite, o divi, veniam precamur,
vivat ut tutus mare qui subegit;
sed furit vinci dominus profundi
　　　regna secunda.

ausus aeternos agitare currus
immemor metae iuvenis paternae　　　　　600
quos polo sparsit furiosus ignes
　　　ipse recepit.

sparkle of gems adorns, with which the hair is encircled. Let my sons bring these as gifts unto the
bride, but let them first be anointed and imbued
with baneful poisons. Now call on Hecate. Prepare
the death-dealing rites; let altars be erected, and let
now their fires resound within the palace.

CHORUS

No violence of fire or of swelling gale, no fearful
force of hurtling spear, is as great as when a wife,
robbed of her love, burns hot with hate; not when
cloudy Auster has brought the winter's rains, and
Hister's floods speeds on, wrecking bridges in its
course, and wanders afield; not when the Rhone
beats back the sea, or when the snows melt into
streams beneath the sun's strong rays and in mid-
spring Haemus has dissolved. Blind is the fire of
love when fanned by rage, cares not to be controlled,
brooks no restraint, has no fear of death; 'tis eager
to advance even against the sword.

595 Have mercy, O gods, be gracious, we beseech
you, that he [1] may live in safety who tamed the sea;
but the lord [2] of the deep is enraged that the second
realm is conquered. The youth [3] who dared drive
the everlasting chariot, heedless of his father's goal,
himself caught the fire which in his madness he
scattered o'er the sky. The familiar path has cost

---

[1] Jason, who first ventured on the sea in the Argo; *cf.*
ll. 318 ff.
[2] Neptune. Jupiter is lord of the sky, Neptune of the sea,
and Pluto of the underworld.   [3] Phaëthon.

constitit nulli via nota magno ;
vade qua tutum populo priori,
rumpe nec sacro, violente, sancta
    foedera mundi.

Quisquis audacis tetigit carinae
nobiles remos nemorisque sacri
Pelion densa spoliavit umbra,
quisquis intravit scopulos vagantes   610
et tot emensus pelagi labores
barbara funem religavit ora
raptor externi rediturus auri,
exitu diro temerata ponti
    iura piavit.

Exigit poenas mare provocatum.
Tiphys in primis, domitor profundi,
liquit indocto regimen magistro ;
litore externo, procul a paternis
occidens regnis tumuloque vili   620
tectus ignotas iacet inter umbras.
Aulis amissi memor inde regis
portibus lentis retinet carinas
    stare querentes.

Ille vocali genitus Camena,
cuius ad chordas modulante plectro
restitit torrens, siluere venti,
cum suo cantu volucris relicto
adfuit tota comitante silva,
Thracios sparsus iacuit per agros,   630
at caput tristi fluitavit Hebro ;
contigit notam Stÿga Tartarumque,
    non rediturus.

no mortal dear; walk thou where 'twas safe for folk aforetime, nor break, rash man, the inviolable covenants of the universe.

607 Whoever handled that daring ship's famous oars and despoiled Pelion of his sacred grove's thick shade, whoever entered between the roaming rocks [1] and, having passed the perils of the deep, moored his vessel on a savage shore, to return captor of foreign gold—all by a dreadful end atoned for the sea's outraged laws.

616 Punishment the challenged ocean claims. First of all, Tiphys, the tamer of the deep, gave up control to an untrained helmsman; dying on a foreign shore, far from his ancestral realm, in a paltry tomb he lies midst unfamiliar shades. For this, Aulis, remembering her lost king, in her becalmed harbour holds ships chafing at delay. [2]

625 That son [3] of the tuneful Muse, at whose sweet melodies the swift stream stood still and the winds were hushed, when the bird, leaving off its own singing, came near him, the whole wood following after—he lay scattered over the Thracian fields, but his head floated down mournful Hebrus; he came to the familiar [4] Styx and Tartarus, never to return.

---

[1] The Symplegades.
[2] *i.e.* Aulis, long after this event, keeps the Greek fleet back from Troy, as if thus taking vengeance on that first fleet which robbed her of her king.
[3] Orpheus.
[4] Orpheus had visited the lower world once before.

Stravit Alcides Aquilone natos,
patre Neptuno genitum necavit
sumere innumeras solitum figuras;
ipse post terrae pelagique pacem,
post feri Ditis patefacta regna,
vivus ardenti recubans in Oeta
praebuit saevis sua membra flammis,   640
tabe consumptus gemini cruoris
    munere nuptae.

Stravit Ancaeum violentus ictu
saetiger; fratrem, Meleagre, matris
impius mactas morerisque dextra
matris iratae. meruere cuncti
morte quod crimen tener expiavit
Herculi magno puer inrepertus,
raptus, heu, tutas puer inter undas.
ite nunc, fortes, perarate pontum   650
    fonte timendo.

Idmonem, quamvis bene fata nosset,
condidit serpens Libycis harenis;
omnibus verax, sibi falsus uni,
concidit Mopsus caruitque Thebis.
ille si vere cecinit futura,
exul errabit Thetidis maritus.[1]
igne fallaci nociturus Argis
Nauplius praeceps cadet in profundum;
occidet proles,[2] patrioque pendet   660
    crimine poenas;

---

[1] *Leo deletes this line, but reads* erravit *with* ω. *Richter retains line and reads* errabit.
[2] *Leo supplies* occidet proles.

284

MEDEA

634 Alcides laid low the sons [1] of Aquilo, he slew Neptune's son [2] wont to take upon him countless shapes; but he himself, after establishing peace on land and sea, after opening up the kingdoms of savage Dis, laid him down, living, on burning Oeta, and gave his body to the devouring flames, consumed by the wasting of the double blood,[3] his wife's offering.

643 The bristling boar,[4] irresistible in his thrust, laid Ancaeus low; thou, Meleager, dost impiously slay thy mother's brother and diest by thine enraged mother's hand. All these deserved the charge [5] for which that tender boy,[6] sought vainly by mighty Hercules, atoned by death—the boy snatched away, alas, midst peaceful waters. Go now, ye brave, plough up the sea, whose streams ye ought to dread.

652 Idmon, though he well knew his fate, was slain [7] by a serpent on Libya's sands; true to all, but false to himself alone, Mopsus fell and saw not Thebes again. If he [8] told truth as to the future, Thetis' husband [9] shall in exile wander. Nauplius, while striving to wreck the Argives by false beacon fires, shall fall headlong into the deep; his son [10] shall perish and pay the penalty of his father's sin; [11] Oileus,[12]

---

[1] Zetes and Calaïs. [2] Periclymenus.
[3] i.e. the commingled blood of the hydra and of Nessus; see Index s.v. "Nessus." [4] The Calydonian boar.
[5] i.e. of violating the sea. [6] Hylas.
[7] He could foresee the fate of others, as of Peleus, but could not foresee and guard against his own.
[8] Mopsus. [9] Peleus. [10] Palamedes.
[11] i.e. of joining in the Argonautic expedition.
[12] Ajax; the father's name is put in place of the son's.

fulmine et ponto moriens Oileus ;
coniugis fatum redimens Pheraei
uxor, impendens animam marito.
ipse qui praedam spoliumque iussit
aureum prima revehi carina,
ustus accenso Pelias aeno
arsit angustas vagus inter undas.
iam satis, divi, mare vindicastis ;
     parcite iusso.

NVTRIX

Pavet animus, horret, magna pernicies adest.   670
immane quantum augescit et semet dolor
accendit ipse vimque praeteritam integrat.
vidi furentem saepe et aggressam deos,
caelum trahentem ; maius his, maius parat
Medea monstrum.   namque ut attonito gradu
evasit et penetrale funestum attigit,
totas opes effundit et quidquid diu
etiam ipsa timuit promit atque omnem explicat
turbam malorum, arcana secreta abdita,
et triste laeva comprecans[1] sacrum manu   680
pestes vocat quascumque ferventis creat
harena Libyae quasque perpetua nive
Taurus cohercet frigore Arctoo rigens,
et omne monstrum.   tracta magicis cantibus
squamifera latebris turba desertis adest.
hic saeva serpens corpus immensum trahit
trifidamque linguam exertat et quaerit quibus
mortifera veniat ; carmine audito stupet
tumidumque nodis corpus aggestis plicat
cogitque in orbes.   " parva sunt " inquit " mala 690

---

[1] *So Leo, with E:* complicans *A:* congregans *Richter:*
comparans *Buecheler:* comprimens *Koetschau.*

286

too, dying midst flame and flood; redeeming from
death her lord[1] of Pherae, the wife[2] shall perish,
giving up her life for her husband's sake. Pelias
himself, who bade the prize of the golden spoil be
brought away in the first ship, seething in boiling
pot, wandering midst waters close confined, perished
by fire. Enough now, ye gods, have ye avenged the
sea; spare him[3] who was ordered to the task.

NURSE [*alone*]

My spirit quakes with horror; some great disaster
is at hand. Monstrously grows her grief, feeds its
own fires and renews its former strength. Often
have I seen her in frenzy and assailing the gods,[4]
drawing down the sky; but greater than such deeds,
greater is the monstrous thing Medea is preparing.
For now that with maddened steps she has gone
out and come to her baleful shrine, she lavishes all
her stores and brings forth whatever e'en she herself long has dreaded, and marshals her whole train
of evil powers, things occult, mysterious, hidden;
and, supplicating the grim altar with her left hand,
she summons destructive agencies, whatever burning
Libya's sands produce, what Taurus, stiff with arctic
cold, holds fast in his everlasting snows, and all
monstrous things. Drawn by her magic incantations,
the scaly brood leave their lairs and come to her.
Here a savage serpent drags its huge length along,
darts out its forked tongue, and seeks against whom
it is to come death-dealing; hearing her incantation,
it stops in amaze, knots its swollen body into writhing
folds, and settles them into coils. "Petty are the
evils," she cries, "and cheap is the weapon which

---

[1] Admetus.   [2] Alcestis.   [3] Jason.
[4] *i.e.* the sun and moon.

et vile telum est, ima quod tellus creat;
caelo petam venena.   iam iam tempus est
aliquid movere fraude vulgari altius.
huc ille vasti more torrentis iacens
descendat anguis, cuius immensos duae,
maior minorque, sentiunt nodos ferae
(maior Pelasgis apta, Sidoniis minor)
pressasque tandem solvat Ophiuchus manus
virusque fundat; adsit ad cantus meos
lacessere ausus gemina Python numina.   700
et Hydra et omnis redeat Herculea manu
succisa serpens, caede se reparans sua.
tu quoque relictis pervigil Colchis ades,
sopite primum cantibus, serpens, meis."

Postquam evocavit omne serpentum genus,
congerit in unum frugis infaustae mala.
quaecumque generat invius saxis Eryx,
quae fert opertis hieme perpetua iugis
sparsus cruore Caucasus Promethei,
et quis sagittas divites Arabes linunt   711
pharetraque pugnax Medus aut Parthi leves,   710
aut quos sub axe frigido sucos legunt   712
lucis Suebae nobiles Hyrcaniis;
quodcumque tellus vere nidifico creat
aut rigida cum iam bruma discussit decus
nemorum et nivali cuncta constrinxit gelu,
quodcumque gramen flore mortifero viret,
quicumque tortis sucus in radicibus
causas nocendi gignit, attrectat manu.

288

deepest earth begets; from heaven will I seek my poisons. Now, now is the time to set in motion some plan deeper than common guile. Hither let that serpent [1] descend which lies like a vast rushing stream, whose huge folds the two beasts [2] feel, the greater and the less (the greater used [3] by Pelasgians; by Sidonians, the less); let Ophiuchus at length relax his choking grip and give the poison vent; in answer to my incantations let Python come, who dared to attack the twin divinities.[4] Let Hydra return and every serpent cut off by the hand of Hercules, restoring itself by its own destruction.[5] Thou, too, ever-watchful dragon,[6] quitting the Colchians, come thou to my aid, thou who through my incantations wast first lulled to slumber."

[705] When she had summoned forth the whole tribe of serpents, she assembled her evil store of baleful herbs. Whatever trackless Eryx produces on his rocky slopes; plants that grow on heights clothed in unbroken winter, the heights of Caucasus, spattered with Prometheus' gore; plants wherewith the rich Arabians smear their arrows, and the bold Mede, girt with his quiver, or the light-armed Parthians; or those juices which, under the cold pole, high-born Sueban women gather in Hyrcanian groves; whatever the earth produces in the nest-building springtime or when frozen winter has stripped the woods of their glory and bound all things with icy fetters; all plants that bloom with deadly flower, and all whose juices breed cause of death in their twisted

---

[1] The constellation Draco, winding between the two Bears.
[2] The Bears.
[3] *i.e.* as a fixed point in sailing.
[4] Apollo and Diana.   [5] See Index *s.v.* "Hydra."
[6] Which guarded the golden fleece.

Haemonius illas contulit pestes Athos,   720
has Pindus ingens, illa Pangaei iugis
teneram cruenta falce deposuit comam;
has aluit altum gurgitem Tigris premens,
Danuvius illas, has per arentes plagas
tepidis Hydaspes gemmifer currens aquis,
nomenque terris qui dedit Baetis suis
Hesperia pulsans maria languenti vado.
haec passa ferrum est, dum parat Phoebus diem;
illius alta nocte succisus frutex;
at huius ungue secta cantato seges.   730

Mortifera carpit gramina ac serpentium
saniem exprimit miscetque et obscenas aves
maestique cor bubonis et raucae strigis
exsecta vivae viscera.   haec scelerum artifex
discreta ponit; his rapax vis ignium,
his gelida pigri frigoris glacies inest.
addit venenis verba non illis minus
metuenda.—sonuit ecce vesano gradu
canitque.   mundus vocibus primis tremit.

MEDEA

Comprecor vulgus silentum vosque ferales deos 740
et Chaos caecum atque opacam Ditis umbrosi domum,
Tartari ripis ligatos squalidae Mortis specus.[1]
supplicis, animae, remissis currite ad thalamos novos:
rota resistat membra torquens, tangat Ixion humum,
Tantalus securus undas hauriat Pirenidas.   745

---

[1] *Peifer puts full stop after* domum, *and corrects* ligatae
squalido: *M* specu | supplicis . . .

roots—all these she handles. Haemonian Athos con-
tributed those baneful herbs, these, mighty Pindus;
on the ridges of Pangaeus that plant was lopped of
its tender foliage with a bloody sickle; these Tigris
fed, checking his deep flood the while; the Danube,
those; these, gem-studded Hydaspes, flowing with
warm waters through thirsty tracts, and the Baetis,
which gave its name to its own country,[1] pushing
into the western sea with languorous flood. These
plants felt the knife while Phoebus was making
ready the day; the shoot of that was clipped at mid-
night; while this was severed by finger-nail with
muttered charm.

[731] She seizes death-dealing herbs, squeezes out
serpents' venom, and with these mingles unclean
birds, the heart of a boding owl, and a hoarse screech-
owl's vitals cut out alive. Other objects the mistress
of evil arts lays out, arranged in separate heaps; in
some is the ravening power of fire; in others numb-
ing frost's icy cold. She adds to her poisons words,
no less fearsome than they.—But listen, her frenzied
step has sounded, and she chants her incantations
All nature shudders as she begins her song.

[*Enter* MEDEA, *singing an incantation.*]

MEDEA

I supplicate the throng of the silent, and you,
funereal gods, murky Chaos and shadowy Dis' dark
dwelling-place, the abysses of dismal Death, girt by
the banks of Tartarus. Leaving your punishments,
ye ghosts, haste to the new nuptials; let the wheel
stop that is whirling his body, and Ixion stand on
earth; let Tantalus in peace drink his fill of the

---

[1] Provincia Baetica, in Spain.

vos quoque, urnis quas foratis inritus ludit labor, 748
Danaides, coite : vestras hic dies quaerit manus. 749
gravior uni poena sedeat coniugis socero mei :   746
lubricus per saxa retro Sisyphum volvat lapis.[1]   747
    Nunc meis vocata sacris, noctium sidus, veni   750
pessimos induta vultus, fronte non una minax.

    Tibi more gentis vinculo solvens comam
secreta nudo nemora lustravi pede
et evocavi nubibus siccis aquas
egique ad imum maria, et Oceanus graves
interius undas aestibus victis dedit;
pariterque mundus lege confusa aetheris
et solem et astra vidit, et vetitum mare
tetigistis, ursae.   temporum flexi vices :
aestiva tellus floruit cantu meo,   760
coacta messem vidit hibernam Ceres ;
violenta Phasis vertit in fontem vada
et Hister, in tot ora divisus, truces
compressit undas omnibus ripis piger.
sonuere fluctus, tumuit insanum mare
tacente vento ; nemoris antiqui domus
amisit umbras, vocis imperio meae
die reducto ; Phoebus in medio stetit
Hyadesque nostris cantibus motae labant :
adesse sacris tempus est, Phoebe, tuis.   770

    [1] *The transposed order of ll. 746–749 is Bothe's : Richter
follows this : Leo, the traditional order.*

Pirenian spring. You, too, whom a fruitless toil mocks with urns full of holes, ye Danaids, come hither: this day needs your hands. On one alone, my lord's new father, let a penalty rest heavier—let the slippery stone roll Sisyphus [1] backward o'er the rocks.

750 Now, summoned by my sacred rites, do thou,[2] orb of the night, put on thy most evil face and come, threatening in all thy forms.[3]

752 For thee, loosing my hair from its bands after the manner of my people, with bare feet have I trod the secret groves and called forth rain from the dry clouds; I have driven the seas back to their lowest depths, and the Ocean, his tides outdone, has sent his crushing waves farther into the land; and in like manner, with heaven's law confounded, the world has seen both sun and stars together, and you, ye bears, have bathed in the forbidden sea.[4] The order of the seasons have I changed: the summer land has blossomed 'neath my magic song, and by my compelling Ceres has seen harvest in winter-time; Phasis has turned his swift waters backward to their source, and Hister, divided into many mouths, has checked his boisterous streams and flowed sluggishly in all his beds. The waves have roared, the mad sea swelled, though the winds were still; the heart of the ancient woods has lost its shadows, when the bright day has come back to them at commandment of my voice; Phoebus has halted in mid-heaven, and the Hyades, moved by my incantations, totter to their fall. The hour is at hand, O Phoebe, for thy sacred rites.

[*She offers various gifts to* HECATE.]

1 Sisyphus was father of Creon, and he alone is not to be relieved of his toil. This toil is even to be increased, and so bring greater anguish to Creon.
2 Hecate as the moon-goddess.
3 Hecate is *triformis, triceps.*   4 See Index *s.v.* " Bears."

Tibi haec cruenta serta texuntur manu,
  novena quae serpens ligat,
tibi haec Typhoeus membra quae discors tulit,
  qui regna concussit Iovis.
vectoris istic perfidi sanguis inest,
  quem Nessus expirans dedit.
Oetaeus isto cinere defecit rogus,
  qui virus Herculeum bibit.
piae sororis, impiae matris, facem
  ultricis Althaeae vides.   780
reliquit istas invio plumas specu
  Harpyia, dum Zeten fugit.
his adice pinnas sauciae Stymphalidos
  Lernaea passae spicula.
sonuistis, arae, tripodas agnosco meos
  favente commotos dea.

    Video Triviae currus agiles,
non quos pleno lucida vultu
pernox agitat, sed quos facie
lurida maesta, cum Thessalicis   790
vexata minis caelum freno
propiore legit. sic face tristem
pallida lucem funde per auras,
horrore novo terre populos
inque auxilium, Dictynna, tuum
pretiosa sonent aera Corinthi.
tibi sanguineo caespite sacrum
sollemne damus, tibi de medio
rapta sepulchro fax nocturnos
sustulit ignes, tibi mota caput   800
flexa voces cervice dedi,
tibi funereo de more iacens
passos cingit vitta capillos,

[771] To thee I offer these wreaths wrought with bloody hands, each entwined with nine serpent coils; to thee, these serpent limbs which rebellious Typhoeus wore, who caused Jove's throne to tremble. In this is the blood which Nessus, that traitor ferryman, bestowed as he expired. With these ashes the pyre on Oeta sank down which drank in the poisoned blood of Hercules. Here thou seest the billet [1] of a pious sister but impious mother, Althaea, the avenger. These feathers the Harpy left in her trackless lair when she fled from Zetes. Add to these the quills of the wounded Stymphalian bird which felt the darts of Lerna.[2]—You have given forth your voice, ye altars; I see my tripods shaken by the favouring deity.

[787] I see Trivia's swift gliding car, not as when, radiant, with full face, she drives the livelong night, but as when, ghastly, with mournful aspect, harried by Thessalian threats, she skirts with nearer rein the edge of heaven. So do thou wanly shed from thy torch a gloomy light through air; terrify the peoples with new dread, and let precious Corinthian bronzes resound, Dictynna, to thy aid.[3] To thee on the altar's bloody turf we perform thy solemn rites; to thee a torch caught up from the midst of a funeral pyre has illumed the night; to thee, tossing my head and with bended neck, I have uttered my magic words; for thee a fillet, lying in funeral fashion, binds my flowing locks; to thee is brandished the gloomy

---

[1] See Index *s.v.* "Althaea."

[2] *i.e.* the arrows of Hercules, poisoned with the gall of the Lernaean hydra.

[3] The moon in eclipse was supposed to be suffering under the spell of magic, which spell might be removed by beating on brazen vessels and by making other loud noises.

tibi iactatur tristis Stygia
ramus ab unda, tibi nudato
pectore maenas sacro feriam
bracchia cultro.   manet noster
sanguis ad aras ; assuesce, manus,
stringere ferrum carosque pati
posse cruores—sacrum laticem   810
percussa dedi.

    Quodsi nimium saepe vocari
quereris votis, ignosce precor ;
causa vocandi, Persei, tuos
saepius arcus una atque eadem est
semper, Iason.

    Tu nunc vestes tinge Creusae,
quas cum primum sumpserit, imas
urat serpens flamma medullas.
ignis fulvo clusus in auro   820
latet obscurus, quem mihi caeli
qui furta luit viscere feto
dedit et docuit condere vires
arte, Prometheus.   dedit et tenui
sulphure tectos Mulciber ignes,
et vivacis fulgura flammae
de cognato Phaethonte tuli.
habeo mediae dona Chimaerae,
habeo flammas usto tauri
gutture raptas, quas permixto   830
felle Medusae tacitum iussi
servare malum.

    Adde venenis stimulos, Hecate,
donisque meis semina flammae
condita serva.   fallant visus
tactusque ferant, meet in pectus

---

[1] Of the yew or cypress, trees naturally connected with
death and the world of death.
296

branch [1] from the Stygian stream; to thee with
bared breast will I as a maenad smite my arms with
the sacrificial knife. Let my blood flow upon the
altars; accustom thyself, my hand, to draw the sword
and endure the sight of beloved blood. [*She slashes
her arm and lets the blood flow upon the altar.*] Self-
smitten have I poured forth the sacred stream.

812 But if thou complainest that too often thou art
called on by my prayers, pardon, I pray; the cause,
O Perses' daughter,[2] of my too oft calling on thy
bows is one and the same ever, Jason.

817 Do thou now [*she takes a phial*] poison Creusa's
robe that, when she has donned it, the creeping
flame may consume her inmost marrow. Within
this tawny gold [*she takes a casket*] lurks fire, darkly
hid; Prometheus gave it me, even he who expiates
with ever-growing liver his theft from heaven, and
taught me by his art how to store up its powers.
Mulciber hath also given me fires which subtly lurk
in sulphur; and bolts of living flame I took from my
kinsman,[3] Phaëthon. I have gifts from Chimaera's
middle part,[4] I have flames caught from the bull's
scorched throat, which, well mixed with Medusa's
gall, I have bidden to guard their bane in silence.

833 Give sting to my poisons, Hecate, and in my gifts
keep hidden the seeds of fire. Let them cheat the
sight, let them endure the touch; let burning fire

---

[2] *i.e.* Hecate; the bow is typical of her aid in magic.
[3] Both Medea and Phaëthon were descended from Phoebus.
[4] *i.e.* the goat part, which vomited fire.

venasque calor, stillent artus
ossaque fument vincatque suas
flagrante coma nova nupta faces.
    Vota tenentur; ter latratus   840
audax Hecate dedit et sacros
edidit ignes face lucifera.

  Peracta vis est omnis; huc natos voca,
pretiosa per quos dona nubenti feras.
ite, ite, nati, matris infaustae genus,
placate vobis munere et multa prece
dominam ac novercam.   vadite et celeres domum
referte gressus, ultimo amplexu ut fruar.

CHORVS

    Quonam cruenta maenas
praeceps amore saevo   850
rapitur? quod impotenti
facinus parat furore?
vultus citatus ira
riget et caput feroci
quatiens superba motu
regi minatur ultro.
quis crèdat exulem?

    Flagrant genae rubentes,
pallor fugat ruborem,
nullum vagante forma   860
servat diu colorem.
huc fert pedes et illuc,
ut tigris orba natis
cursu furente lustrat
Gangeticum nemus.

penetrate to heart and veins; let her limbs melt and her bones consume in smoke, and with her blazing locks let the bride outshine her wedding torches.

⁸⁴⁰ My prayers are heard : thrice has bold Hecate bayed loud, and has raised her accursèd fire with its baleful light.

⁸⁴³ Now all my power is marshalled ; hither call my sons that by their hands thou mayst send these costly gifts unto the bride.

[MEDEA'S *sons are brought in.*]

Go, go, my sons, born of an ill-starred mother, win to yourselves by means of gifts and much beseeching your mistress and stepmother. Begone and quickly come you home again, that I may enjoy one last embrace.

[*Exeunt sons towards the palace ;* MEDEA *in the opposite direction.*]

CHORUS

Whither is this blood-stained maenad borne headlong by mad passion ? What crime with reckless fury is she preparing ? Her distraught face is hard set in anger, and with fierce tossings of her head she haughtily threatens e'en the king. Who would think her an exile ?

⁸⁵⁸ Her cheeks blaze red, pallor puts red to flight; no colour in her changing aspect does she keep long. Hither and thither she wanders, as a tigress, robbed of her cubs, ranges in mad course through the jungles of Ganges.

Frenare nescit iras
Medea, non amores ;
nunc ira amorque causam
iunxere ; quid sequetur ?
quando efferet Pelasgis   870
nefanda Colchis arvis
gressum metuque solvet
regnum simulque reges ?
nunc, Phoebe, mitte currus
nullo morante loro,
nox condat alma lucem,
mergat diem timendum
dux noctis Hesperus.

NVNTIVS

Periere cuncta ! concidit regni status !
nata atque genitor cinere permixto iacent.   880

CHORVS

Qua fraude capti ?

NVNTIVS

          Qua solent reges capi—

donis.

CHORVS

In illis esse quis potuit dolus ?

NVNTIVS

Et ipse miror vixque iam facto malo
potuisse fieri credo.   quis cladis modus ?
avidus per omnem regiae partem furit
ut iussus ignis ; iam domus tota occidit,
urbi timetur.

300

MEDEA

⁸⁶⁶ How to curb her anger Medea knows not, nor yet her love; now that anger and love have joined cause, what will the outcome be? When will the wicked Colchian be gone from the Pelasgian borders and free from terror at once our kingdom and our kings? Now, O Phoebus, speed thy chariot with no check of rein; let friendly darkness veil the light, and let Hesperus, vanguard of the night, plunge deep this fearful day.

[*Enter* MESSENGER, *running from the direction of the palace.*]

MESSENGER

All is lost! The kingdom's props have fallen Daughter and father in commingled ashes lie.

CHORUS

By what snare taken?

MESSENGER

By the common snare of kings—by gifts.

CHORUS

What snare could have been in them?

MESSENGER

Myself, I also marvel, and, though the woeful thing is done, can scarce believe it could be done. What stay is there to ruin? The greedy fire rages through the palace's every part as if 'twere bidden so. Already the whole house has fallen, the city is in peril.

SENECAE TRAGOEDIAE

CHORVS

Vnda flammas opprimat.

NVNTIVS

Et hoc in ista clade mirandum accidit:
alit unda flammas, quoque prohibetur magis,
magis ardet ignis; ipsa praesidia occupat.   890

NVTRIX

Effer citatum sede Pelopea gradum,
Medea, praeceps quaslibet terras pete.

MEDEA

Egone ut recedam? si profugissem prius,
ad hoc redirem. nuptias specto novas.
quid, anime, cessas? sequere felicem impetum.
pars ultionis ista, qua gaudes, quota est?
amas adhuc, furiose, si satis est tibi
caelebs Iason. quaere poenarum genus
haut usitatum iamque sic temet para:
fas omne cedat, abeat expulsus pudor;   900
vindicta levis est quam ferunt purae manus.
incumbe in iras teque languentem excita
penitusque veteres pectore ex imo impetus
violentus hauri. quidquid admissum est adhuc,
pietas vocetur. hoc age et faxis sciant
quam levia fuerint quamque vulgaris notae

MEDEA

Let water put out the flames.

Nay, in this disaster this marvel, too, has happened :
water feeds the flames, and the more 'tis checked,
the more fiercely burns the fire ; the very defences [1]
does it seize upon.

[*Enter* MEDEA, *in time to hear the last words.*]

Quickly begone, Medea, from the land of Pelops;
seek headlong any land thou wilt !

What I—shall I give ground ? Nay, had I fled
already, for this I should return. Strange nuptials
see I here.

[*She becomes absorbed in her own thoughts.*]

Why, soul, dost falter ? Follow up the attack so
well begun. How small a part of thy vengeance
is that in which thou art rejoicing ! Thou dost love
him still, mad one, if 'tis enough for thee that Jason
wifeless be. Seek thou some unaccustomed form
of chastisement, and now thus prepare thyself : let
all right give way ; let honour begone, defeated; light
is the rod which innocent hands uplift. Bend to
thine anger, rouse up thy halting purpose, and with
all thy strength drain from thy heart's very depths
its old-time violence. Let all that has yet been done
be called but piety. To the task ; let them know
how petty, of what common stamp, were the crimes

---

[1] Water, the natural defence against fire.

quae commodavi scelera.   prolusit dolor
per ista noster ; quid manus poterant rudes
audere magnum ?   quid puellaris furor ?
Medea nunc sum ; crevit ingenium malis.   910

   Iuvat, iuvat rapuisse fraternum caput ;
artus iuvat secuisse et arcano patrem
spoliasse sacro, iuvat in exitium senis
armasse natas.   quaere materiam, dolor ;
ad omne facinus non rudem dextram afferes.

   Quo te igitur, ira, mittis, aut quae perfido
intendis hosti tela ?   nescio quid ferox
decrevit animus intus et nondum sibi
audet fateri.   stulta properavi nimis—
ex paelice utinam liberos hostis meus   920
aliquos haberet ! quidquid ex illo tuum est,
Creusa peperit.   placuit hoc poenae genus,
meritoque placuit ; ultimum, agnosco, scelus
animo parandum est.   liberi quondam mei,
vos pro paternis sceleribus poenas date.

   Cor pepulit horror, membra torpescunt gelu
pectusque tremuit.   ira discessit loco
materque tota coniuge expulsa redit.
egone ut meorum liberum ac prolis meae
fundam cruorem ?   melius, a, demens furor !   930
incognitum istud facinus ac dirum nefas
a me quoque absit ; quod scelus miseri luent ?
scelus est Iason genitor et maius scelus
Medea mater.   occidant, non sunt mei ;
pereant—mei sunt.   crimine et culpa carent,

304

I wrought to serve him. In them my grief was but practising; what great deed had prentice hands the power to do? What, a girl's rage? Now I am Medea; my wit has grown through suffering.

911 Glad am I, glad, that I tore off my brother's head, glad that I carved his limbs, that I robbed my father of his guarded treasure,[1] glad that I armed daughters[2] for an old man's death. Seek thou fresh fields, my grief; no untrained hand wilt thou bring to any crime.

916 Whither, then, wrath, art tending, or what weapons art thou aiming at the forsworn foe?[3] A dark purpose my fierce spirit hath resolved within me, and dares not yet acknowledge to itself. Fool! fool! I have gone too fast—would that mine enemy had children by his paramour! [*She pauses and then addresses herself.*] All offspring that thou hast by him are Creusa's brood. Resolved is this way of vengeance, rightly resolved; for a last deed of guilt, I see it now, must my soul make ready. Children that once were mine, do you pay penalty for your father's crimes.

926 Horror has smit my heart! My limbs are numb with cold and my heart with terror flutters. Wrath has given place; the mother has all come back, the wife is banished. Can I shed my children's, my own offspring's blood? Ah, mad rage, say not so! Far, even from me, be that unheard-of deed, that accursed guilt! What sin will the poor boys atone? Their sin is that Jason is their father, and, greater sin, that Medea is their mother. [*She pauses.*] Let them die, they are none of mine; let them be lost—they are my own. They are without crime and guilt, yea, they are

---

[1] The golden fleece.   [2] *i.e.* of Pelias.   [3] Jason.

305

sunt innocentes—fateor, et frater fuit.
quid, anime, titubas ? ora quid lacrimae rigant
variamque nunc huc ira, nunc illuc amor
diducit ? anceps aestus incertam rapit ;
ut saeva rapidi bella cum venti gerunt   940
utrimque fluctus maria discordes agunt
dubiumque fervet pelagus, haut aliter meum
cor fluctuatur. ira pietatem fugat
iramque pietas. cede pietati, dolor.

  Huc, cara proles, unicum afflictae domus
solamen, huc vos ferte et infusos mihi
coniungite artus. habeat incolumes pater,
dum et mater habeat. urguet exilium ac fuga.
iam iam meo rapientur avulsi e sinu,
flentes, gementes osculis. pereant patri,   950
periere matri. rursus increscit dolor
et fervet odium, repetit invitam manum
antiqua Erinys. ira, qua ducis, sequor.
utinam superbae turba Tantalidos meo
exisset utero bisque septenos parens
natos tulissem ! sterilis in poenas fui—
fratri patrique quod sat est, peperi duos.

  Quonam ista tendit turba Furiarum impotens ?
quem quaerit aut quo flammeos ictus parat,
aut cui cruentas agmen infernum faces   960
intentat ? ingens anguis excusso sonat
tortus flagello. quem trabe infesta petit
Megaera ? cuius umbra dispersis venit
incerta membris ? frater est, poenas petit.
306

innocent—I acknowledge it ; so, too, was my brother.
Why, soul, dost hesitate ? Why are my cheeks
wet with tears ? Why do anger and love now
hither, now thither draw my changeful heart ? A
double tide tosses me, uncertain of my course ; as
when rushing winds wage mad warfare, and from
both sides conflicting floods lash the seas and the
fluctuating waters boil, even so is my heart tossed.
Anger puts love to flight, and love, anger. O wrath,
yield thee to love.

945 Hither, dear children, sole comfort of my fallen
house, come hither and link your entwining limbs
with mine. Let your father have you unharmed, so
but your mother may have you too. But exile and
flight press hard upon me ; now, now will they be
torn from my bosom and carried away from me,
midst tears and sighs and kisses.—Let them be
lost to their father ; they are lost to me. My
grief grows again and my hate burns hot ; Erinys,
as of old, claims my unwilling hand. O wrath,
where thou dost lead I follow. I would that from my
womb the throng of proud Niobe had sprung, and
that I had been the mother of twice seven sons !
Too barren have I been for vengeance—yet for my
brother and my father there is enough, for I have
borne two sons.

958 Whither hastes that headlong horde of Furies ?
Whom seek they ? Against whom are they preparing
their flaming blows ? Whom does the hellish host
threaten with its bloody brands ? A huge snake
hisses, whirled with the writhing lash. Whom does
Megaera seek with her deadly torch ? Whose shade
comes there dimly seen, its limbs all scattered ? It
is my brother, and 'tis punishment he seeks. We'll
pay, yes, all the debt. Plunge your brands into

dabimus, sed omnes. fige luminibus faces,
lania, perure, pectus en Furiis patet.

Discedere a me, frater, ultrices deas
manesque ad imos ire securas iube ;
mihi me relinque et utere hac, frater, manu
quae strinxit ensem—victima manes tuos 970
placamus ista.— quid repens affert sonus ?
parantur arma meque in exitium petunt.
excelsa nostrae tecta conscendam domus
caede incohata. perge tu mecum comes.
tuum quoque ipsa corpus hinc mecum aveham.
nunc hoc age, anime ; non in occulto tibi est
perdenda virtus ; approba populo manum.

IASON

Quicumque regum cladibus fidus doles,
concurre, ut ipsam sceleris auctorem horridi
capiamus. huc, huc fortis armiferi cohors 980
conferte tela, vertite ex imo domum.

MEDEA

Iam iam recepi sceptra germanum patrem,
spoliumque Colchi pecudis auratae tenent ;
rediere regna, rapta virginitas redit.
o placida tandem numina, o festum diem,
o nuptialem ! vade, perfectum est scelus ;
308

my eyes, tear, burn; see, my breast is open to
the Furies.

⁹⁶⁷ O brother, bid the avenging goddesses depart
from me, and go in peace to the deep-buried ghosts;
to myself leave me and use this hand, brother,
which has drawn the sword— [*She slays the first son.*]
With this victim I appease thy ghost.—What means
that sudden noise? 'Tis arms they are making
ready, and they seek me for my slaying. To the
lofty roof of our palace will I mount, now the bloody
work hath been begun. [*To her remaining son.*] Do
thou come with me. [*To her dead son.*] Thy corpse
also will I take hence with me. Now to the task,
O soul; not in secrecy must thy great deed be lost;
to the people approve thy handiwork.

[*Exit* MEDEA, *carrying the body of her dead son and
leading the living. Enter* JASON *in the street below
shouting to the citizens.*]

JASON

Ye faithful souls, who mourn your princes' doom,
rally to me that we may take the author herself
of this dread crime. Here, here, my brave band
of warriors, bring weapons, raze this house to the
very ground.

MEDEA

[*Appearing on the house-top.*]

Now, now have I regained my regal state, my
brother, my sire; and the Colchians have once more
the spoil of the golden fleece; restored is my kingdom, my ravished virginity is restored. Oh, divinities,
at last propitious, oh, festal day, oh, nuptial day! On!
the crime is accomplished; but vengeance is not yet

309

vindicta nondum; perage, dum faciunt manus.
quid nunc moraris, anime? quid dubitas potens?
iam cecidit ira.   paenitet facti, pudet.
quid, misera, feci? misera?   paeniteat licet,   990
feci.   voluptas magna me invitam subit,
et ecce crescit.   derat hoc unum mihi,
spectator iste.   nil adhuc facti reor;
quidquid sine isto fecimus sceleris perit.

IASON

En ipsa tecti parte praecipiti imminet.
huc rapiat ignes aliquis, ut flammis cadat
suis perusta.

MEDEA

Congere extremum tuis
natis, Iason, funus, ac tumulum strue;
coniunx socerque iusta iam functis habent,
a me sepulti; natus hic fatum tulit,   1000
hic te vidente dabitur exitio pari.

IASON

Per numen omne perque communes fugas
torosque, quos non nostra violavit fides,
iam parce nato.   si quod est crimen, meum est;
me dedo morti; noxium macta caput.

MEDEA

Hac qua recusas, qua doles, ferrum exigam.
i nunc, superbe, virginum thalamos pete,
relinque matres.
310

complete ; be done with it while thy hands are still about it. Why dost thou delay now, O soul ? Why hesitate, though thou canst do it ? Now has my wrath died within me. I am sorry for my act, ashamed. What, wretched woman, have I done ?—wretched, say I ? Though I repent, yet have I done it ! Great joy steals on me 'gainst my will, and lo, it is increasing. [*She catches sight of* JASON *in the crowd below.*] This one thing I lacked, that yon man should behold. Naught have I done as yet ; whatever crime I've done is lost unless he see it.

JASON [*discovering her*]

See, there she is herself, leaning over the sheer battlement ! Someone bring fire that she may fall consumed by her own flames.

MEDEA

Nay, Jason, heap up for thy sons their last funeral pyre ; build them a tomb. Thy wife and father have already the services due the dead, buried by me ; this son has met his doom, and this shall suffer like fate before thy eyes.

JASON

By all the gods, by our flight together, by our marriage couch, to which I have not been faithless, spare the boy. If there is any guilt, 'tis mine. I give myself up to death ; destroy my guilty head.

MEDEA

Here[1] where thou dost forbid it, where it will grieve thee, will I plunge the sword. Go now, haughty man, take thee maids for wives, abandon mothers.

---

[1] In the body of the living son.

SENECAE TRAGOEDIAE

IASON
Vnus est poenae satis

MEDEA
Si posset una caede satiari haec manus,
nullam petisset. ut duos perimam, tamen   1010
nimium est dolori numerus angustus meo.
in matre si quod pignus etiamnunc latet,
scrutabor ense viscera et ferro extraham.[1]

IASON
Iam perage coeptum facinus—haut ultra precor,
moramque saltem supplicis dona meis.

MEDEA
Perfruere lento scelere, ne propera, dolor:
meus dies est; tempore accepto utimur.

IASON
Infesta, memet perime.

MEDEA
                     Misereri iubes—
bene est, peractum est. plura non habui, dolor,
quae tibi litarem. lumina huc tumida alleva,   1020
ingrate Iason. coniugem agnoscis tuam?
sic fugere soleo. patuit in caelum via:
squamosa gemini colla serpentes iugo

---

[1] *Leo deletes these two lines.*

312

MEDEA

One is enough for punishment.

If this hand could be satisfied with the death of one, it would have sought no death at all. Though I slay two, still is the count too small to appease my grief. If in my womb there still lurk any pledge of thee, I'll search my very vitals with the sword and hale it forth.

Now end what thou hast begun—I make no more entreaty—and at least spare[1] my sufferings this suspense.

Enjoy a slow revenge, hasten not, my grief; mine is the day; we are but using the allotted[2] time.

O heartless one, slay me.

Thou biddst me pity— [*She slays the second son.*] 'Tis well, 'tis done. I had no more atonement to offer thee, O grief. Lift thy tear-swollen eyes hither, ungrateful Jason. Dost recognize thy wife? 'Tis thus[3] I am wont to flee. A way through the air has opened for me; two serpents offer their scaly

[1] Translating *dona* in the sense of *remitte.*
[2] *i.e.* Creon had granted Medea this whole day for her own in Corinth.
[3] By means of a dragon-drawn car which now appears in the air.

summissa praebent.   recipe iam natos, parens;
ego inter auras aliti curru vehar.

IASON

Per alta vade spatia sublimi aethere;
testare nullos esse, qua veheris, deos.

necks bending to the yoke. Now, father, take back thy sons. [*She throws the bodies down to him.*] I through the air on my winged car shall ride.

[*She mounts the car and is borne away.*]

JASON [*calling after her*]

Go on through the lofty spaces of high heaven and bear witness, where thou ridest, that there are no gods.

HIPPOLYTUS,

OR

PHAEDRA

DRAMATIS PERSONAE

HIPPOLYTUS, *son of Theseus and Antiope, an Amazon.*

PHAEDRA, *wife of Theseus and stepmother of Hippolytus.*

THESEUS, *king of Athens.*

NURSE *of Phaedra.*

MESSENGER

SLAVES AND ATTENDANTS.

CHORUS *of Athenian citizens.*

THE SCENE is laid throughout in the court in front of the royal palace at Athens, and the action is confined to the space of one day.

ARGUMENT

THESEUS had wed Antiope, the Amazon, and of their union had been born Hippolytus. This youth grew up to love the chase, austere and beautiful, shunning the haunts of men and scorning the love of women. Theseus had meanwhile slain Antiope, and married Phaedra, Cretan Minos' child.

And now, for four years past, the king has not been seen upon the earth, for, following the mad adventure of his bosom friend, Pirithoüs, he has descended into Tartarus to help him steal away its queen, and thence, men think, he never will return.

Deserted by her lord, the hapless Phaedra has conceived a hopeless passion for Hippolytus; for Venus, mindful of her old amour with Mars, which Phaedra's ancestor, Apollo, had exposed, has sent this madness on her, even as Pasiphaë, her mother, had been cursed with a most mad and fatal malady.

HIPPOLYTVS, or PHAEDRA

Ite, umbrosas cingite silvas
summaque montis iuga, Cecropii!
celeri planta lustrate vagi
quae saxosae loca Parnetho
subiecta iacent, quae Thriasiis
vallibus amnis rapida currens
verberat unda, scandite colles
semper canos nive Rhipaea;
hac, hac alii qua nemus alta
texitur alno, qua prata iacent   10
quae rorifera mulcens aura
Zephyrus vernas evocat herbas,
ubi per graciles levis Ilisos [1]   13
labitur agros piger et steriles   15
amne maligno radit harenas.

Vos qua Marathon tramite laevo
saltus aperit, qua comitatae
gregibus parvis nocturna petunt
pabula fetae; vos qua tepidis   20
subditus austris frigora mollit
durus Acharneus.

Alius rupem dulcis Hymetti,
parvas alius calcet Aphidnas;
pars illa diu vacat immunis,

---

[1] *Leo deletes l. 14:* ubi Maeander super inaequales.

320

HIPPOLYTUS, or PHAEDRA

HIPPOLYTUS

*[In the early morning, in the palace court at **Athens**.
Enter* HIPPOLYTUS *with a large company of huntsmen armed with the various weapons of the hunt,
and leading numerous dogs in leash.* HIPPOLYTUS
*proceeds to assign the various tasks of the day to his
followers.]*

Go, girdle the shadowy woods and the topmost
ridges of the mount, ye sons of Cecrops! With nimble
feet wide wandering, scour the coverts that lie 'neath
rocky Parnes and in the vale of Thria, whose swift-
flowing stream lashes its banks; climb the hills ever
white with Rhipean snow. Here, here let others
lie, where the tall alder-thickets fringe the grove,
where meadows lie which Zephyr soothes with his
dew-laden breath and calls forth the herbage of the
spring, where scant Ilissos flows sluggishly along
through meagre fields, and with ungenerous stream
creeps o'er unfruitful sands.

[17] Go ye by the left path where Marathon opens out
her forest glades, where with their small following
the suckling mothers seek nightly forage; and ye,
where rugged Acharneus tempers his frosts beneath
the warm south-wind.

[23] Let one tread sweet Hymettus' cliff, another,
small Aphidnae; too long unharried is that spot

321

qua curvati litora ponti
Sunion urget.   si quem tangit
gloria silvae, vocat hunc Phlye [1]
hic versatur, metus agricolis,
vulnere multo iam notus aper.   30

At vos laxas canibus tacitis
mittite habenas; teneant acres
lora Molossos et pugnaces
tendant Cretes fortia trito
vincula collo.
at Spartanos (genus est audax
avidumque ferae) nodo cautus
propiore liga.   veniet tempus,
cum latratu cava saxa sonent;
nunc demissi nare sagaci
captent auras lustraque presso   40
quaerant rostro, dum lux dubia est,
dum signa pedum roscida tellus
impressa tenet.

A ius raras cervice gravi
portare plagas, alius teretes
properet laqueos.   picta rubenti
linea pinna vano cludat
terrore feras.
tibi vibretur missile telum,
tu grave dextra laevaque simul
robur lato dirige ferro,   50
tu praecipites clamore feras
subsessor ages; tu iam victor
curvo solves viscera cultro.

Ades en comiti, diva virago,
cuius regno pars terrarum
secreta vacat, cuius certis
petitur telis fera quae gelidum
                    [1] So Leo: Flius MSS.

where Sunium thrusts out the shores of the curving
sea. If any feels the lure of the forest, Phlye calls
for him; there is the haunt of the boar, terror of
husbandmen, famed by now for many a wound.

[31] But do you cast off the leashes from the dogs
that hunt in silence; still let thongs hold the keen
Molossians fast, and let the savage Cretans tug on
the stout bonds with well-worn necks. But the
Spartans (for their breed is bold and eager for the
prey) hold in carefully with a tighter knot. The
time will come when the hollow rocks will re-echo
with their bayings; now, with heads low-hung, let
them snuff the air with keen nostrils, and with
muzzles to earth quest through the forest haunts,
while the light is still dim, while the dewy ground
still retains the well-marked trail.

[44] Let some of you make speed to load your necks
with the heavy, wide-meshed nets, and others with
the smooth-wrought snares. Let a line decked out
with crimson feathers hedge the deer with empty
terror. Thou shalt brandish the dart, thou with right
and left hand together hurl the heavy oak-shaft with
broad iron head; do thou lie in hiding and with
shouts drive the game on in headlong rush; and thou,
when victory is won, shalt free flesh from hide with
thy curved hunting-knife.

[54] And do thou be with thy follower, O manlike
goddess,[1] for whose sovereignty earth's secret places
are reserved, whose darts with unerring aim seek

[1] Diana.

potat Araxen et quae stanti
ludit in Histro.   tua Gaetulos
dextra leones, tua Cretaeas   60
sequitur cervas; nunc veloces
figis dammas leviore manu.
tibi dant variae pectora tigres,
tibi villosi terga bisontes
latisque feri cornibus uri.
quidquid solis pascitur arvis,
sive illud Arabs divite silva
sive illud inops novit Garamans   68
vacuisque vagus Sarmata campis,[1]   71
sive ferocis iuga Pyrenes   69
sive Hyrcani celant saltus,   70
arcus metuit, Diana, tuos.   72
tua si gratus numina cultor
tulit in saltus, retia vinctas
tenuere feras, nulli laqueum
rupere pedes; fertur plaustro
praeda gementi ; tum rostra canes
sanguine multo rubicunda gerunt
repetitque casas rustica longo
turba triumpho.   80
   En, diva, faves : signum arguti
misere canes.   vocor in silvas.
hac, hac pergam qua via longum
compensat iter.

PHAEDRA

O magna vasti Creta dominatrix freti,
cuius per omne litus innumerae rates
tenuere pontum,[2] quidquid Assyria tenus
tellure Nereus pervius rostris secat,

---

[1] *Leo transposes l. 71 to follow l. 68.*
[2] *Leo conjectures* portus.

out the prey which drinks of the cool Araxes or sports on Ister's frozen streams. Thy hand aims at Gaetulian lions, thine at Cretan deer; and now with lighter stroke dost thou pierce swift-fleeing does. The striped tigers face thee, but the shaggy-backed bisons flee, and the wild ox with wide-spreading horns. All things that feed in the lonely fields, whether the Arabian knows them in his rich forests, or the needy Garamantian and the wandering Sarmatian on his desert plains, whatever the heights of the rough Pyrenees or the Hyrcanian glades conceal, all fear thy bow, Diana. If, his offerings paid, thy worshipper takes thy favour with him to the glades, his nets hold the tangled prey, no feet break through his snares; his game is brought in on groaning wains, his hounds have their muzzles red with blood, and all the rustic throng come home in long triumphant line.

[81] Lo, goddess, thou dost hear me: the shrill-tongued hounds have given the sign. I am summoned to the woods. Here, here I'll hasten by the shortest way. [*Exeunt.*

[*Enter* PHAEDRA *from the palace.*]

PHAEDRA

O mighty Crete, the vast sea's mistress, whose countless vessels along every coast have held the deep, yea, whatever lands, e'en to Assyria, making

cur me in penates obsidem invisos datam
hostique nuptam degere aetatem in malis   90
lacrimisque cogis ? profugus en coniunx abest
praestatque nuptae quam solet Theseus fidem.
fortis per altas invii retro lacus
vadit tenebras miles audacis proci,
solio ut revulsam regis inferni abstrahat;
pergit furoris socius, haud illum timor
pudorque tenuit—stupra et illicitos toros
Acheronte in imo quaerit Hippolyti pater.

Sed maior alius incubat maestae dolor.
non me quies nocturna, non altus sopor   100
solvere curis.   alitur et crescit malum
et ardet intus qualis Aetnaeo vapor
exundat antro.   Palladis telae vacant
et inter ipsas pensa labuntur manus;
non colere donis templa votivis libet,
non inter aras, Atthidum mixtam choris,
iactare tacitis conscias sacris faces,
nec adire castis precibus aut ritu pio
adiudicatae praesidem terrae deam:
iuvat excitatas consequi cursu feras   110
et rigida molli gaesa iaculari manu.

Quo tendis, anime ?   quid furens saltus amas ?
fatale miserae matris agnosco malum ;
peccare noster novit in silvis amor.
genetrix, tui me miseret; infando malo

a path for the prows of ships, old Nereus cleaves—
why dost thou force me here, given o'er to an
enemy's house as hostage, wife to my foe, to spend
my days in wretchedness and weeping? Behold, fled
is my lord afar and keeps his bridal oath as is the wont
of Theseus. Through the deep shades of the pool
which none recrosses is he faring, this brave recruit of
a madcap suitor,[1] that from the very throne of the
infernal king he may rob and bear away his wife.
He hurries on, a partner in mad folly; him nor fear
nor shame held back. And there in the depths of
Acheron he seeks adultery and an unlawful bed,
this father of Hippolytus.[2]

[99] But another, greater smart burdens my woeful
breast. No rest by night, no deep slumber frees
me from care. A malady feeds and grows within my
heart, and it burns there hot as the steam that wells
from Aetna's caverns. Pallas' loom stands idle and
my task slips from my listless hands; no longer it
pleases me to deck the temples with votive offerings, nor at the altars, midst bands of Athenian
dames, to wave torches in witness of the silent rites,
nor with pure prayers and pious worship to approach
the goddess[3] who guards the land once granted to
her! My joy is to follow in pursuit of the startled
beasts and with soft hand to hurl stiff javelins.

[112] Whither, my soul, art tending? Why this mad
love of forest glades? I recognize my wretched
mother's fatal curse;[4] her love and mine know how
to sin in forest depths. Mother, my heart aches for

[1] Pirithoüs.
[2] From being merely the assistant of another in an unlawful deed, Theseus is here conceived as the principal in it.
[3] Pallas, patroness of Athens by the assignment of the
gods.
[4] See Index *s.v.* "Pasiphaë."

correpta pecoris efferum saevi ducem
audax amasti; torvus, impatiens iugi
adulter ille, ductor indomiti gregis—
sed amabat aliquid.   quis meas miserae deus
aut quis iuvare Daedalus flammas queat?   120
non si ipse remeet, arte Mopsopia potens
qui nostra caeca monstra conclusit domo,
promittat ullam casibus nostris opem.
stirpem perosa Solis invisi Venus
per nos catenas vindicat Martis sui
suasque, probris omne Phoebeum genus
onerat nefandis.   nulla Minois levi
defuncta amore est, iungitur semper nefas.

NVTRIX

Thesea coniunx, clara progenies Iovis,
nefanda casto pectore exturba ocius,   130
extingue flammas neve te dirae spei
praebe obsequentem.   quisquis in primo obstitit
pepulitque amorem, tutus ac victor fuit;
qui blandiendo dulce nutrivit malum,
sero recusat ferre quod subiit iugum.

Nec me fugit, quam durus et veri insolens
ad recta flecti regius nolit tumor.
quemcumque dederit exitum casus feram;
fortem facit vicina libertas senem.

Honesta primum est velle nec labi via,   140
pudor est secundus nosse peccandi modum.
quo, misera, pergis?   quid domum infamem aggravas
superasque matrem?   maius est monstro nefas;
328

thee; swept away by ill unspeakable, thou didst
boldly love the wild leader of the savage herd.
Fierce was he and impatient of the yoke, lawless in
love, leader of an untamed herd; yet he did love
something. But as for me, what god, what Daedalus
could ease my wretched passion? Though he himself [1] should return, mighty in Attic cunning, who
shut our monster in the dark labyrinth, he could
afford no help to my calamity. Venus, detesting the
offspring of the hated Sun, is avenging through us
the chains [2] that bound her to her loved Mars, and
loads the whole race of Phoebus with shame unspeakable. No daughter of Minos' house hath found
love's bondage light; ever 'tis linked with guilt.

NURSE

O wife of Theseus, illustrious child of Jove, quickly
drive guilty thoughts from thy pure breast, put
out these fires, nor show thyself obedient to this
dread hope of love. Whoever at the outset has re-
sisted and routed love, has been safe and conqueror;
but whoso by dalliance has fed the sweet torment,
too late refuses to bear the accepted yoke.

[136] I know how the stubborn pride of princes, ill
brooking truth, refuses to be bent to righteousness;
but whatever outcome fate shall give I am ready to
endure; freedom near at hand makes the aged brave.

[140] Best is the upright purpose and the unswerving
path; next is the shame, that knows some measure
in transgressing. To what end art thou hasting,
wretched woman? Why heap fresh infamy upon
thy house and outsin thy mother? Impious sin is

---

[1] Daedalus.
[2] See Index *s.v.* " Mars " and " Venus."

nam monstra fato, moribus scelera imputes.
si, quod maritus supera non cernit loca,
tutum esse facinus credis et vacuum metu,
erras; teneri crede Lethaeo abditum
Thesea profundo et ferre perpetuam Styga;
quid ille, lato maria qui regno premit
populisque reddit iura centenis, pater?   150
latere tantum facinus occultum sinet?
sagax parentum est cura.   credamus tamen
astu doloque tegere nos tantum nefas;
quid ille rebus lumen infundens suum
matris parens?   quid ille qui mundum quatit
vibrans corusca fulmen Aetnaeum manu,
sator deorum?   credis hoc posse effici,
inter videntes omnia ut lateas avos?

Sed ut secundus numinum abscondat favor
coitus nefandos utque contingat stupro   160
negata magnis sceleribus semper fides;
quid poena praesens conscius mentis pavor
animusque culpa plenus et semet timens?
scelus aliqua tutum, nulla securum tulit.
compesce amoris impii flammas, precor,
nefasque quod non ulla tellus barbara
commisit umquam, non vagi campis Getae
nec inhospitalis Taurus aut sparsus Scythes;
expelle facinus mente castifica horridum
memorque matris metue concubitus novos.   170
miscere thalamos patris et nati apparas
uteroque prolem capere confusam impio?
330

worse than monstrous passion; for monstrous love
thou mayst impute to fate, but crime, to character.
If, because thy husband sees not the realms of earth,
thou dost believe thy guilt safe and devoid of fear,
thou errest. Suppose that Theseus is indeed held
fast, hidden away in Lethean depths, and must suffer
the Styx eternally; what of him, thy father, who
holds the seas under his wide dominion and gives
laws to a hundred [1] peoples? Will he permit so great
a crime to lie concealed? Shrewd is the care of
fathers. Yet suppose that by craft and guile we do
hide this great wickedness from him; what of him
who sheds his light on all things, thy mother's
sire? [2] What of him who makes the heavens rock,
brandishing Aetnean bolts in his glittering hand,
the father of the gods? Dost believe thou canst
so sin as to escape the all-seeing eyes of both thy
grandsires?

[159] But grant that heaven's kindly grace conceals
this impious intercourse; grant that to incest be shown
the loyalty which great crimes never find; what
of the ever-present penalty, the soul's conscious
dread, and the heart filled with crime and fearful
of itself? Some women have sinned with safety,
but none with peace of soul. Then quench the fires
of impious love, I pray, and shun a deed which no
barbaric land has ever done, neither the Getae,
wandering on their plains, nor the inhospitable
Taurians, nor scattered Scythians. Drive this hideous
purpose from thy chaste mind, and, remembering
thy mother, shun strange matings. Dost purpose
to share thy bed with father and with son, and
receive in an incestuous womb a blended progeny?

[1] The "hundred cities" of Crete.
[2] The Sun.

perge et nefandis verte naturam ignibus—
cur monstra cessant? aula cur fratris vacat?
prodigia totiens orbis insueta audiet,
natura totiens legibus cedet suis,
quotiens amabit Cressa?

PHAEDRA

               Quae memoras scio
vera esse, nutrix; sed furor cogit sequi
peiora. vadit animus in praeceps sciens
remeatque frustra sana consilia appetens.   180
sic cum gravatam navita adversa ratem
propellit unda, cedit in vanum labor
et victa prono puppis aufertur vado.
quid ratio possit? vicit ac regnat furor
potensque tota mente dominatur deus.
hic volucer omni pollet in terra impotens
laesumque flammis torret indomitis Iovem;
Gradivus istas belliger sensit faces,
opifex trisulci fulminis sensit deus,
et qui furentes semper Aetnaeis iugis   190
versat caminos igne tam parvo calet;
ipsumque Phoebum, tela qui nervo regit,
figit sagitta certior missa puer
volitatque caelo pariter et terris gravis.

NVTRIX

Deum esse amorem turpis et vitio furens
finxit libido, quoque liberior foret
332

Then go thou on and overturn all nature with thy
unhallowed fires. Why do monsters cease?[1] Why
does thy brother's[2] labyrinth stand empty? Shall
the world hear of strange prodigies, shall nature's
laws give way, whenever a Cretan woman loves?

PHAEDRA

I know, nurse, that what thou sayest is true; but
passion forces me to take the worser path. With
full knowledge my soul moves on to the abyss and
vainly seeks the backward way in quest of counsels
sane. Even so, when the mariner urges his laden
vessel against opposing seas, his toil goes for naught
and the ship, vanquished, is swept away by the swift-
moving tide. What can reason do? Passion has
conquered and now rules supreme, and, a mighty
god, lords it o'er all my soul. This winged god
rules ruthlessly throughout the earth and inflames
Jove himself, wounded with unquenched fires.
Gradivus, the warrior god, has felt those flames;
that god[3] has felt them who fashions the three-
forked thunderbolts, yea, he who tends the hot
furnaces ever raging 'neath Aetna's peaks is inflamed
by so small a fire as this. Nay, Phoebus himself,
who guides with sure aim his arrows from the bowstring, a boy of more sure aim pierces with his flying
shaft, and flits about, baneful alike to heaven and to
earth.

NURSE

'Tis base and sin-mad lust that has made love
into a god and, to enjoy more liberty, has given to

[1] *i.e.* Why are no more monsters like the Minotaur produced?
[2] The Minotaur. [3] Vulcan.

titulum furori numinis falsi addidit.
natum per omnes scilicet terras vagum
Erycina mittit, ille per caelum volans
proterva tenera tela molitur manu   200
regnumque tantum minimus e superis habet!
vana ista demens animus ascivit sibi
Venerisque numen finxit atque arcus dei.
quisquis secundis rebus exultat nimis
fluitque luxu, semper insolita appetit.
tunc illa magnae dira fortunae comes
subit libido ; non placent suetae dapes,
non tecta sani moris aut vilis scyphus.
cur in penates rarius tenues subit
haec delicatas eligens pestis domos ?   210
cur sancta parvis habitat in tectis Venus
mediumque sanos vulgus affectus tenet
et se coercent modica ? contra divites
regnoque fulti plura quam fas est petunt ?
quod non potest vult posse qui nimium potest.
quid deceat alto praeditam solio vides ;
metue ac verere sceptra remeantis viri.

PHAEDRA

Amoris in me maximum regnum puto
reditusque nullos metuo.   non umquam amplius
convexa tetigit supera qui mersus semel   220
adiit silentem nocte perpetua domum.

NVTRIX

Ne crede Diti.   clauserit regnum licet
canisque diras Stygius observet fores,
solus negatas invenit Theseus vias.

passion the title of an unreal divinity. The goddess of Eryx[1] sends her son, forsooth, wandering through all lands, and he, flying through heaven's void, wields wanton weapons in his boyish hands, and, though least of gods, still holds such mighty empire! 'Tis love-mad souls that have adopted these vain conceits and have feigned Venus' divinity and a god's archery. Whoever rejoices in overmuch prosperity and abounds in luxury is ever seeking unaccustomed joys. Then that dire comrade of high estate, inordinate desire, steals in; wonted feasts no longer please, nor houses of simple fashion or modest cups. Why steals this deadly pest more rarely into humble homes, choosing rather the homes of daintiness? Why doth hallowed love dwell 'neath lowly roofs and the general throng have wholesome impulses? Why hath modest fortune self-control? Why, on the other hand, do rich men, propped on empire, ever grasp at more than heaven allows? He who is too powerful seeks power beyond his power. What becomes one endowed with high estate, thou knowest well; then fear and respect the sceptre of thy returning lord.

PHAEDRA

Love's is, I think, the mightiest sovereignty over me, and I fear no lord's return. Nevermore has he reached sight of the vaulted skies who, once plunged in perpetual night, has gone to the silent home.

NURSE

Trust not in Dis. Though he bar his realm, and though the Stygian dog keep guard o'er the grim doors, Theseus alone finds out forbidden ways.

[1] Venus

SENECAE TRAGOEDIAE

PHAEDRA

Veniam ille amori forsitan nostro dabit.

NVTRIX

Immitis etiam coniugi castae fuit ;
experta saevam est barbara Antiope manum.
sed posse flecti coniugem iratum puta ;
quis huius animum flectet intractabilem ?
exosus omne feminae nomen fugit,   230
immitis annos caelibi vitae dicat,
conubia vitat.   genus Amazonium scias.

PHAEDRA

Hunc in nivosi collis haerentem iugis,
et aspera agili saxa calcantem pede
sequi per alta nemora, per montes placet.

NVTRIX

Resistet ille seque mulcendum dabit
castosque ritus Venere non casta exuet ?
tibi ponet odium, cuius odio forsitan
persequitur omnes ?   precibus haud vinci potest.

PHAEDRA

Ferus est ; amore didicimus vinci feros.   240

NVTRIX

Fugiet.

PHAEDRA

Per ipsa maria si fugiet, sequar.

HIPPOLYTUS

PHAEDRA

He will give indulgence to my love, perchance.

NURSE

Harsh was he even to a virtuous wife; foreign
Antiope found his hand severe. But suppose thou
canst bend thy angry husband; who can bend this
youth's stubborn soul? Hating the very name of
woman, he flees them all, sternly devotes his years
to single life and shuns the marriage tie. Thou
wouldst know him of Amazonian breed.

PHAEDRA

Though he keep him to the peaks of snowy hills,
though he course swiftly 'mongst the ragged rocks,
still through the deep forests, over the mountains, 'tis
my resolve to follow him.

NURSE

Will he stop for thee and yield himself to thy
caresses? Will he lay aside his pure practices for
impure love? Will he give up his hate for thee,
when 'tis for hate of thee, perchance, he repels all
women? By no prayers can he be overcome.

PHAEDRA

Wild is he; but wild things, we have learned,
can be o'ercome by love.

NURSE

He will flee away.

PHAEDRA

Though he flee through the very seas, still will I
follow.

NVTRIX

Patris memento.

PHAEDRA

Meminimus matris simul

NVTRIX

Genus omne profugit.

PHAEDRA

Paelicis careo metu

NVTRIX

Aderit maritus.

PHAEDRA

Nempe Pirithoi [1] comes ?

NVTRIX

Aderitque genitor.

PHAEDRA

Mitis, Ariadnae pater.

NVTRIX

Per has senectae splendidas supplex comas
fessumque curis pectus et cara ubera
precor, furorem siste teque ipsa adiuva.
pars sanitatis velle sanari fuit.

[1] *So A : Leo* Perithoi.

HIPPOLYTUS

NURSE

Remember thy father.

PHAEDRA

My mother I remember too.

NURSE

He shuns the whole race of women.

PHAEDRA

Then need I fear no rival.

NURSE

Thy husband will be here.

PHAEDRA

Yes, comrade of Pirithoüs !

NURSE

And thy father will be here.

PHAEDRA

He will be kind, Ariadne's father.

NURSE

By these gleaming locks of age, by this heart,
worn with care, by these dear breasts, I beg thee
check this mad love and come to thy own relief. The
wish for healing has ever been the half of health.

PHAEDRA

Non omnis animo cessit ingenuo pudor.   250
paremus, altrix.   qui regi non vult amor
vincatur.   haud te, fama, maculari sinam.
haec sola ratio est, unicum effugium mali :
virum sequamur ; morte praevertam nefas.

NVTRIX

Moderare, alumna, mentis effrenae impetus,
animos coerce.   dignam ob hoc vita reor
quod esse temet autumas dignam nece.

PHAEDRA

Decreta mors est ; quaeritur fati genus.
laqueone vitam finiam an ferro incubem ?
an missa praeceps arce Palladia cadam ?   260

NVTRIX

Sic te senectus nostra praecipiti sinat   262
perire leto ?   siste furibundum impetum.
haud quisquam ad vitam facile revocari potest.[1]

PHAEDRA

Prohibere nulla ratio periturum potest
ubi qui mori constituit et debet mori.
proin castitatis vindicem armemus manum.   261

NVTRIX

Solamen annis unicum fessis, era,   267
si tam protervus incubat menti furor,
contemne famam : fama vix vero favet,

---

[1] *Leo deletes this line.*

340

HIPPOLYTUS

PHAEDRA

Not wholly has shame fled from my noble soul.
I yield, dear nurse. Let the love which will not
be controlled be overcome. Fair fame, I will not
suffer thee to be defiled. This is the only way, the
one sole escape from evil: let me follow my husband;
by death will I forestall my sin.

NURSE

Check, O my child, the rush of thine unbridled
spirit; control thy passion. For this cause do I deem
thee worthy life, since thou declarest thyself worthy
death.

PHAEDRA

I am resolved on death; I seek but the manner
of my fate. With the noose shall I end my life, or
fall upon the sword? or shall I leap headlong from
Pallas' citadel?

NURSE

Can my old age permit thee thus to go headlong
to thy death? Resist this mad impulse. No one
can easily be recalled to life.

PHAEDRA

No argument can stay from perishing one who
has resolved to die and ought to die. Wherefore
in protection of my honour let me arm my hand.

NURSE

O mistress, sole comfort of my weary years, if
so unruly a passion weighs on thy soul, scorn thou
this fame; scarcely doth fame favour truth, being

341

peius merenti melior et peior bono.   270
temptemus animum tristem et intractabilem.
meus iste labor est aggredi iuvenem ferum
mentemque saevam flectere immitis viri.

CHORVS

Diva non miti generata ponto,
quam vocat matrem geminus Cupido,
impotens flammis simul et sagittis,
iste lascivus puer et renidens
tela quam certo moderatur arcu !
labitur totas furor in medullas
igne furtivo populante venas.[1]   280
non habet latam data plaga frontem,
sed vorat tectas penitus medullas.
nulla pax isti puero : per orbem
spargit effusas agilis sagittas ;
quaeque nascentem videt ora solem,
quaeque ad Hesperias iacet ora metas,
si qua ferventi subiecta cancro,
si qua Parrhasiae glacialis ursae
semper errantes patitur colonos,
novit hos aestus.   iuvenum feroces   290
concitat flammas senibusque fessis
rursus extinctos revocat calores,
virginum ignoto ferit igne pectus
et iubet caelo superos relicto
vultibus falsis habitare terras.
Thessali Phoebus pecoris magister
egit armentum positoque plectro
impari tauros calamo vocavit.
induit formas quotiens minores
ipse qui caelum nebulasque fecit :   300
candidas ales modo movit alas,

[1] *Leo deletes ll. 279, 280.*

better to the worse deserving, worse to the good.
Let us test that grim and stubborn soul. Mine is
the task to approach the savage youth and bend
the cruel man's relentless will.

[*Exeunt into the palace.*]

CHORUS

Thou goddess, born of the cruel sea, who art
called the mother of both Loves,[1] that wanton,
smiling boy of thine, reckless alike with torches and
with arrows, with how sure bow doth he aim his
shafts ! His madness steals to the inmost marrow,
while with creeping fire he ravages the veins. The
wound he deals has no broad front, but it eats its
way deep into the hidden marrow. There is no peace
with that boy of thine ; throughout the world nimbly
he scatters his flying shafts. The shore that beholds
the new-born sun and the shore that lies at his
far western goal, the land lying beneath the burning Crab and the cold region of the Arcadian Bear,
which sustains its ever-wandering husbandmen, all
know these fires of his. He kindles the fierce flames
of youth and in worn-out age he wakes again the
extinguished fires ; he smites maids' breasts with
unknown heat, and bids the very gods leave heaven
and dwell on earth in borrowed forms.

296 Phoebus as keeper of the Thessalian herd [2]
drove his cattle along and, laying quill aside, called
together his bulls on the unequal reeds. How often did
he put on lower forms, even he [3] who made heaven and
the clouds : now as a bird he fluttered his white wings

---

[1] Ἔρως and Ἀντέρως.
[2] Phoebus kept the herds of King Admetus for a year.
[3] Jupiter, who came to Leda in the form of a swan.

dulcior vocem moriente cygno;
fronte nunc torva petulans iuvencus
virginum stravit sua terga ludo,
perque fraternos nova regna fluctus
ungula lentos imitante remos
pectore adverso domuit profundum,
pro sua vector timidus rapina.
arsit obscuri dea clara mundi
nocte deserta nitidosque fratri   310
tradidit currus aliter regendos.
ille nocturnas agitare bigas
discit et gyro breviore flecti,   313
dum tremunt axes graviore curru;[1]   316
nec suum tempus tenuere noctes   314
et dies tardo remeavit ortu.   315
natus Alcmena posuit pharetras   317
et minax vasti spolium leonis,
passus aptari digitis zmaragdos
et dari legem rudibus capillis;   320
crura distincto religavit auro,
luteo plantas cohibente socco;
et manu, clavam modo qua gerebat,
fila deduxit properante fuso.
   Vidit Persis ditique ferax
  Lydia regno deiecta feri
  terga leonis
  umerisque, quibus sederat alti
  regia caeli, tenuem Tyrio
  stamine pallam.
  sacer est ignis (credite laesis)   330
  nimiumque potens.   qua terra salo
  cingitur alto quaque per ipsum
  candida mundum sidera currunt,
  haec regna tenet puer immitis,

      [1] *Leo has set this line after 313.*

with note sweeter than the dying swan; now with
savage front as a wanton bull he lowered his back for
the sport of maidens and through the strange kingdom
of his brother's waves, using his hoofs in place of pliant
oars, he breasted the deep sea and overcame it, a
ferryman trembling for the prize [1] he bore. The
radiant goddess [2] of the darksome sky burned with
love and, forsaking the night, gave her gleaming
chariot to her brother to guide in fashion other than
his own. He learned to drive the team of night and
to wheel in narrower circuit, while the axle groaned
beneath the car's heavier weight; nor did the nights
keep their accustomed length, and with belated
dawning came the day. The son of Alcmena [3] laid
by his quiver and the threatening skin of the huge
lion, letting emeralds be fitted to his fingers and
law be enforced on his rough locks; he bound his
legs with cross-garterings of gold and within yellow
sandals confined his feet; and in that hand, with
which he but now bore the club, he spun out threads
with flying spindle.

[325] Persia and the rich, fertile realm of Lydia saw
the fierce lion's skin laid aside, and on those shoulders,
on which the royal structure of the lofty sky had
rested, a gauzy cloak of Tyrian web. 'Tis an accursed
fire (believe those who have suffered) and all too
powerful. Where the land is encircled by the briny
deep, where the bright stars course through heaven
itself, over these realms the pitiless boy holds
sovereignty, whose shafts are felt in the lowest

[1] Europa, whom the god, in bull-form, carried over the sea
to Crete.
[2] Diana, or Luna, the moon-goddess, who was in love with
the shepherd, Endymion.
[3] Hercules, smitten with love for Omphale, the Lydian
queen.

spicula cuius sentit in imis
caerulus undis grex [1] Nereidum
flammamque nequit relevare mari.
ignes sentit genus aligerum.
Venere instinctus suscipit audax
grege pro toto bella iuvencus;   340
si coniugio timuere suo,
poscunt timidi proelia cervi.   342
tunc virgatas India tigres   344
decolor horret; tunc vulnificos
acuit dentes aper et toto est
spumeus ore;
Poeni quatiunt colla leones   348
et mugitu dant concepti [2]   343
signa furoris. cum movit Amor,   343[b] 349
tum silva gemit murmure saevo.   350
amat insani belua ponti
Lucaeque boves, vindicat omnem
sibi naturam; nihil immune est,
odiumque perit cum iussit Amor.
veteres cedunt ignibus irae—
quid plura canam? vincit saevas
cura novercas.
    Altrix, profare quid feras; quonam in loco est
regina? saevis ecquis est flammis modus?

NVTRIX

Spes nulla tantum posse leniri malum,   360
finisque flammis nullus insanis erit.
torretur aestu tacito et inclusus quoque,
quamvis tegatur, proditur vultu furor;
erumpit oculis ignis et lassae genae

---

[1] So A: *Leo pervius undis rex.*
[2] *Leo has transposed this line.*

346

depths by the sea-blue throng of Nereids, nor can
they ease their heat by ocean's waters. These
fires the race of winged creatures feel. Goaded on
by love, the bold bull undertakes battle for the
whole herd; if they feel that their mates are in
danger, timid stags challenge to war. At such a
time swart India holds striped tigers in especial fear;
at such a time the boar whets his death-dealing
tusks and his jaws are covered all with foam; African
lions toss their manes and by their roarings give
token of their engendered passion. When Love has
roused them, then the forest groans with their grim
uproar. Love sways the monsters of the raging sea,
sways Lucanian bulls,[1] claims as his own all nature;
nothing is exempt, and hate perishes at the command
of Love. Old grudges yield unto his fires. Why tell
of more? Love's cares o'erwhelm harsh stepmothers.

[*Enter* NURSE *from the inner palace.*]

[358] Nurse, tell the news thou bearest. How stands
it with the queen? Hath her fierce flame any bound?

NURSE

No hope is there that such suffering can be relieved, and no end will there be to her mad fires.
She is parched by a silent fever, and e'en though 'tis
hidden away, shut in her heart, her passion is betrayed in her face; fire darts from her eyes; again,
her weary gaze shrinks from the light; nothing

---

[1] *i.e.* elephants, so called because Italy first saw elephants
in Lucania, in the war with Pyrrhus.

lucem recusant, nil idem dubiae placet
artusque varie iactat incertus dolor.
nunc ut soluto labitur moriens gradu
et vix labante sustinet collo caput,
nunc se quieti reddit et, somni immemor,
noctem querelis ducit ; attolli iubet   370
iterumque poni corpus et solvi comas
rursusque fingi ; semper impatiens sui
mutatur habitus.   nulla iam Cereris subit
cura aut salutis ; vadit incerto pede,
iam viribus defecta.   non idem vigor,
non ora tinguens nitida purpureus rubor ;
populatur artus cura, iam gressus tremunt
tenerque nitidi corporis cecidit decor.[1]
et qui ferebant signa Phoebeae facis
oculi nihil gentile nec patrium micant.   380
lacrimae cadunt per ora et assiduo genae
rore irrigantur, qualiter Tauri iugis
tepido madescunt imbre percussae nives.
    Sed en, patescunt regiae fastigia.
reclinis ipsa sedis auratae toro
solitos amictus mente non sana abnuit.

PHAEDRA

    Removete, famulae, purpura atque auro inlitas
vestes, procul sit muricis Tyrii rubor,
quae fila ramis ultimi Seres legunt.
brevis expeditos zona constringat sinus,   390
cervix monili vacua, nec niveus lapis
deducat aures, Indici donum maris ;
odore crinis sparsus Assyrio vacet.
sic temere iactae colla perfundant comae

<hr />

[1] *Leo deletes ll. 377, 378*

long pleases her unbalanced soul, and her limbs
by ever-shifting pangs are tossed in changeful wise.
Now with failing steps she sinks down as if dying,
and can hardly hold up her head on her fainting
neck; now she lies down to rest and, heedless of
slumber, spends the night in lamentations; she bids
them to lift her up and again to lay her down, to loose
her hair and again to bind it up; her raiment, with
itself dissatisfied, is ever changed. She has now no
care for food or health. She walks with aimless feet,
wasted now in strength. Her old-time sprightliness
is gone, and the ruddy glow of health no longer
shines on her bright face; care feeds upon her
limbs, her steps totter and the tender grace of her
once beautiful form is fallen away; her eyes, which
once shone like Phoebus' torch, no longer gleam
with their ancestral fire. Tears fall down her face
and her cheeks are wet with constant drops, as when
on the top of Taurus the snows melt away, pierced
by a warm shower.

[384] But see, the palace doors are opening, and she
herself, lying on golden couch, all sick of soul, rejects
her wonted garments.

PHAEDRA

Away, ye slaves, with robes bedecked with purple
and with gold; away, scarlet of the Tyrian shell,
the webs [1] which the far-off Seres gather from the
trees. Let a narrow girdle hold in my garments'
unencumbering folds, let there be no necklace at my
throat, let no snowy pearls, the gift of India's ocean,
weigh down my ears, and let my hair hang loose,
unscented by Assyrian nard. So, tossed at random,

[1] A reference to silk and the culture of the silkworm by
the Seres, supposed to be the Chinese.

umerosque summos, cursibus motae citis
ventos sequantur.   laeva se pharetrae dabit,
hastile vibret dextra Thessalicum manus.[1]   397
qualis relictis frigidi Ponti plagis   399
egit catervas Atticum pulsans solum   400
Tanaitis aut Maeotis et nodo comas
coegit emisitque, lunata latus
protecta pelta ; talis in silvas ferar.

CHORVS

Sepone questus ; non levat miseros dolor ;
agreste placa virginis numen deae.

NVTRIX

Regina nemorum, sola quae montes colis
et una solis montibus coleris dea,
converte tristes ominum in melius minas.
o magna silvas inter et lucos dea
clarumque caeli sidus et noctis decus,   410
cuius relucet mundus alterna vice,
Hecate triformis, en ades coeptis favens.
animum rigentem tristis Hippolyti doma ;
det facilis aures.   mitiga pectus ferum ;
amare discat, mutuos ignes ferat.
innecte mentem ; torvus aversus ferox
in iura Veneris redeat.   huc vires tuas
intende ; sic te lucidi vultus ferant
et nube rupta cornibus puris eas,
sic te regentem frena nocturni aetheris   420
detrahere numquam Thessali cantus queant

[1] *Leo deletes :* talis severi mater Hippolyti fuit.   398

350

let my locks fall down upon my neck and shoulders
and, moved by swift running, stream upon the wind.
My left hand shall be busied with the quiver and my
right wield a Thessalian spear.   In such guise as the
dweller by Tanaïs or Maeotis,[1] leaving cold Pontus'
tract behind, led her hordes, treading Athenian soil,
and, binding her locks in a knot, let them flow free,
her side protected by a crescent shield; so will I
betake me to the woods.

CHORUS

Cease thy complainings; grieving helps not the
wretched.   Appease the rustic divinity of our virgin
goddess.

NURSE

O queen of groves, thou who in solitude lovest
thy mountain-haunts, and who upon the solitary
mountains art alone held holy, change for the better
these dark, ill-omened threats.   O great goddess of
the woods and groves, bright orb of heaven, glory of
the night, by whose changing beams the universe
shines clear, O three-formed Hecate, lo, thou art at
hand, favouring our undertaking.   Conquer the unbending soul of stern Hippolytus; may he, compliant,
give ear unto our prayer.   Soften his fierce heart;
may he learn to love, may he feel answering flames.
Ensnare his mind; grim, hostile, fierce, may he turn
him back unto the fealty of love.   To this end direct
thy powers; so mayst thou wear a shining face and,
the clouds all scattered, fare on with undimmed
horns; so, when thou drivest thy car through the
nightly skies, may no witcheries of Thessaly prevail

---

[1] *i.e.* any woman of the race of Amazons.

351

nullusque de te gloriam pastor ferat.
ades invocata, iam fave votis, dea.

Ipsum intuor solemne venerantem sacrum
nullo latus comitante—quid dubitas? dedit
tempus locumque casus; utendum artibus.
trepidamus? haud est facile mandatum scelus
audere, verum iussa qui regis timet,
deponat omne et pellat ex animo decus;
malus est minister regii imperii pudor.   430

HIPPOLYTVS

Quid huc seniles fessa moliris gradus,
o fida nutrix, turbidam frontem gerens
et maesta vultu? sospes est certe parens
sospesque Phaedra stirpis et geminae iugum?

NVTRIX

Metus remitte. prospero regnum in statu est
domusque florens sorte felici viget.
sed tu beatis mitior rebus veni;
namque anxiam me cura sollicitat tui,
quod te ipse poenis gravibus infestus domas.
quem fata cogunt, ille cum venia est miser;   440
at si quis ultro se malis offert volens
seque ipse torquet, perdere est dignus bona
quis nescit uti.   potius annorum memor
mentem relaxa; noctibus festis facem
attolle, curas Bacchus exoneret graves.
352

HIPPOLYTUS

to drag thee down and may no shepherd[1] make boast o'er thee. Be near, goddess, in answer to our call; hear now our prayers.

[HIPPOLYTUS *is seen approaching.*]

424 The man himself I see, coming to perform thy sacred rites, no comrade at his side. [*To herself.*] Why dost thou hesitate? Chance has given thee both time and place. Thou must employ thy arts. Why do I tremble? 'Tis no easy task to dare a crime bidden by another, but whoso fears a sovereign's behests must lay aside and banish from his heart all thought of honour; shame is but an ill servant of a sovereign's commands.

HIPPOLYTUS

Why dost hither wend wearily thy aged steps, O faithful nurse, with troubled brow and face dejected? Surely my sire is safe, Phaedra is safe, and their two sons?

NURSE

Banish thy fear. The realm is in prosperous state, thy house is strong, flourishing under the smile of Heaven. But in this happy lot do thou show thyself less harsh; for distress for thee harasses my anxious heart, seeing that thou in thine own despite dost break thyself with heavy penances. If fate compels, 'tis pardonable to be wretched; but whoso of his own accord surrenders himself to misery and causes his own torment, he deserves to lose the happiness he knows not how to use. Nay, remember thy youth and relax thy spirit; go out o' nights, raising the festal torch; let Bacchus unburden thy weighty cares.

[1] An allusion to Endymion.

Aetate fruere ; mobili cursu fugit.
nunc facile pectus, grata nunc iuveni Venus.
exultet animus.   cur toro viduo iaces ?
tristem iuventam solve ; nunc luxus [1] rape,
effunde habenas, optimos vitae dies   450
effluere prohibe.   propria descripsit deus
officia et aevum per suos duxit gradus ;
laetitia iuvenem, frons decet tristis senem.
quid te coherces et necas rectam indolem ?
seges illa magnum fenus agricolae dabit
quaecumque laetis tenera luxuriat satis,
arborque celso vertice evincet nemus
quam non maligna caedit aut resecat manus.
ingenia melius recta se in laudes ferunt,
si nobilem animum vegeta libertas alit.   460

Truculentus et silvester ac vitae inscius
tristem iuventam Venere deserta coles ?
hoc esse munus credis indictum viris,
ut dura tolerent, cursibus domitent equos
et saeva bella Marte sanguineo gerant ?
quam varia leti genera mortalem trahunt   475
carpuntque turbam, pontus et ferrum et doli !
sed ista credas desse : sic atram Styga
iam petimus ultro.   caelibem vitam probet
sterilis iuventus ; hoc erit, quidquid vides,
unius aevi turba et in semet ruet.   480
providit ille maximus mundi parens,   466
cum tam rapaces cerneret Fati manus,
ut damna semper subole repararet nova.
excedat agedum rebus humanis Venus,
quae supplet ac restituit exhaustum genus :   470
orbis iacebit squalido turpis situ,
vacuum sine ullis piscibus stabit mare

---

[1] *So A : Leo* cursus.

⁴⁴⁶ Enjoy thy life ; 'tis speeding swift away. Now hearts are light, now love to youth is pleasing. Let thy heart rejoice. Why dost lie on a lonely couch ? Free thy youth from gloom ; lay hold on pleasures ; loosen the reins ; let not life's best days escape thee. God has portioned out its proper duties to each time of life and led this span of ours through its own stages; joy befits the young, a serious face the old. Why dost hold thyself in check and strangle thy true nature ? That crop will give to the farmer the best return which in the tender blade runs riot with joyous growth, and that tree with lofty head will overtop the grove which no grudging hand cuts down or prunes away. So will right minds be reared unto a richer fruit of praise, if sprightly freedom nourish the high-born soul.

⁴⁶¹ Wilt thou, as a harsh woods-dweller, ignorant of life, spend thy youth in gloom and let Venus be forgot ? Is it man's allotted task, thinkst thou, to endure hardship, curb horses in their swift course, and wage savage wars in bloody battles ? How various are the forms of death that seize and feed on mortal throngs ! the sea, the steel and treachery ! But suppose these lacking : by thy path we make wantonly for murky death. The unwedded life let barren youth applaud ; then will all that thou beholdest be the throng of one generation only and will fall in ruins on itself. In his providence did yonder almighty father of the universe, when he saw how greedy were the hands of Fate, give heed ever by fresh progeny to make losses good. Come now, let love but be banished from human life, love, which supplies and renews the impoverished race : the whole globe will lie foul in vile neglect ; the sea will stand empty of its fish ; birds will be lacking to the heavens, wild beasts to the woods, and

alesque caelo derit et silvis fera,
solis et aer pervius ventis erit. 474
proinde vitae sequere naturam ducem ; 481
urbem frequenta, civium coetum cole.

HIPPOLYTVS

Non alia magis est libera et vitio carens
ritusque melius vita quae priscos colat,
quam quae relictis moenibus silvas amat.
non illum avarae mentis inflammat furor
qui se dicavit montium insontem iugis,
non aura populi et vulgus infidum bonis,
non pestilens invidia, non fragilis favor ;
non ille regno servit aut regno imminens 490
vanos honores sequitur aut fluxas opes,
spei metusque liber; haud illum niger
edaxque livor dente degeneri petit ;
nec scelera populos inter atque urbes sata
novit nec omnes conscius strepitus pavet
aut verba fingit ; mille non quaerit tegi
dives columnis nec trabes multo insolens
suffigit auro ; non cruor largus pias
inundat aras, fruge nec sparsi sacra
centena nivei colla summittunt boves ; 500
sed rure vacuo potitur et aperto aethere
innocuus errat.
                    Callidas tantum feris
struxisse fraudes novit et fessus gravi
labore niveo corpus Iliso fovet.
nunc ille ripam celeris Alphei legit,
nunc nemoris alti densa metatur loca,
ubi Lerna puro gelida perlucet vado,
sedesque mutas; hinc aves querulae fremunt
ornique ventis lene percussae tremunt

356

the paths of air will be traversed only by the winds.
Follow, then, nature as life's guide; frequent the
city; seek out the haunts of men.

HIPPOLYTUS

There is no life so free and innocent, none which
better cherishes the ancient ways, than that which,
forsaking cities, loves the woods. His heart is
inflamed by no mad greed of gain who has devoted
himself to harmless ranging on the mountain-tops;
here is no shouting populace, no mob, faithless to good
men, no poisonous hate, no brittle favour. No slave
is he of kings, nor in quest of kingship does he chase
empty honours or elusive wealth, free alike from
hope and fear; him venomous spite assails not with
the bite of base-born tooth; those crimes that spawn
midst the city's teeming throngs he does not know,
nor in guilty consciousness does he quake at every
sound, or frame lying words. He seeks not in pride
of wealth to be sheltered by a roof reared on a thousand pillars, nor in insolence plates he with much
gold his rafter-beams. No streams of blood drench
his pious altars, no hecatombs of snow-white bullocks,
sprinkled with the sacred meal, bend low their necks;
but his lordship is over the empty fields, and beneath
the open sky he wanders blameless.

⁵⁰² His only craft is to set cunning snares for the
wild beasts, and, when weary with hard toil, he
refreshes his body in Ilissos' stream, chilled by the
snows. Now he fares along the bank of swift-
flowing Alpheus, now traverses the lofty grove's
deep places, where cool Lerna is transparent with its
crystal shoals, and the silent forest-depths, wherein the
complaining birds make music, and the ash-trees and
ancient beeches quiver, moving gently in the breeze.

veteresque fagi.   iuvit aut amnis vagi   510
pressisse ripas, caespite aut nudo leves
duxisse somnos, sive fons largus citas
defundit undas sive per flores novos
fugiente dulcis murmurat rivo sonus.

Excussa silvis poma compescunt famem
et fraga parvis vulsa dumetis cibos
faciles ministrant.   regios luxus procul
est impetus fugisse.   sollicito bibunt
auro superbi ; quam iuvat nuda manu
captasse fontem ! certior somnus premit   520
secura duro membra versantem toro.
non in recessu furta et obscuro improbus
quaerit cubili seque multiplici timens
domo recondit ; aethera ac lucem petit
et teste caelo vivit.

                Hoc equidem reor
vixisse ritu prima quos mixtos deis
profudit aetas.   nullus his auri fuit
caecus cupido, nullus in campo sacer
divisit agros arbiter populis lapis ;
nondum secabant credulae pontum rates ;   530
sua quisque norat maria.   non vasto aggere
crebraque turre cinxerant urbes latus ;
non arma saeva miles aptabat manu
nec torta clausas fregerat saxo gravi
ballista portas, iussa nec dominum pati
iuncto ferebat terra servitium bove ;
sed arva per se feta poscentes nihil
pavere gentes, silva nativas opes
et opaca dederant antra nativas domos.

Rupere foedus impius lucri furor   540
et ira praeceps quaeque succensas agit
libido mentes ; venit imperii sitis
cruenta, factus praeda maiori minor,
358

Sweet it is to lie on the bank of some vagrant stream,
or on the bare sward to quaff light-stealing slumbers,
be it where some copious spring pours down its hurrying waters, or through budding flowers some brook
murmurs sweetly as it glides along.

515 Fruit shaken from the forest trees stays his
hunger, and berries plucked from the low bushes
afford an easy meal. It is his passion to flee far from
royal luxury. 'Tis from anxious cups of gold that
the proud drink! how sweet to catch up with the
bare hand the water of the spring! Here slumber
more surely soothes as he lays him down, care-free,
on his hard bed. He guiltily plots no stealthy deeds
in secret chamber and on a hidden couch, nor hides
fearfully away in his labyrinthine palace; 'tis the air and
light he seeks, and his life has heaven for its witness.

525 'Twas in such wise, methinks, they lived whom
the primal age produced, in friendly intercourse with
gods. They had no blind love of gold; no sacred
boundary-stone, judging betwixt peoples, separated
fields on the spreading plain; not yet did rash vessels
plough the sea; each man knew only his native
waters. Then cities were not surrounded with massive
walls, set with many towers; no soldier applied his
fierce hand to arms, nor did hurling engines burst
through closed gates with heavy stones. Not yet
did earth, suffering a master's rule, endure the hard
toil of the yoked ox; but the fields, fruitful of themselves, fed nations who asked nothing more; the
woods gave men their natural wealth, and shady caves
afforded natural homes.

540 Unholy passion for gain broke up this peaceful
life, headlong wrath, and lust which sets men's hearts
aflame. Next came cruel thirst for power; the
weaker was made the stronger's prey, and might

359

pro iure vires esse. tum primum manu
bellare nuda[1] saxaque et ramos rudes
vertere in arma. non erat gracili levis
armata ferro cornus aut longo latus
mucrone cingens ensis aut crista procul
galeae comantes; tela faciebat dolor.
invenit artes bellicus Mavors novas   550
et mille formas mortis. hinc terras cruor
infecit omnes fusus et rubuit mare.
tum scelera dempto fine per cunctas domos
iere, nullum caruit exemplo nefas.
a fratre frater, dextera nati parens
cecidit, maritus coniugis ferro iacet
perimuntque fetus impiae matres suos.
taceo novercam; mitior nil est feris.
sed dux malorum femina; haec scelerum artifex
obsedit animos, huius incestis stupris   560
fumant tot urbes, bella tot gentes gerunt
et versa ab imo regna tot populos premunt.
sileantur aliae; sola coniunx Aegei,
Medea, reddet feminas dirum genus.

NVTRIX

Cur omnium fit culpa paucarum scelus

HIPPOLYTVS

Detestor omnes, horreo fugio execror.
sit ratio, sit natura, sit dirus furor,
odisse placuit. ignibus iunges aquas
et amica ratibus ante promittet vada
incerta Syrtis, ante ab extremo sinu   570
Hesperia Tethys lucidum attollet diem

---

[1] *Leo comments: post* nuda *hoc fere desideramus:* tela tum
saeva manu | aptare adorti.

360

took the place of right. At first men fought with
naked fists, [next they began to lay hand to deadly
weapons [1]] and turned stones and rough clubs to the
use of arms. As yet there was no light cornel-shaft,
tipped with tapering iron ; no long, sharp-pointed
sword hung at the side ; no helmets crested with
plumes gleamed from afar ; rage furnished arms. Warlike Mars invented new modes of strife and a thousand
forms of death. From this source streams of blood
stained all lands and the sea grew red. Then crime
stalked unchecked through every home and no impious deed lacked precedent. Brother was slain by
brother, father by the hand of son, husband lay dead
by the sword of wife, and unnatural mothers destroyed
their own offspring. I say naught of stepmothers ;
they are no whit more merciful than the beasts.
But the leader of all wickedness is woman ; 'tis she,
cunning mistress of crime, besets our minds ; 'tis by
her foul adulteries so many cities smoke, so many
nations war, so many peoples lie crushed beneath
the ruins of their kingdoms, utterly o'erthrown. Let
others be unnamed ; Aegeus' wife alone, Medea, will
prove that women are an accursed race.

NURSE

Why make the crime of few the blame of all ?

HIPPOLYTUS

I abominate them all, I dread, shun, curse them
all. Be it reason, be it instinct, be it wild rage : 'tis
my joy to hate them. Sooner shall you mate fire
and water, sooner shall the dangerous Syrtes offer
to ships a friendly passage, sooner shall Tethys from

---

[1] Translating Leo's suggested interpolation.

et ora dammis blanda praebebunt lupi,
quam victus animum feminae mitem geram.

NVTRIX

Saepe obstinatis induit frenos Amor
et odia mutat.   regna materna aspice;
illae feroces sentiunt Veneris iugum.
testaris istud unicus gentis puer.

HIPPOLYTVS

Solamen unum matris amissae fero,
odisse quod iam feminas omnes licet.

NVTRIX

Vt dura cautes undique intractabilis   580
resistit undis et lacessentes aquas
longe remittit, verba sic spernit mea.
  Sed Phaedra praeceps graditur, impatiens morae.
quo se dabit fortuna? quo verget furor?
terrae repente corpus exanimum accidit
et ora morti similis obduxit color.
attolle vultus, dimove vocis moras.
tuus en, alumna, temet Hippolytus tenet.

her far western shore bring in bright dawn, and
wolves gaze on does with eyes caressing, than I, my
hate o'ercome, have kindly thought for woman.

NURSE

Oft-times doth Love put curb on stubborn hearts
and change their hate. Look at thy mother's kingdom; those warlike women feel the yoke of Venus.
Thou bearest witness to this, of her race the only
son.[1]

HIPPOLYTUS

I count it the one solace for my lost mother, that
now I may hate all womankind.

NURSE [aside]

As some hard crag, on all sides unassailable, resists
the waves, and flings far back the flood importunate,
so does he spurn my words.

[583] But Phaedra is hurrying towards us, impatient
of delay. Whither will fortune go? Whither will
madness tend?

[PHAEDRA enters and falls as in a swoon.]

Her fainting body has fallen suddenly to earth and
death-like pallor has overspread her face.

[HIPPOLYTUS hastens to raise her in his arms.]

Lift thy face, break silence. See, my daughter, thine
own Hippolytus embraces thee.

---

[1] It is said that the Amazons were accustomed to kill all
boys born to them. Hippolytus, being the son of Theseus, had
been spared.

SENECAE TRAGOEDIAE

PHAEDRA

Quis me dolori reddit atque aestus graves
reponit animo ? quam bene excideram mihi ! 590

HIPPOLYTVS

Cur dulce munus redditae lucis fugis ?

PHAEDRA

Aude, anime, tempta, perage mandatum tuum.
intrepida constent verba ; qui timide˙rogat
docet negare. magna pars sceleris mei
olim peracta est ; serus est nobis pudor—
amavimus nefanda. si coepta exsequor,
forsan iugali crimen abscondam face.
honesta quaedam scelera successus facit.
en incipe, anime !—Commodes paulum, precor,
secretus aures. si quis est abeat comes. 600

HIPPOLYTVS

En locus ab omni liber arbitrio vacat.

PHAEDRA

Sed ora coeptis transitum verbis negant ;
vis magna vocem mittit et maior tenet.
vos testor omnes, caelites, hoc quod volo [1]— 604

HIPPOLYTVS

Animusne cupiens aliquid effari nequit ? 606

[1] *Leo deletes the fragmentary line* (605): me nolle.

HIPPOLYTUS

PHAEDRA [*recovering*]

Who gives me back to grief and again sets in my soul this fever dire? How blest was my unconsciousness of self!

HIPPOLYTUS

Why dost thou shun the sweet boon of life restored?

PHAEDRA [*aside*]

Courage! my soul, essay, fulfil thine own behest. Fearless be thy words, and firm; who makes timid request, invites denial. The chief part of my guilt is long since accomplished; too late for me is modesty—I *have* loved basely. If I follow up what I have begun, perchance I may hide my sin behind the marriage torch. Success makes some sins honest. Come now, my soul, begin! [*To* HIPPOLYTUS.] Lend ear to me privately a little while, I pray. If any comrade of thine is here, let him withdraw.

HIPPOLYTUS

Behold, the place is free from all witnesses.

PHAEDRA

But my lips refuse passage to the words I seek to frame; some strong power urges me to speak, and a stronger holds me back. I call you all to witness, you heavenly powers, that what I wish—

HIPPOLYTUS

Thy heart desires somewhat and cannot tell it out?

SENECAE TRAGOEDIAE

PHAEDRA

Curae leves locuntur, ingentes stupent.

HIPPOLYTVS

Committe curas auribus, mater, meis.

PHAEDRA

Matris superbum est nomen et nimium potens;
nostros humilius nomen affectus decet;   610
me vel sororem, Hippolyte, vel famulam voca,
famulamque potius; omne servitium feram.
non me per altas ire si iubeas nives,
pigeat gelatis ingredi Pindi iugis;
non, si per ignes ire et infesta agmina,
cuncter paratis ensibus pectus dare.
mandata recipe sceptra, me famulam accipe;
te imperia regere, me decet iussa exsequi [1]
muliebre non est regna tutari urbium;
tu qui iuventae flore primaevo viges   620
cives paterno fortis imperio rege,
sinu receptam supplicem ac servam tege.
miserere viduae—

HIPPOLYTVS

                    Summus hoc omen deus
avertat! aderit sospes actutum parens.

PHAEDRA

Regni tenacis dominus et tacitae Stygis
nullam relictos fecit ad superos viam;

[1] *Leo deletes this line.*

HIPPOLYTUS

PHAEDRA

Light troubles speak; the weighty are struck dumb.

HIPPOLYTUS

Entrust thy troubles to my ears, mother.

PHAEDRA

Mother—that name is too proud and high; a humbler name better suits my feelings. Call me sister, Hippolytus, or slave—yes, slave is better; I will endure all servitude. Shouldst thou bid me walk through deep-drifted snows, I would not shrink from faring along the cold peaks of Pindus; shouldst thou send me through fire and midst deadly battle ranks, I would not hesitate to offer my breast to naked swords. Take thou in my stead the sceptre committed to my care, accept me for thy slave; it becomes thee to bear sway, me, to obey thine orders. It is no woman's task to watch o'er royal cities. Do thou, in the vigour of thy youth's first bloom, rule o'er the citizens, strong in thy father's power; take to thine arms thy suppliant, and protect thy slave. Pity my widowhood—

HIPPOLYTUS

The most high God avert that omen! In safety will my father soon return.

PHAEDRA

The overlord of the fast-holding realm and of the silent Styx has made no way to the upper world

367

thalami remittet ille raptorem sui ?—
nisi forte amori placidus et Pluton sedet.

HIPPOLYTVS

Illum quidem aequi caelites reducem dabunt.
sed dum tenebit vota in incerto deus, 630
pietate caros debita fratres colam
et te merebor esse ne viduam putes
ac tibi parentis ipse supplebo locum.

PHAEDRA

O spes amantum credula, o fallax Amor
satisne dixit ? [1] precibus admotis agam.
Miserere, tacitae mentis exaudi preces—
libet loqui pigetque.

HIPPOLYTVS

Quodnam istud malum est ?

PHAEDRA

Quod in novercam cadere vix credas malum.

HIPPOLYTVS

Ambigua voce verba perplexa iacis ;
effare aperte.

So A: Leo dixi.

once quitted; and will he let the robber [1] of his
couch go back? Unless, perchance, even Pluto sits
smiling upon love!

HIPPOLYTUS

Him surely the kindly deities will bring again.
But while God still holds our prayers in doubt, with
due affection will I care for my dear brothers, and
so deserve of thee that thou shalt not deem thee
widowed, and myself will fill for thee my father's
place.

PHAEDRA [*aside*]

O credulous hope of lovers, O deceitful love! Has
he not said enough? I'll bring my prayers to bear
upon him and attack.

[*To* HIPPOLYTUS.]

[636] Have pity! hearken to the prayers my heart
may not express. I long—and am ashamed—to speak.

HIPPOLYTUS

What, pray, is this thy trouble?

PHAEDRA

A trouble thou wouldst scarce believe could befall
a stepmother.

HIPPOLYTUS

Words of doubtful meaning thou utterest with
riddling lips. Speak out and plainly.

---

[1] See Index *s.v.* "Pirithoüs," and l. 98, note.

PHAEDRA

Pectus insanum vapor   640
amorque torret. intimis fervet ferus [1]
visceribus ignis mersus et venas latens   643
ut agilis altas flamma percurrit trabes.

HIPPOLYTVS

Amore nempe Thesei casto furis?

PHAEDRA

Hippolyte, sic est: Thesei vultus amo
illos priores quos tulit quondam puer,
cum prima puras barba signaret genas
monstrique caecam Cnosii vidit domum
et longa curva fila collegit via.   650
quis tum ille fulsit! presserant vittae comam
et ora flavus tenera tinguebat pudor;
inerant lacertis mollibus fortes tori;
tuaeque Phoebes vultus aut Phoebi mei,
tuusque potius—talis, en talis fuit
cum placuit hosti, sic tulit celsum caput.
in te magis refulget incomptus decor;
est genitor in te totus et torvae tamen
pars aliqua matris miscet ex aequo decus;
in ore Graio Scythicus apparet rigor.   660
si cum parente Creticum intrasses fretum,
tibi fila potius nostra nevisset soror.
te, te, soror, quacumque siderei poli
in parte fulges, invoco ad causam parem.
domus sorores una corripuit duas:
te genitor, at me natus.

---

[1] *Leo deletes l. 642:* penitus medullas atque per venas
meat.

HIPPOLYTUS

PHAEDRA

'Tis burning love scorches my maddened heart. A hot fire glows deep in my inmost vitals and hides darkly in my veins, as when nimble flames dart through deep-set timbers.

HIPPOLYTUS

'Tis with pure love for Theseus thou dost burn ?

PHAEDRA

Hippolytus, 'tis thus with me : Theseus' features I love, those former looks of his which once as a youth he had, when his first beard marked his smooth cheeks, when he looked on the dark home of the Cretan monster, and gathered in the long thread o'er the winding way. How glorious was he then ! Fillets bound his locks, and his young face glowed with the blush of modesty; strong muscles lay beneath the softness of his arms; and his features were as of thy Phoebe or of my Phoebus—or, rather, were thy own. Such, yes, such was he when he won his foeman's [1] favour; just so he bore his head erect. In thee more brightly shines a beauty unadorned; all of thy sire is in thee, and yet some portion of thy mother's sternness blends with an equal charm ; on Grecian face shows Scythian austerity. If with thy father thou hadst come to the shores of Crete, for thee and not for him would my sister have spun the thread. Thee, thee, O sister, wherever amidst the starry heavens thou shinest, I call to aid for a cause like to thine own. One house has ruined two sisters : thee, the father, but me, the son.

[*She kneels to* HIPPOLYTUS.]

i.e. Ariadne, daughter of the foe of Athens.

               En supplex iacet
adlapsa genibus regiae proles domus.
respersa nulla labe et intacta, innocens
tibi mutor uni: certa descendi ad preces;
finem hic dolori faciet aut vitae dies.   670
miserere amantis—

HIPPOLYTVS

             Magne regnator deum,
tam lentus audis scelera? tam lentus vides?
et quando saeva fulmen emittes manu,
si nunc serenum est? omnis impulsus ruat
aether et atris nubibus condat diem,
ac versa retro sidera obliquos agant
retorta cursus. tuque, sidereum caput,
radiate Titan, tu nefas stirpis tuae
speculare? lucem merge et in tenebras fuge.
cur dextra, divum rector atque hominum, vacat   680
tua nec trisulca mundus ardescit face?
in me tona, me fige, me velox cremet
transactus ignis. sum nocens, merui mori;
placui novercae.
             Dignus en stupris ego?
scelerique tanto visus ego solus tibi
materia facilis? hoc meus meruit rigor?
o scelere vincens omne femineum genus,
o maius ausa matre monstrifera malum [1]
genetrice peior! illa se tantum stupro
contaminavit, et tamen tacitum diu   690
crimen biformi partus exhibuit nota
scelusque matris arguit vultu truci
ambiguus infans—ille te venter tulit.

---

[1] *Leo deletes this line.*

⁶⁶⁶ See, a king's daughter lies fallen at thy knees, a suppliant. Without spot or stain, pure, innocent, I am changed for thee alone. With fixed purpose have I humbled myself to prayer; this day shall bring an end either to my misery or my life. Have pity on her who loves—

HIPPOLYTUS

Great ruler of the gods, dost thou so calmly hear crimes, so calmly look upon them? And when wilt thou send forth thy thunderbolt with angry hand, if now 'tis cloudless? Let all the sky fall in shattered ruin, and in murky clouds hide the day; let the stars be turned backward and, wrenched aside, go athwart their courses. And thou, star of stars, O radiant Sun, dost thou behold this shame of thy race? Hide thy light and take refuge in darkness. Why is thy right hand empty, O ruler of gods and men? why is not the world in flames by thy forked lightning? Me let thy thunder smite, pierce me, me let thy swift-darting fire consume. I am guilty, I have deserved to die; I have stirred my stepmother to love.

[*To* PHAEDRA.]

⁶⁸⁴ Look thou! Am I fitted for adulteries? For such crime did I alone seem to thee an easy instrument? Hath my austerity earned this? O thou, who hast outsinned the whole race of women, who hast dared a greater evil than thy monster-bearing mother, thou worse than she who bore thee! She did but pollute herself with her shameful lust, and yet her offspring by its two-shaped infamy displayed her crime, though long concealed, and by his fierce visage the hybrid child made clear his mother's guilt. That was the womb that bore thee. Oh,

o ter quaterque prospero fato dati
quos hausit et peremit et leto dedit
odium dolusque.   genitor, invideo tibi;
Colchide noverca maius haec, maius malum est.

PHAEDRA

Et psa nostrae fata cognosco domus:
fugienda petimus; sed mei non sum potens.
te vel per ignes, per mare insanum sequar   700
rupesque et amnes, unda quos torrens rapit;
quacumque gressus tuleris hac amens agar —
iterum, superbe, genibus advolvor tuis.

HIPPOLYTVS

Procul impudicos corpore a casto amove
tactus.   quid hoc est?   etiam in amplexus ruit?
stringatur ensis, merita supplicia exigat.
en impudicum crine contorto caput
laeva reflexi.   iustior numquam focis
datus tuis est sanguis, arquitenens dea.

PHAEDRA

Hippolyte, nunc me compotem voti facis;   710
sanas furentem.   maius hoc voto meo est,
salvo ut pudore manibus immoriar tuis.

HIPPOLYTVS

Abscede, vive ne quid exores, et hic
contactus ensis deserat castum latus.
374

thrice and again blest of fate are they whom hatred
and treachery have destroyed, consumed, and given
unto death ! O father, I envy thee ; than thy Colchian
stepdame [1] this is a curse, greater, greater far !

PHAEDRA

I, too, recognize the fortune of my house : we
seek what we should shun ; but I am not mistress
of myself. Thee even through fire, through the
mad sea will I pursue, yes, over crags and rivers,
swollen by torrent streams ; where'er thou shalt
direct thy steps, there will I madly rush. Once
more, proud man, I grovel at thy feet.

HIPPOLYTUS

Away with thy impure touch from my chaste
body ! What ? Even rush into my arms ! Out,
sword, and mete her just punishment. See, with
left hand in her twisted hair have I bent back her
shameless head. Never has blood been more justly
spilled upon thy altar, O goddess of the bow.

PHAEDRA

Hippolytus, now dost thou grant me fulfilment
of my prayer ; thou healest me of my madness. This
is beyond my prayer, that, with my honour saved,
'tis by thy hands I die.

[*She grasps the sword and points it at her breast.*]

HIPPOLYTUS

Begone, live, lest thou have thy wish ; and let this
sword, polluted by thy touch, quit my chaste side.

[*He throws his sword from him.*]

[1] Medea, who had tried to murder Theseus.

quis eluet me Tanais aut quae barbaris
Maeotis undis Pontico incumbens mari?
non ipse toto magnus Oceano pater
tantum expiarit sceleris.   o silvae, o ferae!

NVTRIX

Deprensa culpa est.   anime, quid segnis stupes?
regeramus ipsi crimen atque ultro impiam   720
Venerem arguamus.   scelere velandum est scelus;
tutissimum est inferre, cum timeas, gradum.
ausae priores simus an passae nefas,
secreta cum sit culpa, quis testis sciet?

Adeste, Athenae! fida famulorum manus,
fer opem! nefandi raptor Hippolytus stupri
instat premitque, mortis intentat metum,
ferro pudicam terret—en praeceps abit
ensemque trepida liquit attonitus fuga.
pignus tenemus sceleris.   hanc maestam prius   730
recreate.   crinis tractus et lacerae comae
ut sunt remaneant, facinoris tanti notae.
perferte in urbem.   recipe iam sensus, era.
quid te ipsa lacerans omnium aspectus fugis?
mens inpudicam facere, non casus solet.

What Tanaïs will cleanse me, what Maeotis, with its
barbaric waves rushing into the Pontic sea? Not
great Father Neptune's self, with his whole ocean,
could wash away so much of guilt. O woods! O beasts!

[*He rushes off into the depths of the forest.*]

NURSE

Her sin has been found out. O soul, why dost
stand inactive and aghast? We must throw the
crime back on him himself, and ourselves charge him
with incestuous love. Crime must be concealed by
crime. 'Tis safest, when in fear, to force the attack.
Whether we first dared the sin or suffered it, since
it was done in secret, who of his own knowledge is
to testify?

[*She raises her voice in loud outcry.*]

725 Help, Athens, help! Faithful band of slaves,
come to our aid! The ravisher, Hippolytus, with
vile, lustful intent, is after us; he is upon us and
threatens us with death; with the sword he is terrifying our chaste queen—ah! he has rushed headlong
forth and, dazed, in panic flight, has left his sword.
We hold the proof of guilt. But the stricken queen,
revive her first. Let her dishevelled hair, her torn
locks, stay even as they are, the marks of that great
guilt. Bear her to the city. Now come back to
consciousness, my mistress. Why dost tear thyself
and shun the glances of us all? 'Tis thinking makes
impure, not circumstance.   [*Exeunt.*

377

Fugit insanae similis procellae,
ocior nubes glomerante Coro,
ocior cursum rapiente flamma,
stella cum ventis agitata longos
     porrigit ignes.   740
Conferat tecum decus omne priscum
fama miratrix senioris aevi;
pulchrior tanto tua forma lucet,
clarior quanto micat orbe pleno
cum suos ignes coeunte cornu
iunxit et curru properante pernox
exerit vultus rubicunda Phoebe
nec tenent stellae faciem minores.
talis est, primas referens tenebras,
nuntius noctis, modo lotus undis   750
Hesperus, pulsis iterum tenebris
     Lucifer idem.
Et tu, thyrsigera Liber ab India,
intonsa iuvenis perpetuum coma,
tigres pampinea cuspide territans
ac mitra cohibens cornigerum caput,
non vinces rigidas Hippolyti comas.
ne vultus nimium suspicias tuos;
omnes per populos fabula distulit
Phaedrae quem Bromio praetulerit soror.   760

     Anceps forma bonum mortalibus,
     exigui donum breve temporis,
     ut velox celeri pede laberis!
Non sic prata novo vere decentia
aestatis calidae despoliat vapor,
saevit solstitio cum medius dies
et noctes brevibus praecipitant rotis;

HIPPOLYTUS

He fled like a raging tempest, swifter than cloud-collecting Corus,[1] swifter than flame which speeds on its way when a star,[2] driven by the winds, extends its long-trailing fire.

[741] Let fame compare with thee [3] all ancient beauty, fame, admirer of the olden time ; as much fairer does thy beauty shine as gleams more brightly the full-orbed moon when with meeting horns she has joined her fires, when at the full with speeding chariot blushing Phoebe shows her face and the lesser stars fade out of sight. Such as he is the messenger of night, who brings the first shadows back, Hesperus,[4] fresh bathed in ocean ; and when the shadows have been driven away again, Lucifer [5] also.

[753] And thou, Bacchus, from thyrsus-bearing India, with unshorn locks, perpetually young, thou who frightenest tigers with thy vine-clad spear, and with a turban bindest thy hornèd head—thou wilt not surpass Hippolytus' crisp locks. Admire not thou thy beauty overmuch ; story has spread through every nation whom[6] the sister of Phaedra preferred to Bromius.

[761] O beauty, doubtful boon to mortals, brief gift for but a little time, how swiftly on quick foot thou dost slip away !

[764] Not so swiftly are the meadows, beauteous with early spring, despoiled by the hot summer's glow, when with solstitial fire midday rages, and the nights sweep headlong in their brief course.

[1] The north-west wind.
[2] A meteor.
[3] Hippolytus.
[4] The evening star.
[5] The morning star.
[6] *i.e.* Theseus, whom Ariadnè would have preferred to Bacchus (Bromius) had not Theseus deserted her.

languescunt folio ut lilia pallido,
et gratae capiti deficiunt comae
et fulgor teneris qui radiat genis   770
momento rapitur nullaque non dies
formonsi spolium corporis abstulit.
res est forma fugax ; quis sapiens bono
confidat fragili ?   dum licet, utere.
tempus te tacitum subruit, horaque
semper praeterita deterior subit.

    Quid deserta petis ?   tutior aviis
non est forma locis.   te nemore abdito,
cum Titan medium constituit diem,
cingent turba licens Naides improbae,   780
formonsos solitae claudere fontibus,
et somnis facient insidias tuis
lascivae nemorum deae [1]
Panas quae Dryades montivagos petunt
aut te stellifero despiciens polo
sidus post veteres Arcadas editum
currus non poterit flectere candidos.
et nuper rubuit, nullaque lucidis
nubes sordidior vultibus obstitit ;
at nos solliciti numine turbido,   790
tractam Thessalicis carminibus rati,
tinnitus dedimus ; tu fueras labor
et tu causa morae, te dea noctium
dum spectat celeres sustinuit vias.

    Vexent hanc faciem frigora parcius,
haec solem facies rarius appetat ;
lucebit Pario marmore clarius.
quam grata est facies torva viriliter
et pondus veteris triste supercili !
Phoebo colla licet splendida compares.   800

----

[1] *Leo deletes this line.*

As lilies wither and their leaves grow pale, so do our
pleasing locks fall from the head, and the bright glow
which shines on youthful cheeks is ravished in a
moment and no day takes not spoil of our body's
beauty. Beauty is a fleeting thing. Who that is
wise would trust so frail a blessing? Enjoy it while
thou mayest. Time is silently undermining thee,
and an hour, worse than the last, is ever creeping on.

777 Why seek desert places? Beauty is no safer in
pathless regions. Hide thee in the woods when
Titan has brought midday, and the saucy Naïds, a
wanton throng, will encompass thee, wont in their
waters to imprison shapely boys,[1] and for thy slumbers
the frolicsome goddesses of the groves will lay their
snares, the Dryads, who pursue Pans wandering on
the mountains. Or else, looking down on thee from
the starry heavens, the orb[2] that was born after the
old Arcadians[3] will lose control of her white-shining
car. And lately she blushed fiery red, though no
staining cloud obscured her bright face; but we,
anxious for our troubled goddess, thinking her harried
by Thessalian charms, made loud jingling sounds:
yet 'twas thou[4] hadst been her trouble, thou the
cause of her delaying; while gazing on thee the
goddess of the night checked her swift course.

795 This face of thine let frosts more rarely ravage,
let this face more seldom woo the sun; 'twill shine
more bright than Parian marble. How pleasing is
the manly sternness of thy face and the severe
dignity of thine old-seeming brow! With Phoebus
mayst thou match that gleaming neck. Him locks

[1] The poet has in mind the case of Hylas.
[2] Luna. The reference is to Luna and Endymion.
[3] The Arcadians were said to be older than the moon.
[4] The chorus concludes that it was Hippolytus, and not
Endymion, who of late had caused the moon's perturbations.

illum caesaries nescia colligi
perfundens umeros ornat et integit;
te frons hirta decet, te brevior coma
nulla lege iacens. tu licet asperos
pugnacesque deos viribus audeas
et vasti spatio vincere corporis;
aequas Herculeos nam iuvenis toros,
Martis belligeri pectore latior.
si dorso libeat cornipedis vehi,
frenis Castorea mobilior manu   810
Spartanum poteris flectere Cyllaron.
amentum digitis tende prioribus
et totis iaculum dirige viribus;
tam longe, dociles spicula figere,
non mittent gracilem Cretes harundinem.
aut si tela modo spargere Parthico
in caelum placeat, nulla sine alite
descendent, tepido viscere condita
praedam de mediis nubibus afferent.

    Raris forma viris (saecula prospice)   820
inpunita fuit. te melior deus
tutum praetereat formaque nobilis
deformis senii limina transeat.[1]

Quid sinat inausum feminae praeceps furor?
nefanda iuveni crimina insonti apparat.
en scelera! quaerit crine lacerato fidem,
decus omne turbat capitis, umectat genas.
instruitur omni fraude feminea dolus.

    Sed iste quisnam est, regium in vultu decus

---

[1] So A: Leo monstret imaginem.

that will not be confined, streaming o'er his shoulders, adorn and robe; but thee a shaggy brow, thee shorter locks, lying in disarray, become. 'Tis thine with manly strength to dare meet the rough and warlike gods and by the spread of thy huge body to overcome them; for even in youth thou dost match the muscles of a Hercules, art broader of chest than war-waging Mars. Shouldst thou be pleased to ride a horn-footed horse, with hand more agile on the rein than Castor's thou couldst guide the Spartan Cyllarus. Stretch thong with thy first fingers[1] and shoot the dart straight with all thy might; still not so far, though skilled to hurl the dart, will Cretans send the slender shaft. Or should it please thee to shoot thy arrows into the sky, in Parthian fashion, none will come down without its bird, but, deep fixed in the warm breast, will bring prey from the very clouds.

820 To few men hath beauty (scan the ages past) not brought its penalty. May God, more merciful, pass thee by unharmed, and may thy illustrious beauty pass the threshold o'er of shapeless age.

824 What would the woman's headlong madness leave undared? She is preparing outrageous charges against this guileless youth. Behold her guilty wiles ! By her torn hair she seeks to be believed; she disorders all the glory of her locks, bedews her cheeks with tears. She is marshalling her plot by every art that woman knows.

[*A man is seen approaching who proves to be* THESEUS.]

829 But who is this, wearing a regal dignity on his

---

[1] *i.e.* the thumb and forefinger.

gerens et alto vertice attollens caput ?   830
ut ora iuveni paria Perithoo gerit,
ni languido pallore canderent genae
staretque recta squalor incultus coma.
en ipse Theseus redditus terris adest.

THESEVS

Tandem profugi noctis aeternae plagam
vastoque manes carcere umbrantem polum,
et vix cupitum sufferunt oculi diem.
iam quarta Eleusin dona Triptolemi secat
paremque totiens libra composuit diem,
ambiguus ut me sortis ignotae labor   840
detinuit inter mortis et vitae mala.
pars una vitae mansit extincto mihi :
sensus malorum.   finis Alcides fuit,
qui cum revulsum Tartaro abstraheret canem,
me quoque supernas pariter ad sedes tulit.
sed fessa virtus robore antiquo caret
trepidantque gressus. heu, labor quantus fuit
Phlegethonte ab imo petere longinquum aethera
pariterque mortem fugere et Alciden sequi.

Quis fremitus aures flebilis pepulit meas ?   850
expromat aliquis. luctus et lacrimae et dolor,
in limine ipso maesta lamentatio ?
auspicia[1] digna prorsus inferno hospite.

NVTRIX

Tenet obstinatum Phaedra consilium necis
fletusque nostros spernit ac morti imminet.

[1] hospitia *Grotius.*

face and with head borne high? How like the
young Pirithoüs he is in countenance, were his
cheeks not so deathly pale and did not unkempt
squalor stiffen in his bristling hair. See, it is Theseus
himself, restored to the upper world.

THESEUS

At last have I escaped the realm of eternal night,
the dark world which in vast prison-house o'ershades
the dead, and scarcely do my eyes endure the longed-
for light. Now for the fourth time is Eleusis harvest-
ing the bounty of Triptolemus,[1] as many times has
Libra made day equal unto night, since dubious
battling with an unknown fate has kept me between
the ills of death and life. Though dead to all things
else, one part of life remained to me—my sense of ills.
Alcides was the end, who, when he dragged the dog
by violence out of Tartarus, brought me, too, along
with him to the upper world. But my strength is
spent, has lost its old-time vigour, and my steps do
falter. Alas, how hard a struggle it was from lowest
Phlegethon to attain the far realms of air, at once
to flee from death and follow Hercules!

850 But what is this tearful outcry that strikes my
ears? Let someone tell me. Grieving and tears and
woe, and on my very threshold sad lamentation?—
auspices that well befit a guest from hell.

NURSE

Phaedra holds unbending purpose of self-murder;
she scorns our tears and is on the very edge of
death.

1 Wheat: see Index *s.v.* " Triptolemus."

SENECAE TRAGOEDIAE

THESEVS

Quae causa leti? reduce cur moritur viro?

NVTRIX

Haec ipsa letum causa maturum attulit.

THESEVS

Perplexa magnum verba nescio quid tegunt.
effare aperte quis gravet mentem dolor.

NVTRIX

Haut pandit ulli; maesta secretum occulit   860
statuitque secum ferre quo moritur malum.
iam perge, quaeso, perge; properato est opus.

THESEVS

Reserate clausos regii postes laris.
O socia thalami, sicine adventum viri
et expetiti coniugis vultum excipis?
quin ense viduas dexteram atque animum mihi
restituis et te quidquid e vita fugat
expromis?

PHAEDRA

Eheu, per tui sceptrum imperi,
magnanime Theseu, perque natorum indolem
tuosque reditus perque iam cineres meos,   870
permitte mortem.

386

HIPPOLYTUS

THESEUS

What cause for death? Why die, now that her husband is come back?

NURSE

That very cause has brought with it speedy death.

THESEUS

Thy riddling words some weighty matter hide. Tell me plainly what grief weighs on her mind.

NURSE

She discloses it to none; though sorrowing, she hides her secret grief and is resolved to take with her the woe whereof she dies. But come now, I pray thee, come; there is need of haste.

THESEUS

Unbar the closed portals of the royal house.

[*The doors are thrown open and* THESEUS *encounters his wife just within.*]

864 O partner of my couch, is it thus thou welcomest thy lord's return and the face of thy long-sought husband? Come, put away the sword from thy right hand, give me heart again, and whatever is driving thee out of life, declare it.

PHAEDRA

Alas, O Theseus, great of soul, by the sceptre of thy kingdom, by thy children's lives, by thy return, and by my body already doomed to dust, allow my death.

SENECAE TRAGOEDIAE

THESEVS

Causa quae cogit mori?

PHAEDRA

Si causa leti dicitur, fructus perit.

THESEVS

Nemo istud alius, me quidem excepto, audiet.

PHAEDRA

Aures pudica coniugis solas timet.

THESEVS

Effare; fido pectore arcana occulam.

PHAEDRA

Alium silere quod voles, primus sile.

THESEVS

Leti facultas nulla continget tibi.

PHAEDRA

Mori volenti desse mors numquam potest.

THESEVS

Quod sit luendum morte delictum indica.

PHAEDRA

Quod vivo.

HIPPOLYTUS

THESEUS

What cause forces thee to die?

PHAEDRA

If the cause of my death is told, its fruit is lost.

THESEUS

No one else shall hear it, save myself.

PHAEDRA

A chaste woman dreads her husband's ears alone.

THESEUS

Speak out; in my true heart will I hide thy secret.

PHAEDRA

Where thou wouldst have another silence keep, keep silence first thyself.

THESEUS

No means of death shall be granted unto thee.

PHAEDRA

If one wills to die, death can never fail.

THESEUS

Tell me what sin is to be purged by death.

PHAEDRA

That I still live.

SENECAE TRAGOEDIAE

THESEVS

Lacrimae nonne te nostrae movent ?   880

PHAEDRA

Mors optima est perire lacrimandum suis.

THESEVS

Silere pergit.   verbere ac vinclis anus
altrixque prodet quidquid haec fari abnuit.
vincite ferro.   verberum vis extrahat
secreta mentis.

PHAEDRA

Ipsa iam fabor, mane.

THESEVS

Quidnam ora maesta avertis et lacrimas genis
subito coortas veste praetenta optegis?

PHAEDRA

Te, te, creator caelitum, testem invoco
et te, coruscum lucis aetheriae iubar,
ex cuius ortu [1] nostra dependet domus,   890
temptata precibus restiti; ferro ac minis
non cessit animus; vim tamen corpus tulit.
labem hanc pudoris eluet noster cruor.

THESEVS

Quis, ede, nostri decoris eversor fuit ?

[1] *Leo conjectures* ex quibus utrimque.

890

THESEU

Do not my tears move thee ?

PHAEDRA

'Tis best to die a death to be wept by friends.

THESEUS

She persists in silence. Then by scourge and bonds shall her old nurse reveal whatever she will not tell. [*To attendants.*] Bind her with chains. Let the power of the scourge drag forth the secrets of her soul.

PHAEDRA

Hold ! I will myself confess.

THESEUS

Why dost turn away thy sorrowing face and hide with veiling robe the tears that suddenly o'erflow thy cheeks ?

PHAEDRA

Thee, thee, O sire of the heavenly gods, I call to witness, and thee,[1] bright radiance of celestial light, on whom as founder this house of ours depends—though sorely tempted, I withstood his prayers ; to sword and threats my soul yielded not ; yet did my body bear his violence. This stain of shame shall my blood wash away.

THESEUS

Who, tell me, was the destroyer of my honour ?

[1] Phoebus, the father of Phaedra's mother, Pasiphaë.

PHAEDRA

Quem rere minime.

THESEVS

Quis sit audire expeto.

PHAEDRA

Hic dicet ensis quem tumultu territus
liquit stuprator civium accursum timens.

THESEVS

Quod facinus, heu me, cerno? quod monstrum
    intuor?
regale parvis asperum signis ebur
capulo refulget, generis Actaei decus.   900
sed ipse quonam evasit?

PHAEDRA

           Hi trepidum fuga
videre famuli concitum celeri pede.

THESEVS

Pro sancta Pietas, pro gubernator poli
et qui secundum fluctibus regnum moves,
unde ista venit generis infandi lues?
hunc Graia tellus aluit an Taurus Scythes
Colchusque Phasis? redit ad auctores genus
stirpemque primam degener sanguis refert.
est prorsus iste gentis armiferae furor,
392

PHAEDRA

Whom thou least thinkest.

THESEUS

Who is he? I demand to hear.

PHAEDRA

This sword will tell, which, in his panic terror, the ravisher left behind, fearing the gathering of the citizens.

THESEUS

Ah me! What villainy do I behold? What monstrous thing do I see? The royal hilt of ivory, embossed with tiny figures, gleams before me, the glory of the Athenian race. But he, whither has he escaped?

PHAEDRA

The slaves, here, saw him speeding swift away in headlong flight.

THESEUS

O holy Piety, O ruler of the heavens, and thou [1] who with thy billows dost sway the second realm, whence came this infection of infamy in our stock? Was that man nurtured by the land of Greece or by the Scythian Taurus and Colchian Phasis? The breed reverts to its progenitors and debased blood reproduces the primal stock. This, truly, is the madness of that warlike race,[2] to contemn Venus'

---

[1] Neptune. For the "second realm" see Index *s.v.* "Neptune."

[2] The Amazons.

odisse Veneris foedera et castum diu   910
vulgare populis corpus.   o tetrum genus
nullaque victum lege melioris soli!
ferae quoque ipsae Veneris evitant nefas
generisque leges inscius servat pudor.
ubi vultus ille et ficta maiestas viri
atque habitus horrens, prisca et antiqua appetens
morumque senium triste et affectus graves?
o vita fallax, abditos sensus geris
animisque pulchram turpibus faciem induis:
pudor impudentem celat, audacem quies,   920
pietas nefandum; vera fallaces probant
simulantque molles dura.

                                    Silvarum incola
ille efferatus castus intactus rudis,
mihi te reservas? a meo primum toro
et scelere tanto placuit ordiri virum?
iam iam superno numini grates ago,
quod icta nostra cecidit Antiope manu,
quod non ad antra Stygia descendens tibi
matrem reliqui.   profugus ignotas procul
percurre gentes; te licet terra ultimo   930
summota mundo dirimat Oceani plagis
orbemque nostris pedibus obversum colas,
licet in recessu penitus extremo abditus
horrifera celsi regna transieris poli
hiemesque supra positus et canas nives
gelidi frementes liqueris Boreae minas
post te furentes, sceleribus poenas dabis.

laws and to prostitute the long-chaste body to the crowd. O abominable race, yielding to no laws of a better land! Even the very beasts do shun incestuous love, and instinctive chastity guards Nature's laws. Where are those features, that feigned austerity of the man, that rough garb, aping old-fashioned and archaic ways? Where thy stern manners and the sour severity of age? O two-faced life, thou keepest thy true thoughts hidden and dost clothe foul purpose with an aspect fair—chaste bearing hides unchastity; meekness, effrontery; piety, sin unspeakable; false men approve truth and the soft affect hardihood.

⁹²² O thou lover of the woods, the boasted wild man, continent, rough, unstained, is it for me thou keepst thyself in check? With my couch, by such crime as this, was it thy pleasure to make first test of manhood? Now, now I give thanks to the heavenly powers that Antiope fell stricken by my hand, and that, descending to the Stygian pit, I did not leave to thee thy mother. Fugitive, traverse nations remote, unknown; though a land on the remotest confines of the world hold thee separated by Ocean's tracts, though thou take up thy dwelling in the world opposite our feet, though thou escape to the shuddering realms of the high north and hide deep in its farthest corner, and though, placed beyond the reach of winter [1] and his hoar snows, thou leave behind thee the threatening rage of cold Boreas,

---

[1] *i.e.* in the Hyperborean regions.

profugum per omnes pertinax latebras premam;
longinqua clausa abstrusa diversa invia
emetiemur, nullus obstabit locus—   940
scis unde redeam.   tela quo mitti haud queunt,
huc vota mittam.   genitor aequoreus dedit
ut vota prono terna concipiam deo,
et invocata munus hoc sanxit Styge.

En perage donum triste, regnator freti!
non cernat ultra lucidum Hippolytus diem
adeatque manes iuvenis iratos patri.
fer abominandam nunc opem nato, parens;
numquam supremum numinis munus tui
consumeremus, magna ni premerent mala;   950
inter profunda Tartara et Ditem horridum
et imminentes regis inferni minas,
voto peperci.   redde nunc pactam fidem.
genitor, moraris? cur adhuc undae silent?
nunc atra ventis nubila impellentibus
subtexe noctem, sidera et caelum eripe,
effunde pontum, vulgus aequoreum cie
fluctusque ab ipso tumidus[1] Oceano voca.

CHORVS

O magna parens, Natura, deum
tuque igniferi rector Olympi,   960
qui sparsa cito sidera mundo
cursusque vagos rapis astrorum
celerique polos cardine versas,

[1] So Leo: E tumidos.

still shalt thou pay penalty for thy crime. Fugitive,
through all thy hiding-places untiringly will I pursue
thee; regions remote, blocked, hidden away, far
separate, trackless, will I traverse, and no place shall
stop me—thou knowest whence I am returned.
Whither weapons cannot be hurled, thither will I
hurl my prayers. My father of the sea granted me
thrice to fashion prayers whereto the god would bow,
and, calling upon Styx, confirmed the boon.

[*To* NEPTUNE.]

945 Now fulfil the sad [1] boon, O ruler of the sea! Let
Hippolytus see the bright day no more, and in youth
pass to the ghosts that are wrathful with his sire.
Now bring aid, which my soul abhors, O father, to
thy son; never should I squander this last boon [2] of
thine, did not great ills o'erwhelm; in depths of
Tartarus, in presence of dread Dis, and imminent
menace of hell's lord, I was sparing of this prayer.
Keep now thy promised faith. Father, dost thou
delay? Why are thy waves yet silent? Now veil
the night with dark clouds driven by the winds;
snatch stars and sky from sight; pour forth the deep;
and, rising high, summon the floods from Ocean's
self.

CHORUS

O Nature, mighty mother of the gods, and thou,
fire-bearing Olympus' lord, who through the swift
firmament whirlest the scattered stars, and the
wandering courses of the planets, who makest the
heavens on swift axis turn, why dost thou take such

---

[1] Because a father is asking the death of his son.
[2] Theseus has already used two of his wishes, the first when
he set out from Troezen to Athens, and the second when he
was in the labyrinth.

cur tanta tibi cura perennes
agitare vias aetheris alti,
ut nunc canae frigora brumae
nudent silvas, nunc arbustis
redeant umbrae, nunc aestivi
colla leonis Cererem magno
fervore coquant viresque suas   970
temperet annus?
sed cur idem qui tanta regis,
sub quo vasti pondera mundi
librata suos ducunt orbes,
hominum nimium securus abes,
non sollicitus prodesse bonis,
nocuisse malis?
    Res humanas ordine nullo
Fortuna regit sparsitque manu
munera caeca, peiora fovens;   980
vincit sanctos dira libido,
fraus sublimi regnat in aula.
tradere turpi fasces populus
gaudet, eosdem colit atque odit.
tristis virtus perversa tulit
praemia recti; castos sequitur
mala paupertas vitioque potens
regnat adulter.
o vane pudor falsumque decus!

  Sed quid citato nuntius properat gradu
rigatque maestis lugubrem vultum genis?   990

  O sors acerba et dura, famulatus gravis,
cur me ad nefandum nuntium casus vocat?

care to keep perpetual the pathways of the lofty
sky, that now the hoar frosts of winter may strip the
woods, now to the plantations their umbrage come
again, that now in summer the Lion's fervent heat
may ripen the grain and the year regulate its powers?
But why, again, dost thou, who holdest so wide sway,
and by whose hands the ponderous masses of the
vast universe are poised and wheel their appointed
courses—why dost thou dwell afar, all too indifferent
to men, not anxious to bring blessing to the good,
and to the evil, bane?

978 Fate without order rules the affairs of men,
scatters her gifts with unseeing hand, fostering the
worse; dire lust prevails against pure men, and
crime sits regnant in the lofty palace. The rabble
rejoice to give government to the vile, paying high
honours even where they hate. Warped are the
rewards of uprightness sad virtue gains; wretched
poverty dogs the pure, and the adulterer, strong in
wickedness, reigns supreme. O decency, honour,
how empty and how false!

989 But why does yon messenger haste hither with
rapid pace, his sad countenance wet with grieving
tears?

[*Enter* MESSENGER.]

MESSENGER

O lot bitter and hard, O cruel servitude, why calls
fate upon me to bear unutterable tidings?

THESEVS

Ne metue clades fortiter fari asperas;
non imparatum pectus aerumnis fero.

NVNTIVS

Vocem dolori lingua luctifico negat.

THESEVS

Proloquere quae sors aggravet quassam domum.

NVNTIVS

Hippolytus, heu me, flebili leto occubat.

THESEVS

Natum parens obisse iam pridem scio;
nunc raptor obiit.   mortis effare ordinem.

NVNTIVS

Vt profugus urbem liquit infesto gradu   1000
celerem citatis passibus cursum explicans,
celso sonipes ocius subigit iugo
et ora frenis domita substrictis ligat.
tum multa secum effatus et patrium solum
abominatus saepe genitorem ciet
acerque habenis lora permissis quatit;
cum subito vastum tonuit ex alto mare
crevitque in astra.   nullus inspirat salo
ventus, quieti nulla pars caeli strepit
placidumque pelagus propria tempestas agit.   1010
400

HIPPOLYTUS

THESEUS

Fear not to speak out boldly the disaster, cruel though it be; I bear a heart not unprepared for suffering.

MESSENGER

My tongue refuses utterance to the grief-bringing woe.

THESEUS

Tell what mischance weighs down this shattered house.

MESSENGER

Hippolytus, woe is me, lies in lamentable death.

THESEUS

That his son was dead the sire has long since known; now is the ravisher dead. But tell the manner of his end.

MESSENGER

When with troubled steps he left the city, a fugitive, unfolding his swift way with flying feet, he quickly brought his prancing steeds 'neath the high yoke and curbed their mouths with tight-drawn reins. Then much did he utter, communing with himself, and, cursing his native land, called oft upon his sire, and with loose reins fiercely shook the lash; when suddenly from out the deep the vast sea thundered and starward heaved itself. No wind was blowing on the briny sea, from no quarter of the calm sky came the noise, but a self-born [1] tempest stirred the peaceful deep. Not so violently does the

---

[1] *i.e.* the commotion came from within the sea.

non tantus Auster Sicula disturbat freta
nec tam furens Ionius exsurgit sinus
regnante Coro, saxa cum fluctu tremunt
et cana summum spuma Leucaten ferit.
consurgit ingens pontus in vastum aggerem;
tumidumque monstro pelagus in terras ruit.[1]

   Nec ista ratibus tanta construitur lues;
terris minatur. fluctus haud cursu levi
provolvitur; nescio quid onerato sinu
gravis unda portat. quae novum tellus caput   1020
ostendit astris? Cyclas exoritur nova?
latuere rupes numen[2] Epidauri dei
et scelere petrae nobiles Scironides
et quae duobus terra comprimitur fretis.[3]

   Haec dum stupentes quaerimus,[4] totum en mare
immugit, omnes undique scopuli astrepunt;
summum cacumen rorat expulso sale,
spumat vomitque vicibus alternis aquas
qualis per alta vehitur Oceani freta
fluctum refundens ore physeter capax.   1030
inhorruit concussus undarum globus
solvitque sese et litori invexit malum
maius timore, pontus in terras ruit
suumque monstrum sequitur—os quassat tremor.
quis habitus ille corporis vasti fuit!
caerulea taurus colla sublimis gerens
erexit altam fronte viridanti iubam;
stant hispidae aures, orbibus varius color,
et quem feri dominator habuisset gregis
et quem sub undis natus—hinc flammam vomunt 1040
oculi, hinc relucent caerula insignes nota;

       [1] *Leo deletes this line.*
       [2] *So* A : *Leo* numine.
       [3] *Leo deletes ll. 1022–1024.*
       [4] querimur *A.*

south wind distress Sicilia's straits, nor so madly does the Ionian sea swell beneath the north-west's tyranny, when the cliffs tremble under the shock of waves and the white spray smites Leucate's summit. The mighty deep heaves up into a huge mound, and the sea, swollen with a monstrous birth, rushes to land.

1017 Nor is that vast destruction piled up for ships; 'tis the land it threatens. With no light sweep the flood rolls forward ; some strange thing in its burdened womb the heavy wave is carrying. What new land shows its head to the stars ? Is a new Cyclad rising ? The rocks, the sacred seat of the Epidaurian god,[1] were hid, and the cliffs famous for the crime of Sciron, and the land [2] which is hemmed in by two seas.

1025 While we in dumb amaze are wondering what this means, behold, the whole sea bellows, and the cliffs on every hand echo back the sound ; the highest peak is wet with dashed-up spray ; it foams, and then in turn spews back the flood, as when a cavernous whale swims through the deep ways of ocean, spouting back streams of water from his mouth. Then the great globe of waters shivered, shook and broke, and brought to the shore a thing more terrible than our fear ; the sea rushed landward, following its monster. My lips tremble in the telling. How the thing looked ! how huge ! A bull it was, towering high with a dark blue neck, and he reared a high mane upon his verdant crest ; his shaggy ears stood up ; his eyes flashed with changing colour, now such as the lord of a wild herd might have, now such as one born beneath the sea—now his eyes dart flame, now they flash wondrous with cerulean gleam. His

---

[1] These altar-like rocks were sacred to Aesculapius.
[2] Isthmus.

opima cervix arduos tollit toros
naresque hiulcis haustibus patulae fremunt;
musco tenaci pectus ac palear viret,
longum rubente spargitur fuco latus.
tum pone tergus ultima in monstrum coit
facies et ingens belua immensam trahit
squamosa partem.   talis extremo mari
pistrix citatas sorbet aut frangit rates.
tremuere terrae, fugit attonitum pecus   1050
passim per agros nec suos pastor sequi
meminit iuvencos; omnis e saltu fera
diffugit, omnis frigido exsanguis metu
venator horret.   solus immunis metu
Hippolytus artis continet frenis equos
pavidosque notae vocis hortatu ciet.

　　Est alta ad agros collibus ruptis via,
vicina tangens spatia suppositi maris;
hic se illa moles acuit atque iras parat.
ut cepit animos seque praetemptans satis   1060
prolusit irae, praepeti cursu evolat,
summam citato vix gradu tangens humum,
et torva currus ante trepidantes stetit.
contra feroci natus insurgens minax
vultu nec ora mutat et magnum intonat:
" haud frangit animum vanus hic terror meum;
nam mihi paternus vincere est tauros labor."
inobsequentes protinus frenis equi
rapuere currum iamque derrantes via,
quacumque rabidos pavidus evexit furor,   1070
hac ire pergunt seque per scopulos agunt
　　At ille, qualis turbido rector mari
ratem retentat, ne det obliquum latus,

brawny neck with great muscles bulges and his wide
nostrils roar with his gaping draughts of air. His
breast and dewlap are green with clinging moss, and
his long flanks with red seaweed are spotted. His
hinder parts are joined into monstrous shape, and,
all scaly, the huge beast drags his measureless length
along. Such is that sea-monster of the outer ocean
which swallows or crushes swift-flying ships. The
lands quaked with fear; herds fled in frenzy in all
directions through the fields, and the herdsman forgot
to follow his cattle. All beasts fled from their wooded
haunts; all hunters stood trembling, pale with chilling
fear. Hippolytus alone, quite unafraid, with tight
reins holds fast his horses and, terror-stricken though
they are, urges them on with the encouragement of
his familiar voice.

1057 There is a deep passage towards the fields
through the broken hills, hard by the neighbouring
stretches of the sea below. Here that huge creature
sharpens his anger and prepares his wrath. When
he has gained his spirit, and with full trial rehearsed
his wrath, he darts forth, running swiftly, scarce
touching the surface of the ground with flying feet,
and stands, in grim menace, before the trembling
steeds. Thy son, rising up, confronts him with fierce,
threatening look, nor does he change countenance,
but loudly thunders: "This empty terror cannot
break my spirit, for 'twas my father's task to conquer
bulls." But straightway his horses, disobedient to
the reins, seized the chariot and, roaming from the
road, wherever frenzied terror carried them in their
mad flight, there they plunged along and dashed
amid the rocks.

1072 But he, as a helmsman holds his ship steady on
the boisterous sea, lest it give its side to the waves,

405

et arte fluctum fallit, haud aliter citos
currus gubernat.   ora nunc pressis trahit
constricta frenis, terga nunc torto frequens
verbere cohercet.   sequitur adsiduus comes,
nunc aequa carpens spatia, nunc contra obvius
oberrat, omni parte terrorem movens.

Non licuit ultra fugere, nam toto obvius   1080
incurrit ore corniger ponti horridus.
tum vero pavida sonipedes mente exciti
imperia solvunt seque luctantur iugo
eripere rectique in pedes iactant onus.
praeceps in ora fusus implicuit cadens
laqueo tenaci corpus et quanto magis
pugnat, sequaces hoc magis nodos ligat
sensere pecudes facinus—et curru levi,
dominante nullo, qua timor iussit ruunt.
talis per auras non suum agnoscens onus   1090
Solique falso creditum indignans diem
Phaethonta currus devio excussit polo.
late cruentat arva et inlisum caput
scopulis resultat; auferunt dumi comas,
et ora durus pulchra populatur lapis
peritque multo vulnere infelix decor.
moribunda celeres membra provolvunt rotae;
tandemque raptum truncus ambusta sude
medium per inguen stipite erecto tenet,
paulumque domino currus affixo stetit.   1100
haesere biiuges vulnere—et pariter moram
dominumque rumpunt.   inde semanimem secant

and skilfully cheats the floods, in like manner guides
his swift-moving steeds. Now he drags on their
mouths checked by the tight-drawn reins, and now,
oft plying the twisted lash, he forces them to his
will. His companion [1] holds doggedly in pursuit,
now racing alongside the horses, now making detour
to face them, from every side filling them with fear.

[1080] But now they could flee no further; for he
charged full front upon them, that bristling, horned
monster of the deep. Then, truly, the plunging
horses, driven by mad fear, broke from control,
struggled to wrench their necks from the yoke, and,
rearing up, hurled their burden to the ground.
Headlong on his face he plunged and, as he fell,
entangled his body in the clinging reins; and the
more he struggled, the tighter he drew those firm-
holding coils. The horses felt their deed, and now,
with the light chariot, since none controlled, wherever
fear bade on they dashed. Just so, not recognizing
their wonted burden, and indignant that the day had
been entrusted to a pretended Sun, the horses [2] flung
Phaëthon far from his heavenly track. Far and
wide the fields are stained with blood, and his head,
dashed on the rocks, bounds back from them. The
brambles pluck away his hair; the hard stones ravage
that lovely face, and his ill-fated beauty is ruined by
many a wound. The swift wheels drag his dying
limbs; and at last, as he is whirled along, a tree, its
trunk charred into a stake, stays him with its stock
driven right through the groin and holds him
fast, and for a little while the car stands still,
held by its impaled master. Awhile that wound
stays the team—then equally delay and their master,
too, they break. [3] Thereafter the thickets slash his

[1] The monster.   [2] *i.e.* of the Sun.   [3] A bold case of zeugma.

virgulta, acutis asperi vepres rubis
omnisque truncus corporis partem tulit.
errant per agros funebris famuli manus,
per illa qua distractus Hippolytus loca
longum cruenta tramitem signat nota,
maestaeque domini membra vestigant canes.
necdum dolentum sedulus potuit labor
explere corpus.   hocine est formae decus?   1110
qui modo paterni clarus imperii comes
et certus heres siderum fulsit modo,
passim ad supremos ille colligitur rogos
et funeri confertur.

THESEVS

        O nimium potens,
quanto parentes sanguinis vinclo tenes,
natura, quam te colimus inviti quoque.
occidere volui noxium, amissum fleo.

NVNTIVS

Haud flere honeste quisquam quod voluit potest.[1]

THESEVS

Equidem malorum maximum hunc cumulum reor,
si abominanda casus optanda efficit.   1120

NVNTIVS

Et si odia servas, cur madent fletu genae?

THESEVS

Quod interemi, non quod amisi fleo.

[1] *So A :* Haud odere non est quisquam quod voluit potens *E:*
Leo corrects, followed by Richter, Gaudere non est ipse quod
voluit potens.

half-dead body, the rough brambles with their sharp thorns tear him, and every tree-trunk has taken its toll of him. Now bands of his mourning servants are scouring the fields through the places where Hippolytus was dragged, marked in a long trail by bloody traces, and his whimpering dogs are tracking their master's limbs. But not yet has the painstaking toil of his grieving friends availed to fill out his body. Has his glorious beauty come to this? He who but now was the illustrious partner of his father's throne, who but now, his acknowledged heir, shone like the stars, he is being gathered from every hand for his last burning, and collected for his funeral pyre.

THESEUS [*weeping*]

O nature, all too potent, with how strong ties of blood dost thou hold parents! how we cherish thee, even against our wills! Guilty, I wished him dead; lost, I lament him.

MESSENGER

Not rightfully may any weep what he has willed.

THESEUS

Truly I deem this the crowning woe of woes, if fortune makes what we must loathe that we must long for.

MESSENGER

If thou still keepst thy hate, why are thy cheeks wet with tears?

THESEUS

Not that I lost, but that I slew, I weep.

Quanti casus humana rotant!
minor in parvis Fortuna furit
leviusque ferit leviora deus;
servat placidos obscura quies
praebetque senes casa securos.
    Admota aetheriis culmina sedibus
Euros excipiunt, excipiunt Notos,
insani Boreae minas,   1130
imbriferumque Corum.
raros patitur fulminis ictus
umida vallis;
tremuit telo Iovis altisoni
Caucasus ingens Phrygiumque nemus
matris Cybeles.   metuens caelo
Iuppiter alto vicina petit;
non capit umquam magnos motus
humilis tecti plebeia domus.
circa regna tonat.[1]   1140
    Volat ambiguis mobilis alis
hora, nec ulli praestat velox
Fortuna fidem.
hic qui clari laetus vidit [2]
sidera mundi nitidumque diem
nocte relicta, luget maestos
tristis reditus ipsoque magis
flebile Averno sedis patriae
videt hospitium.
    Pallas Actaeae veneranda genti,
quod tuus caelum superosque Theseus   1150
spectat et fugit Stygias paludes,
casta, nil debes patruo rapaci;
constat inferno numerus tyranno.

---

[1] *Leo deletes this line.*   [2] *Leo supplies* laetus vidit.

HIPPOLYTUS

CHORUS

How chance whirls round the affairs of men!
Less does fortune rage midst humble folk, and
more lightly God smites the more lightly blessed.
Unnoticed ease keeps men in peace and a cottage
bestows age untroubled.

1128 The mountain-peaks, lifted to airy heights,
catch east, catch south winds, mad Boreas' threats,
and the rain-fraught north-west gale. Seldom does
the moist valley suffer the lightning's blast; but
Caucasus the huge, and the Phrygian grove of
mother Cybele, quake beneath the bolt of high-
thundering Jove. For in jealous fear Jove aims at
that which neighbours on high heaven; but the low-
roofed, common home ne'er feels his mighty blasts.
Around thrones he thunders.

1141 On doubtful wings flies the inconstant hour,
nor does swift Fortune pledge loyalty to any. He [1]
who with joy beheld the clear, starry skies and
bright day, the night [2] now left behind, in grief is
lamenting his sorrowful return, and finds his welcome to his father's dwelling more doleful than
Avernus' self.

1149 O Pallas, ever to be revered by the Athenian
race, for that thy Theseus looks on sky and upper
world and has escaped from the pools of Styx,
chaste one, thou owest naught to thine uncle, the
all-devouring; unchanged the tale [3] remains for the
infernal king.

---

[1] Theseus, who has but now returned from Hades.
[2] *i.e.* the darkness of the lower world.
[3] *i.e.* if Theseus has escaped Pluto, Hippolytus has gone to
fill his place.

Quae vox ab altis flebilis tectis sonat
strictoque vaecors Phaedra quid ferro parat?

THESEVS

Quis te dolore percitam instigat furor?
quid ensis iste quidve vociferatio
planctusque supra corpus invisum volunt?

PHAEDRA

Me, me, profundi saeve dominator freti,
invade et in me monstra caerulei maris   1160
emitte, quidquid intimo Tethys sinu
extrema gestat, quidquid Oceanus vagis
complexus undis ultimo fluctu tegit.
o dure Theseu semper, o numquam ad tuos
tuto reverse, natus et genitor nece
reditus tuos luere; pervertis domum
amore semper coniugum aut odio nocens.

Hippolyte, tales intuor vultus tuos
talesque feci? membra quis saevus Sinis
aut quis Procrustes sparsit aut quis Cresius,   1170
Daedalea vasto claustra mugitu replens,
taurus biformis ore cornigero ferox
divulsit? heu me, quo tuus fugit decor
oculique nostrum sidus? exanimis iaces?

412

[1154] What voice of wailing sounds from the high palace ? And what would maddened Phaedra with the naked sword ?

[*Enter* PHAEDRA *with a drawn sword in her hand.*]

THESEUS

What fury pricks thee on, wild with grief? Why that sword ? What mean thine outcries and lamentations over the hated corpse ?

PHAEDRA

Me, me, assault, O savage ruler of ocean's depths ; against me send forth the blue sea's monsters, what-e'er in her inmost womb farthest Tethys bears, whate'er in his restless waves' embrace Ocean hides in his remotest flood. O Theseus, always harsh, who never without harm unto thy loved ones dost come back, son and father [1] have paid for thy home-comings by their death. Thou art the destroyer of thy home, hurtful ever, whether through love or hatred of thy wives.[2]

[*Turning to the mangled corpse.*]

[1168] O Hippolytus, is it such I see thy face ? such have I made it ? What savage Sinis, what Procrustes, has scattered thy members so, or what Cretan bull, fierce, two-formed monster, filling the labyrinth of Daedalus with his huge bellowings, has torn thee asunder with his horns ? Ah, woe is me ! whither is thy glorious beauty fled, and thine eyes, my stars ? Dost lie low in death ? Come back for

---

[1] See Index *s.v.* "Theseus."
[2] Theseus had slain Antiope in a fit of anger, and now has destroyed Hippolytus through jealous love for Phaedra.

ades parumper verbaque exaudi mea—
nil turpe loquimur—hac manu poenas tibi
solvam et nefando pectori ferrum inseram
animaque Phaedram pariter ac scelere exuam,
et te per undas perque Tartareos lacus,
per Styga, per amnes igneos amens sequar. 1180
placemus umbras; capitis exuvias cape
laceraeque frontis accipe abscissam [1] comam.
non licuit animos iungere, et certe licet
iunxisse fata.

    Morere, si casta es, viro;
si incesta, amori. coniugis thalamos petam
tanto impiatos facinore? hoc derat nefas,
ut vindicato sancta fruereris toro.
o mors amoris una sedamen mali,
o mors pudoris maximum laesi decus,
confugimus ad te; pande placatos sinus. 1190

 Audite, Athenae, tuque, funesta pater
peior noverca: falsa memoravi et nefas,
quod ipsa demens pectore insano hauseram,
mentita finxi. vana punisti pater,
iuvenisque castus crimine incesto iacet,
pudicus, insons.

    Recipe iam mores tuos.
mucrone pectus impium iusto patet
cruorque sancto solvit inferias viro.

 Quid facere rapto debeas nato parens,
disce a noverca: condere Acherontis plagis.[2] 1200

---

[1] *So ς: Leo abscisam.*
[2] *Leo gives ll. 1199, 1200 to Theseus; but they seem more
naturally to belong to Phaedra. So A.*

a little and hearken to my words—no shameful thing I speak—with this hand will I make amends to thee, in my wicked heart will I thrust the sword and set Phaedra free equally from life and crime. Then through waters, through Tartarean pools, through Styx, through rivers of fire will I madly follow thee. Let me appease thy shade; take the spoils of my head, and accept this lock torn from my wounded forehead. It was not ours to be joined in life, but surely 'tis ours to be joined in death.

[*To herself.*]

1184 Now die, if thou art pure, for thy husband's sake; if impure, for thy love. Shall I seek again my husband's couch by so great crime defiled? The one horror lacking was that, as if pure, thou shouldst enjoy his couch claimed as thy right. O death, thou only solace of evil love, O death, thou chiefest grace to damaged honour, I fly to thee; spread wide thy forgiving arms.

1191 Hear me, O Athens, and thou, his father, worse than baleful stepdame: I have lied to you, and the crime which, crazed with passion, I had conceived in my own mad breast, I falsely charged to him Thou, father, hast punished to no purpose; and the chaste youth, through charge of the unchaste, lies there, all pure and innocent.

[*To* HIPPOLYTUS.]

1196 Recover now thine honour. My impious breast is bare to the sword of justice, and my blood makes atonement to a guiltless man.

[*To* THESEUS.]

1199 What thou, his father, shouldst do, now that thy son is murdered, learn from his stepdame: hide thee in Acheron.

[*She falls upon her sword and dies.*]

415

Pallidi fauces Averni vosque, Taenarei specus,
unda miseris grata Lethes vosque, torpentes lacus,
impium abdite atque mersum premite perpetuis
    malis.
nunc adeste, saeva ponti monstra, nunc vastum mare,
ultimo quodcumque Proteus aequorum abscondit
    sinu,
meque ovantem scelere tanto rapite in altos gurgites.
tuque semper, genitor, irae facilis assensor meae,
morte facili dignus haud sum qui nova natum nece
segregem sparsi per agros quique, dum falsum
    nefas
exsequor vindex severus, incidi in verum scelus. 1210
sidera et manes et undas scelere complevi meo ;
amplius sors nulla restat ; regna me norunt tria.

In hoc redimus ? patuit ad caelum via,
bina ut viderem funera et geminam necem,
caelebs et orbus funebres una face
ut concremarem prolis ac thalami rogos ?
donator atrae lucis, Alcide, tuum
Diti remitte munus ; ereptos mihi
restitue manes.　impius frustra invoco
mortem relictam.　crudus et leti artifex,　　　　　1220
exitia machinatus insolita effera,
nunc ipse tibimet iusta supplicia irroga.
pinus coacto vertice attingens humum
caelo remissum findat in geminas trabes,
416

HIPPOLYTUS

THESEUS

Ye jaws of wan Avernus, ye Taenarean caves,
ye waves of Lethe, welcome to the wretched, ye
sluggish pools, hide ye my impious self, plunge deep
and bury me in unending woes. Come now, savage
monsters of the deep, now, vast sea, and whatever
Proteus has hidden away in the furthest hollow of
his waters, and hurry me off, me who felt triumph
in crime so great, to your deep pools. And thou,
father, who didst e'er give too quick assent to my
angry prayer, I am not worthy of an easy death who
have brought unheard-of destruction on my son and
scattered his mangled limbs throughout the fields;
who, while, as stern avenger, I was punishing an unreal
crime, have myself fallen into true guilt. Heaven,
hell, and ocean have I filled up by my sin; there
remains no further lot; [1] three kingdoms know me.

1213 For this have I returned ? Was the way opened
to the light of heaven that I might look on two
funerals and a double murder, that, wifeless and
childless, I might with one torch light the funeral
pyres of son and wife ? O giver of light that is
but darkness, Alcides, give back his boon [2] to Dis;
give me up again to the ghosts whom I escaped.
Impiously, I make vain prayers for the death I left
behind. Thou bloody man, skilful in deadly arts,
who didst contrive unheard-of, barbarous ways of
death, now upon thyself inflict fitting punishment.
Shall a pine-tree, its top bent down to earth, split
me in two, shot back into the air ? [3] Shall I be

---

[1] A reference to the three lots by which the sons of Saturn
divided the universe among themselves.
[2] Hercules had asked the boon of Dis that he might take
Theseus with him out of Hades.
[3] See Index *s.v.* " Sinis."

mittarve praeceps saxa per Scironia ?
graviora vidi, quae pati clausos iubet
Phlegethon nocentes igneo cingens vado ;
quae poena memet maneat et sedes, scio.

Umbrae nocentes, cedite et cervicibus
his, his repositum degravet fessas manus   1230
saxum, seni perennis Aeolio labor ;
me ludat amnis ora vicina alluens ;
vultur relicto transvolet Tityo ferus
meumque poenae semper accrescat iecur ;
et tu mei requiesce Perithoi pater :
haec incitatis membra turbinibus ferat
numquam resistens orbe revoluto rota.
dehisce tellus, recipe me dirum chaos,
recipe, haec ad umbras iustior nobis via est—
natum sequor.   ne metue qui manes regis ;   1240
casti venimus ; recipe me aeterna domo
non exiturum.   non movent divos preces ;
at si rogarem scelera, quam proni forent !

CHORVS

Theseu, querelis tempus aeternum manet.
nunc iusta nato solve et absconde ocius
dispersa foede membra laniatu effero.

THESEVS

Huc, huc reliquias vehite cari corporis
pondusque et artus temere congestos date.
Hippolytus hic est ? crimen agnosco meum ;
418

hurled headlong over the Scironian cliffs? More dreadful things have I seen which Phlegethon bids imprisoned sinners suffer, compassing them about with his stream of fire; what punishment waits for me, and what place, I know.

¹²²⁹ Ye guilty shades, make room, and on these shoulders, these, let the rock rest, the endless task of the aged son[1] of Aeolus, and weigh down my weary hands; let water, lapping my very lips, mock my thirst;[2] let the fell vulture leave Tityus and fly hither, let my liver constantly grow afresh for punishment; and do thou rest awhile, father[3] of my Pirithoüs—let the wheel that never stops its whirling bear these limbs of mine on its swift-turning rim. Yawn, earth; take me, dire Chaos, take me; this way to the shades is more fitting[4] for me—my son I follow. And fear not, thou who rulest the shades; I come clean-handed;[5] receive me into thy everlasting home, to go forth no more. My prayers move not the gods; but if I asked impious things, how would they bend to answer!

CHORUS

Theseus, time without end awaits thy lamentations. Now pay the rites due to thy son and bury with speed the scattered limbs mangled so shamefully.

THESEUS

Hither, hither bring the remains of his dear body and heap together, as they come, the burden of his limbs. Is this Hippolytus? Mine is the sin, I do

---

[1] Sisyphus. [2] Referring to the torture of Tantalus.
[3] Ixion. [4] *i.e.* than his former journey to the lower world.
[5] *i.e.* with no evil designs on Proserpina, as before.

ego te peremi, neu nocens tantum semel   1250
solusve fierem, facinus ausurus parens
patrem advocavi.   munere en patrio fruor.
o triste fractis orbitas annis malum !
complectere artus, quodque de nato est super,
miserande, maesto pectore incumbens fove.

CHORVS

  Disiecta, genitor, membra laceri corporis
in ordinem dispone et errantes loco
restitue partes.   fortis hic dextrae locus,
hic laeva frenis docta moderandis manus
ponenda ; laevi lateris agnosco notas.   1260
quam magna lacrimis pars adhuc nostris abest !

THESEVS

  Durate trepidae lugubri officio manus,
fletusque largos sistite, arentes genae,
dum membra nato genitor adnumerat suo
corpusque fingit.   hoc quid est forma carens
et turpe, multo vulnere abruptum undique ?
quae pars tui sit dubito ; sed pars est tui.
hic, hic repone, non suo, at vacuo loco.
haecne illa facies igne sidereo nitens,
inimica flectens lumina ? huc cecidit decor ?   1270
o dira fata, numinum o saevus favor '
sic ad parentem natus ex voto redit ?
  En haec suprema dona genitoris cape,
saepe efferendus ; interim haec ignes ferant.

420

acknowledge it; 'tis I who have murdered thee, and, lest once only or alone I might be guilty, when I his father would dare crime, my own sire I summoned to my aid. Behold, I enjoy my father's boon. O childlessness, bitter misfortune for broken years! Come, clasp his limbs and all that is left thee of thy son, thou wretched man, and, in thy sad breast fondling, cherish them.

CHORUS

The scattered parts of his torn body set thou, his sire, in order, and put back in place the random pieces. Here should be his strong right hand, here we must put his left, skilled in managing the reins; traces of his left side I recognize. But how large a part is still lacking to our tears!

THESEUS

Be firm, my trembling hands, for your sad duty; be dry, my cheeks, stay your flowing tears, while a father is portioning out members to his son and fashioning his body. What is this shapeless, ugly piece, with many a` wound torn on every side? What part it is of thee, I know not; but it is a part of thee. Here, here lay it down, not in its own but in an empty place. Is this that face which once gleamed with fire as of the stars, which turned his enemy's eyes aside? Has his beauty fallen to this? O dire fate, O cruel favour of the gods! Thus comes back son to father in answer to his prayer?

[*Placing some ornaments on the torn body.*]

1273 Lo, these are thy sire's last gifts. Take them, O thou who must oft be borne to burial. Now let the fires consume these limbs.

SENECAE TRAGOEDIAE

Patefacite acerbam caede funesta domum;
Mopsopia claris tota lamentis sonet.
vos apparate regii flammam rogi;
at vos per agros corporis partes vagas
inquirite.
      Istam terra defossam premat,
gravisque tellus impio capiti incubet!   1280

HIPPOLYTUS

[To attendants.]

¹²⁷⁵ Open wide my palace, gloomy and foul with slaughter, and let all Athens with loud laments resound. Do you make ready the flames of the royal pyre ; do you seek through the fields for his body's parts still wandering.

[Pointing to PHAEDRA'S *corpse.]*

¹²⁷⁹ As for her, let her be buried deep in earth, and heavy may the soil lie on her unholy head !

OEDIPUS

DRAMATIS PERSONAE

OEDIPUS, *king of Thebes; the son, as he supposed, of Polybus, king of Corinth, and Merope, his wife, but found to be the son of Laïus and Jocasta.*

JOCASTA, *wife of Oedipus, found to be also his mother.*

CREON, *a Theban prince, brother of Jocasta.*

TIRESIAS, *the prophet of Thebes, now old and blind.*

MANTO, *daughter of Tiresias.*

OLD MAN, *sent from Corinth to announce to Oedipus the death of Polybus.*

PHORBAS, *shepherd in charge of the royal flocks of Thebes.*

MESSENGER, *who announces the self-inflicted blindness of Oedipus and the suicide of Jocasta.*

CHORUS *of Theban elders.*

THE SCENE is laid before the royal palace of Thebes; the play opens in the early morning of the day within which the tragedy is consummated.

ARGUMENT

AN oracle once came to Laïus, king of Thebes, that he should perish by his own son's hands. When, therefore, a son was born to him, he gave the infant to his chief shepherd to expose on Mount Cithaeron. But the tender-hearted rustic gave the babe instead to a wandering herdsman of Polybus, the king of Corinth.

Years later a reputed son of Polybus, Oedipus by name, fearing an oracle which doomed him to slay his father and wed his mother, fled from Corinth, that so he might escape this dreadful fate. As he fared northward he met and slew an old man who imperiously disputed the narrow way with him. Upon arriving at the Theban land he read the riddle of the Sphinx, and so destroyed that monster which Juno had sent to harass the land which she hated ; and for this service Oedipus was made the husband of Jocasta, the widowed queen of Laïus (recently slain, so said report, by a band of robbers, on the high road), and set upon the vacant throne.

Now other years have passed, and sons and daughters have been born to the royal pair. But now a dreadful pestilence afflicts the State. Oedipus has sent Creon to consult the oracle, to learn the cause and seek the means of deliverance from the scourge. And while he waits his messenger's return the murky dawn still finds him grieving for his kingdom's wretched plight.

OEDIPVS

OEDIPVS

Iam nocte Titan dubius expulsa redit
et nube maestus[1] squalida exoritur iubar,
lumenque flamma triste luctifica gerens
prospiciet avida peste solatas domos,
stragemque quam nox fecit ostendet dies.
  Quisquamne regno gaudet? O fallax bonum,
quantum malorum fronte quam blanda tegis!
ut alta ventos semper excipiunt iuga
rupemque saxis vasta dirimentem freta
quamvis quieti verberat fluctus maris,   10
imperia sic excelsa Fortunae obiacent.
quam bene parentis sceptra Polybi fugeram
curis solutus exul, intrepidus, vagans [2]
(caelum deosque testor) in regnum incidi.
infanda timeo—ne mea genitor manu
perimatur. hoc me Delphicae laurus monent,
aliudque nobis maius indicunt scelus.
est maius aliquod patre mactato nefas?
pro misera pietas (eloqui fatum pudet),
thalamos parentis Phoebus et diros toros   20
nato minatur impia incestos face;
hic me paternis expulit regnis timor.

---

[1] *So Leo and Richter: Bentley* maestum squalida extollit
iubar.
[2] *So Richter, with A: Leo* vacans, *with E.*

OEDIPUS

Now night is driven away; the hesitant sun returns,
and rises, sadly veiling his beams in murky cloud;
with woeful flame he brings a light of gloom and
will look forth upon our homes stricken with ravening plague, and day will reveal the havoc which night
has wrought.

[6] Does any man rejoice in royalty? O deceitful
good, how many ills dost hide beneath thy smiling
face! As lofty peaks do ever catch the blasts, and as
the cliff, which with its jutting rocks cleaves the vast
deep, is beaten by the waves of even a quiet sea, so
does exalted empire lie exposed to fate. How happily
had I escaped the sceptre of my father, Polybus!
An exile freed from cares,[1] fearless, wandering, upon
a kingdom (be heaven and the gods my witness) I
came by chance. Things unspeakable I fear—that
by my hand my father shall be slain. Of this the
Delphic laurels warn me, and another, still greater
crime they assign to me. Is any wickedness greater
than a murdered sire? O hapless filial love!—I
am ashamed to tell my doom—Phoebus threatens
the son with his father's chamber, with bed made
infamous, defiled by unhallowed passion. 'Twas the
fear of this that drove me from my father's realm.

---

[1] *i.e.* regarding the oracle, whose fulfilment he thought he
had escaped.

non ego penates profugus excessi meos ;
parum ipse fidens mihimet in tuto tua,
Natura, posui iura.   cum magna horreas,
quod posse fieri non putes metuas tamen.
cuncta expavesco meque non credo mihi.

Iam iam aliquid in nos fata moliri parant ;
nam quid rear quod ista Cadmeae lues
in'esta genti, strage tam late edita,   30
mihi parcit uni ?   cui reservamur malo ?
inter ruinas urbis et semper novis
deflenda lacrimis funera ac populi struem
incolumis asto—scilicet Phoebi reus.
sperare poteras sceleribus tantis dari
regnum salubre ?   fecimus caelum nocens.

Non aura gelido lenis afflatu fovet
anhela flammis corda, non Zephyri leves
spirant, sed ignes auget aestiferi canis
Titan, leonis terga Nemeaei premens.   40
deseruit amnes umor atque herbas color,
aretque Dirce, tenuis Ismenos fluit
et tinguit inopi nuda vix unda vada.
obscura caelo labitur Phoebi soror,
tristisque mundus nubilo pallet die.
nullum serenis noctibus sidus micat,
sed gravis et ater incubat terris vapor.
obtexit arces caelitum ac summas domos
inferna facies.   denegat fructum Ceres

430

OEDIPUS

Not as a fugitive[1] did I leave my home ; of my own will, distrustful of myself, O Nature, I made thy laws secure. When thou dreadest some great calamity, though thou thinkst it cannot befall, still do thou fear. I dread all things exceedingly, and I do not trust myself unto myself.

[28] Now, even now the fates are aiming some blow at me ; for what am I to think when this pestilence, so deadly to Cadmus' race, so widespread in its destruction, spares me alone ? For what evil am I reserved ? Midst the ruins of my city, midst funerals to be lamented with tears ever fresh, midst the slaughter of a nation, I stand unscathed—aye ! prisoner at Phoebus' bar. Couldst thou hope that to crimes like thine a wholesome kingdom would be granted ? I have made heaven pestilent.[2]

[37] No soft breeze with its cool breath relieves our breasts that pant with heat, no gentle Zephyrs blow ; but Titan augments the scorching dog-star's fires, close-pressing upon the Nemean Lion's[3] back. Water has fled the streams, and from the herbage verdure. Dirce is dry, scant flows Ismenus' stream, and with its meagre wave scarce wets the naked sands. With paling light glides Phoebus' sister athwart the sky, and the gloomy heavens are wan in the lowering day. No star in clear nights glitters, but a heavy, black fog broods o'er the lands. The citadels of the heavenly gods and their homes on high are veiled in hellish aspect. The ripened corn withholds its fruitful

---

[1] *i.e.* to avoid the consequences of some crime already committed.

[2] *i.e.* " I have caused the gods on my account to work this great destruction " ; or, as Farnabius interprets : " I have infected the very air." This latter interpretation is favoured by l. 79.

[3] The sun is in the constellation of Leo in July.

adulta, et altis flava cum spicis tremat,   50
arente culmo sterilis emoritur seges.
nec ulla pars immunis exitio vacat,
sed omnis aetas pariter et sexus ruit,
iuvenesque senibus iungit et natis patres
funesta pestis, una fax thalamos cremat
fletuque acerbo funera et questu carent.
quin ipsa tanti pervicax clades mali
siccavit oculos, quodque in extremis solet
periere lacrimae.   portat hunc aeger parens
supremum ad ignem, mater hunc amens gerit   60
properatque ut alium repetat in eundem rogum.
quin luctu in ipso luctus exoritur novus
suaeque circa funus exequiae cadunt.
tum propria flammis corpora alienis cremant;
diripitur ignis; nullus est miseris pudor.
non ossa tumuli sancta discreti tegunt.
arsisse satis est; pars quota in cineres abit!
dest terra tumulis, iam rogos silvae negant.
non vota, non ars ulla correptos levant.
cadunt medentes, morbus auxilium trahit.   70

    Adfusus aris supplices tendo manus
matura poscens fata, praecurram ut prior
patriam ruentem neve post omnes cadam
fiamque regni funus extremum mei.
o saeva nimium numina, o fatum grave!
negatur uni nempe in hoc populo mihi
mors tam parata? sperne letali manu
contacta regna, linque lacrimas, funera,

harvest, and though the golden crop waves high
its wheaten ears, the grain dies shrivelled on its
parched stalk. No class is free from death ; but
every age and sex is smitten alike. Young men
with old, fathers with sons, are joined by the deadly
plague ; husband and wife by a single fire are burned,
and funerals lack bitter tears and lamentations. Nay,
the persistent bane of our so great a woe hath of
itself dried our eyes and, as oft in utmost misery,
our tears have perished. Here to the final flames a
stricken father bears his son ; there a crazed mother
carries her child and hastens back to bring another
to the selfsame pyre. Nay more, in their very grief
new grief arises and midst funeral rites their own
rites befall. Anon, with others' fires they burn the
bodies of their own ; yes, fire is stolen, for the
wretched have no shame. No separate mounds cover
the hallowed bones. Mere burning is enough ; how
small a part is turned to ashes ! No ground is left
for tombs ; now woods refuse more pyres. Neither
prayers nor any skill avails the stricken. Healers fall
victims ; the disease drags down those who seek to aid.

⁷¹ Prostrate at the altars, I stretch suppliant hands,
begging my fates to hasten, that I may anticipate
my country's ruin and not fall after all the rest, and
mine become the last funeral of my realm. Oh, divinities too harsh, Oh, heavy fate ! To me alone in all
this people is death denied, so ready for all others ?
Come, fly the land thy baleful hand has tainted,
leave the tears, the deaths, the pest-laden air which

tabifica caeli vitia quae tecum invehis
infaustus hospes, profuge iamdudum ocius— 80
vel ad parentes!

IOCASTA

    Quid iuvat, coniunx, mala
gravare questu? regium hoc ipsum reor—
adversa capere, quoque sit dubius magis
status et cadentis imperi moles labet,
hoc stare certo pressius fortem gradu.
haud est virile terga Fortunae dare.

OEDIPVS

Abest pavoris crimen ac probrum procul,
virtusque nostra nescit ignavos metus.
si tela contra stricta, si vis horrida
Mavortis in me rueret, adversus feros 90
audax Gigantas obvias ferrem manus.
nec Sphinga caecis verba nectentem modis
fugi; cruentos vatis infandae tuli
rictus et albens ossibus sparsis solum;
cumque e superna rupe iam praedae imminens
aptaret alas verbera et caudae movens
saevi leonis more conciperet minas,
carmen poposci. sonuit horrendum insuper,
crepuere malae, saxaque impatiens morae
revulsit unguis viscera expectans mea; 100
nodosa sortis verba et implexos dolos
ac triste carmen alitis solvi ferae.

thou bringst with thee, ill-omened guest; fly quickly'
(long since 'twere well)—even to thy parents! [1]

JOCASTA

[*Who has entered in time to hear her husband's last
words.*]

What boots it, husband, to make woe heavier
by lamentation? This very thing, methinks, is
regal—to face adversity and, the more dubious thy
station and the more the greatness of empire totters
to its fall, the more firm to stand, brave with un-
faltering foot. 'Tis not a manly thing to turn the
back to Fortune.

OEDIPUS

Far from me is the crime and shame of cowardice,
and my valour knows not dastard fears. Should
swords be drawn against me, should the bristling
power of Mars rush on me, against even the fierce
Giants would I boldly bear opposing hands. The
Sphinx, weaving her words in darkling measures, I
fled not; I faced the bloody jaws of the fell prophetess
and the ground white with scattered bones. And
when from a lofty cliff, already hovering over her
prey, she prepared her pinions and, lashing her tail
like a savage lion, stirred up her threatening wrath,
I asked her riddle. Thereupon came a sound of
dread; her jaws crashed, and her talons, brooking no
delay, eager for my vitals, tore at the rocks. The
lot's intricate, guile-entangled words, the grim riddle
of the winged beast, I solved.

---

[1] *i.e.* Polybus, king of Corinth, and Merope, his wife, who,
he supposed, were his parents and from whom he had fled to
Thebes.

SENECAE TRAGOEDIAE

Quid sera mortis vota nunc demens facis?
licuit perire. laudis hoc pretium tibi
sceptrum et peremptae Sphingis haec merces datur.[1]
ille, ille dirus callidi monstri cinis
in nos rebellat, illa nunc Thebas lues
perempta perdit. una iam superest salus,
si quam salutis Phoebus ostendit viam.

CHORVS

Occidis, Cadmi generosa proles,   110
urbe cum tota; viduas colonis
respicis terras, miseranda Thebe.
carpitur leto tuus ille, Bacche,
miles, extremos comes usque ad Indos,
ausus Eois equitare campis
figere et mundo tua signa primo.
cinnami silvis Arabas beatos
vidit et versos equites, sagittis
terga fallacis metuenda Parthi;
litus intravit pelagi rubentis;   120
promit hinc ortus aperitque lucem
Phoebus et flamma propiore nudos
        inficit Indos.
Stirpis invictae genus interimus,
labimur saevo rapiente fato;
ducitur semper nova pompa Morti;
longus ad manes properatur ordo
agminis maesti, seriesque tristis
haeret et turbae tumulos petenti
non satis septem patuere portae.   130
stat gravis strages premiturque iuncto
        funere funus.

[1] *Richter assigns ll. 103–105 to Jocasta.*

OEDIPUS

[103] [*To himself.*] Why too late dost thou now in madness pray for death? Thou hadst thy chance to die. This sceptre is thy meed of praise, this thy reward for the Sphinx destroyed. That dust, that cursed dust of the artful monster is warring against me still; that pest which I destroyed is now destroying Thebes. One only salvation is left us now, if any way of salvation Phoebus shows.

CHORUS

Thou art falling, O noble race of Cadmus, with all thy city. Reft of its tillers thou seest thy land, O pitiable Thebes. Destruction feeds, O Bacchus, on that soldiery of thine, thy comrades to farthest Ind, who dared to ride on the Eastern plains and plant thy banners on the world's first edge. The Arabs, blest with their cinnamon groves, they saw, and fleeing horsemen, the backs of the treacherous Parthians,[1] to be feared for their flying shafts; they pierced to the shores of the ruddy sea,[2] whence Phoebus discloses his rising beams, opens the gates of day, and with nearer torch darkens the naked Indians. [124] We, the offspring of an unconquered stock, are perishing, are falling 'neath the fierce onslaught of fate. Each hour a new train moves on to Death; the long array of a mournful band hastes to the shades; the gloomy procession jams, and for the throng that seeks burial the seven gates spread not wide enough. The grievous wrack of carnage halts and funeral crowds funeral in unbroken line.

---

[1] A reference to the proverbial "Parthian shot," delivered while in flight or seeming flight.

[2] Referring not to our "Red Sea," but to the Indian Ocean. See *Herc. Fur.*, 903; *Thy.*, 371.

    Prima vis tardas tetigit bidentes;
laniger pingues male carpsit herbas.
colla tacturus steterat sacerdos;
dum manus certum parat alta vulnus,
aureo taurus rutilante cornu
labitur segnis.   patuit sub ictu
ponderis vasti resoluta cervix;
nec cruor, ferrum maculavit atra   140
turpis e plaga sanies profusa.
segnior cursu sonipes in ipso
concidit gyro dominumque prono
      prodidit armo.
    Incubant agris pecudes relictae;
taurus armento pereunte marcet;
deficit pastor grege deminuto
tabidos inter moriens iuvencos.
non lupos cervi metuunt rapaces,
cessat irati fremitus leonis,   150
nulla villosis feritas in ursis;
perdidit pestem latebrosa serpens;
aret et sicco moritur veneno.

    Non silva sua decorata coma
fundit opacis montibus umbras,
non rura virent ubere glebae,
non plena suo vitis Baccho
bracchia curvat;
omnia nostrum sensere malum.
    Rupere Erebi claustra profundi   160
turba sororum face Tartarea
Phlegethonque suam mutat ripam;
miscuit undis Styga Sidoniis.

[133] First the plague struck the slow-moving sheep ; to their bane did the woolly flock crop the rich herbage. Ready to smite his victim's neck, the priest had taken his stand ; while his upraised hand aimed the unerring blow, the bull, his horn glimmering with gold, sank dully down. Shattered by the blow of a heavy axe, the neck yawned open ;[1] but no blood, only foul gore, oozing from the dark wound, stained the steel. The prancing steed, slowing in mid-course, fell down and flung his rider over his sinking shoulder.

[145] The abandoned cattle lie stricken in the fields ; the bull pines away amidst his dying kine. The herdsman deserts his dwindling herd, midst his wasting bullocks dying. No more do stags fear ravenous wolves ; subsides the mad lion's roar ; no fierceness now among the shaggy bears. The lurking serpent has lost its bane ; parched and dying he lies, his venom dried.

[154] No more do the woods, crowned with their own foliage, shed dusky shadows on the mountain-sides ; the fields no more grow green with fertile glebe, no more do the vine's full branches bend 'neath the load of its own deity ; all things have felt our plague.

[160] They have burst the bars of abysmal Erebus, the throng of sisters with Tartarean torch,[2] and Phlegethon,[2] changing his own course, has mingled Styx with our Sidonian[3] streams. Dark Death opens

---

[1] The experience with two victims is described. The first bull fell before he was struck ; the second was struck with the axe, but no blood flowed.

[2] In reference to the hot fever of the plague-smit victims. Phlegethon was the burning stream of Hades.

[3] *i.e.* Phoenician. Cadmus, son of Agenor, king of Phoenicia had founded Thebes.

Mors atra avidos oris hiatus
pandit et omnes explicat alas;
quique capaci turbida cumba
flumina servat durus senio
navita crudo, vix assiduo
bracchia conto lassata refert,
fessus turbam vectare novam.   170
quin Taenarii vincula ferri
rupisse canem fama et nostris
errare locis, mugisse solum,
vaga per lucos simulacra ferunt
maiora viris, bis Cadmeum
nive discussa tremuisse nemus,
bis turbatam sanguine Dircen,
nocte silenti
Amphionios ululasse canes.

  O dira novi facies leti,   180
gravior leto! piger ignavos
alligat artus languor, et aegro
rubor in vultu, maculaeque caput
sparsere leves; tum vapor ipsam
corporis arcem flammeus urit
multoque genas sanguine tendit,
oculique rigent et sacer ignis
pascitur artus; resonant aures
stillatque niger naris aduncae
cruor et venas rumpit hiantes;   190
intima creber viscera quassat
gemitus stridens.   iamque amplexu
frigida presso saxa fatigant;
quos liberior domus elato
custode sinit, petitis fontes
aliturque sitis latice ingesto.
prostrata iacet turba per aras
oratque mori—solum hoc faciles

wide his greedy, gaping jaws and unfolds all his wings, and the boatman [1] who plies the troubled stream with roomy skiff, though hardy in his vigorous old age, can scarce draw back his arms wearied with constant poling, worn out with ferrying the fresh throng o'er. Nay more, they say that the dog [2] has burst his chains of Taenarian [3] iron, and is wandering through our fields; that the earth has rumbled; that ghosts go stealing through the groves, larger than mortal forms; that twice have Cadmean forests trembled and shed their snows; twice has Dirce welled up with blood; in the silent night Amphion's hounds have bayed.

[180] O dire appearance and new form of death, far heavier than death! Benumbing languor fetters the listless limbs; the sickly cheeks burn red; small spots overspread the face. Then hot vapours scorch the body's very citadel [4] and distend the cheeks with blood; the eyes stand staring, and accursèd fire [5] feeds upon the limbs. There is a ringing in the ears; black blood drips from the strained nostrils and bursts the swelling veins. Full oft does a grating cough rack the inmost frame. Now they strain cold stones close to their breasts; or where new freedom in the house permits, since the watcher has been borne forth, ye [6] hasten to the springs, and with full draughts feed your fevered thirst. Prostrate the crowds lie at the altars and pray for death—this alone

---

[1] Charon.   [2] Cerberus.

[3] See Index *s.v.* "Taenarus."

[4] *i.e.* the head.

[5] *Sacer ignis* is usually supposed to be erysipelas, "St. Anthony's fire."

[6] He addresses the sick folk who, when the watcher is dead rush to the water, which only inflames their thirst.

tribuere dei ; delubra petunt,

haut ut voto numina placent,   200

sed iuvat ipsos satiare deos.

OEDIPVS

Quisnam ille propero regiam gressu petit ?

adestne clarus sanguine ac factis Creo

an aeger animus falsa pro veris videt ?

CHORVS

Adest petitus omnibus votis Creo.

OEDIPVS

Horrore quatior, fata quo vergant timens,

trepidumque gemino pectus affectu labat ;

ubi laeta duris mixta in ambiguo iacent,

incertus animus scire cum cupiat timet.

Germane nostrae coniugis, fessis opem   210

si quam reportas, voce properata edoce.

CREO

Responsa dubia sorte perplexa iacent.

OEDIPVS

Dubiam salutem qui dat adflictis negat.

442

OEDIPUS

the compliant gods bestow. They seek the shrines,
not that they may appease the divinities with gifts,
but joying to glut the very gods.

[CREON *is seen returning from his mission.*[1]]

OEDIPUS

Who, pray, is he who seeks the palace with hasty
steps? Is Creon at hand, noble in blood and deed,
or does my sick fancy see false for true?

CHORUS

He is at hand, Creon, by all our prayers desired.

[*Enter* CREON.]

OEDIPUS

With dread am I shaken, fearing the trend of fate,[2]
and my fluttering heart wavers betwixt two moods;
where joy with grief commingled lies in doubt, the
uncertain soul fears though it longs to know.
210 O brother of my consort, if to weary hearts
thou bringest any aid, quickly declare thy news.

CREON

Doubtful lies the answer and involved the doom.

OEDIPUS

Who grants a doubtful help to sufferers, grants
none.

[1] See Argument.
[2] *i.e.* of the oracle which Creon had been sent to consult.

CREO

Ambage flexa Delphico mos est deo
arcana tegere.

OEDIPVS

Fare, sit dubium licet.
ambigua soli noscere Oedipodae datur.

CREO

Caedem expiari regiam exilio deus,
et interemptum Laium ulcisci iubet.
non ante caelo lucidus curret dies
haustusque tutos aetheris puri dabit.   220

OEDIPVS

Et quis peremptor incluti regis fuit?
quem memoret ede Phoebus, ut poenas luat.

CREO

Sit, precor, dixisse tutum visu et auditu horrida;
torpor insedit per artus, frigidus sanguis coit.
ut sacrata templa Phoebi supplici intravi pede
et pias numen precatus rite summisi manus,
gemina Parnasi nivalis arx trucem fremitum dedit;
imminens Phoebea laurus tremuit et movit comam
ac repente sancta fontis lympha Castalii stetit.
incipit Letoa vates spargere horrentes comas   230

OEDIPUS

CREON

In mazy riddles is the Delphic god wont to hide his secrets.

OEDIPUS

Speak out, though it be doubtful ; to read riddles to Oedipus alone is given.

CREON

The god bids the king's murder be atoned by banishment and the murdered Laïus be avenged. Not sooner shall the bright sun course the heavens, and give wholesome draughts of unpolluted air.

OEDIPUS

And who was the murderer of the illustrious king ? Tell whom Phoebus names, that he may pay the penalty.

CREON

May it be safe, I pray, to have told of things to sight and hearing dreadful. Numbness has settled through my limbs ; my chill blood freezes. When Phoebus' hallowed shrine I entered with reverent feet and raised pious hands in due supplication to the god, the double peaks of snow-clad Parnassus gave an angry roar ; the overhanging laurel of Phoebus trembled and shook its foliage, and suddenly the holy waters of the Castalian spring stood still. The priestess of Leto's son began to fling loose her

et pati commota Phoebum. contigit nondum specum
emicat vasto fragore maior humano sonus :

Mitia Cadmeis remeabunt sidera Thebis,
si profugus Dircen Ismenida liquerit hospes
regis caede nocens, Phoebo iam notus et infans.
nec tibi longa manent sceleratae gaudia caedis :
tecum bella geres natis quoque bella relinquens,
turpis maternos iterum revolutus in ortus.

OEDIPVS

Quod facere monitu caelitum iussus paro,
funeti cineribus regis hoc decuit dari,   240
ne sancta quisquam sceptra violaret dolo.
regi tuenda maxime regum est salus ;
curat peremptum nemo quem incolumem timet.

CREO

Curam perempti maior excussit timor.

OEDIPVS

Pium prohibuit ullus officium metus ?

CREO

Sphinx et nefandi carminis tristes minae.

446

bristling locks and, deep stirred, to suffer Phoebus.
She had not yet reached the cave, when, with a mighty
roar, words louder than voice of man leaped forth : [1]

" Kind shall the stars return to the Theban city of
    Cadmus,
  If, O fugitive guest, Ismenian Dirce thou leavest,
  Stained with the blood of a king, from infancy
    known to Apollo.
  Brief shall be to thee the joys of thy impious
    slaughter :
  With thee war shalt thou bring, and war to thy
    sons leave behind thee,
  Foully returned once more to the impious womb
    of thy mother."

OEDIPUS

That which, at Heaven's warning, I am now prepared to do should fittingly have been done in honour
of the dead king's dust, that none might treacherously
profane the sacred sceptre. Kings have most need
to guard the life of kings; none hath care for him
when dead whom alive he fears.

CREON

Our care for the dead a greater fear dispelled.

OEDIPUS

Did any fear prevent a pious duty ?

CREON

Aye, the Sphinx and the dire threats of her accursèd
chant.

[1] The oracles were commonly given out in dactylic hexa-
meters.

Nunc expietur numinum imperio scelus.
Quisquis deorum regna placatus vides;
tu, tu penes quem iura praecipitis poli
tuque, o sereni maximum mundi decus,   250
bis sena cursu signa qui vario regis,
qui tarda celeri saecula evolvis rota,
sororque fratri semper occurrens tuo,
noctivaga Phoebe, quique ventorum potens
aequor per altum caerulos currus agis,
et qui carentes luce disponis domos,
adeste: cuius Laius dextra occidit,
hunc non quieta tecta, non fidi lares,
non hospitalis exulem tellus ferat;
thalamis pudendis doleat et prole impia;   260
hic et parentem dextera perimat sua,
faciatque (num quid gravius optari potest?)
quidquid ego fugi.   non erit veniae locus.
per regna iuro quaeque nunc hospes gero
et quae reliqui perque penetrales deos,
per te, pater Neptune, qui fluctu brevi
utrimque nostro geminus alludis solo;
et ipse nostris vocibus testis veni,
fatidica vatis ora Cirrhaeae movens:
ita molle senium ducat et summum diem   270
securus alto reddat in solio parens
solasque Merope noverit Polybi faces,
ut nulla sontem gratia eripiet mihi.

OEDIPUS

Now at Heaven's command let the crime be expiated.

[248] Whoever of the gods dost look with favour upon kingdoms—thou,[1] thou whose are the laws of the swift-revolving heavens; and thou,[2] greatest glory of the unclouded sky, who presidest over the twelve signs[3] in thy changing course, who dost unroll the slow centuries with swift wheel; and thou, his sister,[4] ever faring opposite to thy brother, Phoebe, night-wanderer; thou[5] whom the winds obey, who over the level deep dost speed thy azure car; and thou[6] who dost allot homes devoid of light—do ye all attend: Him by whose hand Laïus fell may no peaceful dwelling, no friendly household gods, no hospitable land in exile entertain; over shameful nuptials may he lament and impious progeny; may he, too, slay his own father with his own hand and do—can aught heavier be entreated?—whatever I have fled from. There shall be no place for pardon. I swear by the sway which I now, a stranger, bear, and by that which I abandoned; by my household gods; by thee, O father Neptune, who in double stream dost play against my shores on either side[7] with scanty waves. And do thou[8] thyself come as witness to my words, thou who dost inspire the fate-speaking lips of Cirrha's priestess: So may my father spend peaceful age and end his days secure on his lofty throne; so may Merope know the nuptial torches of her Polybus alone, as by no grace shall the guilty one escape my hand.

[1] Jupiter.　　[2] Phoebus, the sun.　　[3] *i.e.* of the Zodiac.
[4] Phoebe, the moon.　　[5] Neptune.　　[6] Pluto.
[7] He believes that the Isthmus of Corinth is his native land.　　[8] Apollo.

SENECAE TRAGOEDIAE

Sed quo nefandum facinus admissum loco est,
memorate : aperto Marte an insidiis iacet ?

CREO

Frondifera sanctae nemora Castaliae petens.
calcavit artis obsitum dumis iter,
trigemina qua se spargit in campos via.
secat una gratum Phocidos Baccho solum,
unde altus arva deserit, caelum petens,   280
clementer acto colle Parnasos biceps;
at una bimares Sisyphi terras adit;
Olenia in arva tertius trames cava
convalle serpens tangit errantes aquas
gelidumque dirimit amnis Elei [1] vadum.
hic pace fretum subita praedonum manus
aggressa ferro facinus occultum tulit.

In tempore ipso sorte Phoebea excitus
Tiresia tremulo tardus accelerat genu
comesque Manto luce viduatum trahens.   290

OEDIPVS

Sacrate divis, proximum Phoebo caput,
responsa solve; fare, quem poenae petant.

TIRESIA

Quod tarda fatu est lingua, quod quaerit moras
haut te quidem, magnanime, mirari addecet;

---

[1] *So E : A* Elidis : *Leo conjectures* Aetoli.

²⁷⁴ But tell me, where was the impious crime committed? Did he die in open battle or by treachery?

CREON

Seeking holy Castalia's leafy groves, he trod a way hedged in by close-pressing thickets, where the road, three-forking, branches out upon the plains. One road cuts through Phocis, the land that Bacchus loves, whence lofty Parnassus, leaving the lowlands, by a gentle slope lifts heavenward his two peaks; but one leads off to the land [1] of Sisyphus bathed by two seas; a third into the Olenian fields, through a low valley winding, reaches the vagrant waters and crosses the cool shallows of Elis' stream. Here as he fared, relying on peaceful times, a band of robbers suddenly attacked him with the sword and wrought the crime unwitnessed.

[TIRESIAS *is seen approaching.*]

²⁸⁸ But in the nick of time, stirred by Phoebus' oracle, Tiresias, though slow with trembling limbs, comes hurrying, and with him Manto, leading her sightless father.

[*Enter* TIRESIAS, *old and blind, led by his daughter,*
MANTO.]

OEDIPUS

O thou to the gods consecrate, thou next to Phoebus' self, explain the oracle; tell whom the fates demand.

TIRESIAS

That my tongue is slow to speak, that it craves delay, it behooves thee not, O great-souled Oedipus,

[1] The Isthmus.

visu carenti magna pars veri latet.
sed quo vocat me patria, quo Phoebus, sequar.
fata eruantur; si foret viridis mihi
calidusque sanguis, pectore exciperem deum.
appellite aris candidum tergo bovem
curvoque numquam colla depressam iugo.   300
tu lucis inopem, nata, genitorem regens
manifesta sacri signa fatidici refer.

MANTO

Opima sanctas victima ante aras stetit.

TIRESIA

In vota superos voce sollemni voca
arasque dono turis Eoi extrue.

MANTO

Iam tura sacris caelitum ingessi focis.

TIRESIA

Quid flamma? largas iamne comprendit dapes?

MANTO

Subito refulsit lumine et subito occidit.

TIRESIA

Vtrumne clarus ignis et nitidus stetit
rectusque purum verticem caelo tulit   310
452

to wonder; from the blind much of the truth is hidden. But whither my country, whither Phoebus calls me, I will follow. Let us search out the fates; if my blood were fresh and warm, I would receive the god in my own breast.[1] Drive to the altars a pure white bull and a heifer whose neck has never borne the curved yoke. Do thou, my child, who guidest thy blind father, report the clear tokens of the prophetic sacrifice.

[*The victims are stationed at the altars as directed.*]

MANTO

A perfect victim stands before the sacred altars.

TIRESIAS

To our vows invoke Heaven's presence with the accustomed prayer, and heap the altars with the Orient's gift of frankincense.

MANTO

Now have I heaped incense on the gods' sacred hearth.

TIRESIAS

What of the flame? Doth it already seize upon the generous feast?

MANTO

It flashed up with sudden light, and suddenly died down.

TIRESIAS

Did the fire stand clear and bright? Did it lift a pure, pointed flame straight skyward and, spreading,

---

[1] *i.e.* he would speak directly by inspiration instead of proceeding by the different methods of divination.

et summam in auras fusus explicuit comam?
an latera circa serpit incertus viae
et fluctuante turbidus fumo labat?

MANTO

Non una facies mobilis flammae fuit.
imbrifera qualis implicat varios sibi
Iris colores, parte quae magna poli
curvata picto nuntiat nimbos sinu,
quis desit illi quive sit dubites color,
caerulea fulvis mixta oberravit notis,
sanguinea rursus; ultima in tenebras abit.   320
    Sed ecce pugnax ignis in partes duas
discedit et se scindit unius sacri
discors favilla—genitor, horresco intuens:
libata Bacchi dona permutat cruor
ambitque densus regium fumus caput
ipsosque circa spissior vultus sedet
et nube densa sordidam lucem abdidit.
quid sit, parens, effare.

TIRESIA

                    Quid fari queam
inter tumultus mentis attonitae vagus?
quidnam loquar?   sunt dira, sed in alto mala;   330
solet ira certis numinum ostendi notis.
quid istud est quod esse prolatum volunt
iterumque nolunt et truces iras tegunt?
pudet deos nescio quid.   huc propere admove
et sparge salsa colla taurorum mola.
placidone vultu sacra et admotas manus
patiuntur?

unfold its topmost crest upon the air, or sidewise does
it creep uncertain of its course, and with wavering
smoke fall murkily?

MANTO

Not one appearance only had the changeful flame.
As when rain-bringing Iris entwines her various
colours, who, over a great space of heaven sweeping,
by her painted bow proclaims the storm, so wouldst
thou be in doubt what colour is lacking, what is
present in the flame; dark blue, mingled with yellow
spots, it hovered, then was blood-red, and at last
trailed off in blackness.

321 But see, the combative flame is separating into
two parts and the discordant embers of one sacred
pile are rent in twain—O father, I tremble as I gaze:
Bacchus' gift poured out changes to blood, and dense
smoke wreathes the king's head; denser still it settles
about his very face and with its thick cloud has hidden
light in gloom. O father, tell us what it means.

TIRESIAS

What can I tell, halting mid conflicting voices of
a soul amazed? What shall I say? Dire ills they
are, but hidden in mystery. 'Tis the gods' wont with
clear signs to manifest their wrath. What is it
which they would, and again would not, reveal?
What grim menace are they concealing? Something
which shames the gods. Quick, bring the victims
hither, and with salted meal sprinkle the bullocks
necks. With placid mien do they suffer the rites and
the outstretched hands?

SENECAE TRAGOEDIAE

MANTO

> Altum taurus attollens caput
> primos ad ortus positus expavit diem
> trepidusque vultum solis et radios fugit.

TIRESIA

Vnone terram vulnere afflicti petunt?   340

MANTO

Iuvenca ferro semet imposito [1] induit
et vulnere uno cecidit, at taurus duos
perpessus ictus huc et huc dubius ruit
animamque fessus vix reluctantem exprimit.

TIRESIA

Vtrum citatus vulnere angusto micat
an lentus altas irrigat plagas cruor?

MANTO

Huius per ipsam qua patet pectus viam
effusus amnis, huius exiguo graves
maculantur ictus imbre; sed versus retro
per ora multus sanguis atque oculos redit.   350

TIRESIA

Infausta magnos sacra terrores cient.
sed ede certas viscerum nobis notas.

[1] *So Leo, with E: A* opposito : *Bentley* apposito *vel* impulso.

456

OEDIPUS

Facing the east, the bull, lifting high his head, shrank from the day and turned in terror from the sun's bright face.

TIRESIAS

With one blow smitten do they fall to earth?

MANTO

The heifer threw herself upon the ready steel and with one blow fell; but the bull, twice smitten, hither and yon wanders uncertain and feebly drives forth his scarce-resisting life.

TIRESIAS

Does the blood spurt quick from out a narrow thrust, or does it but slowly o'erflood a deep-driven blow?

MANTO

The blood of one through the proper path, where the breast gapes wide, pours in a stream; the other's grievous wounds are stained with but scanty drops; nay, backward turning, the blood flows copiously through mouth and eyes.

TIRESIAS

These ill-omened sacrifices rouse dread forebodings. But describe to me the sure marks of the entrails.

457

SENECAE TRAGOEDIAE

Genitor, quid hoc est? non levi motu, ut solent,
agitata trepidant exta, sed totas manus
quatiunt novusque prosilit venis cruor.
cor marcet aegrum penitus ac mersum latet
liventque venae; magna pars fibris abest
et felle nigro tabidum spumat iecur,
ac (semper omen unico imperio grave)
en capita paribus bina consurgunt toris;   360
sed utrumque caesum tenuis abscondit caput
membrana, latebram rebus occultis negans.[1]
hostile valido robore insurgit latus
septemque venas tendit; has omnes retro
prohibens reverti limes oblicus secat.
mutatus ordo est, sede nil propria iacet,
sed acta retro cuncta: non animae capax
in parte dextra pulmo sanguineus iacet,
non laeva cordis regio, non molli ambitu
omenta pingues visceri obtendunt sinus.   370
natura versa est, nulla lex utero manet.
scrutemur, unde tantus hic extis rigor.
quod hoc nefas? conceptus innuptae bovis,
nec more solito positus, alieno in loco
implet parentem; membra cum gemitu movet,
rigore tremulo debiles artus micant.
infecit atras lividus fibras cruor,

---

[1] *The punctuation of Farnabius: Leo* membrana: latebram
. . . negans | hostile valido, *etc.*

458

OEDIPUS

MANTO

Father, what is this? With no gentle motion, as is their wont, do the entrails shake and quiver, but my whole hand do they cause to tremble and blood spurts afresh from the veins. The heart, diseased through and through, is withered and lies deep hidden, and the veins are of livid hue. A great part of the entrails is wanting, and from the rotting liver black gall oozes forth, and see—ever fatal omen for sole sovereignty—two heads rise side by side with equal bulge; yet each cloven head is hidden in but thin membrane, refusing a lurking place to secret things. The hostile[1] side rises with sturdy strength and shows seven swelling veins; but all these an intercepting line cuts straight across, preventing their return. The positions have been changed; no organ lies in its own place, but all things are reversed: on the right side lie the lungs all clogged with blood, and with no room for breath; the left is not the region of the heart; no caul with soft covering stretches its rich folds over the entrails. Nature is subverted; even the womb follows not its law. Let us look close and see whence comes this stiffness in the entrails. What monstrosity is this? A foetus in an unmated heifer! nor does it lie in accustomed fashion, but fills its mother in an unnatural place. Moaning it moves its limbs, and its weak members twitch with convulsive rigors. Livid gore has stained the entrails black. [*She ceases her inspection as the bodies of the victims suddenly begin to move.*] The sadly

---

[1] Farnabius, commenting on the passage, says that the haruspices made an imaginary division of the *exta* into two parts; the one, called *familiaris*, they assigned to friendly influences, the other, *hostilis*, to hostile. According to the appearance of both these parts, they foretold coming events.

temptantque turpes mobilem trunci gradum,
et inane surgit corpus ac sacros petit
cornu ministros; viscera effugiunt manum.   380
neque ista, quae te pepulit, armenti gravis
vox est nec usquam territi resonant greges;
immugit aris ignis et trepidant foci.

OEDIPVS

Quid ista sacri signa terrifici ferant
exprome; voces aure non timida hauriam.
solent suprema facere securos mala.[1]

TIRESIA

His invidebis quibus opem quaeris malis.

OEDIPVS

Memora quod unum scire caelicolae volunt,
contaminarit rege quis caeso manus.

TIRESIA

Nec alta caeli quae levi pinna secant   390
nec fibra vivis rapta pectoribus potest
ciere nomen; alia temptanda est via;
ipse evocandus noctis aeternae plagis,
emissus Erebo ut caedis auctorem indicet.
reseranda tellus, Ditis inplacabile
numen precandum, populus infernae Stygis
huc extrahendus. ede cui mandes sacrum;
nam te, penes quem summa regnorum, nefas
invisere umbras.

[1] *Leo deletes this line.*

mangled forms essay to move, and one disembowelled body strives to rise and menaces the priests with its horns; the entrails flee from my hand. Nor is that sound which strikes thy ears the deep lowing of the herd, nor are frightened cattle bellowing anywhere; it is the lowing of the altar-fires, the affrighted murmurings of the hearth.

OEDIPUS

What do these signs of the terrifying rites portend? Declare; with no timid ear will I drink in thy words Extremest ills are wont to make men calm.

TIRESIAS

Thou wilt look with envy upon these ills for which thou seekest aid.

OEDIPUS

Tell me the one thing the gods would have me know: who has defiled his hands with the murder of the king?

TIRESIAS

Neither the birds which on light pinion cut the depths of heaven, nor vitals plucked from still living breasts, can summon up the name. We must essay some other path: the king himself must be recalled from the regions of perpetual night, that, released from Erebus, he may point out his murderer. We must unseal the earth, must implore the implacable divinity of Dis, must draw forth hither the people of infernal Styx. Say to whom thou wilt assign the awful mission; for 'tis not right for thee, whose are the highest powers of state, to look upon the shades.

461

SENECAE TRAGOEDIAE

OEDIPVS

Te, Creo, hic poscit labor,
ad quem secundum regna respiciunt mea.   400

TIRESIA

Dum nos profundae claustra laxamus Stygis,
populare Bacchi laudibus carmen sonet.

CHORVS

Effusam redimite comam nutante corymbo,
mollia Nysaeis armati[1] bracchia thyrsis !
  Lucidum caeli decus, huc ades
  votis quae tibi nobiles
  Thebae, Bacche, tuae
  palmis supplicibus ferunt ;
  huc adverte favens virgineum caput,
  vultu sidereo discute nubila   410
  et tristes Erebi minas
  avidumque fatum.
  te decet cingi comam floribus vernis,
  te caput Tyria cohibere mitra
  hederave mollem
  bacifera religare frontem,
  spargere effusos sine lege crines,
  rursus adducto revocare nodo ;
  qualis iratam metuens novercam
  creveras falsos imitatus artus,
  crine flaventi simulata virgo,   420

[1] Armatus *R E T*: armate ψ : armatae *Gronovius.*

462

OEDIPUS

OEDIPUS

Thee, Creon, this task demands, to whom as next in succession my kingdom looks.

TIRESIAS

While we are loosing the bars of abysmal Styx let the people's hymn sound with the praise of Bacchus.

[*Exeunt* CREON, TIRESIAS, *and* MANTO.]

CHORUS [1]

Bind your streaming locks with the nodding ivy, and in your soft hands grasp the Nysaean thyrsus !

[405] Bright glory of the sky, come hither to the prayers which thine own illustrious Thebes, O Bacchus, offers to thee with suppliant hands. Hither turn with favour thy virginal face; with thy star-bright countenance drive away the clouds, the grim threats of Erebus, and greedy fate. Thee it becomes to circle thy locks with flowers of the springtime, thee to cover thy head with Tyrian turban, or thy smooth brow to wreathe with the ivy's clustering berries; now to fling loose thy lawless-streaming locks, again to bind them in a knot close-drawn ; in such guise as when, fearing thy stepdame's [2] wrath, thou didst grow to manhood with false-seeming limbs,

[1] While the choruses in Seneca's tragedies are often more or less dithyrambic in character, this is his best illustration of the dithyramb. For the explanation of references to various stories connected with the life of Bacchus see Index *s.v.* "Bacchus" and his other names mentioned by the chorus. That the address of these opening lines is to the Bacchant women is clear from the terms employed : *Effusam comam, mollia bracchia.* This gives colour to the reading of Gronovius in line 404, armatae.

[2] Juno's.

lutea vestem retinente zona.
inde tam molles placuere cultus
et sinus laxi fluidumque syrma.
vidit aurato residere curru,
veste cum longa tegeres leones,
omnis Eoae plaga vasta terrae,
qui bibit Gangen niveumque quisquis
  frangit Araxen.
Te senior turpi sequitur Silenus asello,
turgida pampineis redimitus tempora sertis ; 430
condita lascivi deducunt orgia mystae.

te Bassaridum comitata cohors
nunc Edono pede pulsavit
sola Pangaeo, nunc Threicio
vertice Pindi ; nunc Cadmeas
inter matres impia maenas
comes Ogygio venit Iaccho,
nebride sacra praecincta latus 438
thyrsumque levem vibrante manu. 441
tibi commotae pectora matres fudere
  comam [1] 440
iam post laceros Pentheos artus
thyades, oestro membra remissae,
velut ignotum videre nefas.
Ponti regna tenet nitidi matertera Bacchi
Nereidumque choris Cadmeia cingitur Ino ;
ius habet in fluctus magni puer advena ponti,
cognatus Bacchi, numen non vile Palaemon.

Te Tyrrhena, puer, rapuit manus,
et tumidum Nereus posuit mare ; 450
caerula cum pratis mutat freta.

---

[1] *Richter thus transposes ll. 439–441 : Leo deletes l. 439.*
464

a pretended maiden with golden ringlets, with saffron girdle binding thy garments. So thereafter this soft vesture has pleased thee, folds loose hanging and the long-trailing mantle. Seated in thy golden chariot, thy lions with long trappings covered, all the vast coast of the Orient saw thee, both he who drinks of the Ganges and whoever breaks the ice of snowy Araxes.

⁴²⁹ On an unseemly ass old Silenus attends thee, his swollen temples bound with ivy garlands; while thy wanton initiates lead the mystic revels. Along with thee a troop of Bassarids in Edonian dance beat the ground, now on Mount Pangaeus' peak, now on the top of Thracian Pindus; now midst Cadmean dames has come a maenad, the impious comrade of Ogygian Bacchus, with sacred fawn-skins girt about her loins, her hand a light thyrsus brandishing. Their hearts maddened by thee, the matrons have set their hair a-flowing; and at length, after the rending of Pentheus' limbs, the Bacchanals, their bodies now freed from the frenzy, looked on their infamous deed as though they knew it not.

⁴⁴⁴ Cadmean Ino, foster-mother of shining Bacchus, holds the realms of the deep, encircled by bands of Nereids dancing; over the waves of the mighty deep a boy holds sway, new come, the kinsman of Bacchus, no common god, Palaemon.

⁴⁴⁹ Thee, O boy, a Tyrrhenian band once captured and Nereus allayed the swollen sea; the dark blue waters he changes to meadows. Thence flourish the

hinc verno platanus folio viret
et Phoebo laurus carum nemus;
garrula per ramos avis obstrepit.
vivaces hederas remus tenet,
summa ligat vitis carchesia.
Idaeus prora fremuit leo,
tigris puppe sedet Gangetica.
tum pirata freto pavidus natat,
et nova demersos facies habet: 460
bracchia prima cadunt praedonibus
inlisumque utero pectus coit,
parvula dependet lateri manus
et dorso fluctum curvo subit,
lunata scindit cauda mare;
et sequitur curvus fugientia carbasa delphin.
    Divite Pactolos vexit te Lydius unda,
aurea torrenti deducens flumina ripa;
laxavit victos arcus Geticasque sagittas
lactea Massagetes qui pocula sanguine miscet; 470
regna securigeri Bacchum sensere Lycurgi;
    sensere terrae Zalacum [1] feroces
    et quos vicinus Boreas ferit
    arva mutantes
    quasque Maeotis alluit gentes
    frigido fluctu
    quasque despectat vertice e summo
    sidus Arcadium geminumque plaustrum.
    ille dispersos domuit Gelonos,
    arma detraxit trucibus puellis;
    ore deiecto petiere terram   480
    Thermodontiacae catervae,
    positisque tandem levibus sagittis
    maenades factae.
    sacer Cithaeron sanguine undavit

    [1] *A* zedacum: *Rapheling* te Dacum.

466

plane-tree with vernal foliage and the laurel-grove
dear to Phoebus; the chatter of birds sounds loud
through the branches. Fast-growing ivy clings to
the oars, and grape-vines twine at the mast-head.
On the prow an Idaean lion roars; at the stern
crouches a tiger of Ganges. Then the frightened
pirates swim in the sea, and plunged in the water
their bodies assume new forms: the robbers' arms
first fall away; their breasts smite their bellies and
are joined in one; a tiny hand comes down at the
side; with curving back they dive into the waves,
and with crescent-shaped tail they cleave the sea;
and now as curved dolphins they follow the fleeing
sails.

[467] On its rich stream has Lydian Pactolus borne
thee, leading along its burning banks the golden
waters; the Massgetan who mingles blood with
milk in his goblets has unstrung his vanquished
bow and given up his Getan arrows; the realms
of axe-wielding Lycurgus have felt the dominion
of Bacchus; the fierce lands of the Zalaces have
felt it, and those wandering tribes whom neighbouring Boreas smites, and the nations which
Maeotis' cold water washes, and they on whom
the Arcadian[1] constellation looks down from the
zenith and the wagons twain.[1] He has subdued
the scattered Gelonians; he has wrested their arms
from the warrior maidens;[2] with downcast face
they fell to earth, those Thermodontian hordes,
gave up at length their light arrows, and became
maenads. Sacred Cithaeron has flowed with the

---

[1] The two phrases refer to the same constellation, conceived first as bears (see Index *s.v.* "Arctos"), and second as
wagons or wains.
[2] The Amazons.

467

Ophioniaque caede;
Proetides silvas petiere, et Argos
praesente Bacchum coluit noverca.
    Naxos Aegaeo redimita ponto
tradidit thalamis relictam
virginem, meliore pensans
damnum marito.   490
pumice ex sicco
fluxit Nyctelius latex;
garruli gramen secuere rivi,
conbibit dulces humus alta sucos
niveique lactis candidos fontes
et mixta odoro Lesbia cum thymo.
ducitur magno nova nupta caelo;
solemne Phoebus carmen
infusis humero capillis
cantat et geminus Cupido   500
concutit taedas;
telum deposuit Iuppiter igneum
oditque Baccho veniente fulmen.

Lucida dum current annosi sidera mundi,
Oceanus clausum dum fluctibus ambiet orbem
Lunaque dimissos dum plena recolliget ignes,
dum matutinos praedicet Lucifer ortus
altaque caeruleum dum Nerea nesciet Arctos,
candida formonsi venerabimur ora Lyaei.

¹ Referring to Pentheus' death. See Index *s.v.* " Ophion "
² Ariadne, deserted by Theseus.
³ *i.e.* wine. See Index *s.v.* " Nyctelius." The following
468

blood of Ophionian[1] slaughter; the Proetides fled to
the woods, and Argos, in his stepdame's very presence, paid homage to Bacchus.

[487] Naxos, girt by the Aegean sea, gave him in
marriage a deserted maiden,[2] compensating her loss
with a better husband. Out of the dry rock there
gushed Nyctelian liquor;[3] babbling rivulets divided
the grassy meadows; deep the earth drank in the sweet
juices, white fountains of snowy milk and Lesbian
wine mingled with fragrant thyme. The new-made
bride is led to the lofty heavens; Phoebus a stately
anthem sings, with his locks flowing down his
shoulders, and twin Cupids brandish their torches.
Jupiter lays aside his fiery weapons and, when Bacchus
comes, abhors his thunderbolt.[4]

[501] While the bright stars of the ancient heavens
shall run in their courses; while the ocean shall
encircle the imprisoned earth with its waters; while
the full moon shall gather again her lost radiance;
while the Day Star shall herald the dawn of the
morning and while the lofty Bears shall know naught
of caerulean[5] Nereus; so long shall we worship the
shining face of beauteous Lyaeus.[6]

[*Enter* CREON, *returned from the rites of necromancy.*]

lines describe the wonders of nature's bounty in honour
of Bacchus' nuptials.
 [4] See Index *s.v.* "Bacchus."
 [5] Nereus, a sea-god, is here used for the sea itself, and the
description "sea-blue" is literally applied.
 [6] Bacchus.

469

OEDIPVS

Etsi ipse vultus flebiles praefert notas,
exprome cuius capite placemus deos   510

CREO

Fari iubes tacere quae suadet metus.

OEDIPVS

Si te ruentes non satis Thebae movent,
at sceptra moveant lapsa cognatae domus.

CREO

Nescisse cupies nosse quae nimium expetis.

OEDIPVS

Iners malorum remedium ignorantia est.
itane et salutis publicae indicium obrues ?

CREO

Vbi turpis est medicina, sanari piget.

OEDIPVS

Audita fare, vel malo domitus gravi
quid arma possint regis irati scies.

CREO

Odere reges dicta quae dici iubent.   520

OEDIPUS

OEDIPUS

Although thy very face displays signs of woe,
declare by whose life we are to appease the gods.

CREON

Thou bidst me speak what fear would leave
unsaid.

OEDIPUS

If falling Thebes is not enough to move thee,
at least be moved by the tottering sceptre of a
kindred house.

CREON

Thou wilt long not to have known what thou
desirest o'ermuch to know.

OEDIPUS

An idle remedy for ills is ignorance. What ! wilt
e'en bury revelations of the public weal ?

CREON

Where foul the medicine, 'tis loathsome to be
healed.

OEDIPUS

Speak out thy tidings, or, by severe suffering
broken, thou shalt know what the power of an
angered king can do.

CREON

Kings hate the words whose speaking they compel.

OEDIPVS

Mitteris Erebo vile pro cunctis caput,
arcana sacri voce ni retegis tua.

CREO

Tacere liceat.   ulla libertas minor
a rege petitur?

OEDIPVS

                    Saepe vel lingua magis
regi atque regno muta libertas obest.

CREO

Vbi non licet tacere, quid cuiquam licet?

OEDIPVS

Imperia solvit qui tacet iussus loqui.

CREO

Coacta verba placidus accipias precor.

OEDIPVS

Vlline poena vocis expressae fuit?

CREO

Est procul ab urbe lucus ilicibus niger,   530
Dircaea circa vallis inriguae loca.
cupressus altis exerens silvis caput
virente semper alligat trunco nemus,
curvosque tendit quercus et putres situ

472

OEDIPUS

To Erebus shalt thou be sent, a cheap sacrifice for all, unless by thy speech thou disclose the secrets which the rites reveal.

CREON

Let me be silent. Can any less liberty be sought from kings?

OEDIPUS

Often, e'en more than speech, to king and kingdom dumb liberty brings bane.

CREON

When silence is not allowed, what is allowed?

OEDIPUS

He weakens power who is silent when bidden to speak.

CREON

Words forced from me I pray thee hear with calm.

OEDIPUS

Was any ever punished for speech compelled?

CREON

Far from the city is a grove dusky with ilex-trees near the well-watered vale of Dirce's fount. A cypress, lifting its head above the lofty wood, with mighty stem holds the whole grove in its ever-green embrace; and an ancient oak spreads its

473

annosa ramos.   huius abrupit latus
edax vetustas; illa, iam scissa cadens
radice, fulta pendet aliena trabe.
amara bacas laurus et tiliae leves
et Paphia myrtus et per immensum mare
motura remos alnus, et Phoebo obvia,   540
enode Zephyris pinus opponens latus.
medio stat ingens arbor atque umbra gravi
silvas minores urguet et magno ambitu
diffusa ramos una defendit nemus.
tristis sub illa, lucis et Phoebi inscius,
restagnat umor frigore aeterno rigens;
limosa pigrum circumit fontem palus.

Huc ut sacerdos intulit senior gradum,
haut est moratus; praestitit noctem locus.
tum effossa tellus, et super rapti rogis   550
iaciuntur ignes.   ipse funesto integit
vates amictu corpus et frondem quatit.
lugubris imos palla perfundit pedes,
squalente cultu maestus ingreditur senex,
mortifera canam taxus adstringit comam.
nigro bidentes vellere atque atrae boves
retro [1] trahuntur.   flamma praedatur dapes,
vivumque trepidat igne ferali pecus.
vocat inde manes teque qui manes regis
et obsidentem claustra Lethaei lacus,   560
carmenque magicum volvit et rabido minax
decantat ore quidquid aut placat leves

---

[1] *So A : Leo* antro, *with E : Richter* intro.

gnarled branches crumbling in decay. The side of
one devouring time has torn away; the other, falling,
its roots rent in twain, hangs propped against a neighbouring trunk. Here are the laurel with bitter
berries, slender linden-trees, Paphian myrtle, and
the alder, destined to sweep its oarage over the
boundless sea; and here, mounting to meet the sun,
a pine-tree lifts its knotless bole to front the winds.
Midmost stands a tree of mighty girth, and with its
heavy shade overwhelms the lesser trees and, spreading its branches with a mighty reach, it stands, the
solitary guardian of the wood. Beneath this tree a
gloomy spring o'erflows, that knows nor light nor sun,
numb with perpetual chill; an oozy swamp surrounds
the sluggish pool.

548 Hither when the aged priest came, there was no
delay; the place furnished night.[1] Then a ditch is
dug and into it are thrown brands plucked from
funeral pyres. The priest shrouds his body in a
mournful pall and waves a branch.[2] His gloomy
robe sweeps o'er his feet; in the squalid garb of
mourning the old man advances, his hoary hair
bound with a wreath of death-dealing yew. Black-
fleeced[3] sheep and oxen of sable hue are backward
dragged. The flame devours the feast, and the
living victims writhe in the deathly fire. Then he
summons the spirits of the dead, and thee who
rulest the spirits, and him[4] who blocks the entrance
to the Lethaean stream; o'er and o'er he repeats a
magic rune, and fiercely, with frenzied lips, he chants

[1] The proposed rites were ordinarily performed only at
night.
[2] i.e. of some funereal tree, as the yew or cypress.
[3] These features are characteristic of the rites of necromancy
which are here described.
[4] Cerberus.

aut cogit umbras ; sanguinem libat focis
solidasque pecudes urit et multo specum
saturat cruore ; libat et niveum insuper
lactis liquorem, fundit et Bacchum manu
laeva canitque rursus ac terram intuens
graviore manes voce et attonita citat.

    Latravit Hecates turba ; ter valles cavae
sonuere maestum, tota succusso solo   570
pulsata tellus. "audior" vates ait,
"rata verba fudi ; rumpitur caecum chaos
iterque populis Ditis ad superos datur."
subsidit omnis silva et erexit comas,
duxere rimas robora et totum nemus
concussit horror, terra se retro dedit
gemuitque penitus—sive temptari abditum
Acheron profundum mente non aequa tulit,
sive ipsa Tellus, ut daret functis viam,
compage rupta sonuit ; aut ira furens   580
triceps catenas Cerberus movit graves.

    Subito dehiscit terra et immenso sinu
laxata patuit. ipse torpentes lacus
vidi inter umbras, ipse pallentes deos
noctemque veram ; gelidus in venis stetit
haesitque sanguis. saeva prosiluit cohors
et stetit in armis omne vipereum genus,
fratrum catervae dente Dircaeo satae.   588
tum torva Erinys sonuit et caecus Furor   590
Horrorque et una quidquid aeternae creant

a charm which either appeases or compels the flitting
ghosts. He makes libation of blood upon the altars,
burns the victims whole, and soaks the trench with
plenteous blood. Of snowy milk likewise he makes
libation, pours wine with his left[1] hand, repeats his
chants, and, with gaze on ground, summons the ghosts
with deeper tone and wild.

[569] Loud bayed the pack of Hecate; thrice the
deep valley gave out a mournful noise; the whole
place was shaken and the ground was stricken from
below. "My prayers are heard." says the priest;
"prevailing words I uttered; blind Chaos is burst
open, and for the tribes of Dis a way is given to
the upper world." All the wood shrank down, its
foliage bristling; the stout oaks were split and the
whole grove shook with horror; the earth also shrank
back, and from her depths gave forth a groan—whether
Hell brooked it ill that its deep abyss was assailed,
or Earth of herself, that she might give passage to the
dead, with crashing noise burst her close barriers; or
else in mad rage three-headed Cerberus shook his
heavy chains.

[582] Suddenly the earth yawned and opened wide
with gulf immeasurable. Myself, I saw the numb
pools amidst the shadows; myself, the wan gods and
night in very truth. My frozen blood stood still and
clogged my veins. Forth leaped a savage cohort
and stood full-armed, the whole viper brood, the troop
of brothers sprung from Dircaean[2] teeth. Then grim
Erinys shrieked, and blind Fury and Horror, and all
the forms which spawn and lurk midst the eternal

---

[1] Because offered to the malignant infernal powers.

[2] A far-fetched epithet from the fact that it was in Dirce's
cave that the dragon was found which Cadmus slew and from
whose teeth the warriors sprang.

celantque tenebrae : Luctus avellens comam
aegreque lassum sustinens Morbus caput,
gravis Senectus sibimet et pendens Metus   594
avidumque populi Pestis Ogygii malum.   589
nos liquit animus.   ipsa quae ritus senis   595
artesque norat stupuit.   intrepidus parens
audaxque damno convocat Ditis feri
exsangue vulgus.
             Ilico ut nebulae leves
volitant et auras libero caelo trahunt.
non tot caducas educat frondes Eryx   600
nec vere flores Hybla tot medio creat,
cum examen arto nectitur densum globo,
fluctusque non tot frangit Ionium mare,
nec tanta gelidi Strymonis fugiens minas
permutat hiemes ales et caelum secans
tepente Nilo pensat Arctoas nives
quot ille populos vatis eduxit sonus.
avide latebras nemoris umbrosi petunt
animae trementes; primus emergit solo,
dextra ferocem cornibus taurum premens,   610
Zethus, manuque sustinens laeva chelyn
qui saxa dulci traxit Amphion sono ;
interque natos Tantalis tandem suos
tuto superba fert caput fastu grave
et numerat umbras.   peior hac genetrix adest
furibunda Agaue, tota quam sequitur manus
partita regem, sequitur et Bacchas lacer
Pentheus tenetque saevus etiam nunc minas.

shades : Grief, tearing her hair ; Disease, scarce holding up her wearied head ; Age, burdened with herself;
impending Fear, and greedy Pestilence, the Ogygian
people's curse. Our spirits died within us. Even she [1]
who knew the rites and the arts of her aged sire stood
amazed. But he, undaunted and bold from his lost
sight, summons the bloodless throng of cruel Dis.

[598] Straightway, like clouds, the shadowy forms
flit forth and snuff the air of open heaven. Not
as many falling leaves does Eryx show; nor does
Hybla in mid-spring as many flowers produce,
when in close masses cling the swarming bees; as
many waves break not on the Ionian sea; as many
birds, fleeing cold Strymon's threats, leave not the
wintry lands and, cleaving the sky, change Arctic
snows for the warm valley of the Nile ; as were the
throngs which the priest's call summoned forth.
Eagerly the shivering ghosts seek the shelter of the
shady grove. First from the ground, his right hand
grasping a wild bull by the horns, Zethus emerges,
and Amphion, in his left holding the shell which by
its sweet music drew the rocks. And midst her
children Tantalis,[2] at last safe in her pride, holds up
her head with insolent arrogance, and numbers o'er
her shades. A mother worse than she, Agave comes,
still raging ; her the whole band follows who rent
their king in pieces, and after the Bacchanals mangled
Pentheus comes, even now savage and holding to
his threats.

---

[1] Manto   [2] Niobe.

Tandem vocatus saepe pudibundum extulit
caput atque ab omni dissidet turba procul   620
celatque semet (instat et Stygias preces
geminat sacerdos, donec in apertum efferat
vultus opertos)—Laius! fari horreo.
stetit per artus sanguine effuso horridus,
paedore foedo squalidam obtectus comam,
et ore rabido fatur : "O Cadmi effera,
cruore semper laeta cognato domus,
vibrate thyrsos, enthea natos manu
lacerate potius ; maximum Thebis scelus—
maternus amor est. patria, non ira deum,   630
sed scelere raperis. non gravi flatu tibi
luctificus Auster nec parum pluvio aethere
satiata tellus halitu sicco nocet,
sed rex cruentus, pretia qui saevae necis
sceptra et nefandos occupat thalamos patris,
invisa proles—sed tamen peior parens
quam natus, utero rursus infausto gravis ;
egitque in ortus semet et matri impios
fetus regessit, quique vix mos est feris
fratres sibi ipse genuit—implicitum malum   640
magisque monstrum Sphinge perplexum sua.
te, te cruenta sceptra qui dextra geris,
te pater inultus urbe cum tota petam
et mecum Erinyn pronubam thalami traham,
traham sonantem [1] verbera, incestam domum
vertam et penates impio Marte obteram.
   Proinde pulsum finibus regem ocius
agite exulem quocumque funesto gradu ;
solum relinquat ; vere florifero virens

---

[1] *So Gronovius: Leo* sonontes, *with A : Richter* sonantis,
with E : de Wilamowitz trahans silentes, verbere.

⁶¹⁹ At length, when often called, one lifts his shame-stricken head and, shrinking afar from all the throng, seeks to hide himself. The seer presses hard after him and redoubles his Stygian prayers, until he bring out to open view the features that fain would hide—Laïus! I shudder as I tell it. There he stood, a sight of horror, his limbs streaming o'er with blood, his ragged locks matted with foul filth; and with raving lips he spoke: "O savage house of Cadmus, rejoicing ever in kindred blood, brandish the thyrsus, with frenzied hands rend thy sons—'twere better so; for Thebes' crowning crime is—the love of mother. O fatherland, not by the wrath of Heaven, but by sin art thou despoiled. 'Tis not the plague-fraught south wind with its destructive blast, nor yet the earth, too little watered by the rain from heaven, that with its dry breath is harming thee; but thy blood-stained king, who as the price of cruel murder has seized the sceptre and the incestuous chamber of his sire, detested son!—but worse the mother than the son, again pregnant in her unhallowed womb; and to his own origin he returned and brought his mother impious progeny, and (a thing the beasts scarce do) himself begot brothers to himself—entanglement of evil, a monster more confused than his own Sphinx. Thee, thee, who in thy blood-stained hand dost hold the sceptre, thee and thy whole city will I, thy father, still unavenged, pursue; and with me Erinys as bridesmaid of thy nuptials will I bring, yea, I will bring her sounding with her lash; thine incestuous house will I overturn and thy household with unnatural strife will I destroy.

⁶⁴⁷ "Wherefore speedily expel ye the king from out your borders, in exile drive him to any place soever with his baleful step. Let him leave the land;

reparabit herbas, spiritus puros dabit   650
vitalis aura, veniet et silvis decor;
Letum Luesque, Mors Labor Tabes Dolor,
comitatus illo dignus, excedent simul.
et ipse rapidis gressibus sedes volet
effugere nostras, sed graves pedibus moras
addam et tenebo; repet incertus viae,
baculo senili triste praetemptans iter.
eripite terras, auferam caelum pater."

OEDIPVS

Et ossa et artus gelidus invasit tremor;
quidquid timebam facere fecisse arguor—   660
tori iugalis abnuit Merope nefas,
sociata Polybo; sospes absolvit manus
Polybus meas.   uterque defendit parens
caedem stuprumque; quis locus culpae est super?
multo ante Thebae Laium amissum gemunt,
Boeota gressu quam meo tetigi loca.
falsusne senior an deus Thebis gravis?—
iam iam tenemus callidi socios doli:
mentitur ista praeferens fraudi deos
vates, tibique sceptra despondet mea.   670

CREO

Egone ut sororem regia expelli velim?
si me fides sacrata cognati laris
non contineret in meo certum statu,
tamen ipsa me fortuna terreret nimis
482

then, blooming with flowers of spring, shall it renew
its verdure, the life-giving air shall give pure breath
again, and their beauty shall come back to the woods ;
Ruin and Pestilence, Death, Suffering, Corruption
and Distress, fit company for him, shall all depart
together. And he himself with hastening steps
shall long to flee our kingdom, but I will set weari-
some delays before his feet and hold him back. He
shall creep, uncertain of his way, with the staff of
age groping out his gloomy way.[1] Rob ye him of
the earth ; his father will take from him the sky." [1]

OEDIPUS

An icy chill has crept through my bones and
limbs ; all that I feared to do I am accused of having
done. But Merope, still wed to Polybus, refutes
the charge of incest ; and Polybus, alive and well,
cleanses my hands. Each parent clears me from
the charge of blood and incest: what room is left
for crime ? As for Laïus, Thebes mourned his loss
long ere I set foot on Boeotian soil. Is the old priest
lying, or is some god oppressing Thebes ? [2]—Now,
now I hold the confederates of a crafty plot : the
priest invents these charges, using the gods as a
screen for trickery and to thee he promises my
sceptre.

CREON

I, should I wish my sister driven from the throne ?
If sacred fealty to my kindred house held me not
fixed in my present station, yet that high estate
itself, ever o'erfraught with care, would frighten me.
Let it be thine in safety to lay off this burden,

---

[1] Both passages point to Oedipus' self-inflicted blindness.
[2] *i.e.* bringing sedition as well as pestilence.

sollicita semper. liceat hoc tuto tibi
exuere pondus nec recedentem opprimat;
iam te minore tutior pones loco.

OEDIPVS

Hortaris etiam, sponte deponam ut mea
tam gravia regna?

CREO

Suadeam hoc illis ego,
in utrumque quis est liber etiamnum status;   680
tibi iam necesse est ferre fortunam tuam.

OEDIPVS

Certissima est regnare cupienti via
laudare modica et otium ac somnum loqui.
ab inquieto saepe simulatur quies.

CREO

Parumne me tam longa defendit fides?

OEDIPVS

Aditum nocendi perfido praestat fides.

CREO

Solutus onere regio regni bonis
fruor domusque civium coetu viget,
nec ulla vicibus surgit alternis dies
qua non propinqui munera ad nostros lares   690
sceptri redundent; cultus, opulentae dapes,
donata multis gratia nostra salus.
quid tam beatae desse fortunae rear?

nor let it o'erwhelm thee when thou wouldst withdraw. Now more safely wilt thou set thyself in
humbler place.

OEDIPUS

Dost even urge me of free will to lay down the
heavy cares of state?

CREON

Thus would I counsel those to whom the way
e'en yet is open to either choice; but as for thee
'tis necessary now to bear thy lot.

OEDIPUS

Whoso longs to reign, his surest way is to praise
humble life and prate of ease and sleep. Calm is
oft counterfeited by a restless soul.

CREON

Does not my long loyalty plead enough for me?

OEDIPUS

To traitors loyalty gives opening for treason.

CREON

Free from a king's burdens, I enjoy a king's advantages; my home is honoured by throngs of citizens,
and no day rises to dawning from the night on
which my royal kinsman's bounty does not overflow
my house; apparel, rich food, deliverance, all are
granted to many through my favour. What should
I think still lacking to a lot so blest?

SENECAE TRAGOEDIAE

Quod dest; secunda non habent umquam modum.

Incognita igitur ut nocens causa cadam?

Num ratio vobis reddita est vitae meae?
num audita causa est nostra Tiresiae? tamen
sontes videmur. facitis exemplum; sequor.

Quid si innocens sum?

            Dubia pro certis solent
timere reges.

        Qui pavet vanos metus,   700
veros meretur.

        Quisquis in culpa fuit,
dimissus odit; omne quod dubium est cadat.

Sic odia fiunt

        Odia qui nimium timet
regnare nescit; regna custodit metus.

OEDIPUS

OEDIPUS

What still is lacking ;[1] prosperity has no bounds.

CREON

Shall I then, my cause unheard, fall like a criminal?

OEDIPUS

Did ye show due regard unto my life? Did Tiresias hear my cause? And yet ye hold me guilty. Ye set the example; I but follow it.

CREON

What if I am innocent?

OEDIPUS

Doubts as if certainties kings are wont to fear.

CREON

Who trembles with vain fear, true fear deserves.

OEDIPUS

Set free the guilty, and he hates; let all that's doubtful perish.

CREON

Thus is hatred bred.

OEDIPUS

He who fears hatred overmuch, knows not to rule; fear is the guard of kingdoms.

---

[1] *i.e.* royal power.

487

CREO

Qui sceptra duro saevus imperio regit,
timet timentes; metus in auctorem redit.

OEDIPVS

Servate sontem saxeo inclusum specu.
ipse ad penates regios referam gradum.

CHORVS

Non tu tantis causa periclis,
non hinc Labdacidas petunt   710
fata, sed veteres deum
irae secuntur. Castalium nemus
umbram Sidonio praebuit hospiti
lavitque Dirce Tyrios colonos,
ut primum magni natus Agenoris,
fessus per orbem furta sequi Iovis,
sub nostra pavidus constitit arbore
praedonem venerans suum,
monituque Phoebi
iussus erranti comes ire vaccae,   720
quam non flexerat
vomer aut tardi iuga curva plaustri,
deseruit fugas nomenque genti
inauspicata de bove tradidit.
    Tempore ex illo nova monstra semper
protulit tellus:
aut anguis imis vallibus editus
annosa supra robora sibilat,
superatque [1] pinus;

---

[1] *So Richter, with E: Leo* supraque, *with A.*

OEDIPUS

CREON

Who harshly wields the sceptre with tyrannic
sway, fears those who fear; terror recoils upon its
author's head.

OEDIPUS [*to attendants*]

Shut up the guilty man in a rocky dungeon and
guard him well. I to the royal palace will return.

[CREON *is led away by attendants. Exit* OEDIPUS.]

CHORUS

Not thou [1] the cause of our great perils, not on
thy account do the fates assail the house of Labdacus;
nay, 'tis the ancient wrath of the gods that follows
us. Castalia's grove lent its shade to the Sidonian
wanderer [2] and Dirce bathed the colonists from Tyre,
what time great Agenor's son,[2] weary with tracking
Jove's thefts [3] over all the world, in fear halted
beneath our trees, worshipping his sister's ravisher;
and, by the advice of Phoebus, bidden to follow a
straying heifer which had never bent beneath the
plough or the slow wain's curving yoke, he gave over
his quest [4] and named a nation [5] from that ill-omened
heifer.

725 From that time on, our land has e'er produced
strange monsters: either a serpent, rising from the
valley's depths, hisses on high above the ancient
oaks and overtops the pines; ever higher, above the

[1] Oedipus.   [2] Cadmus.
[3] Europa, whom Jove, in bull form, had stolen away.
Agenor had sent Cadmus to find her, with instructions not
to return unless successful.
[4] *i.e.* the quest enjoined upon him by his father.
[5] Boeotia, from βοῦς.

supra Chaonias celsior arbores [1]
erexit caeruleum caput,
cum maiore sui parte recumberet;   730
aut feta tellus impio partu
effudit arma: sonuit reflexo
classicum cornu lituusque adunco
stridulos cantus elisit aere; [2]
non ante linguas agiles et ora
vocis ignotae clamore primum
hostico experti.

  Agmina campos cognata tenent,
dignaque iacto semine proles,
uno aetatem permensa die,   740
post Luciferi nata meatus
ante Hesperios occidit ortus.
horret tantis advena monstris
populique timet bella recentis,
donec cecidit saeva iuventus
genetrixque suo reddi gremio
modo productos vidit alumnos.
hac transierit civile nefas!
illa Herculeae norint Thebae
proelia fratrum!   750

  Quid Cadmei fata nepotis,
cum vivacis cornua cervi
frontem ramis texere novis
dominumque canes egere suum?
praeceps silvas montesque fugit
citus Actaeon agilique magis
pede per saltus ac saxa vagus
metuit motas zephyris plumas
et quae posuit retia vitat;

  [1] *Leo deletes this line.*
  [2] *Leo comments:* post 734 dictum oportuit spartos pugnam
inivisse.

490

Chaonian trees he lifts his dark-blue head, although
his greater part still lies upon the ground; or else
the earth, teeming with impious birth, brings forth
armed men: loud resounded the battle-call from
the curving horn, and the brazen trumpet sent forth
its piercing notes. Their tongues and lips, ne'er
nimble before, were first employed in the battle-
cry of their unfamiliar voice.

[738] The kindred bands filled the plains, and this
offspring, worthy the seed that had been sown,
measured their life by a single day; born after the
passing of the Morning Star, they perished ere
Hesperus arose. The wanderer[1] quaked at prodigies so strange, and fearfully awaited the assault
of the new-born folk; until the savage youth[2] fell in
death, and their mother[3] beheld the children she
had but now brought forth returned to her own
bosom. With this may the horror of civil strife have
passed! May the Thebes of Hercules[4] know those
fratricidal struggles only!

[751] What of the doom of Cadmus' grandson, when
the antlers of a long-lived stag covered his brow
with their strange branches, and his own hounds
pursued their master? Headlong from the woods
and mountains the swift Actaeon fled, and with
feet more nimble, scouring glades and rocky
places, shuddered at the feathers[5] fluttering
in the breeze, and avoided the snares he himself had set; at length he gazed into the still

---

[1] *i.e.* Cadmus, exiled by his father.
[2] The monsters sprung from the dragon's teeth.
[3] The earth.
[4] Hercules was born at Thebes.
[5] Tied to bushes along deer-runs in order to frighten the
animals in the desired direction.

donec placidi fontis in unda 760
cornua vidit vultusque feros.
ibi virgineos foverat artus
nimium saevi diva pudoris!

OEDIPVS

Curas revolvit animus et repetit metus.
obisse nostro Laium scelere autumant
superi inferique, sed animus contra innocens
sibique melius quam deis notus negat.
redit memoria tenue per vestigium,
cecidisse nostri stipitis pulsu obvium
datumque Diti, cum prior iuvenem senex 770
curru superbus pelleret, Thebis procul
Phocaea trifidas regio qua scindit vias.
Unanima coniunx, explica errores precor;
quae spatia moriens Laius vitae tulit?
primone in aevo viridis an fracto occidit?

IOCASTA

Inter senem iuvenemque, sed propior seni.

OEDIPVS

Frequensne turba regium cinxit latus?

IOCASTA

Plures fefellit error ancipitis viae,
paucos fidelis curribus iunxit labor.

OEDIPVS

Aliquisne cecidit regio fato comes? 780

pool's water and saw his horns and his beast-like
countenance. 'Twas in that same pool the goddess [1]
of too stern chastity had bathed her virgin limbs!

OEDIPUS

My soul broods o'er its cares and renews its
fears. That by my crime Laïus fell, gods both of
heaven and hell affirm; and yet my soul, conscious
of innocence and known to itself better than to the
gods, makes denial. Retracing the dim path of
memory, I see one met on the way fallen 'neath
the blow of my stout staff and given o'er to Dis; but
first the old man arrogantly from his car thrust the
younger from the way. Yet that was far from Thebes,
where Phocis' land parts the three-forked roads.

[Enter JOCASTA.*]*

[773] O thou, my soul's own mate, resolve my doubts,
I pray thee; what span of life had Laïus at his death?
In the fresh prime of life died he, or in broken age?

JOCASTA

Midway between age and youth, but nearer age.

OEDIPUS

Did a great throng gird the king about?

JOCASTA

The most mistook the uncertain path and strayed;
a few by faithful toil kept near his car.

OEDIPUS

Did any companion share the royal fate?

[1] Diana.

IOCASTA

Vnum fides virtusque consortem addidit.

OEDIPVS

Teneo nocentem; convenit numerus, locus;
sed tempus adde.

IOCASTA

Decima iam metitur seges.

SENEX CORINTHIVS

Corinthius te populus in regnum vocat
patrium.   quietem Polybus aeternam obtinet.

OEDIPVS

Vt undique in me saeva Fortuna irruit!
edissere agedum, quo cadat fato parens.

SENEX

Animam senilem mollis exsolvit sopor.

OEDIPVS

Genitor sine ulla caede defunctus iacet.
testor, licet iam tollere ad caelum pie   790
puras nec ulla scelera metuentes manus.
sed pars magis metuenda fatorum manet.

SENEX

Omnem paterna regna discutient metum.

494

OEDIPUS

JOCASTA

One did faith and valour cause to share his fate.

OEDIPUS [*aside*]

I have the guilty man; the number tallies, and the place. [*To* JOCASTA.] But add the time.

JOCASTA

Now is the tenth harvest being reaped.

[*Enter an old Corinthian messenger.*]

OLD MAN [*to* OEDIPUS]

The Corinthians summon thee to thy father's throne.   Polybus has gained his everlasting rest.

OEDIPUS

How heartless Fortune assails me on every hand! But tell me by what fate my sire is fallen.

OLD MAN

Soft slumber set his aged spirit free.

OEDIPUS

My father lies dead, and by no violence.   I call to witness that now I may lift clean hands to heaven, hands that need fear no charge of crime.   But the more fearful part of my fates remains.

OLD MAN

All fears thy father's kingdom will dispel.

OEDIPVS

Repetam paterna regna; sed matrem horreo.

SENEX

Metuis parentem, quae tuum reditum expetens
sollicita pendet?

OEDIPVS

Ipsa me pietas fugat.

SENEX

Viduam relinques?

OEDIPVS

Tangis en ipsos metus '

SENEX

Effare mersus quis premat mentem timor;
praestare tacitam regibus soleo fidem.

OEDIPVS

Conubia matris Delphico admonitu tremo.   800

SENEX

Timere vana desine et turpes metus
depone; Merope vera non fuerat parens.

OEDIPVS

Quod subditivi praemium nati petit?

OEDIPUS

OEDIPUS

I would seek my father's kingdom, but from my
mother do I shrink.

OLD MAN

Dost fear thy mother, who, in anxious suspense,
longs for thy coming?

OEDIPUS

'Tis love itself bids me flee.

OLD MAN

Wilt leave her widowed?

OEDIPUS

There dost thou touch on the very thing I fear!

OLD MAN

Speak out; what hidden fear weighs on thy soul?
'Tis my wont to offer kings a loyal silence.

OEDIPUS

Warned by the Delphic oracle, I dread my
mother's bed.

OLD MAN

Then cease thy empty fears, thy horrible forebodings; Merope was not in truth thy mother.

OEDIPUS

What did she hope to gain by a changeling son?

497

SENECAE TRAGOEDIAE

SENEX

Regum [1] superbam liberi astringunt fidem.

OEDIPVS

Secreta thalami fare quo excipias modo.

SENEX

Hae te parenti parvulum tradunt manus.

OEDIPVS

Tu me parenti tradis; at quis me tibi?

SENEX

Pastor nivoso sub Cithaeronis iugo.

OEDIPVS

In illa temet nemora quis casus tulit?

SENEX

Illo sequebar monte cornigeros greges.   810

OEDIPVS

Nunc adice certas corporis nostri notas.

SENEX

Forata ferro gesseras vestigia,
tumore nactus nomen ac vitio pedum.

---

[1] *So Leo with the best MSS.:* Regnum superbam. *etc.,* A.

---

[1] The meaning of this *sententia*, especially in its application
as Merope's reason for secretly adopting a son, is not altogether
clear.   Various suggestions have been offered by commentators

OEDIPUS

OLD MAN

Kings' children hold rude loyalty in check.[1]

OEDIPUS

The secrets of the chamber—tell how thou knowest them.

OLD MAN

'Twas these hands gave thee, a tiny babe, unto thy mother.

OEDIPUS

Thou gav'st me to my mother; but who gave me to thee?

OLD MAN

A shepherd, 'neath Cithaeron's snowy peak.

OEDIPUS

What chance brought thee within that wood?

OLD MAN

On that mountain-side was I tending my horned flocks.

OEDIPUS

Now name also the sure marks upon my body.

OLD MAN

Thy soles had been pierced with iron, and thou hast thy name[2] from thy swollen and crippled feet.

as to the interpretation. Perhaps the simplest interpretation is the best, that royal offspring (and hence the insurance of succession) is the strongest hold upon lagging loyalty which threatens to fall away.

[2] Οἰδίπους, "swollen-footed."

OEDIPVS

Quis fuerit ille qui meum dono dedit
corpus requiro.

SENEX

Regios pavit greges ;
minor sub illo turba pastorum fuit.

OEDIPVS

Eloquere nomen.

SENEX

Prima languescit senum
memoria longo lassa sublabens situ.

OEDIPVS

Potesne facie noscere ac vultu virum ?

SENEX

Fortasse noscam ; saepe iam spatio obrutam   820
levis exoletam memoriam revocat nota.

OEDIPVS

Ad sacra et aras omne compulsum pecus
duces sequantur ; ite, propere accersite,
famuli, penes quos summa consistit gregum.

SENEX

Sive ista ratio sive fortuna occulit,
latere semper patere quod latuit diu ;
saepe eruentis veritas patuit malo.
500

OEDIPUS

Who was he who gave thee my body as a gift? I seek to know.

He fed the royal flocks; there was a humbler band of shepherds under him.

Tell me his name.

An old man's early memory grows faint, failing through weakness and long disuse.

Couldst recognize the man by face and feature?

Perchance I might; some trifling mark oft-times calls back the memory of things that time hath buried and made dim.

Let all the flocks be driven hither to the sacred altars, their guides with them; go, slaves, and quickly summon those with whom is the herds' chief control.

[*The slaves depart on the errand.*]

Whether design or chance conceals these things, suffer to lie hid for ever what has lain hid so long; truth often is made clear to the discoverer's bane.

SENECAE TRAGOEDIAE

OEDIPVS

Malum timeri maius his aliquod potest?

SENEX

Magnum esse magna mole quod petitur scias.
concurrit illinc publica, hinc regis salus,   830
utrimque paria; contine medias manus,
nihil lacessas, ipsa se fata explicent.

OEDIPVS

Non expedit concutere felicem statum; [1]
tuto movetur quidquid extremo in loco est.

SENEX

Nobilius aliquid genere regali appetis?
ne te parentis pigeat inventi vide.

OEDIPVS

Vel paenitendi sanguinis quaeram fidem;
sic nosse certum est.

               Ecce grandaevus senex,
arbitria sub quo regii fuerant gregis,
Phorbas.   refersne nomen aut vultum senis?   840

SENEX

Adridet animo forma; nec notus satis,
nec rursus iste vultus ignotus mihi.

---

[1] *Modern editors have rightly assigned l. 833 to Oedipus,
whereas old editors, with A, gave the line to the Old Man.*

OEDIPUS

OEDIPUS

Can any bane greater than all this be feared?

OLD MAN

Great, be thou sure, is that bane which thou
seekst with toil so great. Here meet, from that side
and from this, the public weal and the king's, and
both are in equal balance. Keep thy hand from
both; challenge thou nothing; let the fates unfold
themselves.[1]

OEDIPUS

'Tis not expedient to disturb a happy state; that
is with safety changed which is at its worst.

OLD MAN

Dost seek for a nobler thing than royal lineage?
Beware lest thou rue the finding of thy parentage.

OEDIPUS

I will seek certainty even of rueful birth; so
resolved am I to know.

[*Enter* PHORBAS. OEDIPUS *to himself.*]

838 Behold the ancient, heavy with years, once
keeper of the royal flocks, Phorbas. [*To* OLD MAN.]
Dost recall the old man's name or features?

OLD MAN

His form comes easily to my memory; but that
face, while not well known, again is not unknown
to me.

---

[1] *i.e.* let well enough alone. The condition of the state is
critical, and Oedipus' personal problem is acute; but wisdom
bids keep hands off and let the fates unfold themselves.

Regnum optinente Laio famulus greges
agitasti opimos sub Cithaeronis plaga?

PHORBAS

Laetus Cithaeron pabulo semper novo
aestiva nostro prata summittit gregi.

SENEX

Noscisne memet?

PHORBAS

Dubitat anceps memoria.

OEDIPVS

Huic aliquis a te traditur quondam puer?
effare. dubitas? cur genas mutat color?
quid verba quaeris? veritas odit moras. 850

PHORBAS

Obducta longo temporum tractu moves.

OEDIPVS

Fatere, ne te cogat ad verum dolor.

PHORBAS

Inutile isti munus infantis dedi;
non potuit ille luce, non caelo frui.

SENEX

Procul sit omen! vivit et vivat precor.

OEDIPUS

[*To* PHORBAS.]

843 While Laïus held the throne, didst ever as a
slave drive rich flocks on Cithaeron's tracts?

PHORBAS

Cithaeron, abounding ever in fresh pasturage, in
summer-time gave feeding-ground for my flocks.

OLD MAN

Dost thou know me?

PHORBAS

My memory falters and is in doubt.

OEDIPUS

Didst thou once give a boy to this man here?
Speak out. Thou falterest? Why do thy cheeks
change colour? Why seekst for words? Truth
scorns delay.

PHORBAS

Thou stirrest matters o'erclouded by long lapse of
time.

OEDIPUS

Speak, lest pain force thee to the truth.

PHORBAS

I did give him an infant, a worthless gift; never
could he have enjoyed the light or sky.

OLD MAN

Far be the omen! He lives and I pray may live.

505

SENECAE TRAGOEDIAE

OEDIPVS

Superesse quare traditum infantem negas?

PHORBAS

Ferrum per ambos tenue transactum pedes
ligabat artus, vulneri innatus tumor
puerile foeda corpus urebat lues.

OEDIPVS

Quid quaeris ultra? fata iam accedunt prope. 860
quis fuerit infans edoce.

PHORBAS

Prohibet fides.

OEDIPVS

Huc aliquis ignem! flamma iam excutiet fidem.

PHORBAS

Per tam cruentas vera quaerentur vias?
ignosce quaeso.

OEDIPVS

Si ferus videor tibi
et impotens, parata vindicta in manu est:
dic vera. quisnam? quove generatus patre?
oua matre genitus?

PHORBAS

Coniuge est genitus tua.

506

OEDIPUS

OEDIPUS

Why dost thou say that the child thou gavest did not survive?

PHORBAS

Through both his feet a slender iron rod was driven, binding his legs together. A swelling [1] engendered in the wound, galled the child's body, a loathsome plague.

OEDIPUS [*to himself*]

Why seekest further? Now doth fate draw near. [*To* PHORBAS.] Who was the babe? Speak out.

PHORBAS

My loyalty forbids.

OEDIPUS

Hither with fire, someone! Now shall flames banish loyalty.

PHORBAS

Is truth to be sought along such cruel ways? Pardon I beg.

OEDIPUS

If I seem harsh to thee, and headstrong, vengeance is in thy hands; speak thou the truth. Who was he? Of what sire begot? Of what mother born?

PHORBAS

Born of thy—wife.

---

[1] See l. 813, note.

OEDIPVS

Dehisce, tellus, tuque tenebrarum potens,
in Tartara ima, rector umbrarum. rape
retro reversas generis ac stirpis vices.   870
congerite, cives, saxa in infandum caput,
mactate telis.   me petat ferro parens,
me natus, in me coniuges arment manus
fratresque, et aeger populus ereptos rogis
iaculetur ignes.   saeculi crimen vagor,
odium deorum, iuris exitium sacri,
qua luce primum spiritus hausi rudes
iam morte dignus.   redde nunc animos acres,[1]
nunc aliquid aude sceleribus dignum tuis.
i, perge, propero regiam gressu pete ;   880
gratare matri liberis auctam domum.

CHORUS

Fata si liceat mihi
fingere arbitrio meo,
temperem zephyro levi
vela, ne pressae gravi
spiritu antennae tremant.
lenis et modice fluens
aura nec vergens latus
ducat intrepidam ratem ;
tuta me media vehat   890
vita decurrens via.
  Cnosium regem timens
astra dum demens petit
artibus fisus novis,
certat et veras aves
vincere ac falsis nimis
imperat pinnis puer,

[1] Animos parens *A; Heinsius suggests* pares, *Bücheler* feros
or truces.

OEDIPUS

Yawn, earth ! And do thou, king of the dark world,
ruler of shades, to lowest Tartarus hurl this unnatural
interchange 'twixt brood and stock. Citizens, heap
stones upon my accursed head ; slay me with weapons.
Let father, let son assail me with the sword ; let
husbands and brothers arm hands against me, and let
the sick populace snatch brands from the pyres and
hurl them at me. The crime of the age I wander,
hate of the gods, destruction of holy law, the very
day I drew the untried air already worthy death.
[*To himself.*] Now be stout of soul, now dare some
deed worthy of thy crimes. Go, get thee to the
palace with hurrying feet; congratulate thy mother
on her house enriched by children. [*Exit.*

CHORUS

Were it mine to shape fate at my will, I would trim
my sails to gentle winds, lest my yards tremble, bent
'neath a heavy blast. May soft breezes, gently
blowing, unvarying, carry my untroubled barque
along; may life bear me on safely, running in middle
course.

892 While, in fear of the Cretan king, madly the
lad[1] sought the stars, in strange devices trusting,
and strove to vanquish true birds in flight, and laid
his commands on pinions all too false, his name he

---

[1] Icarus.

nomen eripuit freto.
callidus medium senex
Daedalus librans iter   900
nube sub media stetit,
alitem expectans suam
(qualis accipitris minas
fugit et sparsos metu
conligit fetus avis),
donec in ponto manus
movit implicitas puer
compede audacis viae.
quidquid excessit modum
pendet instabili loco.   910
      Sed quid hoc ?   postes sonant ;
maestus en famulus manu
regius quassat caput.
ede quid portes novi.

NVNTIVS

  Praedicta postquam fata et infandum genus
deprendit ac se scelere convictum Oedipus
damnavit ipse, regiam infestus petens
invisa propero tecta penetravit gradu.
qualis per arva Libycus insanit leo,
fulvam minaci fronte concutiens iubam ;   920
vultus furore torvus atque oculi truces,
gemitus et altum murmur, et gelidus fluit
sudor per artus, spumat et volvit minas
ac mersus alte magnus exundat dolor.
secum ipse saevus grande nescio quid parat
suisque fatis simile.
                    "Quid poenas moror ? "
ait " hoc scelestum pectus aut ferro petat,
aut fervido aliquis igne vel saxo domet.
quae tigris aut quae saeva visceribus meis
510

robbed the sea of its own name.[1] But shrewd old
Daedalus, balancing a middle path, stopped midway of
the clouds, awaiting his winged son (as a bird flees the
threatening hawk and gathers her scattered and
frightened brood), until the boy in the sea plied
hands enmeshed in the shackles of his daring flight.
Whatsoever exceeds the allotted bounds, hangs in a
place unsure.

[*Enter a messenger from within the palace.*]

911 But what is this? The doors creak open; behold, a servant of the king, stricken with woe, beats
with his hand upon his head. Tell us what news
thou bringst.

MESSENGER

When Oedipus grasped his foretold fate, and his
breed unspeakable, he condemned himself as con-
victed of the crime and, seeking the palace with
deadly purpose, he entered within that hateful roof
with hurried step. As over the fields a Libyan lion
rages, with threatening front and shaking his tawny
mane; so he, his face fierce with passion, with eyes
wild staring, with groans and deep mutterings, limbs
with cold sweat streaming, froths and threatens, and
his mighty, deep-buried anguish overflows. He,
raging in soul, plans some monstrous deed to match
his destiny.

926 "Why do I delay punishment?" he cries;
"let someone with the sword assail this guilty
breast, or overwhelm me with burning fire or stones.
What tigress, what ravening bird will pounce upon

---

[1] The sea was subsequently called after him the Icarian
sea.

incurret ales ?   ipse tu scelerum capax,   930
sacer Cithaeron, vel feras in me tuas
emitte silvis, mitte vel rabidos canes—
nunc redde Agauen.   anime, quid mortem times ?
mors innocentem sola fortunae eripit."

  Haec fatus aptat impiam capulo manum
ensemque ducit.   " itane ?   tam magnis breves
poenas sceleribus solvis atque uno omnia
pensabis ictu ?   moreris—hoc patri sat est ;
quid deinde matri, quid male in lucem editis
natis, quid ipsi, quae tuum magna luit   940
scelus ruina, flebili patriae dabis ?
solvendo non es ! illa quae leges ratas
Natura in uno vertit Oedipoda, novos
commenta partus, supplicis eadem meis
novetur.   iterum vivere atque iterum mori
liceat, renasci semper ut totiens nova
supplicia pendas.   utere ingenio, miser ;
quod saepe fieri non potest fiat diu—
mors eligatur longa.   quaeratur via
qua nec sepultis mixtus et vivis tamen   950
exemptus erres ; morere, sed citra patrem.
cunctaris, anime ? "
               Subitus en vultus gravat
profusus imber ac rigat fletu genas.
" et flere satis est ?   hactenus fundent levem
oculi liquorem ?   sedibus pulsi suis
lacrimas sequantur.   di maritales, satin ?
fodiantur oculi ! "   dixit atque ira furit ;
512

my vitals? Do thou thyself, thou all-holding haunt of crime, O curst Cithaeron, send thy wild beasts against me from thy forests, send thy maddened dogs—once more send Agave.[1] O soul, why shrinkst thou from death? 'Tis death alone saves innocence from fortune.''

935 With this he lays impious hand on hilt and draws his sword. "So then? With brief suffering like this canst atone for so great crimes, and with one blow wilt pay all debts? Thy death—for thy father 'tis enough; what then to thy mother, what to thy children shamefully begot, what to her who with utter ruin is atoning for thy crime, thy mourning country, wilt thou give? Thou canst not pay![2] Let that same Nature who in Oedipus alone reverses established laws, devising strange births, be changed anew for my punishment. Be it thine to live again, to die again, ever to be reborn, that at each birth thou mayst pay new penalties. Now use thy wit, poor wretch; let that which may not oft befall, befall thee long—choose thou a lasting death. Search out a way whereon to wander, not mingling with the dead and yet removed from the living; die thou, but reaching not thy sire. Dost hesitate, O soul?''

952 Lo, with sudden shower a flood o'erwhelms his face and waters his cheeks with weeping. "And is it enough to weep? Only thus far shall mine eyes o'erflow with some few drops? Nay, driven from their sockets, let them follow the tears they shed. Ye gods of wedlock, is it enough? These eyes must be dug out!" He speaks and raves with wrath; his

---

[1] Agave in her madness had helped tear Pentheus in pieces.
[2] *i.e.* by mere death. The Latin is the regular phrase for bankruptcy.

ardent minaces igne truculento genae
oculique vix se sedibus retinent suis;
violentus audax vultus, iratus ferox,　　　　　　960
tantum furentis;[1] gemuit et dirum fremens
manus in ora torsit.　at contra truces
oculi steterunt et suam intenti manum
ultro insecuntur, vulneri occurrunt suo.
scrutatur avidus manibus uncis lumina,
radice ab ima funditus vulsos simul
evolvit orbes;　haeret in vacuo manus
et fixa penitus unguibus lacerat cavos
alte recessus luminum et inanes sinus,
saevitque frustra plusque quam satis est furit.　970
　　Factum[2] est periclum lucis; attollit caput
cavisque lustrans orbibus caeli plagas
noctem experitur.　quidquid effossis male
dependet oculis rumpit, et victor deos
conclamat omnes: "parcite, en, patriae precor;
iam iusta feci, debitas poenas tuli;
inventa thalamis digna nox tandem meis."
rigat ora foedus imber et lacerum caput
largum revulsis sanguinem venis vomit.

CHORVS

　　Fatis agimur; cedite fatis.　　　　　　980
non sollicitae possunt curae
mutare rati stamina fusi.
quidquid patimur mortale genus,
quidquid facimus venit ex alto,
servatque suae decreta colus
Lachesis nulla revoluta manu.
omnia secto tramite vadunt

---

[1] So *Richter:* A cruentus: *Leo with E.* cruentis.
[2] So *Leo:* furit; tantum ω, *corr. Madvig,* II. 19.

cheeks burn threatening with ferocious fire, and his eyeballs scarce hold themselves in their place; his face is full of reckless daring and mad savagery, as of one in boundless rage; with groans and dreadful cries, his hands into his eyes he thrusts. But his starting eyes stand forth to meet them and, eagerly following their kindred hands, rush upon their wound. With hooked fingers he greedily searches out his eyes and, torn from their very roots, he drags both eyeballs out; still stay his hands in the empty sockets and, deep fixed, tear with their nails the deep-set hollows of his eyes and empty cavities; vainly he rages, and with excessive fury raves.

971 The hazard of light is o'er; he lifts his head, surveys the regions of the sky with his empty sockets, and makes trial of the night. The shreds which still hang from eyes unskilfully plucked out he breaks away, and in triumph cries aloud to all the gods: "Spare now my land, I pray you; now have I done justice, I have paid the debt I owed; at last have I found night worthy of my wedlock." A hideous shower drenches his face and his mangled brow spouts streams of blood from his bursting veins.

CHORUS

By fate are we driven; yield ye to fate. No anxious cares can change the threads of its inevitable spindle. Whate'er we mortals bear, whate'er we do, comes from on high; [1] and Lachesis maintains the decrees of her distaff which by no hand may be reversed. All things move on in an appointed path,

---

[1] A Stoic doctrine.

primusque dies dedit extremum.
non illa deo vertisse licet
quae nexa suis currunt causis.   990
it cuique ratus prece non ulla
mobilis ordo.   multis ipsum
metuisse nocet, multi ad fatum
venere suum dum fata timent.

   Sonuere fores atque ipse suum
duce non ullo luminis orbus
molitur iter.

OEDIPVS

Bene habet, peractum est ; iusta persolvi patri.
iuvant tenebrae.   quis deus tandem mihi
placatus atra nube perfundit caput ?   1000
quis scelera donat ?   conscium evasi diem.
nil, parricida, dexterae debes tuae ;
lux te refugit.   vultus Oedipodam hic decet.

CHORVS

En ecce, rapido saeva prosiluit gradu
Iocasta vaecors, qualis attonita et furens
Cadmea mater abstulit nato caput
sensitque [1] raptum.   dubitat afflictum alloqui,
cupit pavetque.   iam malis cessit pudor.
set haeret ore prima vox.

IOCASTA

        Quid te vocem ?
natumne ? dubitas �; natus es ; natum pudet ? 1010
invite loquere, nate—quo avertis caput
vacuosque vultus ?

---

[1] *So Leo and Richter :* censitque *E, corr.* Σ : sensimve raptum
traxit afflictum *A.*

and our first day fixed our last. Those things God
may not change which speed on their way, close
woven with their causes. To each his established
life goes on, unmovable by any prayer. To many
their very fear is bane ; for many have come upon
their doom while shunning doom.

⁹⁹⁵ The gates have sounded, and he himself, with
none to guide and sightless, gropes his way.

[*Enter* OEDIPUS.]

OEDIPUS

All's well, 'tis finished; to my father have I paid
my debt. How sweet the darkness! What god, at
length appeased, has shrouded my head in this dark
veil? Who has forgiven my crimes? I have escaped
the conscious eye of day. Nothing, thou parricide,
dost owe to thy right hand ; the light hath fled from
thee. This is the face becometh Oedipus.

[*Enter* JOCASTA.]

CHORUS

See, there, with hurried step, frantic, beside herself, Jocasta rushes forth, just as, in frenzied rage,
the Cadmean mother [1] tore her son's head away and
realized her deed. She hesitates, longs and yet fears
to speak to the afflicted one. Now shame has given
way to grief; but her first words falter on her
lips.

JOCASTA

What shall I call thee? Son? Dost question
it? Thou art my son; does "son" shame thee?
Though thou wouldst not, speak, my son—why dost
thou turn away thy head, thy sightless face?

[1] Agave.

517

OEDIPVS

Quis frui tenebris vetat?
quis reddit oculos? matris, en matris sonus!
perdidimus operam. congredi fas amplius
haut est. nefandos dividat vastum mare
dirimatque tellus abdita et quisquis sub hoc
in alia versus sidera ac solem avium
dependet orbis alterum ex nobis ferat.

IOCASTA

Fati ista culpa est; nemo fit fato nocens.

OEDIPVS

Iam parce verbis, mater, et parce auribus,   1020
per has reliquias corporis trunci peto,
per inauspicatum sanguinis pignus mei,
per omne nostri nominis fas ac nefas.

IOCASTA

Quid, anime, torpes? socia cur scelerum dare
poenas recusas? omne confusum perit,
incesta, per te iuris humani decus.
morere et nefastum spiritum ferro exige.
non si ipse mundum concitans divum sator
corusca saeva tela iaculetur manu,
umquam rependam sceleribus poenas pares,   1030
mater nefanda. mors placet; mortis via
quaeratur.
518

OEDIPUS

OEDIPUS

Who wills not that I enjoy my darkness? Who restores my eyes? My mother's, lo, my mother's voice! I have worked in vain. 'Tis unlawful that we meet again. Let the vast sea roll between our impious selves, let remote lands separate, and if beneath this world there hangs another, facing other stars and a straying sun, let it take one of us.

JOCASTA

Fate's is that fault of thine: by fate no one is made guilty.

OEDIPUS

Now spare thy words, mother, spare my ears, by these remnants of my mangled body, I beseech thee, by the unhallowed offspring of my blood, by all that in our names is right and wrong.[1]

JOCASTA [aside]

Why art benumbed, my soul? Since thou hast shared his guilt, why dost refuse to share his punishment? Through thee, incestuous one, all grace of human law has been confused and lost. Die then, and let out thy impious spirit with the sword. Not if the father of the gods himself, shaking the universe, with deadly hand should hurl his glittering bolts at me, could I ever pay penalty equal to my crimes—I, a mother accurst. Death is my darling wish; let the way of death be sought.

---

[1] He prays her in the name both of their proper (mother and son) and improper (husband and wife) relations.

Agedum, commoda matri manum,
si parricida es; restat hoc operae ultimum.
  Rapiatur ensis; hoc iacet ferro meus
coniunx—quid illum nomine haud vero vocas?—
socer est. utrumne pectori infigam meo
telum an patenti conditum iugulo inprimam?
eligere nescis vulnus? hunc, dextra, hunc pete
uterum capacem, qui virum et natos tulit.

CHORVS

  Iacet perempta. vulneri immoritur manus   1040
ferrumque secum nimius eiecit cruor.

OEDIPVS

  Fatidice te, te praesidem et veri deum
compello. solum debui fatis patrem;
bis parricida plusque quam timui nocens
matrem peremi; scelere confecta est meo.
o Phoebe mendax, fata superavi impia.
  Pavitante gressu sequere pallentes vias;
suspensa plantis efferens vestigia
caecam tremente dextera noctem rege.
ingredere praeceps, lubricos ponens gradus,   1050
i profuge vade—siste, ne in matrem incidas.
  Quicumque fessi corpore et morbo graves
semanima trahitis pectora, en fugio exeo;
relevate colla. mitior caeli status
post terga sequitur. quisquis exilem iacens
animam retentat, vividos haustus levis

1032 [*To* OEDIPUS.] Come, lend thy hand against thy mother, if thou art parricide; this lacks to crown thy work.

1034 [*To herself.*] Nay, let me seize his sword; by this blade lies slain my husband—nay, why not call him by his true name?—my husband's father. Shall I pierce my breast with this, or thrust it deep into my bared throat? Thou knowest not to choose a place? Strike here, my hand, through this capacious womb, which bore my husband and my sons!

[*She stabs herself and falls dead.*]

CHORUS

There lies she slain. Her hand dies on the wound, and the sword is driven out by strong streams of blood.

OEDIPUS

Thee, O fate-revealer, thee, guardian and god of truth, do I upbraid. My father only did I owe the fates; twice parricide and more guilty than I feared, I have slain my mother; for 'tis by my sin that she is done to death. O lying Phoebus, I have outdone the impious fates.

1047 With quaking step pursue thy darkling ways; with faltering feet grope through blind night with apprehensive hand. Make haste, planting uncertain steps, go, speed thee, fly!—but stop, lest thou stumble and fall upon thy mother.

1052 All ye who are weary in body and burdened with disease, whose hearts are faint within you, see, I fly, I leave you; lift your heads. Milder skies come when I am gone. He who, though near to death, still keeps some feeble life, may freely now draw

521

concipiat. ite, ferte depositis opem ;
mortifera mecum vitia terrarum extraho.
violenta Fata et horridus Morbi tremor,
Maciesque et atra Pestis et rabidus Dolor,   1060
mecum ite, mecum.   ducibus his uti libet !

deep, life-giving draughts of air. Go, bear ye aid to those given up to death ; all pestilential humours of the land I take with me. Ye blasting Fates, thou quaking terror of Disease, Wasting, and black Pestilence, and mad Despair, come ye with me, with me. 'Tis sweet to have such guides.

[Exit.

COMPARATIVE ANALYSES

OF THE TRAGEDIES IN THIS VOLUME AND
THE CORRESPONDING GREEK DRAMAS

COMPARATIVE ANALYSES

THE GREEK DRAMAS

THE *HERCULES FURENS* OF EURIPIDES

Prologue.—The old Amphitryon, before the altar of Jupiter, at the entrance of the house of Hercules in Thebes, relates how Hercules has gone to the lower world to bring thence to the realms of day the triple-headed Cerberus. Meanwhile, Lycus, taking advantage of the hero's absence, has slain king Creon and usurped his throne. The father, wife, and children of Hercules he has reduced to poverty, and holds them in durance here in Thebes, threatening to slay the sons,

> "Lest, when the boys attain maturer age,
> They should avenge their grandsire, Creon's, death."

Amphitryon condoles with Megara, and counsels with her how they may escape the dangers of their present lot.

Parode, or chorus entry.—The chorus of Theban elders, feeble, tottering old men, enters and bemoans the wretched fate that has befallen their city and the household of their prince.

First episode.—Now enters Lycus, the usurper. He insolently taunts his victims on their helplessness, tells them

COMPARATIVE ANALYSES

SENECA'S TRAGEDIES

THE *HERCULES FURENS* OF SENECA

Prologue.—Juno complains that she is fairly driven out of heaven by her numerous rivals, mortal women who have been deified and set in the sky, either they or their offspring, by Jupiter. Especially is her wrath hot against Hercules, against whom she has waged fruitless war from his infancy until now. But he thrives on hardship, and scorns her opposition. She passes in review the hard tasks which she has set him, and all of which he has triumphantly performed. Already is he claiming a place in heaven. He can be conquered only by his own hand. Yes, this shall be turned against him, for a fury shall be summoned up from hell who shall fill his heart with madness; and in this madness shall he do deeds which shall make him long for death.

Parode, or chorus entry.—A vivid picture of the dawning day, when the stars and waning moon fade out before the rising sun; when Toil wakes up and resumes its daily cares; when through the fields the animals and birds are all astir with glad, new life.

But in the cities men awaken to repeat the sordid round of toil, the greedy quest for gold and power. But, whether happily or unhappily, all are speeding down to the world of shades. Even before his time has Hercules gone down to Pluto's realm, and has not yet returned.

First episode.—Megara enters and bewails the fresh woes that are ever ready to meet her husband's home-coming.

527

that Hercules will never return, belittles and scorns the hero's mighty deeds, and announces his intention of killing the sons.

Amphitryon answers the slanders of Lycus against Hercules, and protests against the proposed barbarous treatment of the children, who are innocent of any harm. He reproaches Thebes and all the land of Greece, because they have so ill repaid the services of their deliverer in not coming to the rescue of his wife and children. Lycus gives orders to burn the hated race of Hercules, even where they kneel for refuge at the altar-side : and threatens the elders who would thwart his will, bidding them remember that they are but as slaves in his sight. Yet the old men valiantly defy him, and warn him that they will withstand his attacks upon the children.

But Megara shows them how foolish it is to contend against the king's unbounded power. Let them rather entreat his mercy. Could not exile be substituted for death? But no, for this is worse than death. Rather, let them all die together. Perhaps Lycus will allow her to go into the palace and deck her children in funeral garments? This prayer is granted, though Lycus warns them that they are to die at once. Left alone, Amphitryon chides Jupiter because he does not care for the children of his son :

> "Thou know'st not how
> To save thy friends. Thou surely art a god,
> Either devoid of wisdom, or unjust."

First choral interlude.—The chorus sings in praise of the mighty works of Hercules, describing these in picturesque detail, from the destruction of the Nemean lion to his last adventure, which has taken him to the world of shades, whence, alas, he will nevermore return. And meanwhile, lacking his protection, his friends and family are plunged in hopeless misery.

Second episode.—Forth from the palace, all dressed in the garb of death, come Megara and her children. She is ready for the doom which has been pronounced upon them. She sadly recalls the fond hopes that she and her husband had

She recounts the incidents of his long and difficult career, his heroic suffering at Juno's bidding.

And now base Lycus has taken advantage of her husband's absence in the lower world to kill her father, Creon, king of Thebes, and all his sons, and to usurp the throne—

"And Lycus rules the Thebes of Hercules!"

She prays her husband soon to come and right these wrongs, though in her heart she fears that he will never come again.

Old Amphitryon tries to reassure her by recalling the superhuman valour and strength of Hercules, but without success.

Now Lycus appears, boasting of the power which he has gained, not by long descent from a noble line, but by his own valour. But his house cannot stand by valour alone. He must strengthen his power by union with some princely house —he will marry Megara! Should she refuse, he will give to utter ruin all the house of Hercules.

Meeting her at the moment, he attempts with specious arguments to persuade her to his plan. But Megara repulses his monstrous proposition with indignant scorn. Lycus attempts to defend his slaughter of her father and brother as done through the exigency of war, and pleads with her to put away her wrath; but all in vain, and in the end he bids his attendants heap high a funeral pyre on which to burn the woman and all her brood.

When Lycus has retired, Amphitryon in his extremity prays to heaven for aid; but suddenly checks himself with incredulous joy, for he hears approaching the well-known step of Hercules!

First choral interlude.—Verily fortune is unjust, for while Eurystheus sits at ease, the nobler Hercules must suffer unending hardships. His labours are briefly recapitulated. Now has he gone to hell to bring back Cerberus. Oh, that he may conquer death as all things else, and come back again, as did Orpheus by the charm of his lyre.

Second episode.—Hercules enters, fresh from the lower world, rejoicing that he again beholds the light of day, and exulting in the accomplishment of his latest and most difficult task; when suddenly he notices soldiers on guard,

cherished for these sons. But these bright prospects have vanished now, for death is waiting to claim them all, herself as well. She will fold them in a last motherly embrace, and pour out her grief:

> "How, like the bee with variegated wings,
>   Shall I collect the sorrows of you all,
>   And blend the whole together in a flood
>   Of tears exhaustless!"

But perhaps even yet her absent lord has power to intervene in her behalf, though he be but a ghost. She prays despairingly that he will come to aid. Amphitryon would try the favour of Jove once more in this extremity:

> "I call on thee, O Jove, that, if thou mean
>   To be a friend to these deserted children,
>   Thou interpose without delay and save them;
>   For soon 'twill be no longer in thy power."

But at this juncture, when no help seems possible from heaven or hell, to their amazed joy Hercules himself appears, and in the flesh. He perceives the mourning garments of his family and the grief-stricken faces of the chorus, and quickly learns the cause of all this woe. He at once plans vengeance upon the wretch who has wrought it all. He has, himself, forewarned by a "bird of evil omen perched aloft," entered Thebes in secret; and now he will hide within his own palace and wait until Lycus comes to fetch the victims whom he has doomed to death. But first he briefly replies to Amphitryon's questions as to the success of his errand to the lower world.

Second choral interlude.—The old men sing in envy of youth and complaint of old age:

> "But now a burden on my head
>   Heavier than Aetna's rock, old age, I bear.'

They hold that had the gods been wiser they would have given renewed youth as a reward to the virtuous, leaving the degenerate to fall asleep and wake no more. And yet, though oppressed by age, they still may "breathe the strain Mnemosyne inspires," and sing unceasingly the deeds of Hercules:

and his wife and children dressed in mourning garments. He asks what these things mean. Amphitryon answers briefly that Lycus has killed Creon and his sons, usurped the throne, and now has doomed Megara and her children to death.

Hercules leaves his home at once to find, and take vengeance on, his enemy, though Theseus, whom he has rescued from the world of shades, begs for the privilege himself of slaying Lycus. Left with Amphitryon, in reply to the latter's questions Theseus gives in great detail an account of the lower world, its way of approach, its topography, and the various creatures who dwell within its bounds. After describing in particular the operations of justice and the punishment of the condemned, he tells how Hercules overcame Cerberus and brought him to the upper world.

Second choral interlude.—The chorus, with Theseus' words in mind, dwell in fancy still upon the lower world. They follow Hercules along " that dark way, which to the distant Manes leads," and picture the thronging shades, the " repulsive glooms," and the " weary inactivity of that still, empty universe." They pray that it may be long ere they must go to that dread world, to which all the wandering tribes of earth must surely come. But away with gloomy thoughts! Now is the time for joy, for Hercules is come again. Let animals and men make holiday, and fitly celebrate their

531

"Alcides, the resistless son of Jove,
  Those trophies which to noble birth belong
  By him are all surpassed; his forceful hand,
  Restoring peace, hath cleansed this monster-teeming land."

Third episode.—Lycus enters and encounters Amphitryon without the palace. Him he bids to go within and bring out the victims to their death. To this Amphitryon objects on the ground that it would make him an accomplice in their murder. Whereupon Lycus enters the palace to do his own errand. The old man, looking after him, exclaims:

"Depart; for to that place the fates ordain
  You now are on the road";

while the chorus rejoices that now the oppressor is so soon to meet his just punishment. Now the despairing cries of Lycus are heard within and then—silence.

Third choral interlude.—All is now joy and exultation. Fear has departed, hope has come back again, and faith in the protecting care of the gods is restored. Therefore, let all Thebes give herself up to the rapture and triumph of this hour.

But now two spectres are seen hovering over the palace, one of whom introduces herself to the chorus as Iris, the ambassadress of Juno, and announces that her companion is a fiend, daughter of the night. Their mission hither is, at the command of Juno, to drive Hercules into a madness, in which he shall slay his children. The fiend, indeed, makes a weak protest against such a mission, but speedily yields and goes darting into the palace, where we know that she begins at once her deadly work within the breast of Hercules.

The chorus bemoans the city's short-lived joy, and the new and terrible disaster that has fallen upon their hero's house. Soon they hear the mad shouts of Hercules, and know by these that the fiend has already done her fatal work.

Exode.—A messenger hurries out of the palace, and describes the dreadful scenes that have just been enacted

prince's world-wide victories, and their own deliverance from
their recent woes.

Third episode.—Hercules returns to his house, fresh from
the slaying of Lycus, and proceeds to offer sacrifices of
thanksgiving to Jupiter. But in the midst of the sacrifice
the madness planned by Juno begins to come upon him.
His sight is darkened, and his reason changed to delirium.
Now he catches sight of his children, cowering in fright ;
he thinks they are the children of Lycus, immediately lets
fly an arrow at one of them, and seizes a second, whom he
drags from the scene. Amphitryon, standing where he can
see all that takes place, describes the wretched death of the
second, and then the third, though Megara tries to save
her last remaining child. She also falls before the blow
of her husband, who thinks in his madness that she is his
cruel stepmother, Juno. Hercules, re-entering, exults in his
supposed victory over his enemies, and then sinks down in a
deep faint.

Third choral interlude.—The chorus calls upon heaven,
earth, and sea to mourn for Hercules in this new disaster
that has befallen him. They pray that he may be restored
to sanity. In a long apostrophe to Sleep they pray that the
soothing influences of this god may hold and subdue him
until his former mind returns to its accustomed course.
They watch his feverish tossings, and suffer with him in
the grief which he so soon must realize. They close with a
pathetic lament over the dead children.

Exode.—Hercules wakes up in his right mind, bewildered
and uncertain where he is. His eyes fall on the murdered

there. Hercules was offering sacrifices of purification before Jove's altar, with his three sons and Megara beside him. All was propitious, when suddenly a madness seized on Hercules. He ceased his present sacrifice, declaring that he must first go to Mycenae and kill Eurystheus and his sons, and so make an end of all his enemies at once. In fancy he mounted a chariot and speedily arrived at Mycenae. His own sons seemed to his disordered vision to be Eurystheus' sons; and rushing savagely upon them, he soon had slain them all, and Megara herself. Then did he fall into a deep, swoonlike slumber, prostrate beside a mighty column, to which the attendants tied him securely with cords, lest he should awake and do further mischief.

The palace doors are now thrown open, and the prostrate, sleeping Hercules is seen. Amphitryon warns the chorus not to wake him lest they restore him to his miseries. Soon Hercules awakes, and in his right mind. He seems to himself to have had a dreadful dream. He looks in wonder at the cords which bind his arms, at the fresh-slain corpses lying near, at his own arrows scattered on the floor. He calls aloud for someone to explain these things to him. Amphitryon advances and informs him that in his madness, sent by Juno's hate, he has destroyed his wife and all his sons.

And now Theseus, having heard that Lycus has usurped the throne of Thebes, and grateful for his own deliverance from the world of shades by Hercules, has come with an army of Athenian youth to aid his friend. He is shocked to find the hero sitting in deepest dejection, with head bowed low, and covered with a mourning veil. Quickly he inquires and learns the truth from Amphitryon. With noble and unselfish friendship, he offers his sympathy and help to Hercules, although the latter warns him to avoid the contagion which his own guilty presence engenders. He bids Hercules be a man, and give over his threats of self-destruction.

Hercules gives the reasons why it is impossible for him to live. First, Juno's inveterate hate, which attacked him in his very cradle, pursues him still, relentlessly; but most and worst of all, he has incurred such odium because of the murder of his wife and children that he will be henceforth an outcast on the earth. No land will give him refuge now.

children, though he does not as yet recognize them as his own. He misses his familiar club and bow, and wonders who has been bold enough to remove these and not to fear even a sleeping Hercules. Now he recognizes in the corpses his own wife and children:

> "Oh, what sight is this?
> My sons lie murdered, weltering in their blood;
> My wife is slain. What Lycus rules the land?
> Who could have dared to do such things in Thebes,
> And Hercules returned?"

He notices that Theseus and Amphitryon turn away and will not meet his gaze. He asks them who has slain his family. At last, partly through their half-admissions, and partly through his own surmise, it comes to him that this dreadful deed is his own. His soul reels with the shock, and he prays wildly for death. No attempts of his two friends to palliate his deed can soothe his grief and shame. At last the threat of old Amphitryon instantly to anticipate the death of Hercules by his own leads the hero to give over his deadly purpose.

He consents to live—but where? What land will receive a polluted wretch like him? He appeals to Theseus:

> "O Theseus, faithful friend, seek out a place
> Far off from here where I may hide myself."

Theseus offers his own Athens as a place of refuge, where his friend may find at once asylum and cleansing from his sin:

> "My land awaits thy coming; there will Mars
> Wash clean thy hands and give thee back thy arms.
> That land, O Hercules, now calls to thee,
> Which even gods from sin is wont to free."

Why should he live? Let him die; and let Juno's cup of happiness be full.

Theseus reminds him that no man escapes unscathed by fate. Nay, even the gods themselves have done unlawful things, and yet live on and do not feel the obloquy their deeds should cause. As for a place of refuge, Athens shall be his home. There shall he obtain full cleansing for his crimes, a place of honour, and ample provision for his wants. All that a generous and grateful friend can give shall be his own.

Hercules accepts this offer of Theseus, reflecting also that he might be charged with cowardice should he give in to his troubles and seek refuge in death. He accordingly takes a mournful farewell of his dead wife and children, commends their bodies to Amphitryon for burial, which it is not lawful for him to give, and so commits himself to the hands of his faithful friend:

> "I will follow Theseus,
> Towed like a battered skiff. Whoe'er prefers
> Wealth or dominion to a steadfast friend,
> Judges amiss."

THE *TROADES* OF EURIPIDES

Prologue.—Neptune, appearing from the depths of the sea, briefly recounts the story of the overthrow of Troy, which he laments, states the present situation of the Trojan women, dwells upon the especial grief of Hecuba, and places the blame for all this ruin upon Minerva:

> "But, oh my town, once flourishing, once crowned
> With beauteous-structured battlements, farewell!
> Had not Minerva sunk thee in the dust,
> On thy firm base e'en now thou mightst have stood."

To him appears Minerva, who, though she had indeed helped the Greeks to their final triumph over Troy, had been turned against them by the outrage of Cassandra on the night of Troy's overthrow. She now makes common cause with Neptune, and plans for the harassing of the Greek fleet

536

COMPARATIVE ANALYSES

THE *TROADES* OF SENECA

Prologue.—Hecuba bewails the fall of Troy, and draws from it a warning to all who are high in power :

> "For of a truth did fortune never show
> In plainer wise the frailty of the prop
> That doth support a king."

She graphically describes the mighty power and mighty fall of her husband's kingdom, and portrays the awe with which the Greeks behold even their fallen foe. She asserts that the fire by which her city has been consumed sprang from her, the brand that she had dreamed of in her dream before the birth of Paris. She dwells horribly upon the death of Priam, which she had herself witnessed.

> "But still the heavenly powers are not appeased."

by storm and flood on the homeward voyage. The Greeks
are to be taught a lesson of reverence :

> "Unwise is he whoe'er of mortals storms
> Beleaguered towns, and crushed in ruins wastes
> The temples of the gods, the hallowed tombs
> Where sleep the dead ; for he shall perish soon."

[The two gods disappear.]

Hecuba, lying prone upon the ground before Agamemnon's
tent, gives voice to her sufferings of body and of spirit;
laments her accumulated losses of home, friends, station,
liberty ; blames Helen for all, and calls upon the chorus of
captive women to join her in lamentation.

Parode, or chorus entry.—The chorus with Hecuba indulges
in speculation as to the place of their future home, speaking
with hope of some Greek lands, and deprecating others.

First episode.—Talthybius, the herald, enters and announces that the lots have been drawn, and reveals to each
captive her destined lord : that Cassandra has fallen to
Agamemnon, Andromache to Pyrrhus, Hecuba to Ulysses.
At news of this her fate Hecuba is filled with fresh lamentations, counting it an especial hardship that she should fall to
the arch-enemy of her race. The herald also darkly alludes
to the already accomplished fate of Polyxena,

> "At the tomb raised to Achilles doomed to serve."

Hecuba does not as yet catch the import of these words.

Cassandra now enters, waving a torch, and celebrates in a
mad refrain her approaching union with Agamemnon.
Hecuba remonstrates with her for her unseemly joy ; whereupon Cassandra declares that she rejoices in the prospect of
the vengeance upon Agamemnon which is to be wrought out
through this union. She contrasts the lot of the Greeks and
Trojans during the past ten years, and finds that the latter
have been far happier ; and even in her fall, the woes of
Troy are far less than those that await the Greek chieftains.
She then prophesies in detail the trials that await Ulysses,
and the dire result of her union with Agamemnon :

> "Thou shalt bear me
> A fury, an Erinys from this land."

COMPARATIVE ANALYSES

The captives are to be alloted to the Greek chiefs, and even now the urn stands ready for the lots.

Hecuba next calls upon the chorus of Trojan women to join her in lamenting their fallen heroes, Hector and Priam.

Parode, or chorus entry.—The chorus, under the direction of Hecuba as chorus leader, in true oriental fashion bewails the downfall of Troy, and in particular the death of Priam and Hector.

First episode.—Talthybius announces that the shade of Achilles has appeared with the demand that Polyxena be sacrificed upon the hero's tomb.

Enter Pyrrhus and Agamemnon, the former demanding that his father's request be carried out, the latter resisting the demand as too barbarous to be entertained. It is finally agreed to leave the decision to Calchas. He is accordingly summoned, and at once declares that only by the death of the maiden can the Greeks be allowed to set sail for home. And not this alone, but Astyanax also must be sacrificed— hurled from the lofty Scaean tower of Troy.

Hecuba here falls in a faint and, upon being revived, again recounts her former high estate, sadly contrasts with that her present condition, and shudders at the lot of the slave which awaits her :

> "Then deem not of the great
> Now flourishing as happy, ere they die."

First choral interlude.—The chorus graphically describes the wooden horse, its joyful reception by the Trojans into the city, their sense of relief from danger, and their holiday spirit ; and at last their horrible awakening to death at the hands of the Greeks within the walls.

Second episode.—The appearance of Andromache with Astyanax in her arms, borne captive on a Grecian car, is a signal for general mourning. She announces her own chief cause of woe :

> "I, with my child, am led away, the spoil
> Of war ; th' illustrious progeny of kings,
> Oh, fatal change, is sunk to slavery."

Her next announcement comes as a still heavier blow to Hecuba :

> "Polyxena, thy daughter, is no more ;
> Devoted to Achilles, on his tomb,
> An offering to the lifeless dead, she fell."

Andromache insists that Polyxena's fate is happier than her own ; argues that in death there is no sense of misery :

> "Polyxena is dead and of her ills
> Knows nothing" ;

while Andromache still lives to feel the keen contrast between her former and her present lot.

Hecuba is so sunk in woe that she can make no protest, but advises Andromache to forget the past and

> "honour thy present lord,
> And with thy gentle manners win his soul" ;

COMPARATIVE ANALYSES

First choral interlude.—The chorus maintains that all perishes with the body ; the soul goes out into nothingness :

> " For when within the tomb we're laid,
> No soul remains, no hov'ring shade.
> Like curling smoke, like clouds before the blast,
> This animating spirit soon has passed."

The evident purpose of these considerations is to discount the story that Achilles' shade could have appeared with its demand for the death of Polyxena.

Second episode.—Andromache appears with Astyanax and recounts a vision of Hector which she has had, in which her dead husband has warned her to hide the boy away beyond the reach of threatening danger. After discussion with an old man as to the best place of concealment, she hides Astyanax in Hector's tomb, which is in the near background. Enter Ulysses, who reluctantly announces that Calchas has warned the Greeks that they must not allow the son of Hector to grow to manhood ; for if they do so, the reopening of the Trojan war will be only a matter of time, and the work will have to be done all over again. He therefore asks Andromache to give up the boy to him. Then ensues a war of wits between the desperate mother and the crafty Greek. She affects not to know where the boy is—he is lost. But if she knew, no power on earth should take him from her. Ulysses threatens death, which she welcomes ; he threatens torture, which she scorns. She at last states that her son is "among the dead." Ulysses, taking these words at their face meaning, starts off gladly to tell the news to the Greeks, but suddenly reflects that he has no proof but the mother's word. He therefore begins to watch Andromache more narrowly, and discovers that her bearing is not that of one who has put her grief behind her, but of one who is still in suspense and fear. To test her, he suddenly calls to his attendants to hunt out the boy. Looking beyond her, he

this with the hope that she may be the better able to rear up Astyanax to establish once more some day the walls and power of Troy.

But the heaviest stroke is yet to fall. Talthybius now enters and announces with much reluctance that Ulysses has prevailed upon the Greeks to demand the death of Astyanax for the very reason that he may grow up to renew the Trojan war. The lad is to be hurled from a still standing tower of Troy. The herald warns Andromache that if she resist this mandate she may be endangering the boy's funeral rites. She yields to fate, passionately caressing the boy, who clings fearfully to her, partly realizing his terrible situation. The emotional climax of the play is reached, as she says to the clinging, frightened lad:

> "Why dost thou clasp me with thy hands, why hold
> My robes, and shelter thee beneath my wings
> Like a young bird?"

She bitterly upbraids the Greeks for their cruelty, and curses Helen as the cause of all her woe, and then gives the boy up in an abandonment of defiant grief:

> "Here, take him, bear him, hurl him from the height,
> If ye must hurl him; feast upon his flesh:
> For from the gods hath ruin fall'n on us."

And now what more can happen? Surely the depth of misfortune has been sounded. In the voice of Hecuba:

> "Is there an ill
> We have not? What is wanting to the woes
> Which all the dreadful band of ruin brings?"

Second choral interlude.—The chorus first tells of the former fall of Troy under Hercules and Telamon; and then refers to the high honours that had come to the city through the translation of Ganymede to be the cupbearer of Jove, and through the special grace of Venus. But these have not availed to save the city from its present destruction.

Third episode.—Menelaüs appears, announcing that the Greeks have allotted to him Helen, his former wife, the cause of all this strife, to do with as he will. He declares his intention to take her to Greece, and there destroy her as a warning to faithless wives.

cries : " Good ! he's found ! bring him to me." Whereat Andromache's agitation proves that the boy is indeed not dead, but in hiding. Where is he hid? Ulysses forces her to choose between the living boy and the dead husband ; for, unless her son is forthcoming, Hector's tomb will be invaded and his ashes scattered upon the sea. To her frantic prayer for mercy he says :

> " Bring forth the boy—and pray."

Follows a *canticum*, in which Andromache brings Astyanax out of the tomb and sets him in Ulysses' sight :

> " Here, here's the terror of a thousand ships ! "

and prays him to spare the child. Ulysses refuses, and, after allowing the mother time for a passionate and pathetic farewell to her son, he leads the boy away to his death.

Second choral interlude.—The chorus discusses the various places to which it may be its misfortune to be carried into captivity. It professes a willingness to go anywhere but to the homes of Helen, Agamemnon, and Ulysses.

Third episode.—Helen approaches the Trojan women, saying that she has been sent by the Greeks to deck Polyxena for marriage with Pyrrhus, this being a ruse to trick the girl into an unresisting preparation for her death. This news Polyxena, though mute, receives witn horror.

Hecuba applauds this decision, and thinks that at last heaven has sent justice to the earth :

> "Dark thy ways
> And silent are thy steps to mortal man ;
> Yet thou with justice all things dost ordain."

Helen, dragged forth from the tent at the command of Menelaüs, pleads her cause. She lays the blame for all upon Hecuba and Priam :

> " She first, then, to the ills
> Gave birth, when she gave Paris birth ; and next
> The agèd Priam ruined Troy and thee,
> The infant not destroying, at his birth
> Denounced a baleful firebrand."

Blame should also fall upon Venus, since through her influence Helen came into the power of Paris.

Hecuba refutes the excuses of Helen. She scouts the idea that Venus brought Paris to Sparta. The only Venus that had influenced Helen was her own passion inflamed by the beauty of Paris :

> " My son was with surpassing beauty graced ;
> And thy fond passion, when he struck thy sight,
> Became a Venus."

As for the excuse that she was borne away by force, no Spartan was aware of that, no cries were heard. Hecuba ends by urging Menelaüs to carry out his threat. This, he repeats, it is his purpose to do.

Third choral interlude.—The chorus sadly recalls the sacred rites in Troy and within the forests of Mount Ida, and grieves that these shall be no more. They lament the untimely death of their warrior husbands, whose bodies have not received proper burial rites, and whose souls are wandering in the spirit-world, while they, the hapless wives, must wander over sea to foreign homes. They pray that storms may come and overwhelm the ships, and especially that Helen may not live to reach the land again.

Exode.—Enter Talthybius, with the dead body of Astyanax borne upon the shield of Hector. He explains that Pyrrhus has hastened home, summoned by news of

COMPARATIVE ANALYSES

Andromache bitterly cries out upon Helen and her marriages as the cause of all their woe. But Helen puts the whole matter to this test:

> "Count this true,
> If 'twas a Spartan vessel brought me here."

Under the pointed questions of Andromache she gives up deception, and frankly states the impending doom of Polyxena to be slaughtered on Achilles' tomb, and so to be that hero's spirit bride. At this the girl shows signs of joy, and eagerly submits herself to Helen's hands to be decked for the sacrificial rite.

Hecuba cries out at this, and laments her almost utter childlessness; but Andromache envies the doomed girl her fate.

Helen then informs the women that the lots have been drawn and their future lords determined; Andromache is to be given to Pyrrhus, Cassandra to Agamemnon, Hecuba to Ulysses.

Pyrrhus now appears to conduct Polyxena to her death, and is bitterly scorned and cursed by Hecuba.

Third choral interlude.—The chorus enlarges upon the comfort of company to those in grief. Hitherto they have had this comfort; but now they are to be scattered, and each must suffer alone. And soon, as they sail away, they must take their last, sad view of Troy, now but a smouldering heap; and mother to child will say, as she points back to the shore:

> "See, there's our Troy, where smoke curls high in air,
> And thick, dark clouds obscure the distant sky."

Exode.—The messenger relates with much detail to Hecuba, Andromache, and the rest the circumstances of the death of Astyanax and Polyxena: how crowds of

545

insurrection in his own kingdom, and has taken Andromache with him. He delivers Andromache's request to Hecuba that she give the boy proper burial, and use the hollow shield as a casket for the dead.

Hecuba and the chorus together weep over the shield, which recalls Hector in his days of might, and over the poor, bruised body of the dead boy, sadly contrasting his former beauty with this mangled form. They then wrap it in such costly wrappings as their state allows, place him upon the shield, and consign him to the tomb.

Talthybius then orders bands of men with torches to burn the remaining buildings of Troy; and in the light of its glaring flames and with the crashing sound of its falling walls in their ears, Hecuba and her companions make their way to the waiting ships, while the messenger urges on their lagging steps.

THE *MEDEA* OF EURIPIDES

Prologue.—The old nurse of Medea, alone upon the stage, laments that the Argo was ever framed, and that Medea had ever fled from Colchis. Then had she never been here in Corinth an exile and now deserted even by her husband, Jason. In describing Medea's distracted condition, the nurse first voices the fear of that violence which forms the catastrophe of the play. Enter an old attendant with the two sons of Medea, who announces a new woe—that Creon, the king, has decreed the banishment of Medea and her children. The nurse repeats her warning note, and urges the attendant to keep the children out of the sight of their mother, who even now can be heard raving within, and vowing the destruction of her children and her husband. The attendant retires with the children.

Parode, or chorus entry.—The chorus of Corinthian women comes to the front of the palace to inquire the cause of Medea's cries, which they have heard, and to profess their attachment to her. From time to time Medea's voice can be heard from within as she prays for death and calls down curses upon Jason. The nurse, at the suggestion of the chorus, undertakes to induce her mistress to come forth, that converse with her

Greeks and Trojans witnessed both tragedies, how both sides were moved to tears at the sad sight, and how both victims met their death as became their noble birth.

Andromache bewails and denounces the cruel death of her son, and sadly asks that his body be given her for burial; but she is told that this is mangled past recognition.

But Hecuba, having now drained her cup of sorrow to the dregs, has no more wild cries to utter; she almost calmly bids the Grecians now set sail, since nothing bars their way. She longs for death, complaining that it ever flees from her, though she has often been so near its grasp.

The messenger interrupts, and bids them hasten to the shore and board the ships, which wait only their coming to set sail.

THE *MEDEA* OF SENECA

Prologue.—Medea, finding herself deserted by Jason, calls upon gods and furies to grant her vengeance. She prays for destruction to light upon her rival, and calls down curses upon Jason. She thinks it monstrous that the sun can still hold on his way, and prays for power to subvert the whole course of nature. She finally realises that she is impotent save as she has recourse to her old sorceries, which she has long since laid aside, and resolves upon them as a means of revenge.

Parode, or chorus entry.—A chorus of Corinthians chants an epithalamium for the nuptials of Jason and Creüsa. First, in Asclepiadean strains, they invoke the gods to be present and bless the nuptials. The strain then changes to quick, joyful Glyconics in praise of the surpassing beauty of the married pair. Changing back to Asclepiads, the chorus continues in extravagant praise of Jason and his bride,

friends may soothe her grief. The nurse goes within, leaving the chorus alone upon the stage.

First episode.—Medea comes forth from the palace to explain to the chorus her position and unhappy condition. She deplores the lot of women in general, and especially in relation to marriage, and enlists the sympathy of the chorus in her attempt to secure some revenge for her wrongs. They confess the justice of her cause and promise to keep her secret.

Creon announces to Medea that she must leave his realm at once, for much he fears that she will take her revenge upon him and upon his house. She pleads for grace, and bewails her reputation for magic power; she assures the king that he has nothing to fear from her, and affects compliance with all that has taken place. Creon, while still protesting that she cannot be trusted, yields in so far that he grants her a single day's delay.

Medea tells the chorus that her recent compliance was only feigned, and openly announces her intention before the day is done of slaying Creon, his daughter, and Jason. She debates the various methods by which this may be accomplished, and decides, for her own greater safety, upon the help of magic.

First choral interlude.—The course of nature is subverted. No longer let woman alone have the reputation for falsehood; man's insincerity equals hers. In poetry the fickleness of both should be sung, just as in history it is seen. Though Medea, for her love of Jason, left her native land and braved all the terrors of the deep, she is now left all forsaken and alone. Verily truth and honour have departed from the earth.

Second episode.—Jason reproaches Medea for her intemperate speech against the king, which has resulted in her banishment, and shows her that he is still concerned for her interests. She retorts with reproaches because of his ingratitude, and proceeds to recount all that she had done for him and given up in his behalf. Jason replies that it was not through her help, but that of Venus, that he had escaped all the perils of the past, and reminds her of the advantages which she herself had gained by leaving her barbarous land

congratulates him on his exchange from Medea to Creüsa, and finally, in six lines of hexameter, exults in the licence of the hour.

First episode.—Hearing the epithalamium, Medea goes into a passion of rage. She recounts all that she has done for Jason, and exclaims against his ingratitude. Again, with shifting feelings she pleads Jason's cause to herself and strives to excuse him, putting all the blame upon Creon. Upon him she vows the direst vengeance. Meanwhile the nurse in vain urges prudence.

Creon now enters, manifesting in his words a fear of Medea, and bent upon her immediate banishment. Medea pleads her innocence, and begs to know the reason for her exile. She reviews at length her former regal estate and contrasts with this her present forlorn condition. She claims the credit for the preservation of all the Argonautic heroes. Upon this ground she claims that Jason is hers. She begs of Creon some small corner in his kingdom for her dwelling, but the king remains obdurate. She then prays for a single day's delay in which to say farewell to her children, who are to remain the wards of the king. This prayer Creon reluctantly grants.

First choral interlude.—Apropos of Medea's reference to the Argonautic heroes the chorus sings of the dangers which those first voyagers upon the sea endured; how the natural bounds which the gods set to separate the lands have now been removed—and all this for gold and this barbarian woman. (The chorus is nowhere friendly to Medea, as in Euripides.) The ode ends with a prophecy of the time when all the earth shall be revealed, and there shall be no "Ultima Thule."

Second episode.—Medea is rushing out to seek vengeance, while the nurse tries in vain to restrain her. The nurse soliloquizes, describing the wild frenzy of her mistress, and expressing grave fears for the result. Medea, not noticing the nurse's presence, reflects upon the day that has been granted her by Creon, and vows that her terrible vengeance shall be commensurate with her sufferings. She rushes off the stage, while the nurse calls after her a last warning.

Jason now enters, lamenting the difficult position in which

549

for Greece. He even holds that his marriage into the royal family of Corinth is in her interest and that of her children, since by this means their common fortunes will be mended. He offers her from his new resources assistance for her exile, which she indignantly refuses, and Jason retires from her bitter taunts.

Second choral interlude.—The chorus prays to be delivered from the pangs of immoderate love and jealousy, from exile, and the ingratitude of friends.

Third episode.—Aegeus, in Corinth by accident, recognizes Medea, and learns from her her present grievous condition and imminent exile. She begs him to receive her into his kingdom as a friend under his protection. This he promises with a mighty oath to do.

Medea, left alone with the chorus, explains to it still more in detail her plans. She will send her sons with gifts to the new bride, which, by their magic power, will destroy her and all who touch her. She adds that she will also slay her two sons, the more to injure Jason. The chorus, while protesting against this last proposal, offers no resistance.

he finds himself. He asserts that it is for his children's sake that he has done all, and hopes to be able to persuade Medea herself to take this view. Medea comes back, and at sight of Jason her fury is still further inflamed. She announces her intended flight. But whither shall she flee? For his sake she has closed all lands against herself. In bitter sarcasm she accepts all these sufferings as her just punishment. Then in a flash of fury she recalls all her services to him and contrasts his ingratitude. She shifts suddenly to passionate entreaty, and prays him to pity her, to give back all that she gave up for him, if she must needs flee; she begs him to brave the wrath of Creon and flee with her, and promises him her protection as of old. In a long series of quick, short passages they shift from phase to phase of feeling, and finally Medea prays that in her flight she may have her children as her comrades. Jason's refusal shows how deeply he loves his sons, and here is suggested to Medea for the first time the method of her direst revenge. Jason now yields to her assumed penitence and grants her the custody of the children for this day alone. When Jason has withdrawn, she bids the nurse prepare the fatal robe which she proposes to send to her rival by the hands of her children.

Second choral interlude.—The chorus opens on the text, "Hell hath no fury like a woman scorned," and continues with a prayer for Jason's safety. It then recounts the subsequent history of the individual Argonauts, showing how almost all came to some untimely end. They might indeed be said to deserve this fate, for they volunteered to assist in that first impious voyage in quest of the golden fleece; but Jason should be spared the general doom, for the task had been imposed upon him by his usurping uncle, Pelias.

Third episode.—The nurse in a long monologue recites Medea's magic wonders of the past, and all her present preparations. Then Medea's voice is heard, and presently she comes upon the stage chanting her incantations. She summons up the gods of Tartara to aid her task; recounts all the wonders which her charms can work; describes her store of magic fires and other potent objects. Then breaking into quicker measure, as if filled with a fuller frenzy, she continues her incantations, accompanied by wild cries and gestures. She finally dispatches her sons to Jason's bride with the robe she has anointed with her magic drugs

Third choral interlude.—The chorus, dwelling upon Medea's proposed place of refuge, sings the praises of Athens, sacred to the Muses. It contrasts with this holy city the dreadful deed which Medea intends, and again vainly strives to dissuade her.

Fourth episode.—Medea, sending for Jason, with feigned humility reproaches herself for her former intemperate words to him, and begs only that he use his influence for the reprieve of their children from exile. To assist him in this, she proposes to send the children themselves, bearing a gorgeous robe of golden tissue (which she has anointed with magic poison) as a wedding present to the bride. Upon this errand Jason retires, attended by his little sons.

Fourth choral interlude.—The chorus, with full knowledge of the fatal robe, pictures the delight of the bride at its reception, and laments her fearful doom.

Fifth episode.—This episode is in four parts.

The attendant returns with the children and announces to Medea that her gifts have prevailed for their reprieve. (The attendant retires.)

Medea contrasts the assured career of her children with her own hapless condition; then remembers her resolve and with softening heart laments their dreadful fate. She hastily sends them within the palace. Left alone, she again struggles between her mother-love and her resolve not to leave her children subject to the scorn of her foes. (She here leaves the stage to wait for tidings from the royal house.)

Then follows a monologue by the chorus leader discussing the advantages of childlessness. No reference is made to the passing events.

Medea returns just in time to meet a messenger who breathlessly announces the death of Creon and his daughter. At the request of Medea he gives a detailed account of the reception of the magic robe and crown, the bride's delight, and her sudden and awful death, in which her father also was involved. He urges Medea to fly at once. She announces her intention to do so as soon as she has slain her children; and then rushes into the house.

and charged with her curses. She hastens out in the opposite direction.

Third choral interlude.—The chorus notes and describes Medea's wild bearing, and prays for her speedy departure from their city.

Fifth choral interlude.—This consists of a single strophe and antistrophe in which the chorus calls upon the gods to restrain Medea's mad act. Then are heard within the house the shrieks first of the two children, then of one, then silence, the chorus meanwhile wildly shouting to Medea to desist from her deadly work.

The exode.—Jason appears in search of Medea that he may avenge on her the death of the royal pair ; but most he fears for his children. The chorus informs him that they are already slain within the palace by their mother's hand. He prepares to force an entrance into the house.

But now Medea appears in a chariot drawn by dragons. She defies Jason's power to harm her. Jason replies by reproaching her with all the murderous deeds of her life, which have culminated in this crowning deed of blood. She in turn reproaches him and his ingratitude as the cause of all. A storm of mutual imprecations follows, and Medea disappears with the bodies of her two sons, denying to Jason even the comfort of weeping over their remains.

THE *HIPPOLYTUS* OF EURIPIDES

Prologue.—Venus complains that Hippolytus alone of all men sets her power at naught and owns allegiance to her rival, Diana. She announces her plan of revenge : that Phaedra shall become enamoured of her stepson, that Theseus shall be made aware of this and in his rage be led to slay his son. If Phaedra perish too, it will but add to the triumph of the goddess' slighted power.

Hippolytus comes in from the chase and renders marked homage to Diana. He is warned by an aged officer of the palace "to loathe that pride which studies not to please." Inquiring the meaning of this warning, he is told to recognize the presence of Venus, too, and to include her in his devotions ; but from this advice he turns away in scorn.

COMPARATIVE ANALYSES

The exode.—A messenger comes running in from the direction of the palace, and announces that the king and his daughter are dead. The eager questions of the chorus bring out the strange circumstances attending this catastrophe. Medea enters in time to hear that her magic has been successful, and ignoring the nurse's entreaties to flee at once, she becomes absorbed in her own reflections. And now in her words may be seen the inward struggle between maternal love and jealous hate as she nerves herself for the final act of vengeance. The purpose to kill her children grows upon her, resist it as she may, until in an ecstasy of madness, urged on by a vision of her murdered brother, she slays her first son ; and then, bearing the corpse of one and leading the other by the hand, she mounts to the turret of her house. Here with a refinement of cruelty she slays the second son in Jason's sight, disregarding his abject prayers for the boy's life. Now a chariot drawn by dragons appears in the air. This Medea mounts and is borne away, while Jason shouts his impotent curses after her.

THE *HIPPOLYTUS* OF SENECA

Prologue.—Hippolytus, in hunting costume, appears in the court of the palace, which is filled with huntsmen bearing nets and all sorts of hunting weapons, and leading dogs in leash. The young prince, in a long rambling speech, assigns places for the hunt, and their duties to his various servants and companions. He ends with an elaborate ascription of praise to his patroness Diana, as goddess of the chase, and with a prayer to her for success in his own present undertaking. The whole speech is in lyric strain, the anapaestic measure, most commonly employed by Seneca.

THE TRAGEDIES OF SENECA

Parode, or chorus entry.—The chorus of Troezenian women deplores the strange malady that has befallen the young queen. They relate how

> "This is the third revolving day
>   Since, o'erpowered by lingering pains,
>   She from all nourishment abstains,
> Wasting that lovely frame with slow decay."

At the conclusion of the lyric part of the chorus, the queen, closely veiled, in company with her aged nurse, is seen coming from the palace gates.

First episode.—Full of anxiety, the nurse strives to indulge her mistress' every whim. Phaedra answers feebly at first, but suddenly, to the amazement of her companion, her speech is filled with the language of the chase, and she again relapses into her mute lethargy. At last, under the insistence of the nurse to probe her mystery, Phaedra confesses that the wretched fate of her house pursues her, too, and that she now feels the torments of love; and though she does not speak his name, the truth at last is clear that Hippolytus is the object of her passion. The nurse recoils in horror and shame from this confession.

Phaedra describes how she has struggled against her unhappy love, but in vain, and is now resolved on death in order to save her honour. At this the nurse throws all her influence in the opposite scale, arguing that, after all, the sway of Venus is universal, that it is only human to love, and that this is no reason for casting away one's life. She even proposes to acquaint Hippolytus with her mistress' feelings, and strive to win his love in return. This proposal Phaedra indignantly rejects. The nurse then offers to fetch from the house certain philtres which will cure the queen of her malady. The queen reluctantly consents to this, and the nurse retires into the palace.

COMPARATIVE ANALYSES

Parode, or chorus entry.—The technical chorus entry is entirely lacking in this play. While the chorus may be assumed to have entered and to have been present during the long interview between Phaedra and her nurse, which forms the first episode, still its presence is in no way manifested until the end of this interview.

First episode.—Phaedra bewails her present lot, in that she has been forced to leave her native Crete, and live in wedlock with her father's enemy. And even he has now deserted her, gone to the very realms of Dis, in company with a madcap friend, to seduce and bear away the gloomy monarch's queen. But a worse grief than this is preying on her soul. She feels in her own heart the devastating power of unlawful love, which has already destroyed all the natural interests of her life. She recalls her mother's unhappy passion ; but this was bearable compared with her own. For Venus has, from deadly hatred of her family, filled her with a far more hopeless love. She does not name the object of her passion, but from her guarded references it is clear that Hippolytus, her stepson, is meant.

The nurse urges her mistress to drive this passion from her breast, moralizing upon the danger of delay. Has not her house already known sinful love enough ? Such love is dangerous, for it cannot long be hid. Granting that Theseus may never return to earth, can her sin be concealed from her father ? from her grandsires, both gods of heaven ? And what of her own conscience ? Can she ever be happy or at peace with such a sin upon her soul ? She pictures her mistress' passion in all its hideousness. Besides, it is most hopeless, since Hippolytus, woman-hater that he is, can never be brought to respond to it. Phaedra yields to these arguments and entreaties of the nurse, and says that now she is resolved upon death as her only refuge. Hereupon the nurse (the usual rôle) begs her not to take this desperate course, and undertakes to bend Hippolytus to their will.

First choral interlude.—The chorus prays that love may never come upon its breast with immoderate power, and relates instances of the resistless sway of Venus and her son.

Second episode.—Phaedra, standing near the doors of the palace, suddenly becomes agitated, and utters despairing cries. The chorus, inquiring the cause of these, is told to listen. At first there is only a confused murmur from within; but this soon resolves itself into the angry denunciations of Hippolytus and the pleading tones of the nurse. By these Phaedra learns that the nurse has indeed revealed the fatal secret to Hippolytus under an oath that he will not betray the truth to anyone, and that the youth has received the announcement with horror and scorn. He breaks forth into bitter reproaches against all womankind. He regrets that his lips are sealed by his oath, else would he straightway reveal to Theseus all his wife's unfaithfulness.

Phaedra, on her side, reproaches the nurse for betraying her secret. She angrily dismisses her, and, after exacting an oath of silence from the chorus, goes out, reiterating her resolve to die, and suggests that she has one expedient left by which her name may be preserved from infamy and her sons from dishonour.

Second choral interlude.—The chorus prays to be wafted far away from these scenes of woe; and laments that the hapless queen had ever come from Crete, for then she would not now be doomed by hopeless love to self-inflicted death.

First choral interlude.—The chorus sings at length upon the universal and irresistible sway of love.

Second episode.—On the inquiry of the chorus as to how the queen is faring, the nurse describes the dreadful effect which this malady of love has already produced upon her. Then the palace doors open, and Phaedra is seen, reclining upon a couch, attended by her tiring women. She rejects all the beautiful robes and jewels which they offer, and desires to be dressed as a huntress, ready for the chase.

The nurse prays to Diana to conquer the stubborn soul of Hippolytus and bend his heart toward her mistress. At this moment the youth himself enters and inquires the cause of the nurse's distress.

Thereupon ensues a long debate, in which the nurse chides Hippolytus for his austere life and argues that the pleasures of life were meant to be enjoyed, and that no life comes to its full fruition unless youth is given free rein. The young man replies by a rhapsody on the life of the woods, so full of simple, wholesome joys, and so free from all the cares of life at court and among men. He compares this with the Golden Age, and traces the gradual fall from the innocence of that time to the abandoned sin of the present. He concludes with laying all the blame for this upon woman.

Phaedra now comes forth, and, seeing Hippolytus, falls fainting, but is caught in the young man's arms. He attempts to reassure her and inquires the cause of her evident grief. After much hesitation, she at last confesses her love for him and begs him to pity her. With scorn and horror he repulses her and starts to kill her with his sword ; but, deciding not so to stain his sword, he throws the weapon away and makes off toward the forest.

The nurse now plans to save her mistress by inculpating Hippolytus. She accordingly calls loudly for help, and tells the attendants who come rushing in that the youth has attempted an assault upon the queen, and shows his sword in evidence.

Second choral interlude.—The chorus dwells upon and praises the beauty of Hippolytus, and discourses upon the theme that beauty has always been a dangerous possession, citing various mythological instances in proof of this.

THE TRAGEDIES OF SENECA

Third episode.—A messenger hurriedly enters with the announcement that the queen has destroyed herself by the noose. The chorus, though grieved, manifests no surprise at this, and is divided as to a plan of action. And now enters Theseus, who demands the cause of the lamentations of the servants, which may be heard from within the palace. He learns from the chorus the fact and manner, but not the cause, of Phaedra's death.

The palace doors are now thrown open and the shrouded body of the queen is discovered within. Theseus, in an agony of lamentations, seeks to know the cause of his queen's death. He at length discovers a letter clasped in her dead hand, by which he is informed that Phaedra has slain herself in grief and shame because her honour has been violated by the king's own son, Hippolytus. Thereupon Theseus curses his son, and calls on Neptune to destroy him, offering this as one of the three requests which, in accordance with the promise of the god, should not be denied.

Here enters Hippolytus, hearing the sound of his father's voice. He looks in amazement upon the corpse of Phaedra, and begs his father to explain her death. Theseus, supposing that his son conceals a guilty conscience, makes no direct answer, but inveighs against the specious arts of man. This strange speech, and still more the manner of his father, now show Hippolytus that he himself is connected in his father's mind with Phaedra's death; and he seeks to know who has thus calumniated him. The wrath of Theseus now breaks over all bounds. He charges his son with the dishonour and murder of his wife, and with withering scorn taunts him with his former professions of purity. Hippolytus protests his innocence, but Theseus continues obdurate, and produces the fatal letter in proof of his statements. Then the youth realizes the terrible mesh of circumstances in which he is taken; but, bound by his oath of secrecy, he endures in silence. After Theseus has pronounced the doom of exile upon him, and retired within the gates, he himself goes forth to seek his comrades and acquaint them with his fate.

Third choral interlude.—The chorus reflects upon the precarious life of man, lauds the golden mean, and prays for the blessings of life without conspicuous fame. No man can hope for continued security in life, when such a youth as Hippolytus is driven off by Theseus' ire. It laments that no

COMPARATIVE ANALYSES

Third episode.—Theseus, just returned to earth from Hades, and with all the horrors of the lower world still upon him, briefly refers to his dreadful experiences and his escape by the aid of Hercules. Then, hearing the sounds of lamentation, he asks the cause. He is told by the nurse that Phaedra, for some reason which she will not disclose, has resolved on immediate self-destruction. Rushing into the palace, he encounters Phaedra just within. After urgent entreaties and threats from Theseus, she confesses that she is determined to die in order to remove the stain upon her honour; and without mentioning the name of him who has ruined her, she shows the sword which Hippolytus has left behind in his flight. This is at once recognized by Theseus, who flies into a wild passion of horror, rage, and bitter scorn. He vows dire vengeance upon his son, which shall reach him wherever he may flee; and ends by claiming from Neptune, as the third of the boons once granted him, that the god will destroy Hippolytus.

Third choral interlude.—The chorus complains that while nature is so careful to maintain the order of the heavenly bodies, the atmospheric phenomena, the seasons, and the productiveness of wealth, for the affairs of men alone she has no care. These go all awry. Sin prospers and righteousness is

longer will his steeds, his lyre, his wonted woodland haunts know the well-loved youth; and reproaches the gods that they did not better screen their guiltless votary.

Exode.—The last words of the chorus are interrupted by the approach of a messenger, who hastily inquires for the king. As the latter comes forth from the palace the messenger announces the death of his son. At the king's request he gives a detailed account of the disaster: how Hippolytus was driving his fiery coursers along the shore, when Neptune sent a monstrous bull from out the sea, which drove the horses to a panic of fear; how the car was at length dashed against a ragged cliff, and Hippolytus dragged, bruised and bleeding, by the maddened horses; how, though yet living, he could not long survive. Theseus expresses pleasure at his son's sufferings, and bids that he be brought into his presence that he may behold his punishment.

The chorus interjects a single strophe, acknowledging Venus as the unrivalled queen of heaven and earth.

Diana now appears to Theseus and reveals to him the whole truth, explaining the infatuation of the queen, the fatal letter, and the wiles of Venus. The father is filled with horror and remorse. Diana tells him that he may yet hope for pardon for his sin, since through the wiles of Venus, which she herself could not frustrate, the deed was done.

Here the dying Hippolytus is borne in by his friends. In his agony he prays for death; but by the voice of his loved goddess he is soothed and comforted. After a touching scene of reconciliation between the dying prince and his father, the youth perishes, leaving Theseus overcome with grief.

in distress. Verily, it does not at all profit a man to strive to live uprightly, since all the rewards of life go to the vain and profligate. While the case of Hippolytus is not mentioned, it is clearly in mind throughout.

Exode.—A messenger, hurrying in, announces to Theseus the death of his son. Theseus receives the news calmly and asks for a detailed account. The messenger relates how Hippolytus had yoked his horses to his car and was driving madly along the highway by the sea, when suddenly the waves swelled up and launched a strange monster in the form of a bull upon the land. This monster charged upon Hippolytus, who fronted the beast with unshaken courage. But in the end the horses became unmanageable through fright, and dragged their master to his death among the rocks. The body of the hapless Hippolytus has been torn in pieces and scattered far and wide through the fields; and even now attendants are bringing these in for burning on the pyre. Theseus laments, not because his son is dead, but because it is through his, the father's, act.

The chorus expatiates upon the fact that the blows of fate fall heavily upon men of exalted condition, but spare the humble. The great Theseus, once a mighty monarch, but now so full of woe, is an example of this truth. It has not profited him to escape from Hades, since now his son has hastened thither.

But now their attention is turned to Phaedra, who appears, wailing aloud, and with a drawn sword in hand. She rails at Theseus as the destroyer of his house, weeps over the mangled remains of Hippolytus, confesses to Theseus that her charge against his son was false, and ends by falling upon the sword.

Theseus, utterly crushed by the weight of woe that has fallen upon him, prays only that he may return to the dark world from which he has just escaped.

The chorus reminds him that he will find ample time for mourning, and that he should now pay due funeral honours to his son. Whereat Theseus bids all the fragments be hunted out and brought before him. These he fits together as best he can, lamenting bitterly as each new gory part is brought to him.

He ends by giving curt command for the burial of Phaedra, with a prayer that the earth may rest heavily upon her.

THE TRAGEDIES OF SENECA

THE *OEDIPUS* OF SOPHOCLES

Prologue.—Dialogue between Oedipus and the priest of
Zeus, who discloses the present plague-smitten condition of
the people, and prays the king for aid since he is so wise.
The fatherly regard of Oedipus for his people, in that he has
already sent a messenger to ask the aid of the oracle, is
portrayed.

The answer of the oracle: first reference to an unexpiated
sin. Short question and answer between Oedipus and Creon,
the messenger, bringing out the facts of Laïus' death.

The irony of fate: Oedipus proposes, partly in his own
interest, to seek out the murderer. As yet there is no
foreshadowing of evil in the king's mind. At the end of the
prologue Oedipus remains alone upon the stage.

Parode, or chorus entry.—The chorus enlarges upon the
distresses of the city, and appeals to the gods for aid.

First episode.—The curse of Oedipus upon the unknown
murderer is pronounced, and the charge is made by Tiresias
(who long refuses to speak, but is forced to do so by Oedipus),
"Thou art the man." Oedipus' explanation of Tiresias'
charge: it is a plot between the latter and Creon. The facts
of Oedipus' birth are hinted at. Tiresias prophesies the
after-life of the king, with the name but thinly veiled.

COMPARATIVE ANALYSES

THE *OEDIPUS* OF SENECA

Prologue.—In the early morning Oedipus is seen lamenting the plague-smitten condition of his people. He narrates how he had fled from Corinth to avoid the fulfilment of a dreadful oracle, that he should kill his father and wed his mother. Even here he cannot feel safe, but still fears some dreadful fate that seems threatening. He describes with minute detail the terrors of the pestilence which has smitten man and beast and even the vegetable world. He prays for death that he may not survive his stricken people. Jocasta remonstrates with him for his despair and reminds him that it is a king's duty to bear reverses with cheerfulness.

Parode, or chorus entry.—The chorus appeals to Bacchus, relating how the descendants of his old Theban comrades are perishing. It enlarges upon the distresses of the city, and deplores the violence of the plague. The sufferings of the people are described in minute detail.

First episode.—Creon, returned from the consultation of the oracle at Delphi, announces that the plague is caused by the unatoned murder of Laïus, former king of Thebes. Oedipus anxiously inquires who the murderer is, but is told that this is still a mystery. Creon describes the scene at Delphi in the giving of the oracle. Oedipus declares himself eager to hunt out the murderer and inquires why the matter has been left so long uninvestigated. He is told that the terrors of the Sphinx had driven all other thoughts out of the people's mind.

The irony of fate: Oedipus pronounces a dreadful curse upon the murderer of Laïus and vows not to rest until he finds him. He inquires where the murder took place and how. At this moment the blind old Tiresias enters, led by his daughter, Manto. Tiresias tries by the arts of divination (which are described with the greatest elaboration) to ascertain the name of the murderer, but without avail; and says that recourse must be had to necromancy, or the raising of the dead.

565

First choral interlude.—The chorus reflects upon the oracle and the certain discovery of the guilty one. Ideal picture of the flight of the murderer. While troubled by the charge of Tiresias, the chorus still refuses to give it credence. After all, the seer is only a man and liable to be mistaken. Oedipus has shown himself a wiser man by solving the riddle of the Sphinx.

Second episode.—Quarrel of Oedipus and Creon based upon the charges of the former. Oedipus' argument: The deed was done long ago, and Tiresias, though then also a seer, made no charge. Now, when forced by the recent oracle, the seer comes forward with Creon. This looks like a conspiracy. Creon pleads for a fair and complete investigation. Jocasta tries to reconcile the two, but in vain, and Creon is driven out. Jocasta relates the circumstances of Laïus' death, which tally in all details but one with the death of one slain by Oedipus. A terrible conclusion begins to dawn upon the king. He tells his queen the story of his life and the dreadful oracle, the fear of the fulfilment of which drove him from Corinth. At the end of this episode the death of Laïus at the hands of Oedipus is all but proved, but the relation between the two is not yet hinted at.

Second choral interlude.—Prayer for a life in accordance with the will of heaven. Under the shadow of impending ill, the chorus seeks the aid of God, meditates upon the doom of the unrighteous, and considers the seeming fallibility of the oracle.

Third episode.—A messenger from Corinth brings the news of Polybus' death, the supposed father of Oedipus. The irony of fate: the king is lifted up with joy that now the oracle cannot be fulfilled that he should kill his own father. Step by step the details of the king's infancy come out, which reveal the awful truth to Jocasta. To Oedipus the only result of the present revelation is that he is probably base-born. Jocasta tries to deter Oedipus from further investigation.

Strophe and antistrophe.—A partial interlude, while they wait for the shepherd who is to furnish the last link in the chain of evidence. The chorus conjectures as to the wonderful birth of Oedipus; possibly his father is Pan, or Apollo, or Mercury, or Bacchus.

COMPARATIVE ANALYSES

First choral interlude.—The chorus sings a dithyrambic strain in praise of the wonderful works of Bacchus. No reference is made to the tragedy which is in progress.

Second episode.—Creon returns from the rites of necromancy in which he had accompanied Tiresias, and strives to avoid telling the result of the investigation to the king. Being at last forced to reveal all that he knows, he describes with great vividness of detail how Tiresias has summoned up the spirits of the dead, and among them Laïus. The latter declares that Oedipus himself is the murderer, having slain his father and married his mother. Oedipus, strong in the belief that Polybus and Merope of Corinth are his parents, denies the charge, and after a hot dispute orders Creon to be cast into prison, on suspicion of a conspiracy with Tiresias to deprive Oedipus of the sceptre.

Second choral interlude.—The chorus refuses to believe the charge against Oedipus, but lays the blame of all these ills upon the evil fate of Thebes which has pursued the Thebans from the first.

Third episode.—Oedipus, remembering that he had slain a man on his way to Thebes, questions Jocasta more closely as to the circumstances of Laïus' death, and, finding these circumstances to tally with his own experience, is convinced that he was indeed the slayer of Laïus.

At this point a messenger from Corinth, an old man, announces to Oedipus the death of Polybus, the king of Corinth, and the supposed father of Oedipus. The latter is summoned to the empty throne of Corinth. A quick succession of questions and answers brings to light the fact that Oedipus is not the child of Polybus and Merope, but that the messenger himself had given him when an infant to the Corinthian pair. This announcement removes the chief support of Oedipus against the charges of Tiresias, and now

The shepherd, arriving, also seeks to keep the dreadful truth from the king, but a second time the passion of Oedipus forces the truth from an unwilling witness. At last the whole story comes out, and Oedipus realizes that he has slain his father and wed his mother.

Third choral interlude.—The utter nothingness of human life, judged by the fate of Oedipus, who above all men was successful, wise, and good. It is inscrutable; why should such a fate come to him? The chorus laments the doom of the king as its own.

Exode.—The catastrophe in its final manifestations. A messenger describes the lamentations and suicide of Jocasta, the despair of Oedipus, and the wild mood in which he inflicts blindness upon himself. He comes upon the stage piteously wailing and groping his way. He prays for death or banishment at the hands of Creon, who is now king. He takes a tender farewell of his daughters and consigns them to Creon's care.

The play ends with the solemn warning of the chorus "to reckon no man happy till ye witness the closing day; until he pass the border which severs life from death, unscathed by sorrow."

he rushes blindly on to know the rest of the fatal truth. The shepherd is summoned who had given the baby to the old Corinthian. He strives to avoid answering, but, driven on by the threats of Oedipus, he at last states that he had received the child from the royal household of Thebes, and that it was in fact the son of Jocasta. At this last and awful disclosure Oedipus goes off the stage in a fit of raving madness.

Third choral interlude.—The chorus reflects upon the dangerous position of the man who is unduly exalted, and illustrates this principle by the case of Icarus.

Exode.—Although there is a short chorus interjected here (lines 980-997) on the inevitableness of fate, all the remainder of the play is really the exode, showing the catastrophe in its final manifestation. A messenger describes with horrible minuteness how Oedipus in his ravings has dug out his eyes. At this point Oedipus himself comes upon the stage, rejoicing in his blindness, since now he can never look upon his shame. And now Jocasta appears, having heard strange rumours. On learning the whole truth, she slays herself on the stage with Oedipus' sword. The plays ends as the blind old king goes groping his way out into darkness and exile.